The Italian Puppet Theater

The Italian Puppet Theater

A History

JOHN McCORMICK

with ALFONSO CIPOLLA *and*
ALESSANDRO NAPOLI

McFarland & Company, Inc., Publishers
Jefferson, North Carolina, and London

Every effort has been made to credit the sources of pictures. In a few instances it has been difficult to ascertain ownership of rights. In the case of all pictures, reproduction or further copying by whatever means without permission of the owners or copyright holders is forbidden.

Diagrams by Clodagh McCormick.

LIBRARY OF CONGRESS CATALOGUING-IN-PUBLICATION DATA

McCormick, John, 1938–
The Italian puppet theater : a history / John McCormick ; with Alfonso Cipolla and Alessandro Napoli.
p.   cm.
Includes bibliographical references and index.

ISBN 978-0-7864-4346-8
softcover : 50# alkaline paper ∞

1. Puppet theater — Italy — History.   I. Cipolla, Alfonso.   II. Napoli, Alessandro, 1967–   III. Title.
PN1978.I8M36   2010   791.5'30945 — dc22   2010006954

British Library cataloguing data are available

Cover photograph: The Lupi stage with a late 19th-century Gianduja, courtesy of Teatro Gianduja — Museo della Marionetta di Torino (photograph Roberto Parodi)

Manufactured in the United States of America

*McFarland & Company, Inc., Publishers
Box 611, Jefferson, North Carolina 28640
www.mcfarlandpub.com*

Preface and Acknowledgments

This book grew out of work on *Popular Puppet Theatre in Europe 1800–1914* (Cambridge University Press, 1998), which I wrote in collaboration with Bennie Pratasik. At the time I neither spoke nor read Italian and therefore for that area of our research relied heavily on Bennie, who was a fluent Italian speaker. Having discovered the richness of the Italian puppet tradition, we planned to write the present book. Sadly, Bennie died in 2004 and this book is therefore dedicated to his memory.

The generosity of many people in Italy with their time and expert advice has been outstanding. In the first rank I should like to thank Remo Melloni, Janne Vibaek Pasqualino, Albert Bagno and Pietro Porta, all of whom have provided me with introductions, made available their own personal collections and introduced me to publications that otherwise I would never have encountered. Silvia Corsi has made a very valuable contribution in tracking illustrations and obtaining permission for their use. Roberto Parodi has taken a number of photographs specifically for this book. Other photographers (credited where possible) have allowed their photographs to be used. My wife Clodagh, apart from making carefully observed diagrams, has also been an invaluable collaborator, especially when working on puppets in museums and private collections, and has also been a tireless reader, re-reader and unofficial sub-editor of this book as it has taken shape. Paola Plebani, a puppeteer working with the Museo della Marionetta of Turin, has shared her excellent knowledge of the workings of the Lupi figures, and most especially of the ballet dancers.

Many people, whether scholars or those working in puppet theater, have also been exceptionally helpful and much is owing to their friendship and encouragement: Carmelo Alberti; Luì Angelini; Vincenzo Argento; Cesare Bertozzi; Pino Capellini; Antonella Caruzzi; Claudio Cinelli; Paolo Comentale; Raoul Cristofoli; Mimmo Cuticchio and Eliseo Puleo; Cuticcio family (Cefalu); Cesare De Lucca; Gianluca Di Matteo; Ferrari family; Stefano Giunchi; Alberto Jona; Bruno Leono; Diego Maj; Enzo Mancuso; Alfredo and Daniel Mauceri; Jenaro Melendrez Chas; Luigi Mercuriale; Fabrizio Montecchi; Mauro and Andrea Monticelli; Eugenio Monti-Colla; Antonio Murru; Napoli family (Catania); Paolo Parmiggiani; Donatella Pau; Roberto Piaggio; Bruno Poieri; Mario Sarica; Taccardi family (Canosa di Puglia); Giusepppina Volpicelli; Ugo Vuoso.

In addition I should like to thank the following organizations and their staff: Associazione Grupporiani (Milan); Biblioteca Burchado (Rome); Biblioteca Casanatense (Rome); Biblioteca Nazionale, Rome; Casa Goldoni, Venice; Castello dei Burattini Museo Giordano Ferrari, Parma (CBMGF); Civica Raccolta Bertarelli, Castello Sforzesco, Milan; Istituto per i beni marionettistici e il teatro popolare, Turin (IBMTP); Library of the Seminario Vescovile, Asti; Musée International de la Marionette, Musée Gadagne, Lyon; Museo Biblioteca dell'Attore, Genoa; Museo dell'Opera dei Pupi, Sortino; Museo della cultura popolare padana, San Benedetto Po; Museo Internazionale delle Marionette Antonio Pasqualino, Palermo (MIMAP); Museo Nazionale delle Arti e Tradizioni Populari, Rome; Scuola Civica Paolo Grassi, Milan; Teatro Rossetti, Trieste; Victoria and Albert Museum, London.

This book has involved numerous visits to Italy, and a part of the cost of these journeys has been covered by an annual research travel grant from Trinity College Dublin.

Titles of pieces performed have generally been translated, except where the sense is obvious. Italian forms of names have also been retained: Carlo Magno for Charlemagne, Orlando for Roland, Rinaldo for Renaud, Arlecchino for Harlequin, Pantalone for Pantaloon, and the Dottore for the Doctor. Spellings of some names and titles occur in several forms, so there may not always be total consistency, e.g. Maino, Majno, Mayno; Guerrino (detto) il Meschino, Guerino, Guerin; or opera, opra, op'ra, opira. A glossary has been provided to assist the reader with certain technical terms and Italian words.

Table of Contents

Introduction

Whoever has read Carlo Collodi's *Pinocchio*, whether as a child or an adult, will have associated puppet theater with Italy. The main character is a puppet who strains to become a "real" boy and an especially striking episode is his visit to a puppet show where he is instantly recognized by the other puppets. Puppetry is a major element of European popular culture and as such has usually been theater for the poor. The appalling poverty of much of Italy in the past sent out waves of Italians, from ice-cream vendors to street musicians, to seek their fortunes abroad. Amongst these were numerous puppeteers who found their way as far as Russia, England and North and South America. Poverty often meant invisibility. The occasional marionette shows performed in the palaces of the nobility were comparatively well recorded and this has led theater historians to lend disproportionate importance to them. Today puppet performances still receive less coverage in newspapers than theater with live actors. In the past the only traces of the activity to survive are often requests for permits to perform or prohibitions on performance. In the nineteenth century some marionette theaters began to acquire a degree of respectability and also to be perceived as places to which the middle classes could safely bring their children, but by the twentieth century the popular adult audiences that puppet theater had previously enjoyed had largely vanished.

The first serious attempt to write a history of the Italian puppet theater was Yorick (Pietro Coccoluto Ferrigini) with his *Storia dei burattini* (1884). A useful point of reference, though not entirely reliable and lacking in notes and sources of information, it owes much to Charles Magnin's *Histoire des marionnettes en Europe* (1862) but also contains valuable material on Italian puppet theater of the later nineteenth century. Yorick opened up the field to further researchers, often working on their own geographical area, such as Pandolfini Barberi in Bologna or Pino Capellini in Bergamo. The first to demonstrate that the repertoires of the puppet theater might warrant serious scholarly examination was Pietro Toldo in his 90-page article "Nella baracca dei burattini" (1908). Much research has been the work of folklorists who have approached puppets from the angle of popular culture, which, as they have shown, evolves at a different and often slower rate than "official" culture. When Giuseppe Pitrè of Palermo in his *Usi e costumi — credenze e pregiudizi del popolo siciliano* (1889) examined the Sicilian opera dei pupi, he signalled the reassessment of a genre previously treated as inferior and not worth serious attention.

By the late 1950s there was a depressing feeling that the Italian tradition of puppet theater was dead or dying and there was a rush to record and preserve what could be saved. In Palermo Antonio Pasqualino and his wife Janne Vibaek began to collect material from puppeteers whose activity had ceased and to create what would become the Museo Internazionale delle Marionette. Italy is exceptionally rich in collections of puppets. These range from the private Borromeo collection on the Isola Madre (Lago Maggiore) to the material of the Puglisi family of Sortino, the Ferrari family of Parma and the Lupi family of Turin. Puppets, their stages and scenery are perishable, and few professional companies were in a position to keep obsolete or worn out material. In aristocratic houses it was easier to store such things in attics or cellars and this is one reason for the survival of the eighteenth-century Grimani family puppets, now housed in the Casa Goldoni in Venice, and of the eighteenth-century Venetian figures in the Davia Bargellini museum in Bologna. The Rissone collection at the Museo Biblioteca dell'Attore in Genoa is an outstanding collection of early nineteenth-century figures comparable only to the Borromeo collections.[1] The traveling puppet companies of Emilia-Romagna are well represented in the folk museum of San Benedetto Po. Increased use of modern technology has also allowed for the development of websites, notably one for Emilia (which includes the collection of the Monticelli family of Ravenna), the BUMA site for the collections of the Scuola Civica Paolo Grassi in Milan, largely based on the Preti family, to which Yorick devotes considerable space, and the site for the immense private collection of Maria Signorelli, which is exhibited from time to time, but has no permanent museum.

In 1980 two major exhibitions produced valuable catalogues: *Burattini e marionette in Italia dal cinquecento ai giorni nostri*, at the Palazzo Antici Mattei in Rome, and *Burattini, marionette, pupi* at the Palazzo Reale, Milan. Since then there have been many smaller exhibitions, often restricted to a single company. In 2001 the Istituto per i Beni Marionettistici e il Teatro Popolare (Turin) mounted an exhibition in the Casa del Conte Verde, Rivoli: *I fili della memoria—percorsi per una storia delle marionette in Piemonte*. Further research and publication has been heavily promoted by Pietro Porta and the Associazione Peppino Sarina of Tortona and by the Ravasio foundation of Bergamo. Enormous amounts of material still remain to be exhumed from local archives, and another important step in this direction has been the encouragement of doctoral students of universities to delve into these.

On the puppeteers themselves, brief but essential information has been provided by Cesare Bertozzi and Paolo Parmiggiani in *Il castello dei burattini* (2004). In Naples and Sicily the work of Ugo Vuoso and Antonio Pasqualino has been very valuable. Less accurate, but still useful, is Alessandra Litta Modignani's *Dizionario biografico e bibliografia dei burattinai, marionettisti e pupari della tradizione italiana*. The memoirs of performers, Colla, Cuticchio, Ferrari, Gambarutti, Niemen, Sarzi and others, have provided records of these individuals and their families. Most have been written towards the end of a career and, although colored by memory, point of view and an element of conscious or unconscious myth-making, provide a greater understanding of the practices of the companies with which they have been connected.

Puppeteers had a specific skill as entertainers and employed this to earn enough to keep them and their families. Intermarriage between puppet families also contributed to a puppet culture. Where a company operated over several generations there was a sense of carrying on the work of a father or grandfather, generally following the tried and tested practices of the older generation. Puppets, techniques and repertoires were handed down. There were developments and changes, but evolution was slow and irregular and chronology often relatively meaningless. In many cases a performance of the 1920s was not substantially different from one of the 1860s. In a profession often of an itinerant nature and dogged by poverty, there was little consistent keeping of records or documents. The surviving registers or "libri mastri" of companies such as Lupi, Preti or Colla are incomplete but usually indicate where a company was performing, what piece was presented each night, and the amount of the takings. Some also provide an excellent idea of the running expenses of a company — the cost of oil for lighting, the hire of musicians, and cloth for the booth or scenery.

During the Napoleonic period puppets were classified as a minor form of theater. Attempts to police and control all aspects of society led to more recording of permits granted or refused and these can be of value in mapping the travels of a company. By the latter part of the century there begins to be more material on which to build a history. A number of scripts survive and there are also collections of objects, puppets, scenery, properties and eventually photographs.

The theater review was a form of journalism that came into its own in the nineteenth century, but critics were slow to think puppets worth their notice. Rome was a magnet for foreign travelers, from young aristocrats doing the grand tour in the late eighteenth century to more ordinary travelers, such as Charles Dickens, who spent an extended period in Italy in 1844 with his entire household because it was cheaper than remaining in England. Dickens, William Story, Ferdinando Gregorovius, Stendhal, and Auguste Jal provide first-hand eye-witness accounts of performances that otherwise went totally unrecorded. They often found colorful popular audiences of as much interest as the show itself. In the early twentieth century Festing Jones's descriptions of the opera dei pupi in Sicily are especially valuable for their detailed but less patronizing portrayal of audiences. Artists such as Bartolomeo Pinelli recorded scenes of street activity that included puppet shows. Here too the emphasis was more on the audience than on the show, but it is often possible to extrapolate information about both.

Terminology

Today in English the word "puppet" is broadly understood as a generic term for animated figures. In Italy there is no single word and terminology has always varied according to region, period and usage. "Marionetta" (marionette) is now understood to be a jointed figure operated from above by means of strings. The "pupo" is also a marionette but has acquired the sense of a "rod marionette" as opposed to a figure worked entirely by strings and is associated with the south of Italy. Marionettes and pupi show considerable differences in size, construction and type of control. "Burattino" means a glove-puppet, or figure worn on the hand and operated from below. This is usually a half figure consisting of a head with a costume and absurdly short arms. The glove-puppet's dimensions are governed by those of the human hand and the main physical variations are in the size of the head and the positioning of the arms on the sleeve. In the past "marionetta" and "burattino" were used in a more general sense and this can be confusing.

"Burattino" is a name for the second zanni of the Commedia dell'Arte. In England in 1617 Ben Jonson in his masque *The Vision of Delight* had an anti-masque which included "a she-monster delivered of six Burratines, that dance with six Pantaloons." The word "buratti" was used for itinerant groups of entertainers that moved around Italy in the fifteenth century and may have been precursors of the Commedia dell'Arte. It is even thought that some of these entertainers may have been mendicant monks. One such group, the Compagnia delli Buratti, was described as being always in motion, shaking their heads and dancing as if they could not stop. This evokes the mad dancing groups of the later middle ages performing the "tarantella" (supposedly to cure those bitten by the tarantula). The melancholy that resulted from the bite, it was thought, could be cured only by hours of violent dancing, and bands of musicians wandered through Italy in the summer, playing for this reason.

The term buratti was equated with entertainers who had a variety of skills, one of which was puppetry. In sixteenth-century Spain many were referred to as "jugadors de manos," described in a Spanish-English dictionary of 1599 as meaning those who "juggle or tell a tale with the hand." In this sense the Spanish use of the term is close to that of the Italian "gioco di mano." This corresponds to the word "juggle," which in English referred to legerdemain, conjuring, cheating or deceiving and by extension to performing with glove-puppets.

In Spanish the word "juglar" (juggle) can describe the activity of a "bagateliere." Covarrubias in his dictionary of 1611, the *Tesoro de la lengua castella, o española*, defines the word "bagatelle" as meaning "titere," or puppet. In Catalan-Provençal areas "bavastel," "balastel," "babastel" and "bagastel" all seem to be variants of "bagatelle." In Naples and other parts of Italy that were attached to Spain, the word "bagatelle," by the seventeenth century, had come to mean a glove-puppet show and a "bagateliere" was a puppeteer. In 1550 Girolamo Cardano, who was probably in Lombardy, mentioned "magatellos" as a popular word to describe small wooden figures that performed dancing, singing, fighting and tricks and were accompanied by instruments. The activity of the "magatellos" suggests marionettes or jigging figures and the word is probably cognate with "bagatelle." "Magattej" later became the popular word for glove-puppets in Milanese.

Rope-dancing went hand in hand with puppets until the nineteenth century and troupes of entertainers often boasted both skills. In early seventeenth-century Spain a common word for a rope-dancer was "volatín." John Varey has pointed out that between 1598 and 1628, there are many instances where the words "volatín" and "titere" (puppet) are used as synonyms. Linguistic variants on "volatín" include "volantín," "volatinero," "bolantín" and "buratín." The last of these provides further support to the idea of "burattino" indicating a puppet by the early seventeenth century.

In Italy by this time "burattino" referred to figures given life through human agency, but it did not indicate any specific type of puppet. Ottonelli in the mid-century mentioned how mountebanks used "fantocci," which he defined as figures known as "burattini," and commented on how, with their "fantoccierie" they entertained the humble and plebeian classes on the piazzas.

In 1684 Prince Ferdinando di Medici gave private performances of what were called the "commedia dei Sig.ri Burattini" at the villa di Pratolino. The figures he used were not glove-puppets, but a contemporary description observes that they were the sort of figures that the common people called "burattini," which may imply that the word itself was seen as a popular one. However, in the eighteenth century there are references to "burattini in musica," unambiguously meaning marionettes performing opera. In 1906, Enrico Novelli (Yambo) published a children's book on how to make marionettes and called it *I burattini di Yambo.* Some years later he started his marionette company and replaced the word "burattini" with "fantocci."

Ottonelli had already employed the term fantocci as a generic word for animated figures. Many puppeteers in the eighteenth and nineteenth centuries used it to mean glove-puppets. Italian companies visiting England in the 1770s presented figures controlled from above by wires or strings which they called fantoccini and the word came into general use for figures able to perform tricks. In the 1920s the Italian Giuseppe Concordia was advertising his marionette show as "fantocci meccanici moderne."

The word "marionnette" was well established in France by the mid-seventeenth century, but did not come into current use in Italy before the second half of the eighteenth.[2] Its first recorded use in Italy is in a letter of 1681, written by Francesco Mazzetti, known as "Arlecchino," to her Royal Highness Giovanna Battista di Savoia-Nemours, mentioning that he had been in Turin eight years previously with his "Teatro di Marionette," after which he had toured most of Italy and parts of Germany and performed for the king of Poland and the Emperor. The Savoy court had linguistic and cultural links with France, which may explain the adoption of the fashionable French term "marionnette."[3]

Marionettes (in the sense of articulated figures operated from above by means of strings or wires) were popular in Venice. They were generally referred to as "figure," "figurine" and "bambocci,"[4] but the word "marionetta" does not seem to have been current before the late eighteenth century.[5] In 1860 the Bolognese puppeteer Angelo Cuccoli wrote out a list of the productions of the company, describing them as being performed by "marionette a mano," by which he meant glove-puppets.

"Pupo," cognate with the English "puppet" and related to such words as "popazzo," was widely used by the popular classes in Rome and the south to mean any sort of doll, including a puppet. In early eighteenth-century Rome, the figures in Cardinal Ottoboni's private theater were described as "popazzi" (a diminutive of "pupi").[6] Possibly because "bagatelle" was associated with glove-puppets, "pupo" settled as a term for marionettes. In nineteenth-century Rome the fashionable Fiano Theater was perceived as a "marionette" theater, while some of the more popular ones were thought of as "pupi" theaters. Until well into the twentieth century, many of the "pupari" (puppeteers) of Sicily continued to describe their shows as "marionette" performances. However, by the later years of the nineteenth century a distinction was commonly made between all-string variety figures, which were "marionettes," and figures that retained the head rod, were used for a dramatic or epic repertoire and were referred to as "pupi."

All marionettes and pupi were originally controlled by a head rod and further rods or strings to operate the limbs. Ottonelli mentions four black silk threads to operate the hands and feet. There is a large degree of regional variation in modes of control and technical detail, especially in the length or thickness of the head rod. Some of the eighteenth-century Venetian marionettes and the majority of Sicilian pupi have no leg strings. One leg is marginally shorter than the other and a slight swiveling movement of the grip at the top of the main control rod gives a sense of walking. Leg strings running through the body still exist with Czech marionettes and can be found in a few eighteenth-century figures in the Casa Grimani and Davia Bargellini collections. Before the twentieth century realistic walking was not thought of as important and leg strings were designed for specific attitudes rather than locomotion. In Palermo a string to the left knee enabled some characters to kneel. In

Catania the knees were not jointed and these large puppets had a stately and highly recognizable gait.[7] Both hands of the Roman and Neapolitan pupi were controlled by strings, but in Palermo and Catania a second rod was attached to the sword arm of figures designed for fighting.[8] Where figures had moving mouths, an additional string or wire running through the center of the head was attached to the back of the counterweighted jaw. This was usually restricted to the main comic character, which might have additional strings to operate the eyes.

Prior to the arrival of Holden's in the 1880s with their much imitated and very flexible all-string figures, the distinction between the marionette and the pupo was primarily a semantic one. From this period on they began to be thought of as two different types of puppet. There is a real justification for this. The all-string marionette depends on weight and gravity and its more naturalistic movements are an imitation of a human performer; the pupo, like the glove-puppet, responds more directly to the operator who is able to endow it with stronger and more stylized movements that represent rather than imitate the human. Most of the older marionette companies retained a head rod until the mid- or late twentieth century. In imitation of Holden's, the Lupi company of Turin briefly experimented with all-string figures, but reverted rapidly to the head rod, which it retained throughout the twentieth century. At the top of the rod was a wooden grip or bulb to which other strings were attached, sometimes with leather tags.[9]

"Marionetta," "burattino" and "pupo" are three terms in relatively general use, but today the very definition of a puppet has become a subject of intense discussion. The introduction of new forms, such as bunraku, muppet, table-top, and object theater and the use of mixed media have rendered the question of nomenclature even more confused. Doretta Cecchi, searching for a generic term, reverted to late seventeenth-century terminology when she called her book *Attori di legno*: wooden actors. The puppet center in Cervia refers to itself as the Centro Teatro di Figura. "Figura" (Germanic "Figur") has now been taken up widely amongst the profession, but not really by the general public. Others have preferred to speak of a theater of animation, but this can also imply a type of socio-theatrical activity which has nothing to do with puppets.

In addition to marionettes and glove-puppets there has always been a small and not very well documented tradition of shadow theater. A shadow theater existed in nineteenth-century Turin, but the only traces of its existence are a few figures in that city's cinema museum. In the seventeenth century Ottonelli refers to shadow performances and the performers as "bianti ombranti." The popular term for shadow theater in the eighteenth century was "ombres chinoises," but in England it was also called "Italian shades." At this period Italian shadow performers are also documented in Russia. In the late twentieth century shadow theater enjoyed a renaissance in Italy with the internationally famous Gioco Vita company, and work with shadows has become a constituent element of many productions both with puppets and in the actors' theater.

Popular and Traditional

A very different problem of terminology arises with the use of such loaded terms as "popular" and "traditional." This is further compounded by other words such as "art" and "artistic" and by the entire high culture/low culture debate. There has always been a tendency for the authorities to try and control what is or is not art or culture. The Austrian empire in the 1790s attempted to regularize the theater along the lines of the "Hamburgische Dramaturgei," engaging in a highly negative approach to popular forms, including puppet theater. Post-revolutionary Russia, Nazi Germany and Fascist Italy all attempted to promote the idea of state-approved culture.

Later twentieth-century critics have created a slightly artificial distinction between high and low culture, often based on social and cultural assumptions that were already becoming out of date. The word "popular" is generally used to refer to the "subordinate classes." Low culture was of the "people" (hence popular) and therefore real culture and desirable. High culture was something that was elitist, the prerogative of the ruling classes, and therefore to be dismissed or downgraded. This polarization fails to recognize the mobility of culture or to acknowledge that the context of the performance may often be as important as the material being performed. The so-called popular classes shade off into the middle classes and it is very hard to establish exact boundaries. It is surprising how similar the repertoires of the "popular" puppet theaters and those of the more middle-class ones actually are. The majority of marionette and pupi performers, even if illiterate, saw themselves as bearers of culture (in the sense of high culture), and this explains the rather inflated speech found in so many nineteenth-century puppet scripts and the general confining of dialect to comic figures, who can afford to be vulgar.

Earning a living has always been a main concern of strolling actors and puppeteers. The word "arte" as used for the Commedia dell'Arte performers indicated professional skill or métier. The puppeteer's art likewise implied this and one of the most important skills for him or her was the voice. Franco Gambarutti, referring back to the marionette performers of his own youth in the 1930s, described their vocal performance as being "un tantino urlata" or shouted. This special theater voice may not have been very different from that used by strolling players. The nearly 80-year-old Maura Ferrari, daughter of Italo, interviewed in 2007, performed a glove-puppet scene between Bargnocla and Fagiolino, recalling how her father would have done it, and produced a startlingly deep, resonant and carrying voice that instantly arrested attention and would have easily overcome the acoustic baffle created by stage curtains or panels prior to the development of sound amplification.

Showmen of earlier periods often possessed high artistic standards, but their emphasis was on quality rather than creative originality. Many put considerable effort and skill into the scenery and costumes, but all this was to make the show as attractive as possible to potential audiences. With the twentieth century a new notion of puppetry as an avant-garde art form began to emerge. Social change and cultural development have taken place on an unprecedented scale, and the whole position and nature of puppet theater has had to be redefined. Today puppetry can no longer be considered one of the mass media. Like theater it has become an elite form, but its elitism is not in the face of popular culture, but of mass culture. Eric Hobsbawm in *The Invention of Tradition* has forced a reassessment of the whole notion of "traditional" culture. Folklorists such as Pitrè carried out invaluable research which led to the preservation of much cultural heritage but also to fossilized and even inaccurate assumptions. Those who speak about "traditional puppetry" almost always mean a type of puppetry that was practiced in the nineteenth century. At the worst this goes along with folk dancing and other such activities that are marketed for tourists and are an artificial re-creation with undesirable nationalistic overtones. In this study the word "classical" is used in preference to "traditional" whether we are speaking of the situation before the twentieth century or of twentieth-century exponents who still operate in a manner not dissimilar to that of previous generations.

A study of the twentieth century has had to take into account the decline of "classical" puppet theater as a result of major social and technological changes, including two world wars, the arrival of cinema and then television and a move for many people from near destitution to moderate affluence. Older forms have of course continued even if the performance context has changed. Today's puppeteers have been exposed to a wide variety of outside influences and international developments. Consequently today it is often easier to speak of puppetry in Italy than of Italian puppet theater.

CHAPTER 1

*To the End of
the Eighteenth Century*

Puppets have existed in Italy since classical times but it is only between the sixteenth century and the end of the eighteenth that a fuller picture begins to emerge. Regional divisions led to the development of strong local traditions. Even today we still think of an Emilian tradition of glove-puppets, of a Venetian one of marionettes or of a Sicilian one of pupi. Up to the Napoleonic invasion of 1798, which laid the foundations for the creation of a unitary state, Italy was divided into a number of duchies, republics and kingdoms. Spheres of political influence were constantly changing. The war of the Spanish succession in the early eighteenth century led to a number of shifts (the duchy of Milan passed from being a Spanish dominion to coming under Austria). Naples and the south, including Sicily, also belonged to Spain for much of the time before becoming the kingdom of Naples and the two Sicilies under the Bourbons. The Papal states, extending from Lazio and the area around Rome to the Adriatic coast, took in much of Emilia, with Bologna as the second city. Tuscany and Parma remained independent duchies. The Republic of Venice at the height of its power extended as far as Bergamo but even after its political and economic decline remained a major center of culture and theater. The republic of Genoa was as significant as Venice as a maritime power, while Piedmont, governed by the ambitious house of Savoy (later to be kings of Italy), had Turin as a royal capital.

The Sixteenth Century

Passing references reveal much puppet activity in the sixteenth century, but the concrete documents out of which a history might be written are all but non-existent. Puppet shows were common in Naples in the last two decades of the century, possibly because of the relatively tolerant attitude of the vice-regal authorities and the fact that shows produced revenue as well as providing a form of entertainment that the church found acceptable.[1] Benedetto Croce, in his *Teatri di Napoli*, gives us a lively picture of the activities of the "ciarlatani" (charlatans) and "bagatellisti." The ciarlatani were people trying to sell almost anything, especially potions and medicines of various kinds, or else exercising a profession, such as tooth-pulling. Performances or demonstrations of skill were used to collect a crowd of potential customers, and many charlatans hired entertainers precisely for this purpose.

In the later sixteenth century there are some brief references to the existence of puppet theaters on the piazzas of Venice, indicating that they were a familiar sight there too. Tommaso Garzoni, in his *Piazza universale di tutte le professioni del mondo*, first published in 1585, gives a wonderful description of performers from various parts of Italy that could be found on St. Mark's Piazza. He refers to the well-known figure, Zan della Vigna, who entertained the crowd with various "bagatelle" and made them laugh with "apelike gestures, baboonlike actions and various feats of prestidigitation."[2]

An indirect early reference to the bagatellieri is provided by the traveller Pietro della Valle in 1614, describing a visit to Constantinople, where he had seen shadow shows. He commented on the fact that, unlike the shadow characters in Italy, which were silent, the Turkish ones spoke and there was frequently a substantial amount of obscene language, such as was used by the bagatellieri of the Piazza Navona in Rome and the Largo del Castello in Naples.[3]

"Guattarelle" was another common term for glove-puppets in sixteenth-century Naples and may have originated from an idea of acting or pretending.[4] Later it became "guarattelle," a term still used in Naples today for Pulcinella performances. The word "fraccurrado" might also be used interchangeably with bagatella but seems more frequently to have been a marotte or stick puppet. In 1552 Anton Francesco Doni described a female performer with her "fraccurradi," which, in this case, are unmistakably glove-puppets:

> Fraccurradi is a sort of entertainment for light-hearted company and is performed with certain "fantocci" (figures) on the points of the fingers. They catch each other, play, joke, kill one another and take castles from each other.[5]

A popular street entertainment was the planchette ("tavoletta") puppet show, where a musician with a bagpipe, violin or hurdy-gurdy had a string tied to his leg at one end and to a post sticking up from a board at the other. One or more jointed figures were mounted on this string, and a tensioning of it by moving the leg caused the figures to dance. This form of entertainment has been recorded since medieval times and was still a popular street entertainment in the early 1800s. The players came from poor regions such as Calabria, Naples or Piedmont and often found their way abroad, particularly to France.

Girolamo Cardano gives a full and unambiguous description of two Sicilians with planchette puppets. He then contrasts these with what would seem to be marionettes:

> For I saw many others that were moved with several strings, and these were sometime tense and sometimes slackened, but there is nothing strange about that. Moreover this was interesting because the dances and movements went in time to the music.[6]

A picture by the Turin painter Giovanni Michele Granieri dating from around 1750 shows a planchette performer with what would appear to be a Pulcinella and a female figure dancing.

By the end of the sixteenth century Italian puppet performers were already finding their way abroad, perhaps in the company of the acting troupes of the Commedia dell'Arte. The earliest reference to what is most probably an Italian marionette show in England dates from 1573 and makes reference to allowing "certain Italian players to make show of an instrument of strange motions."[7] The word "motion" commonly designated a marionette show or one with mechanical figures at the time.

"Il Pifferaio," planchette performer with bagpipes in Turin circa 1750 with Pulcinella figure (detail). (Giovanni Michele Granieri. Oil on canvas, inv. n. 631/d. Courtesy of Palazzo Madama = Museo Civico d'Arte Antica, Fondazione Torino Musei.)

The Seventeenth Century

During the seventeenth century, various names of puppet performers begin to emerge. One of the earliest is Giòanin d'ij osei, who reputedly created the character of Gironi (later to develop into Girolamo) and was active at Caglianetto d'Asti (Piedmont) around 1630. The village of Caglianetto was situated at a confluence of several roads, including the route to France, and this made it a place where an entertainer would be sure to find spectators. A sung dialogue published in Treviso in 1642 is attributed to Nicolo Pugnani, known as Zan Bologna who "performs with puppets," and may well have been from Bologna.[8]

The Counter-Reformation resulted in an ambiguous attitude towards theater and puppets. On the one hand theater was encouraged and developed by the church, and on the other condemned by it. Carlo Borromeo, as cardinal, forbade performances by the Gelosi company in Milan, and the governor, who had invited them, had to bow to this, so as not to find himself in mortal sin.[9] In 1689 Prospero Lambertini, the future Pope Benedetto XIV, was happy to play Dottore Balanzone in a production of *La pazzia del Dottore* for the Academia del Porto. A distinction was made between amateurs of a certain status performing for other refined people and those who made their living out of theater and performed for the poorer, and by implication more gullible, popular classes. Puppets sometimes came under a general condemnation of theatrical activity, but often they escaped because they were "only" puppets.

Giulio Rospigliosi, Pope Clement IX (1667–1669), was a highly cultured man with a great interest in theater, and also a friend of Queen Christina. His successors Clement X (1670–1676) and Innocent XI (1676–1689) reversed his liberal policies. Innocent XI banned all performances with an admission charge, but by 1680 puppet shows were beginning to be allowed. It is not clear how effective the pope's ban really was. In 1689 the pope formally allowed puppet shows to take place, provided women did not perform and the language was not indecent.[10] By now women were beginning to appear on the musical stage, although a papal decree of 1588 still required men to play women's parts. The use of puppets may have made it possible for women's voices to be used, provided that women did not appear on the stage. The Venetian Pope Pietro Vito Ottoboni, grand-uncle of Cardinal Ottoboni, whom he raised to the scarlet, succeeded Innocent XI as Alessandro VIII ("papa Pantalone"). An enthusiastic supporter of opera, he restored the carnival (and theater season) of 1690 and 1691. His successor, the Neapolitan Innocent XII ("papa Pulcinella"— 1691–1700), promptly closed the public theaters, although the performance of oratorios was encouraged.

The theologian Gian Domenico Ottonelli's treatise *Della christiana moderazione del theatro. Libro detto l' ammonizione a' recitanti, per avvisare ogni Christiano a moderarsi da gli eccessi nel recitare* deals with problems of morality relating to the art of the performer who uses his skills as a source of income.[11] It is also a rich source of information for the study of puppets and provides a full account of the types of show that could be seen on the piazzas of mid-seventeenth-century Italy. This work was published in 1652, but the practices recorded had been around for a considerable time. Ottonelli describes how puppet shows were used by ciarlatani to attract a crowd to whom they could sell their wares or services. In some cases the ciarlatano was also the puppet performer. Here too the puppets were a way of drawing a crowd, and not a source of income in themselves. Topographical engravings often feature glove-puppet stages, nearly always placed on a platform.[12] An early eighteenth-century view of the Piazza Maggiore in Bologna shows a platform with a puppet stage and next to it a charlatan, accompanied by an Arlecchino and another zanni, peddling his wares. The humbler bagattellieri scraping a living with the show itself were less likely have a platform.

Ottonelli was not unsympathetic to puppets, but makes an interesting distinction between acceptable and unacceptable shows. He mentions that a show could last some two hours and also describes a glove-puppet stage and its figures:

> For this purpose some appear on a platform inside a simulated castle of cloth. Jugglers with various "fantocci," known as "burattini," that is little figures, which make gestures and speak with great force so as to provoke delight and laughter amongst the spectators. This, when it is carried out without obscenity, remains a curious and pleasant, even if idle, form of popular and ple-

Charlatan with a puppet show and actors on the Piazza Maggiore, Bologna, late 17th century. Also a street story-teller with a story board and musician. ("Piazza Maggiore con cantastorie e burattini." Anonymous, Bologna, mid 18th century. Courtesy Collezioni d'Arte e di Storia della Fondazione Cassa di Risparmio, Bologna.)

beian amusement. But when crude words are heard or immoral things are shown, as unfortunately often happens, then the burattini and their booth serve the devil of Hell to destroy many souls, which is a great offence against the Creator, and the Juggler and Ciarlatano is a shameful and infamous minister of immorality and a means of eternal damnation.[13]

Little more than a decade after Ottonelli, Lorenzo Lippi wrote his parody of the *Gerusalemme liberata*, *Malmantile racquistato*. This mentions going to the piazza to the burattini. In 1688 a new edition appeared with a commentary by Paolo Minucci. He, like Doni in the sixteenth century, defines burattini as figures worked on the ends of the fingers. He also refers to the use of "a sort of whistle" to make them speak.[14] Here he is speaking of the "pivetta" or swazzle, a small device placed in the mouth that works on a similar principle as the reed of a musical instrument. It deforms the voice of the showman and is still much in use today with Pulcinella performers.

Ottonelli refers to performers on the piazzas using what he calls "pupazzi." He classifies these under two headings: "rappresentanti figurati" and "comedianti pupazzani." The first describes performances where the "actor" stands and presents a show, using moving figures (generally marionettes) to illustrate the story. This is rather like the street story-teller who points to a picture to illustrate his material. The characters themselves do not pretend to speak. Such a show is similar to the one evoked by Cervantes in *Don Quixote*. Some itinerant showmen told their stories pointing at figures made of cardboard that moved silently across a screen illuminated from behind and illustrated episodes taken from the Old Testament.[15] Such shows were still to be found in the early nineteenth century. In May 1816, father Stefano Giuseppe Incisa, a priest in Asti, noted in his diary the arrival of a Venetian with a machine presenting sacred history and referred to this as "Chinese shadows," the current term at the period.[16] The program included the sacrifice of Noah after leaving the ark, the burning of Sodom, chaste Joseph, Moses saved from the waters, Moses making water spring from the rock, the patience of Job, David and Bathsheba, and Nebuchadnezzar condemning the three young men to the furnace.

When Ottonelli speaks of "comedianti pupazzani" he means actors performing with pupazzi, speaking for them as real characters in an entertainment based directly on live theatrical performance.[17] Having praised their skill, he goes on to describe the stage and the figures with their control rod to the head. He comments on their ability to dance and on the use of a violin or guitar as musical accompaniment. He also mentions an unnamed showman who, with some skillful companions, performed plays at a certain time of year (presumably Carnival). This showman had more than 100 figures. During the performance, two of the group looked after the scene changes. Another member of the team handled the figures, helped by a companion who passed them to him and took those that had been used. The text was read by a speaker who changed his voice as appropriate to the figures. The script was marked by indications in color to show the tone of voice needed: red for women's voices, deep blue for the men and green for the comic characters.

In 1662, Angilo Vignola sought permission to perform in Reggio Emilia with "some skillfully made figures that perform plays."[18] A year later Emilia Pietro Lafarina from Palermo (with four companions) looked for a permit to perform *The Passion of Our Lord Jesus Christ* in Reggio with figures and recitation. In this case the figures probably illustrated the narrative as "rappresentanti figurati."[19]

Indoor performances of puppet shows with paying audiences are first recorded in the second half of the seventeenth century.[20] In Reggio Emilia the names of Domenico Segala and Antonio Ventade appear in 1660 and 1664, in each case requesting the use of the "Salla delle Gride" to perform with their figures (almost certainly marionettes).[21] In Rome in 1679 a Carlo Leone requested a new permit to continue performing little moral pieces with burattini in a hall on the Piazza Navona, a center of popular activity, ciarlatani and entertainments, where he had been for years. He declared that all the members of his company were married, with children, and that their behavior was respectable and not causing scandal. Despite this attempt to reassure the authorities his request was refused.[22] The size of the company and the indoor venue imply a marionette show; the tone of the request suggests a permanent or semi-permanent puppet theater; and the context indicates that this theater was frequented by popular audiences. The same was true of Giacomo Viazzani, who was arrested in 1692 because of a disturbance during the performance at his Comedia dei Burattini in the Tor Sanguigna.[23] The development of puppet theaters for paying audiences should be seen in the light of the development of paying theaters for live performers. In Rome the first public theater with an admission charge was the Tor di Nona which opened in 1661. Puppets were a popular form of entertainment in Rome by the second half of the century and in 1673 Count d'Alibert, director of the Tor di Nona, had the idea of presenting puppet (probably marionette) shows in his theater.[24] D'Alibert was a committed gambler with constant financial problems, and this was clearly one of his expedients when money was short. At some period prior to 1681 Francesco Mazzetti claimed to have spent a couple of years in Rome and to have performed at the "Conte Alberto's" (which is probably d'Alibert).

The San Moïsè theater in Venice owned by the Zane family housed marionettes for three seasons between 1680 and 1682.[25] Nothing is known about the company that presented the puppet performances, but they occupied the San Moïsè at a period when it had fallen into disuse and could probably have been rented quite cheaply. The theater had been celebrated for its spectacular productions with elaborate machinery, but had run into serious problems in the later 1670s. The stage-machinery may have been removed, but this need not have affected the use of the theater for a marionette production. If we are to judge by an engraved frontispiece for *Il Nicomede in Bitinia*, 1677, a play by Giovanni Matteo Giannini with music by Carlo Grossi, the San Moïsè was probably a small theater with a long auditorium, a small stage and three tiers of boxes.[26] Much has been made of the reference to the puppets at the San Moïsè as being actors of wood and wax. The novelty seems to have been the idea of presenting opera in a public theater with "wooden actors." Marionettes themselves were no novelty, but the idea of using them to present an aristocratic form of entertainment to a wider public may well have been.[27]

Bologna was within the papal orbit and governed by a papal legate. It was also a university city with a large number of students. Anton Francesco Ghiselli in his *Memorie patrie* records that in 1694 there were four places where puppet performances were given.[28] Dramatic works were performed by marionettes in the theater in via Galliera, and also in one next to the Mercanzia; operatic performances were presented with marionettes in the Teatro Pubblico and in one attached to the Church of San Paolo. The Teatro Pubblico was under the patronage of the Antiani family who, like the Zanes of Venice, saw the financial advantage of a theater on their premises. There was also a small theater near the two towers where puppets were performing in 1694, while a private theater in the casa Fibia, via Galliera, presented puppet shows during the Carnival of 1697.[29]

The Eighteenth Century

Expanding urban populations led to an increase in the number of puppet shows and companies by the end of the eighteenth century. Marionettes offered the visual delights of opera and musical theater and the excitement, comedy and pathos of drama in a more modest form that was within the pockets of ordinary people. The piazzas of towns were still a magnet for "bagattelieri." In Turin the space in front of the old Palazzo di Città was a favorite haunt of ciarlatani and street performers until they were moved in 1796 to the Piazza Castello because of the disturbances that tended to arise. Marionette performers were dissociating themselves from the street and seeing themselves as serious purveyors of theatrical fare. Where they did not have a booth or were forbidden to erect one, they usually rented or used a room or hall near a popular thoroughfare or place of assembly. Closed booths were a convenient way of containing an audience, collecting an admission charge and avoiding some of the hazards of street disturbances. They also made the presentation of a more serious dramatic repertoire much easier. In addition, a booth allowed for greater

Stage of the San Moïsè theater, Venice, 1677, showing the three tiers of boxes. (Title page and frontispiece of the libretto of *Il Nicomede in Bitinia. Seconda impressione con mutazione di canzonette ed aggionta del Prologo* by Gio. Matteo Giannini. Music by Carlo Grossi. Venice, Francesco Nicolini, 1677. Courtesy Fondazione Musei Civici di Venezia.)

control by the authorities, for whom it could also have pecuniary advantages. In Venice both glove-puppet and marionette shows could be found on all the main piazzas of the city. Until about 1760 the authorities insisted that they take place in closed booths with an admission charge and limited them to the period between sunset and the beginning of the performances in the other theaters.[30] This created real difficulties for the more humble showmen, still associated with the ciarlatani. In 1760 the "puricinei" (Pulcinellas) were exiled from the Piazza San Marco by the "procuratore," and later doge, Marco Foscarini, although the ban was rapidly revoked.[31]

In some cases limitations on live actors could be of advantage to puppet performers. In Naples in 1701 the public mourning for Charles II of Spain meant that the theaters had to close — but the puppet theaters were not affected. During that season a booth on the Largo del Castello called the "Teatro detto de' Bambocchi" presented operas performed by marionettes accompanied by "some Neapolitan virtuosi ladies and gentlemen," who were probably singers out of work because of the royal mourning.[32]

Rome attracted performers from the whole of Italy. The large number of pilgrims and travelers ensured new audiences all the time. In 1701, Francesco Valesio, in his *Diario di Roma*, mentions the "comedia de burattini in musica" (puppet opera) in the strada de' Coronari.[33] The work being performed was *Nersice* by Pioli, and the admission charge was one testone (a small silver coin). On February 17 there was a very small attendance because of the rain, so the few spectators were reimbursed and sent home. The Fico tennis court was also for "burattini in musica," with an admission charge of half a testone. Valesio refers to the "usual" puppets performing in the Palazzo Maculani behind the church of St. Agnes, which implies a permanent puppet theater.

In 1764 a teatrino in the Saponari was restored for the use of "figurine." A Sebasatiano Faldi and his company, the Comici in Figurine, requested permits on various occasions. Between 1770 and 1781, Faldi, known as the "Pulcinella delli burattini," performed at the Serpente in the Borgo S. Angelo in Trastevere, in a granary in the Borgo S. Spirito and in one under the Arch of the Annunciation in Trastevere. He also had a teatrino on the Piazza Navona and an optical show that included "mathematical shadows consisting of various seascapes, gardens, hunting scenes and others all made of paper."[34] By the 1780s a marionette theater existed in the Ornani palace on the Piazza Navona.[35] In 1782 a Nicola Rigacci asked permission to show his marionettes there and a subsequent request of 1785 indicates him as director.[36]

By the end of the seventeenth century, Venice had a score of public theaters and with the city's many visitors these attracted some of the finest artists of the day and could draw larger and probably more mixed theater audiences than elsewhere in Italy. The theater season ran from the end of October or beginning of November to the beginning of Lent. Theater had become a business, but the capital for this was in the hands of a limited number of families (Tron, Grimani, Zane, and Vendramin).[37]

In the early eighteenth century one of the most celebrated glove-puppet performers on the Piazza San Marco was Alberto Borgogna, 1685–1765, whose work was continued by his son Sylvio, 1710–1794.[38] Alberto appears in a painting by Pietro Longhi and the artist takes the license to show him standing at the side of his booth, with some of his puppets on the stage. It was not uncommon for puppet shows to be given in convents, where live actors would certainly not have been acceptable. Visits to the parlor of a convent were social occasions, when the families of girls who were being educated there could visit them and chat with other parents. A well-known painting by Guardi (in the Ca Resonico) depicts a glove-puppet show entertaining both the inmates of a convent and their visitors.

Recent research indicates that by the end of the eighteenth century there was considerable puppet activity in Turin, a busy mercantile town with a population of some 70,000, and in the surrounding area of Piedmont.[39] Between 1740 and 1798 the aristocratic Cavalieri di Torino had a monopoly over all theatrical manifestations in the city, which meant that they could exact a fee of one-fifth of the takings for the right to perform. Their registers are full of details of licenses, prices, times of performance, and requests from performers. Pietro De Feraris, Pietro De Martini and Michele Mazzolino applied for a permit to give 47 performances with marionettes during the Carnival of 1763.[40] In 1764 Feraris, Martini and Mazzolino, this time associated with a tailor, Antonio Vinardi, requested permission for 62 performances. In the same year Antonio Piacentino and Francesco Rebaudengo were licensed to present marionette performances indoors, but were not allowed use a booth or other temporary structure on the piazzas or elsewhere. Vinardi, who described himself as a tailor, possibly because it was a more respectable profession, appeared in every Carnival season between 1764 and 1781. In 1767–1777 the company, now directed by Vinardi, appeared during Carnival in the theater belonging to Count Verrua.[41]

In subsequent years Vinardi's company performed in a booth on the Piazza Susina (Piazza di Savoia). The last reference to the company was in the Teatro San Rocco for the duration of the Carnival of 1784. Here Vinardi was also involved with amateur actors in live productions. His associates included a former marionette partner Francesco Baima and a Felicita Gionnani. In 1788 Felicita Gionnani, with her own company, gave 25 marionette performances at the San Rocco. She was probably the Teresa Gionnani Gandolfo who gave 64 performances in two seasons at the San Rocco in 1789, about 100 in 1790 and 140 in

Il piacevole divertimento di Francesco Rossi

A V V I S O.

FRa gli Spettacoli, che danno oggetto di divertimento al rispettabile Pubblico, dovrebbe considerarsi fra i minori quello dei Burattini, pure osservandolo con occhio di clemenza, vedrassi, che può andar del pari a qualunque altro più nobile Spettacolo. Veder un uomo solo, che in tanti modi alletta il volgo, è oggetto di trattenimento alla Nobiltà, ed in ben picciola situazione fa vedere fatti Tragici, Comici, con decorazioni, trasformazioni, a pari di qualunque Nobil Teatro.

Da varj Sovrani d'Europa fu aggradito questo picciolo abbozzo di tutta la Comica forza, il che fa sperare a FRANCESCO ROSSI, che potrà meritare non applauso, ma compatimento da questo Pubblico per natura benefico, e cortese. Si rappresenta nel Teatro in casa Malabaila la sera di Sabbato 14. corrente a mezza ora precisa. Il prezzo sarà nella Loggia fs. 5., nella Platea fs. 2. 6.

Bill for the show of Francesco Rossi, 1788. The earliest illustration of glove-puppets presented with elaborate painted scenery. Commedia dell'Arte figures: Arlecchino, Pantalone, Tartaglia and Brighella. ("Il piacevole divertimento del signor Francesco Rossi." Included with the Incisa diaries. Courtesy of Seminario Vescovile di Asti.)

1791.[42] She paid a tax of three lire a performance, which was about three times that normally paid by a marionette proprietor, and this suggests how important her show was.[43]

The San Rocco, also known as the Teatro alla Torre, was in the courtyard in front of the church of that name (and may well have belonged to it). For the first half of the nineteenth century it remained one of the two main puppet theaters in Turin. From 1784 it was occupied for five years by Francesco Rossi with his glove-puppets. His permit obliged him to finish his performances at 6:30 in the evening, when the show started at the town's main dramatic theater, the Carignano. The last request from him was to be allowed to perform little plays with simple puppets in the "usual" ground-floor hall situated in front of the church of San Rocco.[44] Like many, Rossi claimed to have traveled widely and to have performed for the various sovereigns of Europe.[45] He visited Asti in June 1788 and gave nine performances at the Teatro Malabaila. The publicity indicated that this single performer (presumably with assistants) could delight the masses, but also the nobility, presenting in miniature the full repertoire of the live theater. Rossi's exact repertoire, almost identical to a marionette one, is listed by Incisa in his diary and is the earliest extant list of this nature for a glove-puppet company.[46]

On a subsequent visit in 1791 Rossi offered tragedies, comedies, tragi-comedies, fables, and spectacular scenic actions "all decorated with the respective costumes of every nation with necessary scene changes, transformations and metamorphoses for works involving magic or illusion." Another attraction was land and sea battles with live fire. He emphasized the moral value of his show and the decency of the language and suggested a father could bring his children to it (a very early awareness of the potential of the juvenile market).

Rossi's shows in Asti were in total contrast to the more usual street shows of the bagatellieri. In 1788 a group of 16 or 18 entertainers arrived in Asti. Three women sang and danced on the piazza, while others went through the town and its inns. The group included a glove-puppet performer and a girl who practiced conjuring tricks and a balancing act. Glove-puppet shows occurred both on the piazza, where a collection would be taken, and under the arcades of the market, which offered some protection against bad weather and where audiences could be charged one soldo.

Eighteenth-century Milan had nearly twice the population of Turin. In 1744 the Jesuit father Francisco Saverio Quadrio published his *Della storia, e della ragione d'ogni poesia*. From Quadrio one can deduce that puppet shows were a relatively common form of entertainment there. A section of a chapter is devoted to puppets, described as a type of performance commonly known as "burattini."[47] He uses the newer term of "marioneta" and then goes on to distinguish between marionette and glove-puppet shows in the modern sense, as would Incisa in the 1780s. Quadrio sometimes repeats Ottonelli verbatim, but his work is not a moral treatise written at the period of the Counter-Reformation. He advocates honesty of speech and jokes, by which he means the avoidance of obscenity. What is new is an interest in more literary matters when he speaks of the correctness and regularity of the subject treated. He applies neo-classical critical values to the repertoire of the marionette theater, thus reinforcing the view of marionettes as substitute actors. It also emerges from Quadrio's writing that by this date Milan had audiences from a fairly wide social spectrum.[48] Quadrio makes a specific mention of Massimo Romanini (Massimo Bertelli, 1680–1750), who delighted the populace on the big piazza in Milan. Romanini was noted for his use of the swazzle and his ability to adapt his voice to each character. His son Giovanni (1725–1783) followed him and often worked in conjunction with the ciarlatano Buonafede Vitali. The Romanini were so well known that "romanitt" became a Milanese term for a puppet.[49]

The Po Valley from Bologna to the Adriatic, northwards toward Venice, Verona, Brescia or Bergamo or westwards through Parma and on to Piedmont, saw a huge amount of puppet activity in the eighteenth century, and a surprising number of puppeteers had links with Bologna. Corrado Ricci found notices for public performances of marionette operas in theaters in the Angelelli and Bargellini palaces in Bologna in 1710. In 1711 marionette operas and dramatic pieces were staged at the Angelelli. In 1778, *Lo stordito deluso* (The Absent-minded Man Disappointed), a musical intermezzo for three voices, first staged with live actors at the Teatro del Pubblico in 1758, was performed with marionettes at the Legnani Palace.[50] Marionette performances are also recorded there in 1779, 1782, 1784, 1785, 1786 and 1787. There are various references to the "usual" marionettes, which suggest that the Legnani had become a permanent or semi-permanent marionette theater.[51]

In Bologna, any street activity that might involve groupings of members of the popular classes was watched closely by the papal police. Members of the educated middle classes, excluded from positions of power if they were not clerics, were becoming restless, and large organized groups of bandits from the nearby mountains represented a very real threat to the stability of the town itself. In 1729 a puppet performance was given without a license. The authorities intervened and rounded up about 30 dubious individuals, who were also armed.[52] The showman was probably quite innocent of anything more than a few satiric barbs aimed at the unpopular papal authorities, but anything that caused a gathering in the street was suspect and an unlicensed show was a good excuse for intervention.

A company that visited the city of Reggio Emilia in 1791 described itself as a company of actors with a very fine "edifizio di marionette" (marionette fit-up). They saw themselves as actors performing with marionettes and set up in the foyer of the theater for a score of performances, changing their program daily. No titles were given, but they mentioned that they performed comedies, tragi-comedies, tragedies, and "burlette dell'Arte comica" (farces) together with a different musical piece or "ballo" every evening. The latter ranged from a short ballet d'action, with a mythological theme and transformations or scenic effects, to simple dances of figures of various nationalities.[53]

The state archive of Parma contains a number of references to itinerant puppet shows from the 1780s. In June 1788, a Carlo Moncalvo from Milan, a classic ciarlatano, obtained a 20-day license to show puppets and sell a soap to remove stains. The governor issued a ruling in 1790 which ordered any ciarlatani operating without a license to be put in prison.[54] There are various requests for permits to "far ballare i burattini," but it is not always clear whether these were glove-puppets or marionettes.[55] In 1789 a Venetian showman, Pietro Sesselin, obtained a permit to "far ballare i burattini," and then proceeded to look for a separate permit to present plays in a "casotto di fantocci," or puppet booth. "Fantocci" seems to imply a glove-puppet show or maybe one using rod or stick figures. In 1787 an Evangelista Fratti of Parma received a permit to show the biblical story of the Samaritan woman at the well with different moving figures. In all probability this was some type of mechanical theater and not a marionette show. In 1792 and 1793 there are references to moving wax figures that may also have been marionettes.[56] Increasingly the word "marionetta" became the standard one for figures operated from above by rods and strings. Francesco Tomasi from Ferrara had a "divertimento di marionette" in 1787, and in May 1788 Francesco Nardi, from Camerino, applied for a three-month license for the city and state to give performances using marionettes. In June of that year, Stefano Cortesi of Florence applied for a 20-day license to perform plays with marionettes.

Many traveling showmen visited Asti. In 1779 Gigli Toscano (whose name probably indicates that he was from Tuscany) performed between January 23 and February 16, the day before Lent, when all entertainments ceased. He changed programs every night and only two pieces received a second performance, the spectacular and popular *Enchantments of Circe* and *The Stone Guest* (Don Juan). Friday was a day of fasting, abstinence and religious observance. Toscano gave one Friday performance, but this was in a private house for Count Rocca Quazzolo, and according to Incisa the company was well treated and well paid.

Between May 13 and June 25, 1780, a "Bolognese" ran a marionette season in the Alfieri Palace in Asti in a hall belonging to the Cavaliere Malabaila.[57] The extensive repertoire scarcely overlapped that of Toscano, apart from a religious piece, *Innocence Defended by Heaven*, and the inevitable *Stone Guest*. Between January 6 and March 4, 1783, if we are to judge by the almost identical repertoire, the same showman, now calling himself a Bolognese "machinista," provided entertainment for Carnival with his marionettes in the Malabaila Theater. After Easter he paid a brief return visit in the last week of April.[58] On January 26, 1791, Modesto Clerici announced his arrival with marionettes and remained in Asti until Lent. The similarity of his program to that of the Bolognese "machinista" suggests that they were one and the same person. A marionette company (obviously Clerici's) returned in 1792, but atrocious weather virtually wiped out Carnival that year and the audiences would have been very disappointing. The French invaded Savoy in September and Incisa provides a fascinating record of this period, but for some years puppets become less important. Finally, in 1795, a theater for marionettes was created in the palace of the Marquis Roero di San Severino. This had a pit (admission 5 soldi) and a balcony (admission 7 soldi, 6 denari). Performances started in October and ran until November 14. On December 27 Incisa indicates that the marionette company was starting to work again and would continue until Lent, an indication that it was now resident in the theater.[59] In 1796 the theater was remodeled with the provision of two rows of boxes (four on either side on the first floor and a total of nine on the second).[60] On April 27, 1800, Incisa mentions Modesto Clerici as manager of the San Severino marionette theater. Unfortunately times and fashions change. In January 1801, amateur theatricals were the rage in Asti and Clerici had to close his season at the end of January. In January 1802 he was performing again, but this time in a ground-floor room in the post office.

In Naples and the south there had been plenty of puppet activity since the sixteenth century, but few documents survive before the nineteenth. In eighteenth-century Palermo, during the summer months, dismountable wooden show booths proliferated on the Piano Marina, a large open space close to the harbor and also to a densely populated part of the city and to some of the more aristocratic palaces. The first document relating to the legalization of show booths in Palermo dates from 1774.[61] The first specific reference to a puppet booth dates from 1792 and is an application by a Neapolitan, Crispino Zampa, to erect a wooden one to perform comedies and tragedies with wooden pupi as in previous years.[62] In 1797 Sebastiano Cortese (a Sicilian) received a permit to tour through the kingdoms of

Naples and Sicily throughout 1798, presenting a program of acrobatics, feats of strength, balancing acts and performances with pupi "con tenue prestazione."[63] Some shows continued beyond the summer season and had slightly more permanent installations in nearby warehouses or in the houses of the poorer quarters nearby.[64] The usual term for the marionettes was "pupi di legno" (wooden puppets), but there are also references to "pupi di pezza" (cloth puppets), which may be glove-puppets.[65]

Private Performances

Like the actors of the Commedia dell'Arte, marionette companies got engagements with the nobility whenever they could and then boasted of these as publicity. Some of the nobility began to think of having their own private marionette theaters, and in many cases the performers for these theaters may have been recruited from already existing troupes, while the figures used were almost certainly made by practicing performers or their providers. These performances were generally of an occasional nature, but have been relatively well documented through memoirs and printed libretti. Histories of theater have of necessity focused on them although they represent only a small proportion of the puppet activity that was taking place.

In Rome during the Carnival of 1668, in the second year of the pontificate of Clement IX (Giulio Rospigliosi), Domenico Filippo Patriarca, known as the "famous Patriarca," and his company of "burattini" (marionettes in this context) were engaged to play at the Rospigliosi palace. He received 36 scudi for the performance of four plays.[66] That same year Giulio Rospigliosi's own drama *La comica del cielo* or *La baldassara*, a piece about an actress who abandons her profession, converts, becomes a hermit and dies a saint, was presented in the Ludovisi palace, almost certainly by live actors.[67] Later that year Patriarca was engaged by princess di Rossano to give puppet performances of this piece at the entrance to the convent of Campo Marzio for the benefit of the nuns, who probably watched it through the grille.

Ferdinando Raggi mentioned a private performance of *Il Giasone* (by Filippo Acciajoli), presented by Cavaliere Ricciardi with his own puppets in Rome in 1678. This company appeared in a number of private houses performing plays with music. Ricciardi may have been no more than an enthusiastic amateur, but there is at least a hint that this was a professional company. Many such performances occurred in the circle of Queen Christina which, in matters of culture and entertainment, corresponded to other royal courts of Europe. Filippo Acciajoli (c. 1637–1700) was a central figure in this circle. The third son of a princely Florentine family and the brother of a cardinal, his skills extended to writing, music and scenography. He trained at a seminar in Rome and later became a member of the order of Malta. In his youth he traveled widely in Europe and also chartered a ship and visited England, Spain, parts of Africa, Asia and America. From 1668, most of his life was spent between Rome, Florence and Venice. He is credited with saying that he preferred a comedy to a tragedy, a farce to a comedy, a pantomime to a farce, and puppets to everything else.[68]

Acciajoli was fascinated by everything to do with theatrical machinery, and the puppet stage provided an ideal medium for his scenographic inventions. In the early 1670s he was much involved with the Tor di Nona Theater, where his machinery was greatly admired. One of his best-known works was *Il Girello* (1668) which was performed with live actors in Bologna, Florence, Naples, Livorno, Modena, Reggio and eventually reached the marionette stage for the first time in Venice at the San Moïsè theater in 1682. Two of Acciajoli's other operas, *Damira placata* and *Ulisse in Feaccia*, were also presented by marionettes at the San Moïsè. All these works make heavy scenic demands and one may assume that he was a prime mover in that venture.[69]

Acciajoli moved happily between performances of his work with live performers and performances with puppets. Three operas, for which there is no record of puppet performances, are *The Nut-tree of Benevento; or The Witches' Coven*, performed in the private theater of Don Lorenzo Colonna in Rome, *The Elysian Fields* at the Tor di Nona and *The Inferno* at the Capranica Theater. All would have made ample use of machines and transformations. Scenes of witches, of the gods of Olympus and of hell were part and parcel of the language of baroque staging, and rapidly found their way to the marionette stage.

The type of puppet used to perform Acciajoli's work remains a vexed question. At the San Moïsè marionettes were probably used. However, Acciajoli also devised his own large-scale model theater according to the principles of Bartolomeo Neri, who is credited with having invented a sort of mechanical theater where the figures and machines for scenic effect were operated by a system of counterweights, and therefore without visible control rods.[70] This sounds very like a system described by Bernadino Baldi in 1589 when he tries to distinguish between an automat and a marionette:

> I think that there is none the less a difference between the Automat, that moves on its own, that is where the artist does not pull the string, but the hidden counterweight, and that where the "neuropasti" (string-puller) himself pulls first this string then that to move the figure's arm, hand, foot, head, or the eyes, as we see in those little figures that are sometimes given to children to play with.[71]

Ottonelli describes Neri's theater as having a stage of "normal" dimensions with channels along which figures, half a "braccio" (20–25 cms) high and made of card, could move from the side to the center and towards the back. Limited gestures, such as raising an arm, were managed by means of a wire or string concealed behind the figure and attached to a counterweight. Ottonelli mentions the use of this type of mechanical theater to present religious pieces, with the performers concealed and the singers hidden from the audience by a curtain, and claims that Neri was responsible for many mechanical theaters of this nature.[72]

In 1684 Filippo Acciajoli was in Florence with his "little figures commonly known as burattini" to entertain the 21-year-old Ferdinando, grand-prince of Tuscany. The performance involved 24 changes of scene and 124 figures, and Acciajoli was said to have managed the entire show himself, apart from some help in preparing the scenes and fixing the figures in the channels in which they moved and in setting up the machines used in the prologue and the intermezzi.[73] This sounds very ambitious, but, since the figures were probably cut out of flat card and were already mounted on wooden laths, they did not need to be supported and could be moved as the action required. Figures for dance entries were probably mounted as groups and moved as set pieces. The intermezzi had their more spectacular scenic effects and cloud machines, following in the steps of Buontalenti's entertainments for the Medicis in the previous century.

A letter from father Enrico di Noris mentions that clever craftsmen had come from

Rome and created a good company of actors, speaking with the voices of other people and moving them by means of a very fine wire. He also commented on the admirable gestures of these lifeless statuettes.[74] The company of actors was of course speakers and singers, but Noris is possibly incorrect in assuming that they were responsible for operating the figures too. He added an amusing but perceptive comment that, unlike the theater of live performers, this one entailed lesser outlay in preparing the scenes and less spent on the costumes, and that the only cost of lodgings was a trunk like the one he used for traveling.

The show was set up in a hall of the Pitti Palace. Amongst the drawings of the architect Diacinto Maria Marmi are three extraordinarily interesting sketches of this temporary theater.[75] The first is a rough ground plan showing the seating arrangement of the audience, including a box for the ladies at the back and a pit arranged as a court theater, with the most important people seated in the center. In front of this is the orchestra, and quite clearly marked on the stage itself is the puppet stage. This invaluable document also includes a pen and pencil annotated drawing of the stage with two figures on it. A note on the side provides the exact date (May 18, 1684) and indicates the hall that was used, which has been identified as a space in the central part of the palace overlooking the piazza on the second floor.[76] A further note mentions channels in the floor through which the figures were operated and the communication between the below-stage space and the orchestra. The hidden orchestra, the space backstage for singers or speakers, and the clear indication of the channels in which the figures move correspond almost exactly to the Ottonelli description of three decades earlier. It is hardly surprising that the young prince was fascinated by this elaborate toy theater, the value of which was calculated at 20,000 scudi, and he must have been delighted when it was subsequently given to him. Later he had it set up in the Villa Pratolino and gave his own performances.

In Rome Acciajoli was certainly known to the young cardinal Pietro Ottoboni (1667–1740), who was much involved with the Tor di Nona and Capranica theaters and also used puppets as an outlet for his literary and musical talents. In January 1691, at the Casa Savelli, Ottoboni presented the first of his own works performed by puppets, with a company consisting of four of his staff.[77] This was *Columbus, or The Discovery of India*, in which Colombo (Columbus) crosses the seas and falls passionately in love with his own wife. Performances were interrupted when Carnival was cut short by plague and the death of the pope. The "hit" show of the Carnival of 1696 was Cardinal Ottoboni's puppets in a piece called *Heroic Love amongst Shepherds*.

The earthquake of 1703 was regarded by Pope Clement XI (1700–1721) as a punishment for the sins of Romans, and measures against prostitution and public immorality were taken. Opera was banned for some years. Cardinal Ottoboni, vice-chancellor of the papal court, tried to reconcile aesthetic tastes with his position. Puppets were a way of presenting a musical and visual entertainment, generally with a devout theme, but without the appearance of human performers on a stage. After his initial puppet performances in the 1690s, he wrote a libretto and commissioned music from Alessandro Scarlatti, Cesare Bononcini and others for *La pastorella*, a pastiche opera performed by puppets at Palazzo Venezia in 1705.[78] In the early 1700s a private theater to which only a select number of people might be invited was an ideal arrangement for those with artistic tastes and the means to support them. Ottoboni employed the architect Filippo Juvarra from Messina to create a little theater at the Cancellaria palace where operas could continue to be performed. Three

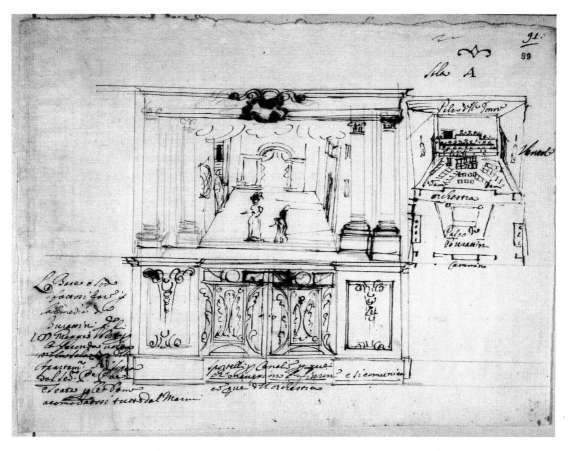

Puppet stage set up in the Pitti Palace, Florence, by Jacinto Marmi, 1684. Stage with figures moving in grooves. Also (right) the plan of the arrangement of the theater with seating, concealed orchestra and puppet stage. ("Teatro dei burattini e teatro delle dame"; Jacinto Marmi, BNCF, Magl. II. I. 380, c. 89. Courtesy Ministero per I Beni e le Attività Culturali della Repubblica Italiana/Biblioteca Nazionale Centrale di Firenze.)

surviving libretti of operas that Ottoboni wrote for this theater are *Costantino Pio* (1710), with music by Carlo Francesco Pollaroli, *Teodosio il Giovane* (1711), with music by Filippo Amadei and *Il ciro* (1711), with music by Alesssandro Scarlatti. When Ottoboni died in 1740, leaving heavy debts, probably as a result of his musical and theatrical enthusiasms, his theater at the Cancellaria was dismantled and the material sold for 150 scudi.

In Venice during the Carnival of 1746, 1747 and 1748 the abbé Angelo Maria Labia, a member of one of the wealthier Venetian families, created a marionette theater to entertain his friends. Called the S. Girolamo, this was in a wooden pavilion in a garden in the Cannareggio.[79] It was a miniature version of the neighboring S. Giovanni Grisostomo theater and reproduced on a small scale the stage, boxes, and other decorations, and also the machinery. Only the acoustics seem to have been disappointing. The actors were described as figures of wax and wood that walked, gestured and moved almost like humans. In the orchestra were more little figures as musicians, and in the boxes were masked figures, while further puppet spectators could be found in the pit of the theater, holding miniaturized versions of the libretto in their hands.[80]

The first works to be performed were *Il cajetto* by the 21-year-old Ferdinando Bertoni and Pier Jacopo Martello's *The Sneeze of Hercules*. Labia wanted to draw attention to himself as a Maecenas. Apart from the free tickets he served the best refreshments and provided his guests with a printed libretto of the works performed. In 1746, a company of good musicians, male and female, concealed backstage, worked the figures and sang accompanied by a large orchestra and gave the fullest satisfaction.[81] The suggestion that they were capable of both working the figures and singing for them probably implies a professional marionette company specially engaged by Labia.[82]

In the later eighteenth century the Grimani, Contarini and Loredan families of Venice are all recorded as having their own marionette theaters.[83] Some were probably not much more than an amusement for the children, while others offered full-scale operatic performances. Carlo Goldoni, in his memoirs, mentions that his father gave him puppets to play with as a child. In 1726, as a young man, he was staying with Count Lantieri at his country villa near Gorizia. He found that the family possessed a set of puppets and he organized what is thought to be the first staging of *The Sneeze of Hercules*, a "bambocciata" specifically for marionettes, which was done as a play, not an opera. In his memoirs he recalled having had a giant puppet made for the Gulliver-like figure of Hercules. In fact the Martello text requires no more than the nose and finger of Hercules, which are sufficient to suggest his size in relation to the pygmies. Goldoni's own plays suited the practice of amateur theatricals popular in the later eighteenth century. Such pieces could often be staged with an all-purpose interior scene or salon and an exterior one (St. Mark's Square, Venice), and examples of both can be found as puppet scenery. The surviving eighteenth-century figures in Venice and Bologna could very plausibly have been used for the staging of various Goldoni plays by a domestic puppet theater.

In Milan the Borromeo family had their own theater, together with ones in their summer residences on the Isola Bella and the Isola Madre on Lago Maggiore. An inventory for the family in 1690 mentions a rectangular chest containing 14 "bambocci" to perform burlesque comedies, dressed according to their parts and equipped with an iron control rod and a spool to support them.[84] Unfortunately there is no further reference to the Borromeo puppets until 1796, when a Gaetano Magni was employed to make a set of marionettes. This included a number of bodies, a Pantalone head with a "mobile beard" and an Arlecchino with an opening mouth. One of Magni's bills is for dressing and painting the hands and faces of 45 marionettes. He also lists string and silk cord, iron rods, small pieces of wood (extra control bars, perhaps for leg strings or strings for special movements), turned wood grips to hold the figures, hats and an assortments of swords and sabers. Amongst other things, he had to provide costumes for a magician, a lackey, a comic figure, Doctor Balia, two soldiers, Tartaglia, an old woman, Beltrame, two servants and Arlecchino.[85]

Italians Abroad

Ciarlatani, bagatellieri, and commediants were all part of a traveling culture. Some established themselves on a fairly regular basis in towns, others traveled widely in search of audiences, and in many cases their travels took them beyond the bounds of Italy. According to the dramatic records of Sir Henry Herbert, Master of the Revels, Italian groups toured through England between 1619 and 1640.[86] One company consisting of three men and a boy showed "an Italian motion with divers and sundry stories in it" at Coventry.[87] The word "motion" could simply refer to some sort of show with mechanical figures, but here it sounds like a puppet show, since it refers to a repertoire of stories.

In 1649 the Maltese Blasius Manfredi, a celebrated water-drinker, presented his show in Nuremberg, adding a performance of "PolliZenello" with small puppets to his other feats.[88] It is uncertain whether he was using marionettes or glove-puppets. Hans Richard Purschke has noted a number of Italians seeking permits in Germany for their Pulcinella shows in the later seventeenth century. Stefan Landolfi, calling himself a "Pollicinell" player, received a permit to perform in Innsbruck in 1688.[89] He is also recorded in Saxony in 1668 and on the Judenplatz in Vienna in 1669.[90] Vienna was both geographically and politically a place towards which puppeteers from Italy might come. Pulcinella, with a variety of spellings (Bouicinella, Politinel, Pollizinell, Policinello), became a generic term for a puppet show, and later this spread to the Low Countries, where it still survives today with the "Poesje" of Antwerp.[91] German performers also began describing themselves as Pulcinella players when seeking licenses.

The most celebrated marionette performers in seventeenth-century France were the Briochés, who are thought to have introduced the puppet character of Pulcinella, gallicized into Polichinelle.[92] The Briochés' real name was Datelin. Pierre Datelin, alias Jean Brioché (1566–1671), performed on the Pont Neuf in Paris in the 1630s. His official profession when he died was that of musician. Nothing is known about Pierre Datelin's shows apart from a famous anecdote about his ape, Fagotin, which had the misfortune to be killed by the irascible Cyrano de Bergerac, who thought it was making fun of him.[93]

Pierre Datelin's son François (1630–1681), also known as Brioché, was sufficiently celebrated to be invited to perform at court in 1653 for the "menus plaisirs du roi" and in 1670 he was appointed "joueur ordinaire des menus plaisirs du roi et du dauphin."[94] In 1657 he received a permit from the "lieutenant civil" to show his puppets at the fair of Saint Germain.[95] In 1676, when Bossuet, in keeping with the spirit of the Counter-Reformation, was denouncing entertainments, the minister Colbert sent a letter to the lieutenant of police ordering him to respect and protect François Brioché and his wooden figures.[96]

Anthony Hamilton, in the first volume of his works, in an epistle to Princess Mary, daughter of James II of England, praised (François) Brioché's Pulcinella, which he had seen at the fair of Saint Germain[97]:

> Là le fameux Polichinelle,
> Qui du théâtre est le héros,
> Quoi qu'un peu libre en ses propos,
> Ne fait point rougir la donzelle
> Qu'il divertit de ses propos.[98]

Magnin found two separate entries in the royal family accounts for 1669. The first related to a payment of 820 "livres" to François Datelin, marionette player, for entertaining the Dauphin over a period of 56 days spent at St. Germain en Laye (20 livres a day between July 17 and August 15, and 15 livres a day for the rest of the month). The second was a payment of 1,365 livres to Brioché, marionette player, for entertaining the royal children at St. Germain en Laye during the months of September, October and November.[99] This led him to assume that there were two separate puppeteers, Datelin and Brioché. The confusion is clarified by a baptismal register. A daughter of Pierre Datelin married Jean-Baptiste Archambault (another entertainer and puppeteer). In 1664 when a son, Antoine, was baptized, the godparents were Jeanne Datelin, born in 1652 and described as the daughter of Brioché II and therefore a cousin of the child, and François Datelin I. François Datelin I is also Brioché II (his father Pierre being Brioché I). A Brioché descendant was still active in Paris in the mid-eighteenth century.

Arguably Pierre Datelin was a French performer.[100] However Auguste Jal,[101] Charles Magnin and Charles Nodier all claimed that Brioché was of Italian origin and Yorick amplified this, making Pierre Datelin's sons, François and Jean, originate in Bologna as Francesco and Giovanni Briocci. Brioché is almost certainly a stage name, a little like Toone in Brussels. The adjective "brioché" was a popular neologism in seventeenth-century Paris, meaning something exciting or tasty, and deriving from "brioche," a refined bread that became popular at the time.

The Italian provenance of Pietro Agiomonti of Bologna is much clearer. In December 1655 he applied for a permit to continue presenting his "little figures" at the Palazzo Comunale of Reggio Emilia.[102] In 1656 he was in Munich accompanied by two other showmen, Carlo Archonati and Leonardo Tauinaeti.[103] Agiomonti's name appears in a variety of guises: Pietro Gimonde (Gimonte, Gemunde), Pietro Agiomonti (Aggimondi, Apimon). In Frankfurt in October 1657, he applied for a permit to present his "Policinello" show.[104] He was appearing at the Alten Schmidstube (an inn), obviously with some success. Three weeks later he requested permission to remain a further two weeks. Gimonde refers to his "kleine docken" or little figures, which would seem to have been marionettes.[105] That this was a substantial show is indicated by a printed bill with four categories of admission charge and by the fact that members of the town council visited it.[106] In 1658 Gimonde visited Vienna, where his "Comedianten der Bambozen" (bambocci) performed on the Judenplatz, much used by entertainers. He also appeared in Innsbruck in 1658 and possibly in Nuremberg. In 1659 he was in Cologne, referred to as Peter Gemundi, known as "Bologna," suggesting his provenance. From then on Signor Bologna remained his professional name and a reference to his "comedias" implies that he was performing a dramatic repertory.

By May 1662, "Signor Bologna, alias Pollicinella" had reached London and the show was seen by Samuel Pepys, who recorded it in his diary as an "Italian puppet play at Covent Garden."[107] Pepys also noted that there was a small orchestra, which included violins and a dulcimer. This may have been Pulcinella's first appearance as a puppet in England. The following October the show was set up at Whitehall to perform for the king and Bologna received a gold chain and a medal worth 25 pounds.[108] The scale of the show can be surmised from the fact that at Whitehall a stage was built measuring just over six meters by five. Bologna was probably the "sieur de Bologne" who appeared with his "Italian marionettes" in Paris in 1678 at the fair of Saint Laurent. A surviving bill announces Molière's *Tricks of Scapin* with changes of scene and several machines, and the appearance of "our Roman Polichinel."[109] The bill also announces a forthcoming full-scale spectacular production of Molière's *Imaginary Invalid*.

Another Italian showman, Antonio Devoto, set up his booth at Charing Cross, London, and was visited by Pepys and his wife in November 1662. Pepys felt that the puppets were better than Bologna's, but that the "motion" (probably the manipulation) was less good.[110] In 1667 Pepys visited the Pulcinella at Charing Cross three times, which suggests that the booth had become semi-permanent. The proprietor of the show appears as Mons Devone, later Anthony Devotte and Anthony Devolto. He managed to obtain royal patronage and received permission to use his booth for live actors. His license refers to him as "Antonio di Voto, punchenello."[111]

Towards the end of 1666, Pietro Resoniero, with his "Italianische Marioneta sPill," arrived in Vienna on his way to Prague, where he obtained permission to perform in the Malastrana district. Resoniero (1640–1735), originally from Vicenza, returned to Vienna in 1667 and set up his show in a booth on the Judenplatz, close to the large one where the rope-dancers performed. The wooden booths were of a semi-permanent nature, and he may even have used the same one as Bologna a few years previously. There is little information about Resoniero, but his theater survived for some 40 years.[112]

Foreign performers also visited Italy. In March 1664, Antonio Ventade from Paris and three companions who "earned their living by traveling the world and making a number of little figures dance" requested permission to present their show in Reggio Emilia. They offered to present various "balli" and other entertainments in the French style. In November 1666 a Bernardo "ditto il Todesco" (which probably means that he was German) also visited Reggio with his "banbocini" or "bambocci." Another term used in these requests is "figurine di legno" (little wooden figures).

Italian puppeteers continued to spread through Europe during the eighteenth century. Sebastiano Da Scio (1680–1750) from Vicenza appeared in Prague in 1700 with his company of Italian actors. In 1705, describing himself as the renowned Italian Harlequin, he sought permission to play in Brno. The first mention of him specifically as a marionette performer is in 1703 when he presented *Faust* at the town hall in Berlin.[113] His "Venetian" marionettes were 70 centimeters high, and his show traveled with a small orchestra.[114]

In October 1770, Carlo Perico opened a highly successful season of nearly 21 months in London with his "Italian fantoccini."[115] Performances were in Italian and French, which, coupled with relatively high admission charges, indicates that the show was intended for a fashionable audience. There were two houses each evening and the repertoire included a number of pantomimes with Arlecchino as the central figure and a collection of trick acts. The latter included a family of Pierrots (possibly a producer puppet of the sort that survives in the Borromeo collections) and Arlecchino eating a dish of spaghetti, a shepherdess playing a mandolin, accompanied by a shepherd on a violin, a black man balancing a spontoon or halberd, an expanding and contracting figure, "savages," a Spanish lady dancing, a tumbler, a rope-dancer, and a sketch in which a Hussar took off his cap and cloak, which were then stolen by Arlecchino.

A company of Italian fantoccini, described as coming from Venice, reached London in 1776, performing at the Little Theatre in the Haymarket. Their chief piece was *The Birth of Harlequin from the Egg*, but they likewise offered a number of tricks and transformations. They were brought over as a speculative venture by a singer called Signor Cardarelli. In 1777 he transferred his contract to a Signor Briochi, who sent them to Dublin, where they appeared in April at the Capel Street Theatre. Here too admission charges indicated a moderately affluent audience. The venture was a failure economically, and the company was stranded in Dublin. Briochi disclaimed all responsibility and in October the managers of the Capel Street Theater lent the theater free of charge for a few nights, which enabled the company to raise enough money to pay their way back to England.[116]

In 1779 another company of Italian fantoccini appeared in London. Their main piece was *Harlequin Great Sorcerer; or The Birth of Harlequin from an Egg*. Interludes included Harlequin and his little horse, a Turk with his wife in a basket, and Harlequin eating a dish of macaroni and drinking a glass of wine. There was also a character whose arms, legs, head and body transformed into six other figures which then danced a cotillion.[117] In 1780 a company arrived from Bologna and remained for two seasons. Harlequin pieces were a staple of the repertoire, but they also performed Pergolesi's *La serva padrona* and Piccinni's *La buona figliuola*. The chief machinist and manipulator of the company was a Joseph Martinelli and in the 1790s he was still active with fantoccini (trick marionettes), which became a very popular street entertainment in England.

In 1776 Ambrogio Sanquirico appeared with his "Ombres Chinoises" in Saint Petersburg, where he remained from September to November, appearing in Moscow the following February. His three-act Chinese shadows had an "English ballet" (probably marionettes) at the end of act two, and at the end of the third act there was rope-dancing (presumably with live performers).[118] In 1788, a showman called Speransoni was offering performances in Moscow in French and Italian of *The Dwarfs of Lilliput,* a marionette piece, which, like *The Sneeze of Hercules*, exploited differences of scale.[119] He also presented shadow shows. The following year, an Italian called Fiandini appeared, combining conjuring tricks with "burattinas." The latter were probably glove-puppets and included the stock characters of Pulcinella, Brighella, Pantalone and the Doctor.[120] In 1797 a Giuseppe Ferre arrived in Moscow and advertised for shows in private houses with his "small burattinas." His emphasis on his figures being of the latest design implies they were marionettes.[121] Various other Italians made their way to Russia with automata, mechanical shows and optical views.

The street glove-puppet show with Pulcinella could be found through much of Europe by the mid-eighteenth century and eventually merged with Kasperl, Petrushka and others. Piacenza-born Giovanni Piccinni arrived in England in the 1780s and is generally credited as being the father of the English Punch and Judy. Henry Collier visited him in the late 1820s and persuaded him to present a performance with the puppets he had abandoned for some time. Collier published this with a number of illustrations by the artist George Cruikshank and it became the "official" Punch and Judy script that is still the basis of performances today. In some cases street shows continued to be associated with the sale of medicines or used by dentists to attract clients. Laurent Mourguet, creator of the French Guignol, is thought to have accompanied his tooth-pulling with a Polichinelle show.

CHAPTER 2

The Golden Age: Glove-Puppets

The golden age of puppet theater in Italy was from the end of the eighteenth century to the early part of the twentieth. Glove-puppets were a ubiquitous form of street entertainment and the performers' livelihood depended on whatever contributions audiences might make. Social segregation was not absolute and puppeteers hoped for the presence of some more affluent spectators. In some cases an open-air enclosure or even a hall might be used and an admission charge levied. It was quite common for poorer audiences to pay for admission in kind with an egg or a handful of nuts, which the performer would resell.

Glove-puppets require the simplest and most portable fit-up. The height of the stage makes for easy visibility, with the player holding the figures close to head height. The attention span of a street audience is shorter than that of an audience in a theater, and there are also other distractions. The performer therefore must have a strong voice and good communication skills. In the street context the carrying power of the swazzle is an excellent means of attracting attention. In Palermo Pulcinella shows, often on the Piazza Marina, in the nineteenth century were called "tutuì," an onomatopoeic word for the squeaky sound of the swazzle.[1]

The glove-puppet evokes rather than imitates a human figure. It has no body as such but has to allow for the anatomy of the hand on which it is placed. Audiences have to imagine the lower half of the figure and certain conventions of movement imply the use of legs.[2] The player's hand and wrist movements form the basis for most of the attitudes and the flexibility of the thumb and fingers determines other possibilities of gesture. Because the glove-puppet is a direct extension of the performer, it can receive energy from the performer more easily than can a marionette.

In order to focus attention, glove-puppet heads are often disproportionately large with oversized eyes. The central element of the glove-puppet show is speech. Head movement, and often eye contact and focus, helps persuade audiences that the puppet is really speaking. Many are carved unevenly so that a movement or change of angle of the profile can suggest movement of the features or give the illusion of a change of mood.

The smallest glove-puppets are the guarattelle of Naples. They have heads about eight centimeters high and six centimeters in diameter, with a full but lightweight costume without any under-sleeve. Lack of resources made for a simple costume unsupported by an under-sleeve and the heads were generally only roughly carved. These figures are very light and their movements are rapid and flexible.[3]

The standard puppets of Emilia Romagna are much larger, more realistic and sculpted in far more detail. The glove, forming the body, is a stout material, often heavy cotton,

31

Top: Gioppino with double expression to allow for changes of mood. (Courtesy Istituto per I Beni Marionettistici e il Teatro Popolare. Photograph Roberto Parodi.) *Above:* Brighella from Bergamo, Sandrone from Emilia and Neapolitan-style Pulcinella (by Gianluca di Matteo), showing respective sizes. (Glove-puppets from Bergamo and Emilia. Courtesy Istituto per I Beni Marionettistici e il Teatro Popolare. Neapolitan "guarattella." Courtesy Gianluca di Matteo. Photograph Roberto Parodi.)

over which the costume is worn. They move more slowly than the guarattella and the rhythm of the performance is closer to that of real life.

In Bergamo puppet heads could be exceptionally large, some weighing as much as four kilos and controlled by means of a short handle that was grasped in the palm of the puppeteer's hand.[4] This led to a more deliberate style of performance, enhanced by the slower mountain speech of the Bergamask puppeteers. In more recent times for practical reasons the size of the puppet heads has been reduced to something commensurate with the Emilian ones, but the unhurried rhythm has remained.

Simple rod puppets, often called "burattini a bastone," are quite often combined with glove-puppets. Also operated from below, the most basic ones correspond to what is known in France as a "marotte," a figure mounted on a stick, with the arms left to swing free, or occasionally operated by separate rods.[5]

The "burattini a bastone" can twirl around easily and are ideal for the final dance that winds up the show. Most commonly they are used for the female partner of the central male

Margì, wife of Gioppino, rod puppet with long arms (skirt removed to show stick). Second half of 19th century. ("Margì, burattino a bastone." Courtesy Istituto per i Beni Marionettistici e il Teatro Popolare. Photograph Roberto Parodi.)

figure. In Naples Pulcinella has Teresina or Colombina and in Bergamo Gioppino has Margì. Peppino Sarina in Tortona used such figures for Angelica (beloved of Orlando) and also for the enchantress Bethzabea.[6] A glove-puppet cannot really have a slender waist, but a figure mounted on a rod rather than the hand of the puppeteer can have a more recognizably feminine shape.[7] Devils were another category of figure for which a rod puppet was not unusual.

Rod puppets probably come from a tradition of crib plays and may have been more widely used than is realized today.[8] A recently discovered script belonging to the Turin showmen Bellone and Sales and dating from the 1820s reutilizes paper from an older script on which there appear to be indications of the use of some form of rod puppet or "fantoccio."[9] When Gualberto Niemen (1904–2003) presented his first show in 1921 he used a collection of 30 rod figures he had acquired from a 90-year-old tinker for the sum of 30 lire.[10] As a solo performer near Alessandria, and later in the Varese region, Niemen used rod figures far more extensively than most. Easy to stick in position on the stage, and also to pick up, they allowed Niemen to present large-cast productions without assistants.

Luigia Salici, daughter of Ferdinando, the creator of the famous marionette company, and her husband Giovanni Stignani formed the Salici-Stignani company. After the First World War they gave up give marionette shows and converted some of the family's fine collection of marionettes into rod puppets, equipping them with a central support rod and rods to the hands. These were referred to as "burattette" (a composite of "burattini" and "marionette") and were generally used as extras, while the main parts were performed by glove-puppets.[11]

Street Shows

The simplest glove-puppet show revolves around a central figure that interacts with both the other characters and the audience. There is no real plot and such a show can be extended or compressed according to the audiences and their readiness to contribute. Scenic requirements are minimal. The poorest performers probably did not even use a stage.

One engraving of the late eighteenth century suggests that the puppeteer used his puppet directly and kept additional figures in a pouch hung from his waist.[12] An improvised stage was sometimes made by hanging a curtain over a cord near the top of a doorway and performing above it.[13] Pietro Aretino in 1534 describes a crude farce performed this way.[14] Andrea Sarina (1828–1902) initially combined puppets with selling pots and pans and other domestic wares on fairgrounds. He is said to have used his old army cloak as a "stage" for his performances.[15] Cloak stages were current in Spain and Portugal and probably widespread in Italy too.

Fights with stout sticks provide climactic moments to most glove-puppet shows. Pulcinella was prepared to use his stick on almost everyone he encountered. At the turn of the nineteenth century many new comic figures were created in the north of Italy, but unlike Pulcinella these characters used their sticks more sparingly and primarily to punish those of whom the audience disapproved. Physical combat was more closely linked to plot development and usually had the more clearly defined dramatic purpose of resolving the dramatic action.

The basic guarattella show involves a series of encounters between Pulcinella and other characters: Teresina (the wife or girlfriend), a more aggressive other male character (Scaramuzzia or in more recent times a camorrist), a large dog with ferocious jaws (a vestige of the medieval mouth of hell), the law in the form of a carabineer, a hangman (who ends up being hanged) and death. Vigorous fights have always been the most popular element of this type of show and almost every encounter ends with one. The solo performer has only two arms and a fight provides the simplest way of concluding a scene and disposing of a character so that the next one can appear. An especially popular routine, much practiced by Nunzio Zampello, was a comic encounter between Pulcinella, who has just killed the camorrist and placed him in a coffin, and death, who plays a number of comic tricks, such as moving the body. Even the coffin is called into use as a grotesque weapon.[16]

The Neapolitan guarattella performers were extremely poor and left very few traces. Their shows with tiny stages and less than a dozen small figures were extremely portable. The showman who earned his living directly from puppets depended on the "piattino" or collection bowl. This was generally held by a companion who had to encourage contributions, chat up the audience, catch those who tried to escape, and often exchange cracks with the puppets, or even play a musical instrument.

Harbors were bustling, populous places and therefore a favorite pitch for puppet shows. Street shows sometimes moved indoors because of the weather or used a room where admission could be charged. Michele Barone, the best-known Pulcinella performer of the early nineteenth century in Naples, performed in the most miserable of little rooms and in the homes of the nobility. Carriages would stop and watch his show in the street, and he also followed the fairs.[17]

The legendary Gaetano Santangelo, known as Ghetanaccio (c. 1782–1832), was a well-known figure and was often to be seen on the Piazza Navona in Rome. He was consumptive and died in abject poverty, and virtually nothing is known about him for certain.[18] Famous for his powerful voice and mordant satirical comments, he could produce a wide range of voices and dialects and even animal noises. He is said to have used the swazzle for the voice of Pulcinella, but the real mouthpiece for his talent was the more recently invented character of Rugantino. Like many good street performers, he was engaged from time to time to perform privately for aristocratic patrons, who enjoyed his satirical wit in what was a closed and tightly controlled society.[19]

In *Il volgo di Roma*, Filippo Chiappini gathered together some of the many anecdotes that circulated about him.[20] In 1825, when Pope Leo (Leone) XII was trying to close down entertainments, and thus threaten his livelihood, one of Ghetanaccio's puppets converted the expression "Coraccio de leone!" (courage of a lion) into "Core de cane! Core de boja! Core de leone!" (heart of a dog, heart of an executioner, heart of a lion). This play on the pope's name supposedly led to one of the many occasions of Ghetanaccio's imprisonment by the papal police. A popular diversion in Rome was the Pasquinade, which took the form of satirical poems or epigrams that appeared mysteriously in public places, and Ghetanaccio was a sort of walking Pasquino.

The Milanese equivalent of Ghetanaccio was Lampugnani, who is recorded with his glove-puppet stage on the Piazza del Duomo between 1848 and 1859.[21] Lampugnani's target for satire was the Austrians, then in control of Lombardy, who were regarded as occupiers. Lampugnani referred to them as "coo di legn" (wooden heads), and they regularly received a beating from Arlecchino. One anecdote describes an occasion when Arlecchino laid about him with special vigor, declaring "Te conscierro come nel quarantott'" (I'll get

Napoli.   Ritorno

Napoli.   Pulcinella.   Naples.   Marionettes.

Early 19th-century popular print of Neapolitan "guarattella." (Courtesy Istituto per i Beni Marionettistici e il Teatro Popolare.)

to know you as I did in '48)[22] but that suddenly the puppets were put down on the playboard and Lampugnani departed, escorted by two soldiers.

Expression of popular sentiment is part of the mythology of street puppet theater. Ghetanaccio and Lampugnani were indeed outspoken, but a large part of their income depended on coming out with things that were subversive or daring, to the delight of their audiences. In most cases a blind eye was turned, but every so often the bounds of tolerance were overstepped or a punctilious official decided to exercise his power and drastic action was taken (usually a night or two in prison).[23]

Riva degli Schiavoni, Venice, with booths including a puppet show, circa 1850. Quaysides were bustling places and much used by entertainers. (Engraving by A. Martinotti from R. and R.M. Leydi, *Marionette e burattini* [Milano: Collana del "Gallo Grande," 1958].)

Glove-Puppets of the Po Valley

The prosperous plains between the Alps, the Apennines and the Adriatic, had numerous towns and villages and comparatively easy and safe transport (often by the river Po). A rich glove-puppet culture evolved there in the nineteenth century. The guarattella made way for shows where two or more puppeteers could present a piece with a dramatic rather than an episodic structure and have a larger number of figures on the stage.[24]

Where possible, audiences were seated on planks or benches (and occasionally chairs in the front) and the performance was in a screened enclosure where a charge might be levied. Showmen often set up in sheltered places such as the arcades under public buildings. In the winter months some moved indoors to a barn, hall or even a theater. The proprietor of a large glove-puppet fit-up enjoyed a status not very different from the director of a marionette company and often played for predominantly middle-class audiences. Carlo Cuniberto, who visited Asti several times between 1811 and 1817, performed in the open under a portico or in a courtyard, but then moved indoors to a hall and finally offered his show on the stage of the Berruti Theater, which he occupied from December 16, 1816, until February 7, 1817.[25] In 1811 the charge had been 2 soldi for an open-air performance (a marionette

Pulcinella in Rome, 1830. The figure of Rugantino on top of the booth suggests this is Ghetanaccio's show. This image depicts simultaneously the stage with puppets and the performer outside the booth. ("Burattini," drawn and engraved by Bartolomeo Pinelli. Romano, 1830. *Costumi di Roma* [Rome: La Calcografia Camerale, 1831]. Courtesy Civica Raccolta delle Stampe, "A. Bertarelli, Milan" [Albo H 2 tav.30].)

show cost 3 or 4 soldi, and a show with live actors 7 or 10 soldi). A bill for 1817 indicates the importance of the scenery and costumes and admission charges of 2 soldi and 6d. for the pit and 4 soldi for the boxes (as opposed to 7 soldi 6d. and 15 soldi for admission to the Opera Buffa).[26] One of the shows offered by Cuniberto was *The Dragon of Transylvania; or Gironi Turned into a Ridiculous King*, a piece equally popular in the repertoires of marionette companies. Cuniberto is also known to have erected a temporary booth on the Piazza Castello when he visited Turin.[27]

In 1808 the associates Gioacchino Bellone and Giovan Battista Sales established a more permanent glove-puppet theater in Turin's via Doragrossa (today's via Garibaldi), probably in a hall attached to the church of San Rocco. Around 1811 they occupied another location, the Teatro Gallo. They were in Milan at the San Romano in 1814–1815, but back in the San Rocco by 1816. A contemporary account describes the San Rocco as spacious and having a gallery and boxes and performing to a well-dressed audience.[28] In 1819 the guide *Turin et ses curiosités* listed three fixed puppet theaters in the city. These were the Gianduja Theater (previously San Rocco) of Bellone and Sales, and two marionette theaters, that in the Paesana Palace (via della Consolata), used by the Lupi family, and the San Martiniano, to which the Lupi and Franco company moved in 1823.[29] The productions of Bellone and Sales involved elaborate staging and, like Rossi, they presented a repertoire based on that of the theaters. By the late 1820s they had branched out as impresarios and opened a circus, the Circo Sales. Around 1843 they graduated from glove-puppets to marionettes, perhaps to compete with their great rivals, the Lupis.

The epicenter of the north Italian glove-puppet tradition is Emilia-Romagna, notably in and around the cities of Bologna, Mantua and Modena. Most puppeteers followed a specific circuit. Their children, if they established separate shows, usually carved up the territory or ventured further afield to avoid competition with other family members. A puppeteer established in a larger town might have more than one pitch there and also visit the surrounding countryside.

Luigi Rimini di Campogalliani (1775–1839), the reputed creator of the character of Sandrone, came from Carpi and was probably of Jewish origin.[30] In the 1790s he abandoned a wife and four children and set off as a traveling puppeteer through the north of Italy, accompanied by a blind musician and story-teller. His second family included two sons and two daughters who also became puppeteers.[31] His son Francesco (1803–1851) later worked the circuit of Trieste, Padua and the Veneto and his grandson, Ugo (1862–1951), was well known through much of Italy, especially in Romagna. Luigi's second son Paolo (1805–1851) was the father of Cesare, whose sons Arturo (1866–1943) and Francesco (1870–1931) also continued the family tradition. Arturo worked for a number of years in Mantua and sometimes collaborated with Francesco, who became one of the most celebrated performers of his generation. Francesco established his own show in 1890.[32] Generally he worked as a solo performer, and such assistants as he did use were close family members.[33] He operated around Piacenza and then increasingly in the province of Mantua. Between November 1896 and March 1897 he worked at the Teatro della Varietà in Mantua. Campogalliani wished to raise the status of the glove-puppet theater at a period when it was often dismissed as being merely for children or at best an ephemeral street entertainment. With the aim of transforming it into a part of the avant-garde, he polished and improved what he had inherited through several generations, but targeted more middle- and upper-class audiences. In 1900–1901 he returned to the same theater with the expressed purpose of achieving a high artistic level, and his performances began to receive serious attention from critics.

Campogalliani's shows were enriched by poems and songs written by himself. After the main play a characteristic element of the performances was a comic duet between Sandrone and the popular comic character of Fasolino. The Commedia dell'Arte was beginning to be "rediscovered" and his work was perceived as a worthy continuation of that tradition. In 1904–1905 he had another season in Mantua, this time at the more prestigious Andreani Theater, where ticket sales were high. This season spread his reputation and launched him on a tour of Italy.

Campogalliani saw himself as a moralist and satirist who, like Molière, used laughter as his method.[34] The idea of the morally improving aspect of puppet theater had been growing since the mid–nineteenth century. This was a move towards respectability, but it was also seen as a way of attracting the patronage of the children of the middle classes. The church retained an ambiguous attitude towards puppets, but they were sometimes acceptable as a way in which children might receive religious education. Puppets made or commissioned by enthusiastic priests still survive today. The "blessed" Luigi Palazzolo (1827–

1886) of Bergamo used the popular character of Gioppino in an educational context to teach catechism to children, but managed to do so in a lively manner that sometimes shocked the more orthodox.

The booth of Giulio Preti (1804–1882) carried the slogan "morality, instruction, progress."[35] The word "progress" had political overtones that were not always acceptable to the church of the time. Preti, the son of a cabinet-maker and puppeteer in Rolo, studied landscape painting at the ducal academy of Modena. He was apprenticed to a Sante Lucini, who taught him mechanics, pyrotechnics and even singing, and was already giving glove-puppet shows with his friends when he joined Paolo Campogalliani's company. In 1830 he married Ermengilda Campogalliani (1810–1884), a daughter of Luigi, and they set up their own portable show. They rapidly acquired a reputation on the piazzas and in the inns of Emilia and eventually reached Modena, where they also performed in theaters.[36] The Preti and Campogalliani companies renewed the repertoire, playing comedies, tragedies and farces and offering a daily change of program. They normally remained in one place for between a fortnight and a month. One of their more regular venues was the spa at Salsomaggiore. Giulio Preti wrote his own scripts and scenarios and satire of manners and politics was an important ingredient of the show. Four of his sons, Gugliemo (initially trained as a teacher), Carlone, Enrico and Emilio continued the family tradition.

In the twentieth century the heavy-handed tactics of the Fascists were often unfavorable towards puppeteers, and the uncomfortably close ties between the Fascists and the church created problems and pushed many puppeteers, especially in Emilia and the north, into taking a more definable political stance. Through these difficult years many puppeteers steered a path that avoided any political reference, but that was not always enough.[37] Enrico Preti was doing excellent business on the piazza of a small town when a company of actors arrived, who were well known to the Fascist mayor. The puppeteer was told to move on. That evening, when Sandrone announced that the show had had to move, a voice demanded why, and Sandrone quipped back, "Because the big puppets give orders to the little ones."[38]

In the early 1920s Attilio Salici, who had no particular political involvement, had a performance interrupted by the Fascists bursting into the theater. Such episodes discouraged people from coming to the shows, and this had dire economic consequences.[39] Totally depressed, he committed suicide in 1925, whereupon his widow and children were put out of the lodging they were renting and neither the mayor nor the priest would offer any assistance. When Monaldesca Gozzi, widow of Attilio Salici and a devout Catholic, was dying in 1952 she dismissed the priest who came to offer the Eucharist, declaring that she would take it from God, but never from a priest.[40] Her half brother, Pirro Gozzi, died in 1940 and indicated in his will that he would curse anyone who even thought of calling a priest or taking his body to a church.[41] Of the countless anecdotes relating to this period, many are probably apocryphal, but they give a flavor of the climate in which puppeteers worked. Gualberto Niemen on one occasion had official permission to set up on a town square in front of the church, but the parish priest objected to the proximity of a puppet show and Niemen found himself in the middle of a dispute between a Catholic priest and a lay mayor.[42] Ciro Bertoni (1888–1986) had a story that he allowed Fagiolino to say the devil did not exist. The following day the Curia newspaper mentioned this, but said it was all right, since everyone knows that Fagiolino has a wooden head. The next night, from the stage, Fagiolino announced that this was not to say much, since not even Dante has been able to give us the address of hell and therefore of the devils who, according to certain priests, would be at home there.[43] Until quite late in the twentieth century a puppeteer might even be refused burial in consecrated ground.

Two celebrated performers in Bologna were Filippo Cuccoli (1806–1872) and his son Angelo (1834–1905). Originally a silk-weaver, Filippo lost his employment because of the decline in that trade and turned to puppets. He set up his stage on the *Piazza Maggiore* in 1831, performing in the morning in front of the church of St. Petronio. In the afternoon and evening (9:00 P.M.) he moved to the arcades of the nearby *Palazzo del Podestà*. The audience sat on planks available after the end of the market, but later Cuccoli bought seating and the arcades became his regular pitch. An old woman puppet requested contributions of a "bacherone" (half a baiocco) to be placed in a tin in front of the stage. At night the main puppet, Sandrone, often made a spectacular exit in an apotheosis of fireworks and Bengal fire — sliding up a wire attached to the neighboring *Palazzo dei Banchi*.[44] Cuccoli carried his puppets to his pitch each day in a basket, "il paniron di Cuccoli." He was such a familiar figure that in 1863–1864 the popular satirical paper *Il diavolo zoppo* portrayed Louis Napoleon as Cuccoli.[45] Satire aimed at the papal authorities was a part of Bolognese life and there were legends about Cuccoli's attacks on the cardinal legate and the gonfaloniere (chief magistrate), and of the nights he spent in prison. These were later discounted by his son. He was, however, occasionally reprimanded for his comments. Once he alluded to the colors red, white and green and this was instantly suppressed by the police because of the potential reference to the tricolor flag of Italian nationalism.[46]

Angelo Cuccoli's career began with the traveling mechanical theater of Angelo Sutto performing *The Passion of Christ*. In 1857 he set up in Minerbio as a glove-puppet performer, but joined his father in Bologna soon after. When Filippo died Angelo acquired a new partner in Augusto Galli (1861–1949), who developed the repertoire and introduced new characters, but gave up street puppet shows for acting in 1883.[47]

Urban development and social changes created problems for the street puppeteer. In 1877 the Piazza Maggiore (Vittorio Emanuele) of Bologna was cleaned up and the traders had to leave. Angelo Cuccoli was eventually forced to move to the less central Piazza San Francesco because the crowds attracted by his show encouraged traders to drift back to the Piazza Maggiore.[48] In 1885 he was on the Piazza de'Marchi in the mornings, but the residents objected to the noise of laughter and the disturbance made by the dismantling of his seating.[49] In the same year the shopkeepers of the arcade of the palace claimed that his stage made it hard for customers to get into the shops. Cuccoli's performances were restricted to evenings and holidays. A campaign in the press led to the finding of a hall complete with a piano in a converted riding school but Cuccoli had lost his main audiences and the show did not transplant well to an indoor space. A sick man, he returned in a limited capacity to the Piazza de'Marchi and the arcade, where he struggled on until 1903, sometimes performing only to a group of friends. During these last years, the charge for a seat on the few rows of benches was 10 cents on workdays and 15 on holidays, and this was collected by his wife before the performance.

The great modern exponent of the Bolognese tradition is Romano Danielli, who began his career in 1953, working with various companies and setting up his own in 1964. He has phenomenal vocal skills as an actor and these he has channeled towards a dialect theater presented by puppets. He has used his literary talent to rewrite the classic scenarios derived

Back view of Angelo Cuccoli's stage erected under arcades of the Palazzo del Podestà, Bologna. (From Antonio Pandolfini Barberi, *Burattini e burattinai bolognesi* [Bologna: Nicola Zanichelli, 1923].)

from the Commedia dell'Arte and make them relevant to today's audiences. For five years (1989–1994) he also had a children's program on television, *La banda dello Zecchino*.

Bologna, politically one of the most left-wing cities in the twentieth century, maintained its anti-clerical and subsequently Communist tradition. This was strongly represented by the Sarzi family. The "dynasty" began with Antonio Sarzi (1863–1948), son of a sacristan and a peddler, who in 1882 abandoned work as secretary to the Commune of San Giorgio di Frassine in the province of Mantua to become a puppeteer. His five children, several of his grandchildren and a great-grandson followed in his footsteps. Antonio Sarzi roamed the provinces of Verona and Mantua with a donkey and cart onto which he loaded his show and basic household equipment. The show was announced with his own handmade posters. His wife collected entrance money and organized the pitches, permits and lodging, but never performed.[50] He had received a basic education that enabled him to write his own versions of such popular pieces as *The Moon of the Thirteenth of March*, *Fagiolino Lawyer* and *The Brigand Musolino*. In addition he could speak a number of dialects.

Antonio usually performed in halls and theaters in the winter, but also used the porticoes of houses. In the summer he performed on town squares, but he preferred enclosed courtyards where it was possible to levy an entrance charge. He seldom performed on Friday, as takings were usually slim, and never performed in Holy Week. Saturday was payday for many workers, and Saturday and Sunday were the best days of the week for audiences. Working mainly in rural areas, he had to take account of seasonal rhythms. During the main agricultural period of the summer, when people might have to work 16 hours a day, he did not perform. Antonio's sight deteriorated badly and in the early years of the twentieth century he was assisted by his son Francesco (1893–1983), who organized his pitches, put up the publicity, negotiated permits, and set up the booth.[51] Francesco often paid the fare for Antonio, who would arrive by tram or bus for the show. In the later years Francesco placed the puppets in the hands of his father, who could recognize each one by its weight and feel and perform as normal with it.

Angelo Cuccoli. Fagiolino on his right hand and the Dottore on his left. The famous basket for carrying the puppets each day is in the background. (Angelo Cuccoli, puppeteer [1834 —1905]. Courtesy Biblioteca dell'Archiginnasio di Bologna [foto cartone 17, fascicolo 81, carta 01].)

Francesco Sarzi enjoyed a reputation as an amateur actor. During the First World War he used puppets to entertain his comrades and patients in the military hospitals. After the war he performed with his father's puppets. Most of his traveling was on a bicycle, and he often performed in inns, where his show brought additional custom, which obviated the need to pay rent for the space. The admission charge for his shows was 20 cents (a newspaper cost between 10 and 15 and a cup of coffee 5).[52] His son Otello later became one of the most influential performers of the twentieth century.

The Maletti family, originally carpenters in Modena, became involved with puppets in the latter part of the nineteenth century. Alberto Maletti (1901–1952), as a boy, joined a Venetian puppeteer, Giacinto Storati, who worked in Modena between 1913 and 1915, and in 1920 he worked with Gustavo Preti. He founded his own company with two of his brothers in 1928.[53] In 1935 he moved to Genoa for a couple of years, apparently because of problems with strict political censorship. He acquired the marionettes of the Cagnoli family and alternated marionette and glove-puppet shows. With the war the activities of the company ceased. Alberto's son Cesare joined the partisans between 1943 and 1945. With peace, Maletti and his sons resumed performances and found engagements in Modena in the lay schools. The generally reactionary political and religious climate of Modena was unsympathetic to Maletti, so he made for the Adriatic coast, briefly joining forces with Otello Monticelli in 1947 but then moving with two of his sons to Rimini, where he died in 1952.[54] In Modena the Maletti tradition continued with Alberto's son Cesare and his grandson Mario.[55]

Bergamo

The comparative prosperity of the Po valley rapidly gave way to poverty in the adjacent mountainous country. In the old city of Bergamo a local puppet, Gioppino, emerged in the early nineteenth century. The earliest showman to be recorded is Battaglia, who, like Lampugnani in Milan, is said to have ended up in prison regularly for his anti–Austrian gibes.[56] He was active from 1820 until about 1835.[57] His pupil Pasquale Strambelli (1804–1865) followed similar lines and often used a stolid and hungry Austrian soldier as a foil to Gioppino.[58] Strambelli probably performed on the Piazza Vecchia of the high town, perhaps under the covered arches of the Palazzo. Another player, Angelo Fatutti (1812–1888), usually set up his stage on the Haymarket. In the winter he also performed in inns and in the summer he traveled further afield, possibly introducing Gioppino to the Milanese.[59] Bernardo Moro (1838–1902), also from Bergamo, was well known for his performances in restaurants in Milan. The Gioppino show spread throughout Lombardy and could be found in Brescia, parts of Emilia and Piedmont and Canton Ticino in Switzerland.

In the early twentieth century Giovan Battista Locatelli (1884–1923) combined puppets with work as a painter and decorator. His career was cut short by bad health, but he was especially well known for his sharp and brilliant wit, and was consulted by Vittorio Podrecca when the latter wished to set up a puppet theater.[60] It was difficult for puppeteers in Bergamo to make a decent living from puppets alone. Irmo Milesi, who operated for years at the Mutuo Soccorso (workmen's club) of Bergamo, learned his skills from Locatelli but also had a job at the Institute of Graphic Arts.[61] Luigi Cristini, who had trained with Milesi, attempted to be a full-time puppeteer between 1932 and 1935, but failed and returned to his previous work.[62]

Luigi ("Bigio") Milesi, active in Bergamo between 1918 and the mid–1970s, was a younger cousin of Irmo Milesi and combined puppetry with work as a confectioner.[63] In 1915 a Bergamask who had carved some glove-puppets to entertain the troops sent a bag full of these to the Milesi household where the young Bigio played with them.[64] When he came to do his own military service, he too performed with puppets for his comrades. Bigio Milesi was a solo performer with an assistant and his performances were arranged to have only two characters on stage at any one time. Like many he prided himself on the number of different voices he could produce. The assistant's job was to pass the puppets up to him and to produce sound effects, such as gun shots, or to operate a flame pipe for the appearance of the devil.

Luigi Nespoli (d. 1951), originally an itinerant tinker, became one of the best-known exponents of Gioppino and for several seasons received engagements from King Umberto to entertain his guests.[65] In the winter he could often be seen in Bergamo, but in better weather he traveled throughout Lombardy and for years had very profitable seasons at the various spas, where he might remain for up to five weeks. His repertoire was extensive enough to allow for a change of show each day. Despite a brief upswing after the Second World War, his later years saw a huge decline in audiences and engagements and he died in poverty.

The mantle of Nespoli with the classic Gioppino show was taken on by Benedetto Ravasio (1915–1990). In the after-war period he performed in restaurants, in the open air and in church halls. Television brought his activities to a stop for a couple of years, but

Carlo Sarzetti stage, Bergamo. An example of a larger booth allowing for more than one performer. (On loan to the Fondazione Bergamo nella Storia — Museo Storico di Bergamo. Courtesy the Scuri family, Bergamo. Photograph Domenico Lucchetti. Courtesy Archivio Privato Famiglia Domenico Lucchetti.)

then he struggled on, working much of the time in Milan, and appearing on television in 1972. Ravasio became the complete puppeteer, making his puppets, painting his scenery, writing his texts, and playing as happily for audiences of adults as for children. His work was not fundamentally different from that of his predecessors, but his awareness of it was. He arrived at a moment when classic puppet theater was beginning to be reassessed and when work could be mechanically recorded for posterity. In 1980 the young Daniele Cortesi, who had been performing with puppets for about three years, met Ravasio and decided to work in the Bergamask style. Cortesi revitalized the Bergamo tradition and represented a new breed of puppeteer with a background of theater training.[66]

South of Bergamo puppet companies traveled through towns in Emilia Romagna and eastward towards Brescia, Verona, Padua and the Veneto and, before the First World War, down the Illyrian coast of Slovenia and Croatia. Amedeo Costantini (1903–1967) of Bologna came from a family of traveling actors, possibly linked to the Costantini family, well known in the history of the Commedia dell'Arte. In the 1930s this proprietor of a fairground shooting gallery bought the complete puppet show of Brandisio Lucchesi (1906–1970), which included figures acquired from Carlo Sarzetti of Bergamo.[67] Costantini ceased to appear at fairs as the ambient noise made it difficult to hold the concentration of audiences for performances of plays. During the post-war years he retained the shooting gallery as an added attraction in the afternoon, on holidays and after the show for an hour or two.[68] He often used courtyards and audiences brought their own seats. Sometimes benches were borrowed from chapels, and later the company acquired its own raked seating. In Brescia during the winter months they played indoors in schools and chapels. Most shows required two performers (with sound effects provided by the younger son Carlo). Publicity consisted of posters painted in powder color on thick paper and these were stuck on walls or glued onto boards each morning and placed on the piazza, in the main shop and often at a crossroad. Towards 5:00 P.M. the two Costantini sons paraded through the town or village with a board and announced the show with a megaphone.

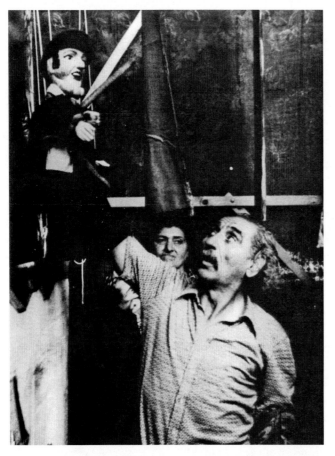

Benedetto Ravasio performing in Bergamo with Gioppino. His wife Pina is in the background. (Courtesy Fondazione Ravasio di Bergamo. Photograph Domenico Lucchetti. Courtesy Archivio Privato Famiglia Domenico Lucchetti.)

In the early days they traveled with a horse-drawn cart, but in 1951 they bought a truck which enabled them to cover longer distances and visit many more small towns and villages in the region. They lived in a caravan that was towed by the truck and a second truck was used to pull their trailer of equipment. Before the spread of television audiences were still more adult than juvenile in composition and were not yet very mobile, so a move from one pitch to another might be no more than five kilometers, and a halt might vary from two or three days to a couple of weeks. The immediate post-war years were ones of general poverty and this led to a brief revival of classic puppet theater. As in many places, admission was often paid in kind except in the autumn, when people sometimes had a little more money after the harvest.

Following a general trend, the Costantinis acquired their own 500-seat portable theater in the 1950s and worked with this until 1958–1959.[69] This large canvas structure (20 meters by 40) had an iron frame and a curved roof. They usually arrived at a new pitch on a Friday and set up in readiness for the weekend.[70] By the later 1950s there was a sharp decline in business. The portable theater was no longer viable and had to be sold. School performances now became a main source of income and engagements for a fee began to replace reliance on the box office.

Costantini never mastered the dialect of Bergamo, but his son Sandro (1930–1997) became a noted Gioppino player. Sandro's memoirs provide one of the best pictures of the situation of the glove-puppet players in the north between the 1940s and late 1960s. After his marriage he set up his own smaller show and performed on Saturdays and Sundays. In the late 1960s he acquired a car, which allowed him to load his equipment onto the roof rack. When he had worked as his father's assistant it was easy to have four puppets onstage at one time, but he subscribed to the idea of the glove-puppet performer as a solo artist, since he felt this made improvisation easier.

Italo Ferrari (1877–1961) came from a poor peasant family in Casalfoschino, near Parma. His father apprenticed him to a shoemaker, but puppets proved too strong an attraction and he set out on an unsuccessful venture as a showman with a friend. He briefly became a barnstorming actor before finding work as an assistant to Arturo Campogalliani, who passed him on to his brother Francesco, who impressed on him the need to speak literate Italian. In 1905 he married Ebe Avanzi, who taught him to read and write, performed with him and made costumes.[71] Like Francesco Campogalliani, Italo Ferrari frequently performed in theaters and also had long seasons at the spa of Salsomaggiore. In 1914 he created his own character, Wladimiro Falesi, called "Bargnocla" (barnacle), who was an instant success and became the stock puppet of Parma. Unusually, the Ferraris used glove-puppets with opening mouths, and this, coupled with a highly distinctive style of carving and a fondness for strong colors, made their figures instantly identifiable. The Ferraris offered a classic glove-puppet show but the style of presentation and the physical appearance of the figures were distinctly contemporary. Italo's son Giordano (1905–1987), a gifted puppeteer and puppet maker, worked with him and later continued the family show but lost the use of speech in his later years. Giordano's sons Luciano (1934–1978) and Italo, known as Gimmi (1940–2006), and now his grandchildren have kept the family tradition alive.[72]

Piedmont

The area south of Turin with such towns as Alessandria was a hub of glove-puppet activity. The Lyonnais Guignol of Laurent Mourguet has much in common with glove-puppets in this region. His name evokes the town of Chignolo (in nearby Pavia province) and may have been imported from here during the Napoleonic period.

One of the most important puppet families was the Sarinas. Antonio (1857–1922), son of the already mentioned Andrea, had considerable artistic skills and developed his father's very basic performance into something far more elaborate, with a stage, scenery, painted publicity, music and a large number of puppets. In 1882 he married Maria Adelaide Palamede, from Broni, who came from a rather bohemian middle-class family with considerable musical and scientific talents, and this led to a further development of the artistic and technical quality of the show.[73] The literary interests of the Palamedes may explain why Antonio Sarina developed a specific interest in chivalrous material more generally associated with the pupi of Sicily.

Italo Ferrari e alcuni dei suoi.......attori

Italo Ferrari and some of his "actors." Publicity postcard. (Courtesy Castello dei Burattini/ Museo Giordano Ferrari.)

Antonio's son Giuseppe, known as Peppino (1884–1978), and daughter Teresa (1885– 1980) carried the show forward to the latter half of the twentieth century.[74] Teresa not only looked after the box office and made costumes but also performed with her brother. In 1920 she married Virginio Scotti, a carpenter at the theater in Tortona who helped Peppino design and build a sophisticated dismountable stage.[75] Peppino Sarina was an autodidact.

Giordano Ferrari and Bargnocla. (Courtesy Castello dei Burattini/Museo Giordano Ferrari.)

He wrote his own scripts and browsed bookstalls regularly and his extensive personal library included an early edition of *Orlando furioso.* His artistic skills ranged from designing his own scenery and costumes to painting frescoes, creating a gothic family tomb, composing his own music and even writing *I Bersaglieri,* a short opera for glove-puppets. The main area covered by the Sarina family was south of the river Po between Alessandria and Piacenza.[76] The courtyard of Peppino Sarina's house in Tortona was also used as a theater.

The Niemen family of puppeteers and circus artistes performed widely through Piedmont with an open-air fit-up and ancillary attractions such as shooting galleries. Gualberto Niemen first presented puppets around 1922, but continued to work with the family acrobatic show until his military service in Bologna in 1924, which he combined with puppet shows in the evenings. In Bologna he encountered Aldo Rizzoli (1885–1968), an excellent interpreter of the local characters of Sandrone, Fagiolino and Dr. Balanzone, who also impressed him with his ability to perform with ten puppets on stage at the same time. In Bologna Niemen found a puppet maker from whom he commissioned a set of eight new puppets. He also acquired a great many books that later served as sources for puppet productions.[77] Back in Piedmont in early 1927, he worked in the area around Alessandria and obtained his first official license to perform on public squares throughout Italy. In winter he gave shows in inns, church halls and for family circles (local community groups), for which a different license was required. Like Costantini he avoided fairs because of the difficulty of holding the attention of the audiences and the small size of contributions. On one occasion he had all his puppets stolen from the booth by children. A woman's bicycle with reinforced handlebars provided an affordable mode of transport, especially for journeys of less than 20 kilometers. He placed the box of puppets on the front carrier and the canvas and scenery on the back one. The poles for the structure, weighing about 30 kilos, were carried on his shoulders and held with one hand while he steered with the other. Later he hired a cart to take his material from one village to another.[78]

In the early 1930s Niemen's stage was 3 meters wide and 2.5 meters high. A seated audience of 100 occupied ten rows of planks on trestles and paid 20 cents each (10 cents for children). The takings, including a collection from those standing around, averaged 25 lire per show. In 1936 he constructed a new and solid stage and replaced acetylene lamps with electric ones.[79] A couple of years later he acquired loudspeakers which made it possible to play to larger audiences. In 1948 he built an "arena," or enclosure, for summer performances. This had canvas walls and raked planks for spectators, with more comfortable seats in the front. It could contain nearly 500 people and admission was 50 cents for adults, 30 cents for children, and 80 cents for the front seats.[80] In the 1950s he introduced amplification to play gramophone records and publicize the show, which he often did by driving round a town in his recently acquired car. By now many of the halls used by Niemen had installed television sets and were less available for outside performances. He acquired his own portable theater, measuring 6 by 18 meters and containing nearly 400 people, and traveled with that until 1964. In later years he presented occasional performances with a smaller setup in cinemas, church halls and family circles and supplemented his income by working as a painter.

The extensive Niemen family of entertainers also includes the Gran Teatro dei Burattini dei Fratelli Niemen that travels throughout Piedmont today under Eliseo Bruno Niemen (b. 1957). They are amongst the last of the itinerant puppeteers whose income depends entirely on the box office. In summer they set up in the open air and in winter they hire large halls into which they may cram 1,000 spectators. With Gianduja as their main figure, they still perform a repertoire that has almost disappeared.

Glove-puppets to Marionettes and Back

Marionettes had a higher status than glove-puppets and a number of nineteenth-century glove-puppet performers graduated into marionette showmen. By 1920 a changing economic climate affected the viability of the large marionette fit-ups. Attilio Salici, with his sister Pia, continued for a time the marionette company of their father, Ferdinando, but then turned to glove-puppets.[81] Attilio's brother Ermengildo Augusto (1869–1914) also became a glove-puppeteer. His children continued until 1931 as the Compagnia dei Burattini Fratelli Salici and reduced Ferdinando's repertoire to scenarios suitable for glove-puppets.[82]

After the death of the marionette showman Vittorio Monticelli (1868–1926), his widow Genoveffa Peli married his collaborator and scene painter Agostino Galliani Serra and together they set up a glove-puppet company.[83] Vittorio's son Vasco (1907–1967) continued the family marionette tradition and then joined with other families in a company called I Pupi which traveled for some years in Europe and visited Brazil. He then turned to glove-puppets and settled in Reggia Emilia, but by the 1960s was having difficulty making a living. His brother Otello (1905–1991) also transferred from marionettes to glove-puppets, but for a long time he was active in both fields. In 1934 he and his wife joined the Fantocci Lirici di Yambo and remained with that company until it was dissolved in 1951.[84] Together with his son William he worked with the Piccoli of Vittorio Podrecca between 1955 and 1961, after which he became a full-time exponent of the classic Emilian glove-puppet repertoire with the figures of Fagiolino, Sandrone and Sganapino. The old marionettes and scenery of the Monticelli marionette company were adapted accordingly.[85] From 1979 onwards William's sons Andrea (b. 1958) and Mauro (b. 1961) have continued the glove-puppet work of their grandfather, but have also branched out into more contemporary forms of puppetry under the title of the Teatro del Drago.

The classic glove-puppet theater involves a way of working that is not vastly different from that of 100 years ago. For some the glove-puppet remains the ideal form of expression, but it is also chosen because it involves only a simple fit-up and can be presented by a single performer.

CHAPTER 3

The Golden Age: Marionettes and Pupi

Shapes and Sizes

The portable street shows described by Ottonelli had very small figures and seem to be very similar to the "fantoccini" brought to England in the late eighteenth century. The shape and size of marionettes and pupi can be a rough indication as to their age and provenance, but there may also be considerable variation from one showman to another. There is also a difference according to whether they are used primarily to tell a story or to reproduce actors' theater. In the former the figures are often proportionately large in relation to the stage, in the latter there is more of an attempt to make them relate in scale to the scenery.

Most marionettes datable from before 1850 are smaller than those in use at the end of the nineteenth century. Many of those that survive were for use in private marionette theaters. The house puppets of the Grimani family measure between 35 and 40 centimeters. Most of those in the Davia Bargellini museum and a few in the Signorelli collection are close to this height.[1] Some have rods well over a meter in length, which suggests that they were used for a more scenic performance, and this is confirmed by the height of surviving scenery. It is possible to find figures from the late eighteenth or early nineteenth century that measure around one meter and were almost certainly used by traveling companies and by the more popular theaters. Two large figures now in the museum of Novara have well-carved heads and hands, made by a professional carver, but relatively crude bodies.[2] This suggests that they were used by a professional troupe, where it was common practice for the showman to purchase heads and hands and to make up the bodies himself. The Museo delle Arti e Tradizioni Popolari in Rome has about 50 figures from one of the pupi theaters in Rome. Most measure between 80 and 90 centimeters and a few, including the dog-headed Pulicane, as much as 97 centimeters. Equipped with short, stout head rods, they must have been nearly as tall as the stage opening and used in performances where the main concern was with telling a story rather than producing miniaturized theater.

In 1812 Giuseppe Medici and Domenico Uccelli applied (unsuccessfully) for permits for an open-air marionette show in Bologna. They indicated the size of their puppets: 22.5 "once" (about 56 cms).[3] The Rissone figures, designed for the scenic stage and probably used by the traveling company of Onofrio Samoggia in the 1820s, are slightly smaller, being between 45 and 48 centimeters. Stendhal referred to the figures of the Fiano Theater in Rome as being about a foot high (30 cms) and another contemporary indicates a fairly similar measurement of 14 inches, but this is merely the impression they gave.[4] With scenery and accessories to scale it can be very difficult for audiences to assess the height of marionettes, but 30 to 35 centimeters is a plausible size for marionettes using a more scenic stage and that is certainly comparable to the Casa Grimani figures. At the time the Fiano was using figures that belonged to the Ottoboni family.[5] A reference in a prologue to the production of *L'Italiano in Algeri* (1833–1834 season) mentions the main character, Cassandrino, as having grown by a palm, which would suggest that by now the average height of the Fiano figures had increased to a little over 50 centimeters.[6] In the same period the marionettes of the Lupi and Fiando theaters of Turin and Milan measured between 50 and 60 centimeters.[7] By the later nineteenth century the general height of marionettes in the north of Italy was between 70 and 80 centimeters. The Palermitan pupi settled at a height of about 80 centimeters, but some earlier figures are smaller. The Neapolitan pupi at between 80 and 90 centimeters are similar in size to the Roman ones. By the later years of the nineteenth century Catanian figures grew to 1.2 meters or even 1.4 meters and armored ones could weigh 35 kilograms.[8]

The shape of the torso of a marionette is a better indication as to its age than is its height. The pupi of the Rome collection have unpadded long and narrow-waisted bodies and pronounced hips which help date them to the eighteenth century or the early decades of the nineteenth. Giordano Ferrari had two Neapolitan figures said to have belonged to Donna Peppa. One, in the Castello dei Burattini, has the more tapered body which suggests that it was made no later than about 1850. The second figure, an old man in sixteenth-century costume (now in the Zanella-Pasqualini collection), is similar. The long torso and narrow waist is a feature of some of the Grimani and Davia Bargellini figures and can also be found with several of the possibly Venetian figures in Lyon's Musée Gadagne.[9]

By the mid–nineteenth century

Nineteenth-century Neapolitan pupo. Military figure attributed to Donna Peppa. (Courtesy the Castello dei Burattini/Museo Giordano Ferrari.)

most marionettes had unisex bodies (except where a woman's breast had to be visible). In many cases bodies were quite crude, but padding was used to give a shape. The two "Peppa" figures are less heavily padded than later Neapolitan figures, but the legs are encased in a tube of scrim which limits knee movement. By the twentieth century Neapolitan pupi were exceptionally heavily padded and this often led to a very wide chest and shoulders, regardless of sex. The limbs were rounded with padding which reduced the flexibility of the figure.

The head rod was the standard control throughout Europe in the eighteenth century but in Italy today has become a means of distinguishing between marionettes and pupi. A flexible connection to a staple on the top of the head permits a wide range of movements from bowing to flying. In Sicily this is usually limited to comic figures, angels, devils, animals and some women. In earlier times a rod embedded in the head was much used. This rod can be found with some Roman and Neapolitan figures and is general for the armored Sicilian pupi, where it runs through the head and emerges at the neck with a bend that hooks onto a staple between the shoulders and then returns to a second hole in the neck that locks it.[10] To free the head for removal is merely a matter of depressing the rod into the neck socket. These heads are easily interchangeable and in this way a company can economize on the number of figures by switching heads and bodies in the long cycles where characters are regularly killed off and new ones appear. Saracen common soldiers are regularly decapitated on stage. A deep groove in the back of the head takes the head rod which ends in the customary bend. An upward blow from a sword releases the head and it falls off.

The Roman pupi figures already mentioned and the Neapolitan ones were operated by a short stout head rod and both arms were controlled by strings. The Catanian pupi were operated by shorter, and generally heavier, rods than the Palermitan ones and usually had no wooden hand grip. In both cases the shield arm was operated by a string, and the sword (right) one by an iron rod.

In the nineteenth century it was common for marionettes to have the right hand closed or half-closed to take a property and the left hand open for more expansive gestures. Women and unarmed characters in the opera dei pupi often have both hands open. The Roman pupi in the Museo delle Arti e Tradizioni Popolari mostly have both hands open. This is even the case for soldiers, which suggests that any weapons were tied on as necessary. Hands of Neapolitan pupi are presented open rather than closed and a hole running straight up the wrist and into the forearm allows for the insertion of a sword, dagger or gun. In Palermo and sometimes in Naples a special string running through the hand allows the sword to be drawn. The sword is permanently fixed in the hand of the Catanian puppet. The manner of holding a sword has a direct impact on fights. In Palermo and Catania it tends to point downwards, which makes for a more stylized manner of fighting. In the Neapolitan tradition it points in the direction of the arm. The style of fighting is also affected by whether the sword arm is controlled by a rod or a string. In Palermo armed figures often had an additional string to raise and lower the visor.

Traveling Marionette Companies in the North of Italy

In the eighteenth century most marionette activity was in towns but the Incisa diaries indicate that traveling marionette companies were a part of provincial life by the later years of that century. Companies began to travel widely through the provinces in search of audiences. According to Yorick, some 400 traveling marionette companies were active at the end of the nineteenth century. Most operated a circuit within a given region, offering what was often the only available form of theater. Where audiences warranted a company might settle down for a longer period and even open a permanent or semi-permanent theater.

Onofrio Samoggia was an important showman of the early nineteenth century, but few traces of his activity remain. The *Gazzetta di Bologna* of February 3, 1820, refers to his company presenting the finest ballets of Gioia and Viganò with magnificent scenery.[11] On October 22, 1820, what were probably Samoggia's marionettes performed the tragedy of *Ulderico and Prezzeva* and the heroic ballet *The Arrival of Scipio in Rome* at the Nosadella Theater of Bologna.[12] Samoggia's name can be found on some of the scripts in the Rissone collection, which suggests that this material may have been his originally.[13]

Ireneo Nocchi's company had great success at the Teatro San Gregorio in Bologna in January 1812 with Vigano's ballet *Prometeo*.[14] In February 1812 he visited Asti with a fantasmagoria with the "usual magicians, shadows, skeletons, mummies, specters, skulls, serpents, dragons and devils" and a number of other presentations of a quasi-scientific nature.[15] On July 10 Nocchi applied for a permit in Parma to open a "padiglione volante" (a temporary booth) on the Piazza delle Vecchie Beccherie to show two machines called "Venus" and the "Oracle" (probably automata).[16] Three years later he reappeared in Parma and received a permit for marionettes.[17] In 1819 he visited Asti, still with his fantasmagoria, the "oracle," a "mechanical clock," a "hydraulic woman" and "the magnetic tubes." This was introduced with a lecture on magnetism and hydraulics. The bill does not mention marionettes but at this period scientific "tricks" were replacing the sleight of hand of the "bagatellieri." The juxtaposition of popular science and marionettes was common at the time.[18] In 1824 a "new heroic spectacular ballet" called *The Triumph of Caesar in Rome* appeared at the Fiando Theater in Milan.[19] "Composed and directed by Ireneo Nocchi of Rome," it included the Roman character of Rugantino.[20] This ballet, together with *Beautiful Judith* and *The Chinese Rites*, was presented by Nocchi on August 27, 1827, at the Teatro Comunale of Modena. Nocchi's was a major touring company but he is also mentioned as having a theater in via Pelletier in Livorno.[21] The standing of the Nocchi company is indicated by the fact that a newspaper bothered to review it when it visited Rome in 1833. The company arrived by sea, probably from Livorno, disembarking at the port of Fiumicino. Performances were given in the Argentina theater, which had been going through a difficult period and was available for anything from an equestrian show to marionettes. The boxes and pit of the Argentina were packed, but the reception was not an unmitigated success. The 30 beautifully painted scenes elicited considerable applause, but the two ballets presented in the first program failed to satisfy everyone. The reviewer indicated he was looking forward to their other ballets with lots of music and scenery, and then added that he had devoted enough space to a mere marionette show.[22] The Nocchi company also appeared regularly in Venice at the Sala di Calle Larga in the 1830s and in August 1836 was in the open-air theater in the public gardens.[23]

The Zane family, possibly related to the owners of the San Moïsè theater, originated in Venice. They spanned two generations, Luciano (1815–1903) and his son Rinaldo (1849–?), and ceased activities around 1904. Charles Dickens described in detail a performance of the Zane company at the Teatro delle Vigne in Genoa in 1844.[24] A few years later, Théophile

Gautier found them in a more modest hall in Domodossola and persuaded them to stage an additional performance for his benefit. The text was in Italian, but parts were in dialect. From Piedmont to Sicily showmen saw themselves as transmitters of culture. Serious action was presented in Italian and dialect was used for popular scenes and comic characters.

From 1882 onwards the Zanes presented long and lavish seasons at the Gerolamo (Fiando) Theater in Milan.[25] An initial triumph was Eugène Scribe's comedy *Les diamants de la reine* with Gerolamo, and a ballet. In the spring of 1883 they resumed touring but returned to the Gerolamo in the autumn, with yet more large-scale spectacular performances. In the spring of 1885 they transferred to the Nuovo Politeama Theater, but were back at the Gerolamo in 1892, this time under Rinaldo Zane, who outdid his father with the scenic splendor of his productions. Their last big production was Louis Varney's operetta version of Dumas's *The Musketeers in the Convent* in 1904. They also traveled abroad and, like an increasing number of companies, visited South America.

Venetian-born Antonio Reccardini (1804–1876) and his wife described themselves as actors when they were married in 1827. The first surviving reference to using marionettes was in Trieste in 1832.[26] A bill of 1846 announces a performance in the foyer of the theater in Trieste with Arlecchino as a miser and Facanapa, a character he invented, as a cook. A live performance of a farce with Reccardini and six of his young children followed the marionettes. Reccardini had a good bass voice and usually closed the show with an operatic aria.[27] A review noted the audience as being composed of the upper classes of Triestine society.[28] Reccardini visited Austria and Germany but his zone of activity was broadly that in which Venetian dialect could be understood and ranged from Padua, Verona and Gorizia to the Dalmatian coast.[29]

The most permanent base of the company was Udine, where in summer they had an open-air enclosure with seating and in winter used the Teatro Minerva.[30] Antonio's son Leone (1844–1914) continued the company and by 1878 was using a complete portable theater, later known as the Teatro Fenice or "Phoenix," after the opera house in Venice. A bill from 1900 indicates a pit, a gallery and boxes and there is a note to the effect that it was covered and sheltered, which allowed performances whatever the weather.[31]

From at least 1837 until 1866 the company performed annually and with great success at the little Sala di Calle Larga Theater in Venice. The San Moïsè had closed in 1818, but was converted into a marionette theater in 1871 by the De Col brothers (Venetian marionettists). This theater changed its name to the Minerva in 1889. In the early 1900s it briefly became a cinema and was then demolished.[32] It was here that the Reccardinis gave their last performances in 1898, before abruptly ceasing to function in 1900.[33]

The two companies with the most complete records and the most extensive collections of material are the Lupis and the Collas. Both benefited from sustained periods in a fixed theater. According to tradition the Collas were a prosperous Milanese family who had furnished the Austrian army with wood, charcoal and forage, and had continued to do the same for the French, but had fallen on hard times with the return of the Austrians in 1814 and are said to have taken to the roads with their own private marionette theater. Gaspare Carlo Gioachimo Colla, known as Giuseppe (1805–1861), is generally accepted as the founder of the dynasty. However a permit dated September 3, 1814, was granted to a Giovanni Colla to open a theater for marionettes in the Palazzo dei Crociferi in Parma. This was for 20 performances and was dependent upon payment of the appropriate tax for "spettacoli e balli" to the Uffizio di Beneficenza and performances had to finish before those of the Teatro Grande began.[34] The name Colla in Parma may be sheer coincidence, but it is also conceivable that a marionette company already existed and that this Giovanni Colla was a relative whom the young Giuseppe joined at some point after 1814.[35]

The Collas are next heard of in 1835, when their registers indicate them as a firmly established company under the leadership of Giuseppe Colla.[36] Most of their traveling was in Piedmont and in the region around Pavia. On the death of Giuseppe his three surviving sons, Antonio (d. 1907), Carlo (1832–1906) and Giovanni, divided the materials and formed three separate companies. Giovanni's company was continued by his son Giacomo (1860–1948), grandson Giovanni (Gianni) and great-granddaughter Cosetta. Antonio had a number of seasons at the Gerolamo theater, Milan, between 1885 and the early 1900s, but his company died with him. He was at the Gerolamo in the spring of 1886 when the celebrated English company of Thomas Holden was at the Teatro Milanese. Holden was much imitated and many companies boasted they were now doing things in the Holden manner. Antonio Colla almost certainly borrowed what he could. He abandoned the head rod for the English control where the head was supported by wires or strings attached to a horizontal bar. In England all the strings were attached to one or more bars (one of which might be in the shape of a T). The Collas later developed this principle and evolved their own horizontal control or "crociera" that could be held in one hand.

Carlo Colla called his company Carlo Colla e Figli and moved to Emilia Romagna in 1863 and then to the area south of the Po. In 1889 he was struck with a serious throat problem and his sixteen-year-old son, Carlo II (1873–1962), took over management. Carlo II admired his uncle Antonio and probably introduced his innovations to his own company. By 1880 the touring pattern was changing, with stays in larger towns which could sustain a company for a longer period. Urban audiences required a more up-to-date repertoire and better production values. Between 1899 and 1906 the Carlo Colla company had seasons at the Gerolamo and in 1911 they finally became the resident company, performing every day except Friday, and twice on Thursdays, Sundays and holidays.

With the closure of the Gerolamo the Carlo Colla company ceased to function in 1957, but it was revived in 1966 by Eugenio Monti (a nephew of Carlo II) and his cousin Carlo Colla III. Monti made a virtue of productions that used the full resources of the large nineteenth-century marionette theater, with richly painted scenery, magnificent costumes and sometimes as many as 14 operators on a high bridge. He revived some of the great successes of the company, such as *Ballo Excelsior*, *The Last Days of Pompei* and *Around the World in 80 Days*, and created new productions in a similar style.[37] The company no longer has its own theater, but often performs in the small auditorium of Milan's Piccolo Teatro. Much of the company's income now comes from special performances for schools, sometimes with workshops attached, and from engagements at festivals.

Ariodante Monticelli was born around 1820. His company traveled through Piedmont, Lombardy and Emilia. The family's main area of activity was around Mantua, until eventually they settled in Ravenna. Little documentation survives apart from some puppets and scenery and an important collection of scripts written by Ariodante. The Monticello family has been active with puppets for over 150 years, worked with major marionette companies of the twentieth century, including Yambo and Podrecca, but today the classic glove-puppet is their main source of income.

The Ajmino, Pallavicini, Burzio and Gambarutti families of Liguria and Piedmont are examples of the traveling companies that toured mainly in their own region, visiting many communities that might otherwise have been deprived of live entertainment. Carlo Ajmino (1820–1870), a printer from Turin, started a marionette company that was continued by his sons Antonio and Luigi. Luigi's daughter, Clotilde, married Pietro Pallavicini (1874–1957) in 1899 and the Pallavicini company came into existence. Pallavicini came of a middle-class background but had worked with marionettes with the Genoese showmen Ugo Ponti and Giovanni Pavero. From the latter he acquired much of the material that he would use as a showman. In 1928 his son Raffaele (1906–1968) took over the company. Raffaele briefly worked with Yambo in the 1930s and was also involved with the company set up by GIL, the fascist organization for the training of youth, in Rome between 1941 and 1943. The Pallavicinis had a huge repertoire of dramas, but, like many, in their last years concentrated more on variety acts. In the 1960s they were engaged to give performances for schoolchildren in the little theater of Genoa's piazzetta Santa Mari degli Angeli.[38] By 1968 Raffaele's two sons had ceased to perform and much of the material was sold.

The Burzio family, also of Piedmont, began with Gaetano Burzio, recorded as a glovepuppet performer in 1750.[39] His son Giuseppe married Giovanna Marengo, of a marionette family, and this was the start of the Burzio marionette company. Cesira Burzio (1880–1958) married Rafaele Gambarutti in 1899 and the company changed names accordingly. When Franco Gambarutti began his career in the 1950s, he developed a variety program accompanied by gramophone records and pre-recorded sound.[40]

One of the latest of the classical traveling marionette companies in Piedmont was that of Giuseppe di Luigi Concordia (1882–1962) of Vercelli. Concordia had been an amateur actor and puppeteer until his marriage with Tersite Benente, who belonged to a puppet family. When he established his company he used the stock Piedmontese characters of Gianduja and Famiola.[41] He presented the standard pieces of the marionette repertoire, but he was especially noted for operas and operettas, a strong variety program, and for the attention given to the more technical aspects of staging, particularly the lighting, and such innovations as a revolving stage and rotating scenery.[42]

The Prandi brothers of Brescia are recorded as paying a successful visit to Verona in 1870 and were at the Mercadente Theater in Naples in 1888.[43] In the same year they had a well-patronized season from June to October in London at the Italian Exhibition in West Brompton. They paid another visit to London in 1893, this time performing at the Crystal Palace. The main mover of the company was Ettore Prandi (b. 1865), described as the "Napoleon of marionette entrepreneurs"; the company also included his father, two women "of a certain age," a girl of about 16 and four male assistants, all part of a family group.[44] The scale of the show, with some 400 figures, was similar to those of the Lupis, Collas or Holdens. They delighted foreign audiences with a musical and variety program. When they ceased to function as a company is unclear but they may have merged with the Gorno Dall'Acqua one.[45] In 1928 the Mariani-Gorno troupe visited London's Scala theater. Top of the list of performers was Ada Prandi, possibly a daughter of Ettore. A fire at Wembley film studios that year destroyed the Mariani-Gorno material and possibly that of the Prandis.

The Salici family originated with Ferdinando Salici (1840–1923), who left his job in the municipality of Menaggio (Lake Como) and traveled with puppets in Lombardy and Piedmont. Hunchbacked due to an accident in his youth, he was often referred to as "il

Il diavolo zoppo (Lame Devil), 62 cms. Ajmino-Pallavicini company. The "mouth of hell" back-cloth was popular for diabolical scenes on the puppet stage. (Courtesy Istituto per i Beni Marionettistici e il Teatro Popolare. Photograph Dario Lanzardo.)

gobbo Salici." Around 1854 he was involved with the company of Luigi Zubiani, active around Rovereto, Trento and Trieste, and married Maria Zubiani.[46] Their son Enrico (1864–1943) left the family company in 1880 and went to England for four years.[47] He was struck by the naturalism of the movements of the English marionettes and picked up the English mode of operating all-string figures and probably the use of cloth joints at the waist and hip, which gave great flexibility of movement. Back in Italy, Enrico set up on his own, later being joined by some of his siblings. In October 1889 he left Genoa for a brief tour of Australia, where the company appeared in Sydney and Melbourne as the "Imperial Marionettes."[48]

By the early 1900s the company, which ran to over a dozen members, many of them relatives, was known as the "Fantocci Lirici di Enrico Salici." Its highly polished professional shows were enjoyed by smart audiences. Sydney Jones's operetta *The Geisha*, presented at the Teatro Filodrammatico of Milan with enormous success in 1912, brought the company to national attention, and this was followed by Franz Lehar's *Merry Widow*, *La mascotte*, and Caballero's *The Five Parts of the World*. Fresh from triumphs in Bologna, Venice and Genoa, the company departed for a tour of Argentina, Columbia, Venezuela and Peru.[49] For the duration of World War I it remained in South America. In 1921 it joined the recently created "Fantocci di Yambo" for a season. Enrico Salici found the political climate of the later 1920s unsympathetic and the economic situation was becoming increasingly difficult. In 1931 the company visited Buenos Aires and subsequently made an extensive tour of South America. In July 1934 it was in Mexico, and by August was appearing at the Chicago Fair. Now known as "Salici's Puppets" the group performed at New York's Radio City Theater, where it presented a variety show. Salici retired in 1936, at the age of 72, and returned to Italy. Four sons and a daughter continued the show in America, but it was now reduced to a series of items making up an act of less than 30 minutes that could be inserted into a music hall program. When they returned to Italy in 1950 they found much of their older material had been destroyed in the bombing of Genoa and a further 500 puppets, scenery and props placed in storage in New York were subsequently lost.[50] Enrico's sons Gino and Adolfo continued, but on a much reduced scale. Their three large vans of the 1920s and 1930s were now reduced to two trunks containing the Can-Can and Eva the smoker, the pianist Paderewski, a gypsy violinist, a clown, a drinker and rumba dancers.[51] They appeared in Paris at the Gaumont Palace and in Cairo for the wedding of King Farouk (May 8, 1951). They also visited Belgium and Germany and toured through the United Kingdom (Belfast, the London Paladium, Glasgow, Manchester, Liverpool and the Isle of Man). By 1954 Adolfo, his wife Clara and nephew Ernesto Bruschi were the company and Britain, where they had slots in the main music-halls, remained their base until 1960. There was a third tour of Australia and New Zealand in 1955–56 and a visit to Italy in 1957. In the last years they presented musical-hall numbers, appeared on the BBC, and even on the Ed Sullivan show in New York. The company finished with the death of Adolfo in 1964.

Places of Performance

Throughout the nineteenth century companies performed in theaters, barns or granaries, disused chapels and parish halls. In the early 1900s many small theaters and halls were turned into cinemas. Parish halls were in the remit of the priest, some of whom were hostile to anything theatrical. Giuseppe Concordia often performed in cinemas, but also used church halls, and in these cases emphasized the educational and extremely moral nature of his shows. Gianni Colla mentions how, in his youth, the first thing to do on reaching a town or village was to visit the priest to negotiate a venue. A showman with children sent them to church to sit in the front and show zeal.[52] Saints' plays and ones about Christian heroes were often performed first to assure the good offices of the church, after which the rest of the repertoire was brought out.[53]

Portable theaters, many little more than tents, had long been associated with traveling puppeteers. A self-contained theater complete with seating saved on the cost of renting and allowed a company to perform wherever an audience might be found. In the summer

The Cuticchio stage on the beach at Mondello (Palermo), 1955. (Courtesy the Compagnia Teatro Arte Cuticchio.)

months many companies, especially in the south, used an open-air screened enclosure or "arena" to which audiences paid an admission charge. The Di Giovannis were doing this in Naples in the mid–1950s and Girolamo Cuticchio in Sicily presented shows in the summer on town squares and camp sites.[54] Like the guarattella booths, marionette and pupi stages were sometimes set up on beaches and contributions were collected.

As late as the 1940s traveling marionette theaters in the north of Italy might remain in one place for up to three weeks. Almost daily changes of program were the norm and the most frequent performance days were Thursday, Saturday and Sunday.[55] After 1918, hired horse-drawn carts were gradually replaced by lorries. Most companies used a couple of vehicles, one for the theatrical material and the other for all their household equipment. Upon arrival in a town they would hire rooms for the projected length of the stay and arrange a pitch for the show. The word "piazza" was used for this, but did not necessarily mean the town square. Local helpers might be taken on for a big show. In the 1930s when

Perozzi family marionette booth. Piedmont, 1950s. The Perozzi company also used an uncovered "arena" surrounded by a fence. (Archival photograph. Courtesy Archivio dell'Associazione Peppino Sarina di Tortona [Al].)

the Gambaruttis had large-scale productions such as *I promessi sposi* (The Betrothed) or *Cristopher Colombus* involving more than 100 figures, these helpers would pass the puppets to the performers stage right using long poles with a hook and collect and hang them up again stage left after they had crossed the stage.

Fixed Theaters

In the later eighteenth century noblemen might let out disused parts of their palaces to entertainers and some of these became permanent puppet theaters. After 1798 deconsecrated religious buildings also became available. By the nineteenth century larger towns often had theaters that were used regularly or at least periodically by marionette companies and there was an increasing middle-class audience prepared to go to respectable marionette theaters, if not to back-street ones.

Giuseppe Fiando moved from Turin to Milan in the mid–1790s.[56] He is thought to have performed in a room in a house on the Piazza Duomo of Milan and later in a larger one in the Palazzo del Pretorio. In 1806 he moved into the former Bellarmino oratory, near the cathedral, and was probably responsible for its conversion into a 700-seat theater generously provided with exits.[57] The same year, the viceroy, Eugène de Beauharnais (stepson of Napoleon), ordered the newspapers to list theatrical entertainments, as was done in Paris. Newspaper circulation was mainly amongst the liberal bourgeoisie and the use of newspaper publicity gave a new status to the marionette theater. On June 18, the *Giornale Italiano* mentioned Fiando's Teatro delle Marionette, "known as Gerolamo."[58] The first show announced was Metastasio's *Themistocles in Susa*, followed by a "brilliant farce" with Gerolamo. The advertisements give an excellent idea of the repertoire of the theater and the name of Gerolamo appears in a variety of guises in the title or subtitle of many of the pieces performed.[59]

In 1808 Fiando tried to turn the Gerolamo into a minor theater with live actors and singers, but was rapidly reminded that the licenses for minor theaters and itinerant shows did not permit them to perform at the same time as the main theaters.[60] In 1816, when Lombardy was an Austrian province, he received a license allowing performances with live actors on the stage of the Gerolamo, but it remained pri-

Title page of the script of *Il mostro turchino* (The Blue Monster) by Carlo Gozzi, adapted for the Fiando Theater, 1815. Stamped with police authorization. (Courtesy the Compagnia Carlo Colla e Figli.)

marily a marionette theater. Between 1825 and 1830, his activity was at its height, and shows became increasingly spectacular and included *The Last Days of Pompei*, with the eruption of Vesuvius and Gerolamo as a gardener.[61]

The Gerolamo continued to be used for marionettes until 1857. After its demolition in 1865 a new 600-seat theater was erected by the firm of Rivolta and Pellini, who also became the owners. This opened on January 29, 1868, re-sited on the nearby piazza of the Palazzo della Giustizia and functioning as the main puppet theater of Milan. The Fiando family remained the resident marionette company until 1881, with Giuseppe Fiando's widow directing productions.[62] It then closed for refurbishment and when it reopened in 1882 the entrance was lit by electricity. By 1887 all the lighting was produced by electricity, only four years after La Scala. The Gerolamo became the permanent home of the Carlo Colla company after 1911. It was damaged by bombing in 1943 and the company had to move out for a time. In 1952, Carlo II handed over the management to his nephew Giuseppe. The economic climate was now difficult and in 1957 the building was scheduled for demolition

The Fiando Theater, Milan, circa 1820. (Courtesy Civico Archivio Fotografico, Milan.)

for reasons of town planning (which did not occur). The theater closed its doors and the extensive collection of material and equipment was put in store.

Apart from Fiando's theater, there were at least two others in Milan in the early 1800s. One was in the former monastery of San Antonio and its director was an ex-shoemaker, Carlo Ré, later to become a major theater director. In 1798 Carlo Torelli opened his Lentasio

Interior of the 1868 Teatro Gerolamo seen from the stage. (From *Il Germano — c'era una volta un teatro di marionette...* [Milan: Strenna dell'Istituto Ortopedico Gaetano Pini, 1975].)

marionette theater and in 1805, he moved into a former Benedictine convent near the Porta Romana. Another marionette theater was active at S. Romano and in 1814 this housed the Sales and Bellone glove-puppet company from Turin. Their performances, according to the *Corriere delle dame*, were well staged and avoided crude language so that it was safe for parents to bring their children to these shows.[63] References to the Fiando in the 1830s make quite clear that children had become an important part of its audience too. Two other marionette theaters were in existence in Milan by 1830, one run by Antonio Macchi and Maddalena Rossi, also with Gerolamo as the main character. In the S. Simone quarter of the city Giuseppe Frattini opened his theater in the 1840s and this was occupied for a time by the Maggi company from Brescia.[64]

Genoa's wooden Teatro delle Vigne dated back to the early eighteenth century as a theater for live actors. Despite its huge capacity (2,500), it was much used by marionette companies until its demolition in 1881.[65] Auguste Jal mentioned seeing a performance by

Andrea Maggi's company there in 1834. The piece being presented was the *Siege of Antwerp*, accompanied by a ballet which he felt was poorly executed.[66] He found the whole show inferior to the marionettes of Milan. In the early nineteenth century a popular Genoese showman was Nicola Tanlongo, whose successor, Il Cincinina (Luca Bixio, 1801–1879), had a little marionette theater in vico dei Santi in the Portoria district and reputedly created the comic characters of Barudda and Pippia, and also introduced hungry cats onstage in his *Barudda Devoured by Wild Beasts*.[67]

The Nosadella was the main marionette theater of Bologna and was established in a deconsecrated convent chapel.[68] It was also much used by amateur acting companies and became known as the Teatro Nazionale. In 1929, after a closure of 15 years, it reopened for four months as a glove-puppet theater, but then became a cinema.[69] The Teatro San Saverio, situated in a former college in Bologna, was also frequently used for marionette performances. In 1825 a company presented Silvio Pellico's *Francesca di Rimini* accompanied by a ballet, *The Rape of the Sabines*.[70]

Naples

One of the earliest documents concerning a puppet theater in Naples is a request in 1792 from a Crispino Zampa for a permit to perform with his "pupi di legno."[71] The first Stella Cerere theater is thought to have existed in the eighteenth century and was situated on the Piazza del Carmine, near the harbor, an area where puppet shows had been established for many years. During the last decade of the nineteenth century this area was developed and the puppet theaters moved to neighboring districts and then to the outskirts. Many relocated themselves to the south-east of Naples, Torre del Greco, Torre Annunziata and Castellammare di Stabia and some took to touring in an attempt to find new audiences. Initially companies played complete cycles lasting several months, but by about 1930 the impact of cinema and social changes made them condense material into single performances for audiences who might well come to see only one show.[72]

In Naples the proprietor of a puppet show was known as a "puparo."[73] The most famous was Donna Peppa (Maria Giuseppina d' Errico, 1792–1867). She came of a theatrical family.[74] Her husband, Salvatore Petito, was the Pulcinella at the San Carlino theater and their son Antonio Petito (1822–1876) became the most celebrated Pulcinella of the century. Peppa herself was a focus for myths and was erroneously credited with introducing the pupi to Naples. Probably employed by the Partenope theater when she first arrived in that city, she later became director of a little theater at the Porta del Carmine. Her productions were noted for the richness of the staging and costumes, but whether she used puppets or live actors from the start is unclear. By 1859 her repertoire included two major heroic cycles, *Kings of France* and *Gerusalemme liberata*. One of her operators was Giovanni De Simone (1830–1906), who opened his own theater at the Porta del Carmine in the

Opposite: **Performance of *Cinderella* at the Gerolamo Theater, 1950s. "Orchestra" of violin and piano. ("An Afternoon at the Gerolamo." Courtesy Compagnia Carlo Colla e Figli. Photograph from *Teatro Gerolamo* [Milan: Pubblicazione a cura dell'Ufficio Stampa del Comune di Milano, 1967].)**

Facade of Stella Cerere theater, Naples, circa 1900. The large painted posters ("cartelloni") on either side of the door indicate the day's program. (Courtesy CEIC Centro Etnografico Campano.)

mid–1850s, taking over the now disused title of Stella Cerere. Filippo and Domenico Buonandi, Nicola Corelli, Luigi Di Giovanni and Gaetano La Rocca, all members of De Simone's company, went on to create their own shows after the De Simone one ceased in 1889–1890. Domenico Buonandi's son Pasquale established himself at Torre del Greco around 1900, and his son Alfredo remained there until 1954. Domenico's brother, Salvatore, moved into the former Ercole theater, which he renamed the Piccolo San Carlino after the demolition of the old San Carlino, and this was continued by his son Giuseppe.

    Luigi Di Giovanni (1869–1944) created his Grande Compagnia Italiana dei Fantocci in 1907 and like the Salicis specialized in marionette variety acts requiring technical virtuosity. He traveled through Italy and in 1911 visited Buenos Aires. Between 1926 and 1940 he performed regularly in the big store, Rinascente, in Naples. His sons and grandsons continued as pupari and maintained some marionettes. In the 1940s they worked at the Piccolo San Carlino and finally closed their show in the 1960s.[75]

    The first decades of the twentieth century were the apogee of puppet activity in Naples. Large numbers of "pupanti" (or "pupari") and also "manianti" (manipulators) are known of, but few details have been recorded. Nicola Corelli (1855–1925), a grandson of Donna Peppa, began his career as an actor, but then moved to the Stella Cerere as a pupante. In 1888 he saw the Prandi company at the Mercadente Theater. This inspired him to set up a company performing the spectacular marionette repertoire of the north Italian companies with such major shows as *The Flood* and the immensely popular *Ballo Excelsior*, but he also retained the Neapolitan pupi for performances from the heroic cycles (*Orlando, Guerin Meschino*). In the early years he had no fixed theater, but he eventually built one at Torre Annunziata where he could present both the pupi and a more modern marionette repertoire.[76] His son Vincenzo (1901–1970) also used both pupi and marionettes and worked in various collaborations with his siblings.[77] Vincenzo's companion and associate was Giovanna Furiati, and their children, as they grew up, became part of the family business. In the early 1950s he built a portable theater, the "Carro di Tespi" (Car of Thespis) and toured in the area around Naples, and later throughout Calabria, Basilicata, Abruzzo, Molise and Puglia, offering plays with live actors followed by puppets.[78] His base remained Torre Annunziata, but in 1969, the "Carro," together with some 200 puppets, was destroyed in a fire and Corelli himself died a month later, in January 1970.

After Vincenzo's death the Corelli Furiati children called themselves the Fratelli Corelli and performed in various halls around Naples. In 1971 they opened their Teatrino Corelli in Torre Annunziata and continued to present heroic material in single self-contained episodes with increased emphasis on the staging. As live actors, they appeared under the title "Compagnia d'Arte Varia Corelli." In 1975 Vincenzo's son Nicola Furiati went to work in a Milanese factory, but continued to make pupi to sell and occasionally worked with his brother. In 1980 Lucio Furiati closed the theater, but earned his living as a puppet maker and house-painter. Nicola re-established himself in Naples in 1985, creating a workshop for pupi, marionettes and stage design, and also had a small company with his wife and family, performing mainly for festivals and events or in schools. His eldest son, Vincenzo, went to art school and introduced a more consciously "artistic" approach, including more stylized figures.

Ciro Perna (1879–1956), the son of a fisherman, was first employed by Giovanni de Simone and later set up his own show first in Herculaneum and later in Casoria. Like the Corellis and the Di Giovannis, he operated with both live actors and puppets. In 1930, after a brief attempt to make his fortune in America, he set up a little theater at the Carmine in Naples. He had a series of "teatrini" and also toured extensively in Campania. His son Giuseppe (1905–1974), noted for his vocal skills, took over the show after the war and moved to Frattamaggiore. Giuseppe's son, also Ciro (1931–2000), set up a show in 1945. Throughout the 1960s he worked mainly in Campania and specialized in stories of the Camorra. By the 1970s his traveling "San Carlino" theater was the last of its sort, and after 1980 it was the only opera dei pupi in the Naples area. By the 1980s the company was reduced to performing for schools and taking engagements. The usual program was a compressed version of the heroic material or else of the "borghese" (Camorra) one, followed by a farce, with Pulcinella, and the very popular "fantocci" (variety marionettes). Perna built up an important collection of material from other puppeteers who had abandoned the profession. His last years were darkened by poverty, blindness and the deaths of two of his sons.

In the late 1930s the Fascist authorities instructed the pupanti of Naples to stop performing pieces to do with the Camorra or brigands, which were what the popular audiences wanted to see, and concentrate on the heroic repertoire with Orlando, Rinaldo and the paladins.[79] This was perceived as educational, promoting positive values with the regular emphasis on the triumph of good over evil, and therefore less likely to encourage violence.[80] The "borghese" repertoire was in dialect and frequently pitted the Camorra against the forces of law and order.[81] Vincenzo Corelli was known for his anti–Fascist views, which led to suspension of his performances for a time and even a brief stay in prison. He invented a harmless piece called *Tom Mix* that was a coded way of announcing a "borghese" one. If the authorities came in sight the puppets promptly reverted to a scene from this.[82] In another case a company announced *New History of Napoleon Bonaparte*, a Camorra piece in which the emperor was only a minor figure. Companies readily, and transparently, re-baptized Camorra figures with such names as Murat.

Faced with the competition of cinema, the little theaters in Naples were already vanishing. Some pupanti took to the province, where they could still scrape a living. There was a brief revival after the war. The long cycles were shortened and reduced to the most significant episodes, but shows had lost their social context and become just another diversion for audiences increasingly familiar with the mass media.[83] Francesco Schioppa abandoned the opera dei pupi in 1951, and his last shows were given in the street without even a stage. The Piccolo San Carlino closed down in 1958. Some puppeteers hired out puppets and equipment. Gaetano, known as Ferrariello, active for a short time after the Second World War, rented puppets from Ciro Perna. Many companies also began to sell everything. The Ferraiolo family of Salerno and the Abbate of Caserta moved into glove-puppets. In the early 1990s the San Martino Museum of Naples received a large donation of decaying pupi that had been found in a house scheduled for demolition, where an unknown pupante had died some 20 years earlier.

The average teatrino in Naples held between 100 and 120 spectators, though the Partenope and the Stella Cerere were larger. In the 1930s individual seats in the stalls cost 12 soldi (60 centesimi), while the "scanni" (benches) cost 6. In cinemas there were three prices: 14, 8 and 4 soldi, with prices raised for popular films.

The Corellis, like many Neapolitan puppeteers, both read the text and worked the figures. Many pupanti worked "al incrocio" with the voice for a puppet provided by one of the other manipulators. Sometimes voices were provided by non-manipulators and assistants might be taken on purely as voices.[84] In the 1930s the average puppeteer could call on about six voices plus that of a woman (usually a man using a falsetto voice).[85] These were the "generico" or all-purpose actor, the comic, the first and second roles, "il generico primario" or character actor and the "parrucca" (bewigged character), who was probably the announcer.[86] In the Perna company Maria, sister of Giuseppe, and Adele, his daughter, ranked amongst the finest female voices of the twentieth century.

From Naples companies traveled through Basilicata and Calabria and on to Sicily; others moved northwards via Rome. Many traveled through Puglia and some remained for a number of years.[87] In 1882 Lorenzo Dell'Aquila (1863–1939) of Barletta created his Aurora company. According to oral tradition he had accompanied his father, a draper, on a business trip to Naples, seen a performance at the San Carlino and later returned to Naples, where he acquired some scripts and a set of about 15 "small" puppets.[88] He and his wife toured the villages of Puglia with a small cart for the equipment. Just after the First World War they created a theater next to the church of San Francisco in Canosa di Puglia. This former wine cellar easily contained 150 spectators on benches and had a stage measuring 6 by 6 meters.[89] The primary audience was agricultural workers. Performances, of which there could be as many as four, each lasting an hour and a quarter, began at 4:00 P.M. In July and August they toured nearby villages, playing in the open air.[90] Like the Neapolitans, they used marionettes as well as pupi and their repertoire also reflected that of the bigger marionette theaters.[91] Performances of heroic material included the *History of Count Orlando* in 108 episodes, *Buovo D'Antona* and *Guerin Meschino*.

The nine Dell'Aquila children were all part of the company. Ruggiero (1899–1945), a primary school teacher, succeeded his parents. He was a gifted artist and improved the quality of the staging and the technical aspect of the puppets. When he died the company was taken over by his niece, Anna Dell'Aquila (1921–1992), one of the finest pupari of the twentieth century, ably seconded by her family, especially her husband Giuseppe Taccardi and her son Sante, but with her death the theater ceased to function.

Sicily

The pupi probably arrived in Sicily from Naples, but here they acquired a significance they did not have on the mainland. De Felice described the opera dei pupi as one of the most characteristic forms of Sicilian theater.[92] Pitrè, despite an absence of hard evidence, liked to think it had existed in Sicily for hundreds of years.[93] The extraordinary development and flowering of the opera dei pupi around the middle of the nineteenth century resulted from a combination of a style of puppet theater with a particular historical moment and social climate. It was absorbed by a popular culture and recreated as a unique phenomenon. Sicily had not appreciated becoming part of the kingdom of the two Sicilies, with Naples as its capital. The unification of Italy increased the sense of remoteness from central government.[94] In a desire to maintain its own identity it looked back to its golden age as a Norman kingdom, when Ruggiero (Roger) had reconquered it for Christendom and such monuments as the palace in Palermo and the cathedral of Monreale had been built. This gave a new immediacy to the medieval chivalric material, making it a point of reference for Sicilian patriotism and therefore placing it in a different postion from that which it had in Rome and Naples.[95] The opera dei pupi also fitted into the Mediterranean folk traditions of Moors and Christians. A performance was closer to a ritual than an entertainment and audiences did not usually applaud.[96] Recent Ottoman expansionism and pirate raids from North Africa emphasized the proximity of the Islamic world and tradition was reinvented, with popular retellings of the stories of Christian knights forever in conflict with the Saracen enemy. This was expressed in a remarkable outburst of folk painting that ranged from the decoration of carts to the glories of the puppet theater. The Sicilian pupi are physically similar to the Roman and Neapolitan ones. They are distinguished by the armor, the mode of delivery of the text and the continuing emphasis on the chivalric repertoire. Armor in most of Italy was in papier-mâché or else consisted of only a few elements of vaguely embossed metal. Many Sicilian pupari developed techniques of metalsmiths and each knight could have armor made of over 50 separate pieces riveted together. On a base of brass or German silver the armorers applied decorative work with other metals such as copper and the whole thing was highly polished. Every major figure had recognizable emblems and the general point of reference was the late Renaissance, with the wildest of fantasy prevailing. Common soldiers, of course, were more lightly armed, usually having no more than a weapon and a shield.

If audiences started to decline or there was serious competition pupari moved on to another town, and this is one of the reasons for the spread of the pupi throughout the island.[97] It was the practice for traveling companies to establish themselves in a town or village for an entire (winter) season of six months and this might remain their base for two or three years. They often found a vacant building and spent a couple of weeks setting up relatively permanent theaters with planks fixed to the walls for seating. Instead of a different drama each night they offered a new episode of a lengthy narrative and this could be stretched over the entire season. By the 1960s, most companies had abandoned serial presentation and often remained no more than a few days in any one place. In some cases they went to Sardinia or Tunisia (Tunisian puppeteers developed their own version of the opera dei pupi). Others traveled to Rome and even to North and South America.[98] Once performances in schools became a significant source of income many companies began to work from a fixed base using a light fit-up and a van.

Western Sicily

Nineteenth-century Palermo had a large and very poor population and puppet theaters satisfied a need for cheap entertainment. The teatrini were situated in back-streets and seldom contained more than 100 spectators. In many cases puppets were an additional source of income for a family and the family living-room was also the theater. They catered to a very local public whose few cents or contributions of food enabled the performers to live.[99] The association of the pupi with the poorest sections of society meant that they were always regarded with suspicion by the authorities, especially during periods of social unrest. Audiences were mostly male and knife fights easily broke out, which led to a perception of the "teatrini" as encouraging murder and the propensity of the Sicilian people for violence.

Claims to have been the "first" to introduce the armed pupi to Sicily have been made for Gaetano Greco and Alberto ("Liberto") Canino, both active in Palermo, and also for Giovanni Grasso and Gaetano Crimi of Catania.[100] Gaetano Greco (1813–1874) was the son of a puparo, possibly Giovanni Greco, active in Palermo between the late eighteenth century and the beginning of the nineteenth. He is generally supposed to have come from Naples and may have been confused with Giovanni when credited with opening a teatrino in 1826 (at the age of 13?).[101] Pulcinella and Colombina were his main figures. For a time Greco transferred to Messina, then Catania and Acireale, but later returned to Palermo and opened his theater on the Piazza Nuova (the market).[102]

Luigi Canino, a successful tailor originally from Trapani, moved to Palermo in the early nineteenth century. His son Alberto specialized in small cylinder pianos ("pianini") which he imported from Fasoni of Naples. He may have sold one to Gaetano Greco, but whether he was already involved with puppets before this is not clear. Alberto Canino turned out to be a skillful maker of figures and with the help of his son Luigi also made puppets for other performers. His jointed figures were more flexible than the standard Neapolitan pupi and he developed ones whose heads could be cut off, or which could be split into two halves in battle scenes.[103]

The Caninos left Palermo and moved to Partinico.[104] After a period in Alcamo Luigi departed for Buenos Aires in 1914, leaving his son Gaspare (1900–1977) with an uncle. Gaspare ran away, worked for a time with Mariano Pennisi in Acireale and after this worked with his father, who had returned to Alcamo. He was wounded in the First World War, but in 1921 he opened his own show in Balestrate and for eight years performed in the winter months and worked as a painter in the summer.[105] He then came back to Alcamo to his father and later took over the show. The local theater, disliking the competition, forced him to move. He used 400 lire inherited from his father to transport his show to San Giuseppe Iato and later to nearby Sancipirello and Terrasini. Eventually he set up his teatrino in via Dante, Alcamo, and usually gave three shows a day. After an interlude in Sciacca he opened another theater with 30 to 40 seats in Alcamo (via Manzoni). Audiences were diminishing but he struggled on until the 1970s, when he sold all his material to Antonio Pasqualino for the International Puppet Museum in Palermo.[106]

Gaetano Greco's family continued with his sons Nicolo and Achille (1856–1937), who had teatrini in the Ballarò and Vuccira quarters of Palermo. In 1890 Achille went to Argentina for a few years, but then returned to Palermo and continued to work there with his sons Alessandro (b. 1883) and Ermengildo (b. 1887). In the 1920s they had a teatrino on the Piazza San Cosimo.[107] In 1930 they moved to Rome and played at the Teatro Quattro Fontane before opening a little theater in the via XX Settembre, which continued until 1953.[108] The Greco tradition was also carried forward by Francesco Sclafani (1911–1991), who had worked with them in Rome, and above all by the Cuticchio family.

Giacomo Cuticchio (1917–1985), the son of a fruit seller, had followed performances at Achille Greco's teatrini in Palermo. He opened his own in 1934 and quickly received the imprimatur of the pupari of Palermo with a performance of the episode of the death of Milone (the father of Orlando). At the time pupi were operated only by men, but Cuticchio's sister Rosalia disguised herself as a boy and unobserved sneaked backstage to assist him.[109] A bomb demolished the family's home in 1943 and Cuticchio began to tour around Sicily. After the war, in 1944, Cuticchio started up again in the devastated city of Palermo, this time with his young brother Girolamo (b. 1933), who turned the handle of the cylinder piano. In the difficult years of the 1960s Giacomo replaced the serial mode of presentation with a single more self-contained performance. The show became a piece of folklore for the benefit of audiences generally unfamiliar with the subject matter or cultural context and understanding little Italian. After Giacomo's death, his wife, Pina, and son Nino continued his Ippogrifo theater, while his son Mimmo struck out on his own.[110]

Girolamo Cuticchio also wished to become a puparo, and in 1947 he successfully replaced his brother for a performance. Finally he opened his own theater in 1954, but also traveled through Sicily until 1960, when he sold his equipment and puppets and found a job as a lorry driver. However, a few years later he began to buy up material from pupari who were giving up, acquiring some from the puppet maker Paolo di Giovanni, and in 1970 he opened a little theater at Terrasini, where he too began to give shows aimed mainly at audiences of tourists. By 1974 he had a full-time teatrino at Termini Immerese, and his young family worked as assistants. In the late 1970s the company developed a close relationship with the International Puppet Museum of Palermo, where it performed on a regular basis until the end of the century. It also acquired a caravan and visited many schools. Finally the company found large modern premises at Cefalù where it could perform and exhibit their puppets, painted posters, old cylinder pianos and other material.

Antonino Mancuso (1910–1988), grandson of a puparo, Nunzio Barone of Partinico, worked as an assistant to Giovanni and Antonino Pernice, who had a teatrino in the Borgo of Palermo. In 1928 he opened his first theater with small puppets, but also worked as a bricklayer and lorry driver. As his family grew they all worked with him and the company traveled through western Sicily. His son Pino (1941–2001) set up his own show in 1970 and became one of the major pupari of the period. Another son, Nino (b. 1934), was gifted, but turned to other ways of earning a living. However, his son Enzo drew him back to the pupi when he created his own teatrino in via del Collegio Maria in the Vecchio Borgo, where the Pernices had had their theater. Today, together with Mimmo and Nino Cuticchio, he is one of the finest living exponents of the Palermitan pupi, showing how dramatically exciting they can still be. In recent years he has reverted to mini-cycles spread over several performances, though not to the full serials that could last many months.

Eastern Sicily

The mountainous nature of the terrain and endemic banditry made communication between western and eastern Sicily difficult. This led to the development of two recognizable styles. In Palermo the male puparo exercised full control over the show, generally producing all the voices and working the main figures.[111] In Catania voice and action were separated (as they often were in marionette theaters). The speakers or "parlatori" were a principal attraction and usually better paid than the figure workers or "manianti."[112] The speaker(s) dictated the rhythm of the performance and also communicated with the "manianti," giving them the appropriate signals.[113] Speech might be improvised, or read from a script, and was generally split amongst two or three voices, including a woman, the "parlatrice" ("parratrice"), who covered the female roles. In 1949, Natale Napoli married Italia Chiesa, who became one of the greatest parratrici of the twentieth century.

The eastern Sicilian style covered the provinces of Siracusa and Ragusa as well as Messina, and even parts of Calabria.[114] Messina had been a center of puppet activity before the 1908 earthquake destroyed most of the theaters.[115] Catania was a commercial city with a more developed middle class. It had its teatrini like Palermo, but also had larger pupi theaters and catered to a more middle-class public. In Catania Gaetano Crimi (1807–1877) opened his theater in 1835.[116] Crimi was well educated and his wife Laura Aleotti was the daughter of a puppeteer.[117] Emphasizing the educational value of the show, he aimed at more middle-class audiences, including women and a large student element. In his case voices were provided by actors from amateur dramatic societies. He wrote his own scripts and preferred to work from a full text rather than a scenario. As more sophisticated urban audiences tired of the older repertoire, he invented a new one, but retained the medieval idiom.

Crimi's first theater was in vico San Filippo near today's Piazza Mazzini and he stayed there until 1840. Between 1840 and 1845 he worked in via Castello Ursino, then from 1845 to 1851 near the university. From 1851 to 1858 he toured the province of Catania and performed in the capital at the casa Bruno in Piazza Carmine. In 1858 he was at the casa Fernandez, via Lincoln (today San Giuliano), and in 1861 in casa Rizzari near the church of San Michele. From 1863 he settled at a theater in via Montesano, which was called the Parnaso in 1868. He redecorated it, added two tiers of boxes, and improved technical facilities for lighting and scenery. Puppets sometimes made way for live actors (family members and Crimi's pupils). His teenage sons Peppe (Giuseppe, 1854–1937) and Ciccio (Francesco, 1851–1897) were trained in fencing so that they could appear as knights in the *Gerusalemme liberata*.[118] The Crimi tradition was also continued through Gaetano's daughter, Clementina, who married a former assistant, Raffaele Trombetta (1858–1932), who is also credited with introducing a new technique for nickel-plating the armor.[119] Between 1900 and 1914 they ran their Teatro Mazzini in the suburbs of Catania. The company was continued by their daughter, Giuseppina (1892–1990), and her husband Pasqualino Amico (1890–1957).[120]

Rivalry between the Crimis and the other great puppet family of Catania, the Grassos, was such that their respective supporters disrupted performances until an official truce was called in 1864. According to his marriage certificate in 1830, Don Giovanni Grasso (1792–1863) was a "comediant" or strolling player.[121] Oral tradition says that he was in trouble for smuggling skins and in 1859 had to depart for Naples, where he was employed at the Stella Cerere theater. Having bought some figures from the owner of the show, he returned to Catania in 1861 and opened a theater in the Cortile delle Grotte.[122]

Grasso's son Angelo (1834–1888) operated in various parts of Catania.[123] In 1861 he opened his "Opira di Don Angelo" in the cellar of the Palazzo Sangiuliano. In 1864 this 500-seat theater was rechristened Teatro Macchiavelli and admission was 10 cents for the pit, 15 for boxes, and 50 for seats in boxes at side of stage.[124] This was relatively expensive in comparison with Palermo, where the admission charge was usually 2 cents, though it might shoot up to 30 or even 40 for a few special performances, such as the battle of Roncisvalle and the death of Orlando. Don Angelo's most popular production was the story of *Buovo d'Antona*, and one of the attractions was the half-man half-dog figure of Pulicane. He did not use female performers and his actors were drawn more from the popular classes than were those of Gaetano Crimi.[125] Like Crimi, and possibly as early as 1859, he sometimes replaced puppets with juvenile amateur actors. A performance around 1880 was noted for the inept stage fighting and the amount of real blood shed.[126] When Angelo Grasso died, his widow, Donna Ciccia, abandoned the puppets and turned the Machiavelli into a variety theater. Their son Giovanni (1873–1930), a splendid speaker for the puppets and a talented dialect performer, went on to become one of the most celebrated Sicilian actors of the first half of the twentieth century.[127] In 1903 the Machiavelli burned down, with the puppets. Rebuilt, it continued until 1920 with the dialect performances of Giovanni Grasso and Angelo Musco.[128]

In 1890 Angelo Grasso's eldest son Gregorio (Don Crioli) took over the Teatro Sicilia, the former Parnaso of Gaetano Crimi. Don Crioli was known for the splendor of the costumes and the armor of the puppets.[129] He spoke for the main noble characters, male and female, while Don Ciccio Rasura, the town treasurer, who had a fine baritone voice and had previously been with Gaetano Crimi, spoke for the others. Don Crioli presented two houses a night and his repertoire included farces and variety items, as well as plays with live actors.

Gaetano Napoli (1877–1968), a saddler by trade, opened his Etna Theater in 1921. Two of his sons, Pippo (1912–1983) and Natale (1921–1984), rapidly became an integral part of the company. A third, Rosario (1914–1934), was a noted painter of "cartelli." The Napoli family had considerable artistic gifts, especially for the making and dressing of figures and for the painting of scenery and cartelli. After occupying a variety of small premises they settled down in via Canfora, where they stayed for about 30 years.[130] The Napoli performed throughout the winter season with puppets, but in the summer the theater was given over to live actors. With the death of Natale, his son Fiorenzo revived the family tradition and led it in a new direction, improving production values, introducing more sophisticated scenery and lighting effects and bringing the pupi closer to theater while maintaining what he regarded as their essential features. The size of the puppets was reduced to 80 centimeters and pre-recorded music allowed audiences to hear a full orchestra playing Wagner as a background to the paladins. In the early 2000s the city of Catania built a theater for the Napoli company, but then allocated it for other purposes.

In the 1880s Mariano Pennisi traveled around Sicily because of his work and saw performances of the opera dei pupi in Palermo. He spent some time studying the opera of Catania. In 1897 he took over the theater that Paolo Messina had established in the stores of the Palazzo Modo in Acireale in 1890. Broadly speaking, his puppets were in the Catanian style, with unjointed knees, but he used a higher bridge. His 1.2-meter figures had long head rods and a number were provided with opening mouths. He adopted Emanuele Macri (1906–1974), an orphan of the Messina quake, and in due course Macri continued the theater, which became very important in the mid–twentieth century and also traveled through much of Italy.

Giacomo Longo, probably from Calabria, visited Siracusa in 1875. Francesco Puzzo (1857–1936) saw his show and created his own.[131] He operated a 100-seat theater, the Eldorado, but in 1917 sold his material and went back to his original activity as a painter, sculptor and decorator. In 1924 his sons Ernesto and Luciano opened the Eden Theater, in a hall measuring 17 by 12 meters and incorporating a stage 5 by 5 meters. This could seat about 170, with a further 70 spectators on a balcony. Disagreements between them closed the theater, but Luciano Puzzo reopened it on his own for a brief and not very successful period before departing to run a cinema in Noto. Ernesto, also a painter, opened his San Giorgio theater in 1928 and continued with his pupi until 1944.[132] In 1948 he gave a final special performance and his material was acquired by Ignazio Puglisi from Sortino.[133] The Puglisi family has been associated with the province of Siracusa since the later nineteenth century. Giovanni Puglisi (1860–1917) was the son of a puparo, Ignazio Puglisi I. His son Ignazio II (1904–1986) became a major puppeteer of the region. After his death the Commune of Sortino acquired his material and set up a rich museum. In 1995 the Associazione Culturale Don Ignazio Puglisi was created by some of his friends and former associates to perpetuate his work. Puglisi's grandson Manlio set up a separate company to continue the family tradition.

Rome

In 1816, Stendhal observed sardonically that the Pope in the interest of the moral purity of the Italians of Rome allowed theater to happen only during Carnival, while for the rest of the year they had the wooden actors.[134] The restricted nature of the Roman theatrical season allowed the puppets unusual importance. In the popular theaters of the Piazza Navona and Trastevere, the chivalrous repertoire provided the staple fare, while the Fiano, on the Corso, catered to a public of a higher social stratum and was comparable to the Fiando or Lupi theaters.[135] A sonnet of Giuseppe Gioacchino Belli written in 1832 refers to the main puppet theaters in Rome, the Fiano, the Ornani and "Er Nufragio" (Il Naufragio), later to become Il Fenice. He also mentions the "Pasce" (Pace) and the Pallacorda, which housed puppet shows from time to time. The latter was converted for this purpose in 1805, but was also used for live actors. To Belli's list one might add the Teatro del Pavone on the street of the same name, the Teatro delle Muse on vicolo del Fico, the Teatro of the Piazza

Montanara and the Valetto, near the Piazza di Sant'Andrea della Valle. One of the last of the popular marionette theaters in Rome was the Aurelio near the Arco dei Saponari, where audiences were known for throwing vegetables. Even the Capranica presented marionettes in the nineteenth century and the Mausoleum of Augustus was turned into a theater for various entertainments, including circuses and marionettes.[136] When Toldo reviewed the situation in 1908 these theaters had mostly vanished.[137]

Performances in the popular theaters of Rome were known locally as "infornate" (oven batches), referring to the large number of spectators crammed into a hot and ill-ventilated space.[138] It was usual to have two houses in the course of an evening. The first, the "lunga camerata" or long show, cost more than the second, the "corta camerata" or short show.[139] In 1847 the Emiliani (formerly Ornani) gave one performance after the Ave Maria and a second one at 10:00 P.M. In some cases a teatrino might have three or even four "infornate" in a day.

The Fiano Theater was situated at number 418 of the Corso on the corner of the Piazza S. Lorenzo di Lucina and opposite the Caffè Nuovo, which functioned rather like a gentlemen's club. The clientele of the Caffè included artists, intellectuals, members of the nobility and even prelates, not to mention many foreign travelers, and a visit to the marionettes where they were sure to catch up on topical allusions and gossip in improvised additions to the script was a huge attraction. The Ottoboni family, dukes of Fiano, acquired the former Ludovisi palace in 1690.[140] Towards the end of the eighteenth century they converted part of the ground floor into a theater and let it out. In addition to the rent, they received a sixth of the takings and were able to retain a box for themselves and a number of seats.[141] By 1812 the theater was known as the marionette theater and was a profitable economic venture. Accounts include the takings between 1812 and 1820 and a list of those involved in the theater with the payments they received.[142] Manager for much of the time between 1816 and 1832 was Liborio Londini, who also had some shows of his own including an automat, described as a "matematica meccanica figura" of a conjuror. One of his partners for some years was Giovanni Bianchi, a former manager of the Pallacorda Theater.[143] The Fiano had about 19 employees in addition to its managers, who each received a salary of 50 baiocchi. The leading spirit until the 1830s was the goldsmith, Filippo Teoli (1771–1844), who received 40 baiocchi. An Adriano Valeri got 35 and a Gugliemo Reggiani 25. These three were probably the main actors, who provided the voices. Three unnamed figure-workers were of a lower status. One received 20 baiocchi and the others 10 each. Three Londinis also appear on the payroll (probably the wife and children of Liborio). The remaining 10 people included musicians (who might change quite frequently), assistants, stage hands and perhaps box office attendants.

Between 1832 and 1844–1845 the Fiano's manager was Vincenzo Jacovacci, later to become director of a number of major theaters.[144] There are many anecdotes about this colorful figure, including the assertion that the papal censors obliged him to put blue knickers onto his marionette ballerinas, as pink ones were too suggestive. Under Jacovacci there was a shift away from satire towards a more spectacular repertoire. The Fiano survived as a marionette theater until 1845–1846, and eventually closed in 1850.[145]

In 1813 the interior of the Fiano was remodeled with equipment bought from the dismantled private theater of the Duke of Lante.[146] Contracts indicate the dimensions of the Fiano stage as 38.3 palms wide (8.56 meters) and 30 palms deep (6.7 meters). Stendhal spoke of a marionette stage with a proscenium opening measuring 3.5 meters by 1.5 meters high and this could easily have been set up on that stage. The footlights were equipped with 14 double flame burners with 12 brass reflectors and there were 24 wing lights. This was a small theater for live actors that became exclusively a marionette one because of the enormous success of Cassandrino.

The Ornani functioned regularly as a marionette theater from the Napoleonic period until 1822. After this there were marionette shows in the afternoon and ones with live actors in the evening.[147] A description of it in a novella by Wilhelm Waiblinger in 1830 describes a colorful audience of street urchins, fruit sellers, shoe-blacks and others, noisy, half-naked, ragged and chewing chestnuts,[148] a very different clientele from the Fiano. The main repertoire was the chivalric one, with Pulcinella as the comic figure. By 1847 the Ornani had been restored and was lit by gas. Renamed the Emiliani, it had evening performances of popular farces with live actors and marionette shows during the day. William Story, who perceived it as belonging to the popular classes, also recorded the admission charges of two baiocchi for the pit, three for the balcony, and five for seats in private boxes.[149] After the closure of the Fiano in 1850, the Emiliani became Rome's main puppet theater and its productions were aimed at juvenile audiences. It closed in 1867.[150]

Ferdinand Gregorovius's comments on the puppet theaters in Rome in 1853 resemble those of Story.[151] He mentions the little theaters of the piazzas San Apollinare and Montanara (near the Arco dei Saponari).[152] He contrasts the insalubrious and noisy Montanara with the San Appollinare, which had "civilized" puppets, educated audiences, a small and elegant stage with well-painted scenery, good costumes and a repertoire that included ballets (it may also have staged performances with live actors). With its emphasis on production values, the Appollinare partially filled the gap left by the Fiano. The main repertoire at the Montanara was the chivalric one with Pulcinella as comic squire to Orlando. Every episode had its furious battle and ended with the triumph of a paladin, or else a lazzo from Pulcinella.

Extensive documentation exists about the organization of puppet theaters in early nineteenth-century Rome. With the setting up of the Roman Republic by the French in 1798, the theater season extended to the whole year, excluding Lent. In 1800 Pope Pius VII, following the French model, set up a system for granting licenses. The responsibility for this was vested in the Deputazione dei Pubblici Spettacoli, a group of six Roman nobles, whose duties included the censorship and the policing of the theaters. Their main concerns were with anything touching on religion, morals or politics.[153] They also had to check five times a year that theaters were structurally sound. Many were in overcrowded rooms, some on the first floor of granaries, and the potential for a disaster was constant. In 1823 the Fiano passed the test but the Pallacorda had to carry out major repairs, while the Pace was not allowed open for the season.[154] Health and hygiene were another concern, and this ranged from instructions about cleanliness to maintaining fire buckets full of water.

The Deputazione decided which days of the week theaters might function, and ensured that they closed for Lent or when the papacy was vacant, or on the occasion of a Holy Year, such as 1825. The main theater season ran from autumn to Carnival (the summer months were generally seen as too hot). Theaters had to deposit an annual sum of caution money that could be used to pay actors or figure-workers if the director failed to do so. In the event of performances being officially cancelled for the death of a pope, the theaters were reimbursed. In 1823 the Fiano Theater petitioned the governor of Rome for a reimbursement of 20 scudi because performances had been stopped following the death of Pope Pius VII.[155]

As in France, the license for the theaters was a monopoly and the license-holder could use this to his financial advantage, whether to exact payments or to prevent competition. In 1819–1820 the license holder, Sig. Cartoni, was to make sure that no theaters other than the one for which he was responsible should function.[156] This included the marionette theaters, but by 1825 the description of the duties and privileges of the monopoly holder had a paragraph inserted which read:

> The holder of the license for the theaters will allow the two theaters of the Fiano and Ornani palaces to function throughout the year without requiring any payment from their directors.[157]

The quasi-official status of the Ornani led its director in 1827 to prevent the opening of another marionette theater "in premises known as the Torellino, near the porch of S. Agnese."[158] During the 1820s regulations governing the theaters fixed the number and prices of tickets to be sold and also included punishments for audience members for entering into discussion with the actors, changing their places or blocking the aisles, keeping their hats on, standing up during the performance or creating disturbances with or without arms. The stocks were set up outside theaters for the immediate punishment of those who infringed these laws. Alessandro Moroni, writing in 1882, commented on the extent to which the puppet theaters of the Piazza Navona, of the Piazza del Fico, and the Fiano, could resemble political meetings as audience members started discussions with the actors.[159]

Scripts were submitted for preventative censorship, but Filippo Teoli habitually inserted pieces of improvised dialogue that the audience could instantly appreciate. In 1838 the censor refused permission for *Cassandrino the Conjuror*, noting that the Fiano treated known people with ridicule, but that this could not always be inferred from the text submitted. A mythology built up about the number of times that Teoli spent the night in prison for his outspoken comments. According to Stendhal it was also common practice to make the police inspectors drunk before the show so that they could not carry out their censorship duties.

The "italiana" of Rossini's *L'Italiana in Algeri* had to be changed in the title to "italiano" to avoid any potentially immoral overtones. "Eunuchs" in the stage directions were converted into "slaves," and replaced by "guards" in the text. An observation by Taddeo (Cassandro) that "here wives are kept by the day" was bowdlerized into "here wives are kept as slaves." In spite of all this, every double-entendre of the original libretto was reinforced in the marionette version. In 1826 Giovanni Giraud's piece *Cassandrino the Bridegroom's Journey on a Donkey*, specially written for Filippo Teoli, has a title that puns on the name of the papal censor, Somai, and "somari," a donkey.[160] The same joke is found in *Cassandro in the Kingdom of the Great Mogul and Condemned to the Harpies*, in which Astolfo arrives on his flying horse to give Cassandro a horn to chase away the harpies who are starving him to death (act four).[161] It is implied that he is a bringer of liberty, chasing the harpies back into their dark lairs deep in the center of the earth. This reference was cut by Somai, almost certainly because it could hint at some of the more obscurantist practices of the Church. The association of puppets with irreverent and satirical comments on church and state led to a variety of satirical publications, especially around 1848–1849 with the proclamation of the

Republic of Rome. These carried titles such as *Cassandrino* or *Rugantino* and published caricatures of important people, presenting them as puppets or puppeteers.[162]

Changing Times

The last two decades of the nineteenth century and the first of the twentieth were the glittering apogee of the marionette theater. These were the years of such spectacular productions as *Ballo excelsior* and the successes of the Prandi and Gorno Dall'Acqua companies.[163] The near perfection achieved by Collas, Lupis and others brought its own problems that only became apparent with the spread of mass media. Arguably a natural cycle of development had been completed and there were limits to the directions in which the classical marionette theater could go. The Holden visits of the 1880s led to huge technical developments, notably the abandonment of the head rod, especially for trick figures.[164] They also coincided with the great rise of the variety theater and of a program made up of acts with an emphasis on virtuosity.

The negative impact of cinema is undeniable, but cinema and puppets went hand in hand for a long time. Francesco Campogalliani often performed in cinemas and combined his glove-puppet program with a film.[165] The Grasso Sicilia Theater in Catania in the early 1900s concluded the program with a cinema show. The film projector was even used as a special effects spotlight during the pupi performances. In the 1930s Antonino Mancuso's traveling show also combined opera dei pupi and cinema.[166] Cinema proprietors often hired a puppeteer to give a performance before the film. Giacomo Colla's company had an engagement of this sort at the Gustavo Modena cinema in Milan in 1922.[167] Some cinema proprietors perceived the pupi as a threat to them. Gaspare Canino opened a theater in San Giuseppe Iato, but the local cinema created a great deal of trouble for him, and finally he had to move on. In the south, many pupari used open-air arenas that also served as cinemas in the summer.

Fausto Braga (1864–1932), active in and around Udine during the first decades of the twentieth century, also combined a film with marionettes. At one point the family split into two companies and the reels of film were passed back and forth (by bicycle) between them. The stage was placed at one end of the hall and a screen at the other. After the marionettes, the audience simply turned round and a projector was mounted on the stage. In February 1928, one company was performing in Moriago in an upstairs loft, with many barred windows and only a narrow access staircase. The film caught fire, and although it was quickly put out there was a panic which led to the deaths of 37 persons. Fausto, who was not present, received a suspended sentence of a year and a half. His son Pirro (1899–1974) spent a couple of weeks in prison and received a suspended sentence of two years. This marked the end of the Braga company, which had been active since Napoleonic times. Pirro continued with his own company, the Teatro della Commedia in Trieste, but joined Podrecca in 1931. The disaster of Moriago (coupled with other cinema fires) led to tightening up of security and the closing down of unsafe venues. This may have been a further factor that pushed so many companies into traveling with portable theaters in the 1950s.

The north had a growing number of industrial workers with more disposable income for entertainment, and they filled the cinemas. Many films took over the subjects of the older repertoires of the marionette theaters and provided similar effects of pathos, terror or excitement, but more realistically. On the other hand, films sometimes provided a source of new material for the puppet theater. The highly successful *Marcellino pane o vino* was adapted by Bianca Burzio for the Gambarutti company as a three-episode marionette drama.[168]

The spread of television in the 1950s was a serious blow to marionette shows. It could be enjoyed by people in their own homes, watched in bars and even set up by priests in parish halls. Throughout Italy improving economic conditions led to a new consumerist culture. The days of the really large marionette companies were finished. Classical puppet theater was based on the idea of a family economy and this left very little disposable income for sons or daughters at a period when their peers were beginning to enjoy a better standard of living. Consequently they began to look for other employment. The 1960s and 1970s were the nadir. However, almost in defiance of this trend, a generation of younger puppeteers with a new self-confidence has emerged since the 1980s. Some are completely new to the art, but many are the children and grand-children of puppeteers and they have given a fresh vitality to the art form. The Sicilian pupi achieved international recognition in 2001 when UNESCO proclaimed them a "masterpiece of the oral and intangible heritage of humanity." Classical puppet theater has moved from being dismissed as something suitable for children and the uneducated to being seen as a significant component of Italian culture. It has often merged with more experimental forms but still remains a basic point of reference.

CHAPTER 4

The Commedia dell'Arte and the Puppet Stage

The ethnomusicologist Roberto Leydi once declared that he gained a greater under-standing of the Commedia dell'Arte by watching Otello Sarzi perform *Sandrone at the Baths of Salsomaggiore,* based on a scenario of Francesco Campogalliani, than by reading erudite works on the subject. The term Commedia dell'Arte was coined in the eighteenth century to describe the professional theater that emerged in sixteenth-century Italy. In the later eighteenth century, because of the use of masks and stock characters and a fondness for improvisation, it was commonly known as the Comedy of Masks, but was regarded as a lit-tle out of date by proponents of a more literary theater. The stock figures of the puppet stage paralleled those of the Commedia dell'Arte but Arlecchino, Brighella, Pulcinella, Pan-talone, Tartaglia and the Dottore (doctor) managed to enjoy an autonomous existence long after these masks had vanished from the actors' stage.

Napoleon disliked the popular theater and under him the masked characters were strongly discouraged. The wearing of Carnival masks in the street could conceal anti-social or subversive behavior too. In January 1801, in Bologna, permission was given for masks only in the theaters and for festivals and balls. This ruling continued with a forbidding of the costumes of Arlecchino, Pantalone, Brighella and of objects relating to religious prac-tices or institutions.[1]

Dialect and Puppet Theater

The geographical configuration of Italy, bisected by the chain of the Apennines, made communications difficult, and the situation was not helped by endemic banditry. The enor-mous distance between north and south and the division into a number of states, mostly controlled or ruled by Spain, Austria, France or the Papacy, made for a high degree of lin-guistic diversity. Italian had been the literary language from the later Middle Ages and flour-ished in Tuscany, but the general level of literacy was so low that it impinged little on the lives of ordinary people. German, French and Spanish all played their part as the languages of officialdom. Piedmontese, Venetian and Sicilian, to mention only a few, were virtually independent languages and often incomprehensible to outsiders. In the south it was pos-sible to find Greek-speaking communities. Ferdinando II (1815–1859), king of the Two Sicilies, nicknamed the lazzarone king because of his fondness for association with the lower classes, was barely competent in anything other than Neapolitan.

The earlier Commedia masks had all been localized and actors and puppeteers exploited linguistic diversity.[2] When Arlecchino and Brighella from Bergamo moved to Venice they blended easily with the enormous servant class and changed dialect accordingly. The use of dialect enabled the masked characters to relate instantly to their audiences. When a company or a character moved outside its own linguistic area dialect was often reduced to a regional accent, retaining only a few words with specific local color. Pulcinella, in Rome, kept much of his Neapolitan dialect, which could be more or less understood there and simply appeared comic. In Adone Finardi's pieces for the Montanara puppet theater in Rome in the 1840s Pulcinella used a comic mixture of Roman, Neapolitan and Marchigiano. In Naples, at the popular San Carlino Theater, the Pulcinella actor Antonio Petito continued the tradition of dialect, but by 1900, the puppet player Pasquale Ferraiolo of Salerno retained dialect only for the title of a piece, a song and a few odd words for flavor.

In the early nineteenth century amateur acting groups sprang up to foster the continuation of a dialect theater that had all but disappeared from the live stage. In 1816 the Fiando Theater of Milan was sometimes available for live performances of dialect plays and one of the actors was Giusepina Fiando. In Rome in the 1830s the Pace, Pallacorda and Ornani theaters all presented dialect pieces, in which the popular puppet figures of Pulcinella and Cassandrino appeared as live actors. Dialect remained a significant part of puppet theater to such an extent that in Bologna in 1869 a group of actors and puppeteers began to play the productions of the Cuccoli puppet repertoire with live actors in the open-air summer theaters. They were referred to as "burattini in persona" and took the roles of the popular puppet characters of Balanzone (the Dottore), Fagiolino and Sganapino using dialect and improvisation rather than a fixed script.[3]

The surge of nationalism that brought Garibaldi to power took its toll on regional variation. The Italian language became a symbol of unification and pressure to abandon dialect grew. In 1861 only 22 percent of the population (mostly in the north) was literate and it has been calculated that about 160,000 people out of a population of 20 million were really Italian speakers.[4] In the first 30 years of the twentieth century, the educated and sophisticated Francesco Campogalliani owed much of his renown to his amazing gift for varying his voice and mastering a wide range of dialects, which he deliberately used in opposition to attempts to standardize the Italian language. Once the Fascists came to power one of their aims was to create a strong unitary state, and the use of dialect was frowned on. In 1930 a speaker in the parliament declared that "dialect in Italy is delaying the process of Italianization of the language.... The Italian language must, in the shortest possible time, become the only voice of the Italian people."[5] At this period the stock characters of the Commedia dell'Arte and of the puppet theater appeared in children's books all speaking standard Italian. The comando generale of the GIL in the early 1940s spoke in no uncertain terms of putting an end to the theater of masks.[6] The censorship required the production of scripts to be checked, and this created further problems for puppeteers, many of whom were only semi-literate and worked to a scenario with improvised dialogue.

As late as the 1950s only about 18 percent of the population was fully Italian speaking.[7] After 1960 the explosion of the mass media led to the spread of Italian. Dialect was no longer discouraged by the authorities, but many audiences were ceasing to understand it. Glove-puppeteer Carlo Salici (1899–1992), for example, used the stock characters of Fagiolino, Sandrone and Facanapa, speaking Bolognese, Modenese and Venetian, but instead

of being a source of comedy, these dialects were often incomprehensible to audiences outside those areas. Sicily was one of the last regions to retain the use of dialect for the farce
performed by the pupi, but in more modern times the farce itself largely disappeared as
audiences changed and few could speak or understand Sicilian.

Pulcinella

Two masks inextricably linked with puppets are Pulcinella and Burattino. Tommaso
Garzoni refers disparagingly to Burattino in 1585 as a live actor whose only gesture is to
put his beret on his head.[8] The Flamminio Scala scenarios of 1611 mention Arlecchino,
Burattino, Pedrolino and occasionally another Zanni, but not Pulcinella.[9] The Locatelli
ones put together in Rome in 1617 and 1622 mention Burattino, Coviello and sometimes
simply a Zanni. Burattino left no trace as a puppet character, but became a generic word
for a puppet.

Pulcinella probably originated in Acerra, close to Naples. The first specific reference
to him as a theatrical role is a late sixteenth-century portrait by Ludovico Caracci of a certain Paoluccio della Cerra "commonly known as Pulcinella."[10] Pulcinella was an established
rural folk type and as such may have existed for some time as a puppet.[11] Silvio Fiorillo, the
well-known interpreter of the braggart Spanish captain, the Matamoros, gave a new currency to Pulcinella as a burlesque version of that character.[12] His Pulcinella, probably created in Naples by 1598, was seen in Paris in 1608 and then passed into a wider European
context.[13] Jacques Callot visited Naples in 1622 and produced his series the *Balli di Sfessa-
nia*, in which Pulcinella is depicted wearing a baggy white costume (similar to the other
performers, especially Pascariello) and equipped with a very large wooden sword, a hat with
two points, and a bristling moustache. As both a glove-puppet and a marionette in Italy,
Pulcinella retained the baggy white smock and Phrygian cap. The Neapolitan, Pulcinella,
also known as "Policinella" became Polichinelle in France. In the 1680s, the Pulcinella of
the Italian company at the Hôtel de Bourgogne, Michelangelo Francanzani (nephew of the
painter Salvator Rosa) added a hump to the back and a protruding stomach. The Dutch
engraver Jacob de Geijn portrayed Francanzani in a white, rather baggy costume with very
long sleeves and a very tall hat, anticipating the gamboling Venetian Pulcinellas of Tiepolo.
Other illustrations of the Italian actors in Paris show him in the heavily padded parti-col-
ored outfit that has since become associated with French Polichinelle and English Punch
puppets. This humpbacked character has aspects of the court fool, many of whom were
physically misshapen, but the costume is also reminiscent of the well-padded doublet of
the traditional Spanish Captain.

Pulcinella is a more fluctuating character than the other masks of the Commedia del-
l'Arte. His behavior varies from scenario to scenario and from performer to performer. He
rapidly became ubiquitous as a character in the Italian marionette and glove-puppet theater. By the 1640s the name was used by Italians traveling abroad to describe their show
and in Venice before the end of the seventeenth century puppets were often referred to gener-
ically as "i puricinei" (the Pulcinellas).[14]

Pulcinella became the central and omnipresent protagonist of the of the guarattella
show, which was to be found throughout Italy by the eighteenth century. A trained animal

was often an adjunct to the entertainment. Pietro Longhi depicts Pulcinella in Venice in the 1760s, holding a stick and facing a live dog on the playboard. This survived in the Punch and Judy show in England. From the various illustrations of Roman street scenes by Bartolomeo and Achille Pinelli in the early nineteenth century it is possible to piece together many of the episodes of a guarattella performance. One shows Pulcinella beating a live cat, an animal also to be found at the time on the Polichinelle stages in Paris. Pulcinella has a wife, Colombina, with whom he has an initial scene and later a dance to conclude the show. Pulcinella, as a parent, appears with a basket on his back containing two little Pulcinelli. This may relate to the idea popular in Naples of the parthenogenetic Pulcinella with numerous offspring.[15] However a comic poem by Giacopo Feretti, "Il burattinajo ambulante per Roma," mentions Pulcinella's numerous family and the complaints of his wife that he is always drunk or beating her.[16] In one engraving, like English Punch, he holds his baby out to the audience. A similar one depicts him holding the child and talking to Colombina, but also shows an angry puppeteer

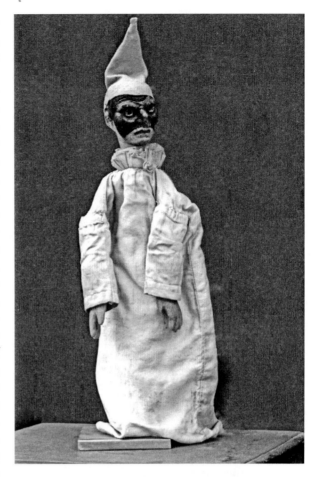

Pulcinella, glove-puppet belonging to Ghetanaccio (Gaetano Santangelo), early 19th century. 40 cms. (Courtesy Collezione Maria Signorelli. Photograph Maristella Campolunghi.)

emerging from the booth and trying to chase off some disruptive boys and waving a devil puppet with fowls' legs.[17] A figure of Rugantino, a puppet associated with Ghetanaccio, sits on top of the stage and this suggests that the performer may be Santangelo himself. Bull fights were popular in Rome at the time, and one of Ghetanaccio's more popular routines was a lively fight between Rugantino and a bull. In Achille Pinelli's large watercolor of 1830 Pulcinella is center stage, facing Rugantino. Colombina stands behind him, while behind Rugantino is a devil. This may be the scenario evoked by G.G. Belli in a sonnet that describes Rugantino beating up his wife Rosetta, who calls on the devil for help. The devil appears in a flash (probably produced by lycopodium), and this is followed by some comic quips between Rugantino and the devil about marriage.[18] In another print Pulcinella gives a thrashing to the devil. There is also a scene where Pulcinella is beating a crouching Rugantino while a devil stands behind him with its arms raised. The presence of more than two characters on the stage suggests that perhaps the booth contained both the puppeteer and an assistant, but may be no more than the artist's attempt to conflate episodes.

Until the 1970s Nunzio Zampello in Naples was performing the simpler street show that parallels the Piccini one still used by British Punch and Judy professors. Much of the language consists of onomatopoeic sounds, distorted by the swazzle. First Pulcinella has an encounter with a dog which nearly swallows his arm, then one with the aggressive owner of the dog, with whom he has a lengthy and highly rhythmic fight in which the latter is eventually killed. After much comic business trying to stuff the corpse into a coffin, Pulcinella sets out for the cemetery. The second part starts with an encounter between Pulcinella and a police officer who is very suspicious of the coffin, which, he is told, contains rags and bones. After prolonged comic play, Pulcinella is arrested. Then two characters appear for a comic dialogue and bring in the gallows. The policeman and Pulcinella re-enter and Pulcinella is given a last request for a meal. He also asks for a confessor and there is play on the word Capuchin (friar) and cappuccino (coffee). A jailer brings in a friar and there is a burlesque confession scene. There follows a much expanded scene with the hangman, who eventually has to demonstrate to Pulcinella how to put his head in the noose and is promptly hung. Pulcinella then encounters death, who plays a variety of tricks on him, fights with him and eventually if not exactly defeated, leaves the stage so that our hero can complete the show by dancing with his girlfriend Teresina.[19]

In Naples the sketches and farces of Antonio Petito often transferred to the guarattella stage. Pasquale Ferraiolo in the early twentieth century set out to create a new Pulcinella repertoire. In his classic piece *A Terrible Night* (Na nuttata è guai) Pulcinella is about to go

Head of Pulcinella as a "pupo" with articulated mouth, 20th century. Compagnia Aurora, Canosa di Puglia. (Courtesy Paolo Comentale, Teatro Casa di Pulcinella, Bari.)

to bed on a stormy night.[20] There is the classic puppet business of arranging the bedding and getting into bed. He is awoken by his friend Felice, who has shut himself out of his house and is in a bad mood because he has seen his fiancée Gilda at the opera with a soldier. As he relates the story he gets so excited that he throws all the furniture, including the bed, out of the window and manages to get his head stuck in the chamber pot. Gilda arrives looking for him, and it transpires that the soldier is her brother. Apart from the element of slapstick and constant indications of lazzi in the script, there is also verbal humor involving distortion of language, as when Felice hears he has inherited two millions from his uncle, and Pulcinella translates this as two melons.

In Naples and Rome Pulcinella as a marionette took over the role of the Zanni or servant. This Pulcinella could be the victim of tricksters and a figure of fun, but he was also endowed with homely good sense and used to contrast natural man with civilised man. In Rome in Adone Finardi's puppet versions of the *Orlando furioso* and the *Orlando innamorato*, Pulcinella has an extended role as a squire to Orlando.[21] Normally Pulcinella's dialogue is improvised, but in this case, exceptionally, there is a fully written text. He acts as a frame-breaker and commentator on the heroic action in which he is involved willy-nilly. The central comic figure, whether Pulcinella or another, was often the only one to have a moving mouth and this was designed as much for direct address to the audience as for dialogue with other characters.[22]

Arlecchino, Brighella and Older Men

The Zanni Arlecchino and Brighella both originated in the Bergamo area. Brighella was the trickster and generally presented as an urban figure, while Arlecchino, who emerged in the Val Brembana near Bergamo, was, at least initially, the simpleton and the countryman. This is the classic coupling of the clever and the stupid slaves of Roman classical comedy. Bergamo was Venetian territory and like many poor people, Arlecchino and Brighella went to Venice to find work as porters, servants or any other menial employment and rapidly adapted to that city. The Zanni belonged to an impoverished underclass and were always the first to be in need in times of hardship or famine. Arlecchino is constantly shown trying to satisfy the pangs of hunger. On the puppet stage, making him eat spaghetti was a favorite trick with showmen (the same was also true for Pulcinella in Naples). North of Rome Arlecchino was ubiquitous. When the Nardi marionette company appeared at the theater near Milan's Porta Romana in 1808 Arlecchino was their principal mask.[23]

On the marionette stage Arlecchino detached himself from his erstwhile companions and, like Pulcinella, became the mouthpiece for the showman and also served as an announcer. He often retained a servant's role, becoming the comic hero and bridging the gap with the audience. Girolamo Renzi (referred to as Johan Rizzi in his application for a permit to the authorities in Prague in 1777) and his partner Francesco Laratta, both from Venice, published bills for their show in both Italian and German.[24] The list of plays performed is almost the same, but on the Italian bills Pulcinella is given as the comic figure in the titles, while on the ones in German it is Arlecchino. This indicates that it is less the physical appearance of the mask that defines the character than the function in the performance. Audiences in Prague may have been more familiar with Arlecchino than Pulcinella and the change of name is little more than an attempt to take this into account.

Arlecchino and Brighella, together with Pantalone and the Dottore (and sometimes the stuttering Venetian Tartaglia), were the longest surviving Commedia masks. All continued to appear on the glove-puppet stage right through the twentieth century. The Dottore remained the most significant of the older masks in Bologna and found a marvelous exponent in Filippo Cuccoli.[25] Because of his strong voice Cuccoli was also employed as a town crier and at Carnival donned the costume of the Dottore and paraded in the streets.[26] Francesco Campogalliani was well known for the virtuosity of his long and rapidly delivered tirades for the Dottore and in more recent times Romano Danieli has maintained the distinctive profile of the character.

The New Masks

The process that gave birth to the masked figures of the Commedia dell'Árte was an ongoing one. The term "maschera" (mask) continued to be used to indicate a stock type

Dottore and Arlecchino (approx. 30 cms). Eighteenth-century Venetian marionettes. (Courtesy Collezione Maria Signorelli. Photograph Maristella Campolunghi.)

even when not masked. Many new "masks" were no more than local variations of existing stock types, but some emerged directly from the theater or popular writing. These include Meneghino (who first appeared in a comedy by Carlo Maria Maggi in the mid–seventeenth century and was subsequently a major figure both in the dialect theater and on the puppet stages of Milan), Meo Patacca of Rome and Stenterello (created by the celebrated Florentine actor Del Buono in the last years of the eighteenth century). Goldoni's Tonin Bella-grazia (Buongrazia) from *Il frappatore* (1747) became a popular puppet figure in Emilia Romagna, evolving into Filippo Cuccoli's Tonin Bonagrazia, who spoke Venetian and dressed in an eighteenth-century costume. Augusto Galli used him as a replacement for Tartaglia in scenes with Dottore Balanzone and Francesco Campogalliani placed him alongside Fasolino (Fagiolino) and Sandrone.

By the end of the eighteenth century the Commedia masks had lost their immediacy in the actors' theater and had become merely theatrical characters, dressed in costumes that belonged to another era. Audiences wanted characters to which they could relate more directly. Non-masked characters were created in response to the needs of the moment and in relation to the profound social changes of the time. They belonged to a new world imbued with the ideas of the French Revolution and with a growing sense of their own identity amongst the popular classes. Most evolved out of recognizable contemporary peas-ant or servant characters, were dressed accordingly and spoke a local dialect. Audiences per-ceived them as their contemporaries, although as time went by even they became a little out of date. Most started life as glove-puppets, probably in street shows, and later trans-ferred to the marionette stage. Unlike the Commedia figures they started life as puppets and there was no sense of an actor disguised by a mask.

Fagiolino, like many popular characters, has a name that evokes food, in this case beans. He became ubiquitous in Emilia Romagna and beyond, even being found in Greece as "Fasulis."[27] Also known as Fagiolino Fanfani, Fasolino, Fasulein or Fasol, he is an urban figure first recorded in late eighteenth-century Bologna with the showman Cavallazzi, who had his pitch in the Corte Galuzzi. On his black hair he wears a long pointed cap with a tassel whose weight allows him to swing it around vigorously to emphasize or punctuate what he is saying. On his right cheek is a growth typical of earlier Zanni masks. Unlike the amoral Zanni, he was created as a contemporary figure believing in natural justice and mak-ing abundant use of his hefty stick when it was a matter of righting wrongs. Like Arlecchino and others he is a joker and there are many anecdotes that treat him as if he were a real per-son.

The original Sandrone was a rustic figure but once he began to appear in the towns he took on the more specific characteristics of the recent urban dweller.[28] Giulio Preti may have given Luigi Campogalliani's creation the appearance we associate with him today, a slightly older man missing some teeth, and wearing a long tasseled red or striped red and white nightcap similar to that of Fagiolino. Sandrone in Bologna would have been laughed at for his country ways, but audiences also identified with his common sense attitudes. With his slow speech, he proved an ideal companion for the cleverer and more urban Fagiolino, but could become a butt of jokes. Filippo Cuccoli supposedly developed the character of Sandrone because his Fagiolino could not really compete with that of Cavallazzi.

Fagiolino and Sandrone formed a nucleus around which further figures accrued. Giulio Preti in Modena invented Pulonia, Sandrone's wife. His Sandrone was initially the cunning servant type but Preti later introduced a son Sgorghiguelo, at which point Sandrone's slow-wittedness was opposed to his son's cleverness and Fagiolino often became a foil to San-drone.[29] Angelo Cuccoli had a character called La Vecchia (old woman), who probably derived from the older folk tradition, but appeared in a number of pieces.[30] Around 1875 he created Flemma, who was always complaining about something, and whose favorite line was "I'll go and tell my mother." Further characters were gradually introduced, including Ghittara and Spadace (two carabinieri), who were later conflated by Cuccoli into a single puppet who wore a uniform similar to those of the Piedmontese carabinieri around 1820, and generally came off the worse in his encounters with Fagiolino. Augusto Galli, who joined Angelo Cuccoli in 1876, may have been the creator of a new Bolognese character, Sganapino Posapiano.[31] Sganapino's bright red hair, black and white check coat and cap with an enormous peak provided a contrast to Fagiolino. His speech was slow compared to the more definite delivery of Fagiolino and he was a simpler character whose main function was simply to amuse the audiences for an hour or so. Many puppeteers came to prefer Sganapino to Fagiolino, and he often replaced him, taking over the stick as well. By the mid–twentieth century he had acquired a much younger face and had become a great favorite with juvenile audiences.

Each puppeteer had his own group of masks, though this selection might also be affected by where performances were given. Sandro Costantini performing mainly in Lombardy had Gioppino and Brighella as his main characters, but switched to Fagiolino and Sandrone when he played in Emilia. Rosa Sarzi remembered her father Antonio using Gioppino, Meneghino, Brighella, Sandrone and Fagiolino, but the central comic figure always seems to have been Fagiolino.[32] Romano Danielli became one of the greatest interpreters of Fagiolino and when he wrote his memoirs of a career of 50 years in 2004, he called them *Fagiolino C'è*.

The rapid development of Piedmont, including the absorption of Genoa, and the putting together of the Lombardo-Veneto area by Austria in the first half of the nineteenth century had an impact on the characters created and the territorial extent covered by them. The great Piedmontese mask was Gerolamo (Girolamo), whose origins may reach back to the seventeenth century. In Carlo Cuniberto's publicity of 1816, he was described as the Piedmontese Zanni, and also as the "second" Zanni, an indication that he was taking on the function of Arlecchino.[33] In 1817, for his performances at the Teatro Berruti in Asti, Cuniberto referred to himself as "known as Gironi," thus assimilating himself with his comic figure. Audiences perceived the puppet in the same way as a real actor taking different roles in different plays. The publicity for a performance of *La bella Maghe-lona* indicated that "Gironi will play the part of a pilgrim at the Saracen port."[34] Of small stature and sporting a bump on his face reminiscent of Arlecchino, Gironi spoke the local dialect, in which his name was Giròni d'la Cri-na. "Cri-na" refers to a stringed instrument and suggests that he had a high-pitched voice, perhaps pointing to the use of the swazzle when he first appeared.

Angelo Cuccoli's Fagiolino and Filippo Cuccoli's Sandrone. (From Antonio Pandolfini Barberi, *Burattini e burattinai bolognesi* [Bologna: Nicola Zanichelli, 1923].)

The Gerolamo or Gironi that

we know today was probably created in the last years of the eighteenth century. According to tradition, Giovan Battista Sales had been performing with him in Genoa, but the last Doge was also called Gerolamo, unfortunate allusions were seen and Sales had to leave. He transferred to Turin, where performances were stopped in 1806 and Sales and his associate Gioachino Bellone had to leave the city. The direct cause of the problem may have been the announcement of a piece based on Francesco Ringhieri's tragedy, *Artabano, or the Tyrant of the World,* subtitled *King by Chance.* Gerolamo, as confidant to the tyrant, acquired a throne, which seemed a transparent allusion to the elevation of his namesake, Napoleon's brother Jerome Bonaparte, to the throne of Westphalia.

Giuseppe Fiando first brought Gerolamo to Milan in the 1790s, and obviously did not run into the same problems as Sales and Bellone did in Turin. In 1806 the *Giornale Italiano* observed:

> What a pleasant rogue is this character of Gerolamo, who appears in all the performances. Even if he is no more than a Piedmontese rustic he will always attract big audiences thanks to the originality of his character as much as his blunt and biting outspokenness, the real comic effect of his popular dialect and his clumsy behavior.[35]

The writer of the article also observed that Gerolamo was being transformed into a pure Milanese character. Gerolamo was taken up by many companies in the region. When Charles Dickens visited Genoa in 1844 he saw the Zane company and commented on the comic marionette (probably Gerolamo) with exceptionally flexible legs who winked at the audience. Over time Gerolamo's roles on the marionette stage ranged from Guerrino Meschino's squire to a brigand in *Majno della Spinetta,* a Burmese idol in *A Journey in a Balloon,* the brigadier in *Musolino the Brigand,* and the priest Don Abbondio in *I promessi sposi.* In *Ginevra degli Almieri* he appeared variously as a faithful servant, a matchmaker, a grave-robber and a lawyer for the defense.[36] In 1816 the Fiando repertoire was still offering a number of pieces with Arlecchino or Brighella in the title roles, and sometimes they alternated with Gerolamo.

When they left Turin Sales and Bellone removed themselves to Cagliasnetto d'Asti, where they created a new character, Gianduja (Giôan d'la duja,

Giuseppe Fiando's Girolamo. (Figure designed for drinking.) (Courtesy Compagnia Carlo Colla e Figli.)

which, in Piedmontese, means Giovanni of the tankard). Probably based on a local character, Gianduja was little more than Gerolamo with a different name. The new puppet was
dressed in exactly the same way as Gerolamo, with a brown waistcoat and breeches, red
stockings, a three-cornered hat and a pigtail with a red ribbon. Gianduja later became a
marionette, and also acquired a wife, Giacometta. This peasant gradually became urbanized in Turin until eventually, when taken up by the Lupi company as a marionette in the
1860s, he became virtually a symbol of the city and gradually replaced Arlecchino, who had
been the mask of that company. Even today his name survives on chocolate labels.

The other popular Piedmontese mask was Famiola. In 1811 he appeared on a bill with
Arlecchino for performances in Asti by the Rizzi family of Turin. They indicated that the
repertoire of their great marionette show would be from the best Italian authors, enlivened
by comic scenes with Famiola.[37] On a visit in 1816 one of the pieces offered was *Famiola
Supposed Prince to the Despair of His Ministers*. By now Famiola had taken on Arlecchino's
central role. His classic costume was breeches with a red waistcoat and coat with white edg-
ings, stockings in red and white stripes, black shoes with eighteenth-century buckles, a red
cap and a large green bow. This evoked the Italian tricolor flag and the Napoleonic "kingdom" of Italy. The name Famiola implies hunger, a concern shared with Arlecchino. Famiola was the mask of the Colla and Monticelli families. When the Carlo Colla e Figli company
moved into the Gerolamo theater in 1911 it substituted Gerolamo for Famiola. Like the
Lupi's Gianduja, its Gerolamo was a more bourgeois positive character with whom their
solidly middle-class audiences could identify.[38] Giacomo Colla continued to use a Famiola
until his show was destroyed in the bombing of the Teatro Bordoni in Pavia during the Second World War.[39] After this he abandoned the character, as he felt it had lost its linguistic
currency and no longer had any great relevance for audiences.

In the Veneto in the 1830s Antonio Reccardini created a local variant of Gerolamo
with Facanapa.[40] Arriving relatively late on the scene, Facanapa was an urban figure whose
name evoked the idea of poking his nose into things and whose knee breeches and tricorn
might have been those of the servants of the early nineteenth century. This small and not
very courageous figure was noted for a stock movement of raising his right leg and pirou-
etting round in a half circle.[41] To emphasize his speech he would give a little jump and stamp
his foot noisily on the stage (an effect akin to Gioppino banging his head on the playboard).
He was immensely popular with Reccardini's predominantly juvenile audiences. Bills for
Reccardini's 1837-1838 season in Venice make special mention of Arlecchino and Facanapa
as foils to one another. In *Guerrino il Meschino at the Trees of the Sun*, Arlecchino and
Facanapa are together squires to the hero. Facanapa was adopted by a number of other com-
panies in the Veneto.[42] In Reggio Emilia, the Muchetti family also used him with Arlecchino.
They later introduced their own mask of Cecchino, a modification of a Facanapa puppet.
He had a title role in *The Dialogue of Pancrazio and Cecchino* and appeared alongside
Arlecchino and Brighella in *The Enchanted Castle* but he never became firmly established.[43]

The distinctive Bergamask glove-puppet tradition centers on Gioppino (a diminutive
of Giuseppe). Much of his appeal was his use of the local dialect but he often appeared far
beyond his home city. Possibly created by Battaglia, one of the earliest performers with the
character, he originated in the lower town of Bergamo but his costume evokes the countryman. He sports a large triple goiter (which he sometimes refers to as his potatoes), possibly a variant of the growths on the faces of other comic characters. Gioppino's wife (Margì)

Famiola, his son Famiolino and an ass. Archival photograph. These figures in the Gianni Colla Collection were used by Giacomo Colla in the early 20th century. (Courtesy Il Teatro di Gianni e Cosetta Colla. From G. Colla and G. Bonora, *Il popolo di legno* [Milano: Imago, 1982]. Photograph Gianni Renna.)

and his entire family all sport this triple goiter. A dietary deficiency made goiter prevalent in the area around Bergamo, especially amongst the poor, but Gioppino's triple one might also be a parodic allusion to the three balls on the coat of arms of the powerful local Colleoni family.[44] Like Fagiolino, Gioppino was nearly always a glove-puppet and because of this remained resolutely a man of the people and did not suffer the embourgeoisement that marked the marionette Gerolamo. He appeared in dramas adapted from the actors' theater, including brigand plays like *Paci Paciana*. Topical events were also utilized as source material. Garibaldi appeared in *Revolution in Palermo*; *Gioppino in Africa* coincided with Italian colonialism in the early twentieth century; and later it was possible to see a Mussolini look-alike accompanying Gioppino.[45]

Like Fagiolino, Gioppino is a positive character and a righter of wrongs. Arlecchino, who continued alongside him, slipped into second place, but he was also coupled with Brighella. Bigio Milesi's *Gioppino in the Counterfeiter's Castle* opens with a graveyard scene where Gioppino and Brighella plan to rob graves for jewels but are very jumpy and startled by someone else with the same idea that they take for a ghost. Gioppino defeats (and kills) a gang of counterfeiters, who had tried to appear as ghosts to persuade people the cellars of a castle were haunted, and is rewarded with the hand of the daughter of the owner.[46] Milesi's Gioppino figured in many pieces that were much closer to the farces of the Commedia dell'Arte. In *Brighella and Gioppino without a Master* the two rascals have stolen from their employers Tartaglia and Pantalone. Brighella comes up with the idea that each should approach the other's former employer for work. Unfortunately the two old men have already discussed their servants. Gioppino is treated to a beating by Tartaglia, but after three or four blows gets hold of the stick and beats him. Brighella is less lucky with Pantalone and receives a sound thrashing. At the end Gioppino, to be fair, offers to give the blows he has not received to Brighella to make things even.

In early nineteenth-century Rome Pulcinella was joined by Rugantino, who was a thoroughly urban figure and apparently untouched by the ideas of the Enlightenment. He emerged from the popular classes of Rome as a puppet. One of his antecedents was Meo Patacca, a Roman equivalent of Coviello (a variant of the Captain), who appeared on the mid–seventeenth-century stage, and, thanks to a celebrated poem by Giuseppe Berneri, "Meo Patacca" (1695), became a part of Roman folklore.[47] Patacca was accompanied by a swaggering (and often cowardly) braggart, Marco Pepe or Marco Spacca. Marco Pepe was far closer to the ordinary man in the street and the people of Rome identified easily with him in popular farces.[48] Filippo Tacconi (1805–1870), nicknamed Pippo il Gobbo because of his small stature and humpback, was a popular actor in a whole series of Meo Patacca pieces and as such gave greater importance to the part of Marco Pepe. It is suggested that the "terribile Meino" of the marionette theater of the piazza Navona was based on this pint-size Meo Patacca.[49]

Rugantino, whose name implies arrogance, was a parody of a Roman bully, as represented by Meo Patacca and Marco Pepe, but he also carried overtones of the popular Roman figure of Pasquino, whose wisecracks were greatly appreciated. A frequent victim of beatings, he usually triumphed with the sharpness of his tongue. His large head topped a deformed and squat body, his legs were bowed and his long dangling arms could reach his feet. His face, too, was deformed by bumps. He had the classic pigtail of the eighteenth-century servant, a large hat rather like that of a carabiniere (which carried a hint of the papal police), a red wool jacket with breeches and waistcoat of the same color, buckled shoes and a couple of rusty cutlasses at the waist. More courageous in his speech than his actions, one of his familiar expressions was "Me n'ha date, ma je n'ho dette!" (he gave it [blows] to me but I said it to him!). His other great expression was "sangue d'un dua" ('Sblood). Pinelli depicts Rugantino with a guitar, which suggests that like Scaramuzzia (another bravo) he may have sung from time to time. A contemporary, Filippo Chiappini, who described some of Ghetanaccio's farces, related an anecdote about the puppeteer taking revenge on a grocer who had cheated him. Ghetanaccio set up his stage next to the grocer's shop and brought on Rugantino, weeping because he has three sons and a gypsy has told him that one will kill, the second will be killed and the third will be a thief. A spirit (equipped with chicken wings) appears and tells him that he must make his first son a doctor, so that he can kill as many people as he wishes, the second son a soldier, so that he can die with honor defending his country, and the third a grocer, so that he can rob with impunity. Rugantino then turned to the grocer's shop and informed the audience that the grocer had sold him short when buying some sausage that morning. Accompanied by loud whistles, the humiliated shopkeeper beat a hasty retreat.[50]

The earliest clear reference to Rugantino as a puppet (probably a marionette or pupo) is in a prose comedy called *The Basilisk of Bernagasco with Arlecchino as a Merchant* performed during the summer of 1807 by Adriano Valeri at the Mausoleum of Augustus.[51] In this play Arlecchino is an illiterate merchant. For four months of the year he cannot read, for four he cannot write and for four he can do neither. Rugantino, who speaks in dialect, appears as a debt collector, backed by a group of police. He beats Arlecchino, but then is beaten in turn by the "Basilisk," who goes under the name of Girone or Girolamo and comes from Livorno. At the Montanara theater Rugantino sometimes alternated with Pulcinella as Orlando's squire but never became as fully established. An amusing fantasy staged at the Emiliani in 1851 was *The Great Demogorgon; or the Walnut tree of Benevento* "with Rugantino persecuted by the witches and protected by the fairy Lirina."[52] Rugantino as a comic servant is reminiscent of Hanswurst in the German Faust plays. He rides a donkey, is pursued by devils and ends up with a good beating.

Between 1812 and 1816, Arlecchino, occasionally accompanied by Pulcinella, was the main comic mask of the Fiano Theater. Cassandro had existed with the Gelosi troupe in the sixteenth century as an old man, but had been overshadowed by Pantalone. He resurfaced in the eighteenth century as an elderly bourgeois figure, often short-sighted and close-fisted or simply as a kindly uncle. His first appearance as a marionette on the Fiano stage was in 1814 in *The Ridiculous Loves of Cassandro with Arlecchino as an Amorous Adviser*. The title alone intimates the aspect of the character that would be emphasized at that theater. Within a couple of years Cassandro had become the main mask of the Fiano, in both comedies and "balli," or musical pieces. He was used in a similar way to Gerolamo in Milan, but was socially of a class that related to the Fiano's more refined audiences. Cassandrino's improvised barbs had a very sharp satirical edge in the restrictive climate of papal Rome but were addressed to a social group that would regard them as "in" jokes. The diminutive form of his name, Cassandrino, probably indicated the reduction of the figure from a human to a marionette. A contemporary reference to the sound of a drum and the sharp and nasal voice of Cassandrino apprising audiences that the show was about to begin could imply the use of a swazzle.[53] What distinguishes Cassandrino is the association with the wickedly satirical Filippo Teoli. Once he ceased to be a mouthpiece for Teoli he faded very rapidly. His distinctive costume was a coat and breeches in fine red silk, a white satin waistcoat with yellow dots, a tricorn, impeccable white linen and silver buckles on his shoes. He boasted that the fabric of his outfit was made in France, his breeches were from England (noted for its tailoring) and that his watch had cost him 100 guineas from the best clock-maker in London. Teoli's Cassandrino was distinguished by his attraction to younger members of the opposite sex, but apart from this foible, which could land him in difficult situations, he was an intelligent and witty man of the world.

Early records of theatrical activity in Sicily are scarce. Around 1718 there are references to a traveling theater, the Teatro dei Traviglini, that had a booth on the Piano della Martorana (Piazza Bellini) in Palermo. The two main masks of this company were the clown Travaglino and the servant Ferrazzano, who may have been local variants of masks of the Commedia dell'Arte.[54] In the show booths of Palermo's Piazza Marina in the last 30 years of the eighteenth century actors presented short farces in which the main figures were porters from the nearby harbor.[55] The porters were known as "vastasi" and these farces, referred to as "vastasate," transferred readily to the puppet stage.[56] A central figure in these was 'Nofriu (Onofrio), described as a mixture of a fool and trickster. He probably became a puppet character towards the end of the eighteenth century, and by the end of the nineteenth, as a glove-puppet, he had slipped into parts played by Pulcinella, notably *The Ninety-nine Misfortunes of Onofrio* and *The Birth of Onofrio from an Egg*.

Pulcinella probably came to Sicily with Neapolitan showmen in the early years of the nineteenth century. When Pitrè described the "tutui" or glove-puppet stages of Palermo in the last years of the century, the main characters were "Poulcinella" (Pulcinella), "Colombrina" (Colombina), "Tartagghia" (Tartaglia), "la Morti" (Death), Birlicchi and Birlacchi (devils) and sometimes a hound.[57] A stock performance involved rivalry between Pulcinella and Tartaglia over Colombina. After a fight Pulcinella feigns dead to test Colombina's love, then revives just in time for a notary to marry them. Pulcinella enjoyed an independent existence, but his companion was often 'Nofriu.

In the early 1900s in Palermo, Festing Jones saw a pupi performance of *Samson* that revolved around Samson's rivalry with the Philistine champion, Accabo, for a lady he had rescued from a lion. A comic interlude involving "the common people of Palermo" was inserted "to amuse the boys" and involved rivalry between 'Nofriu, "Peppiniu" and Rosina.[58]

Peppenino (Peppininu) has much in common with the new "masks" of the Napoleonic period. He shares with them a pigtail and a costume that evokes an eighteenth-century livery: a curly powdered wig with a pigtail, a jabot, a tailcoat, knee breeches, shoes with buckles and, earlier, a tricorn. Like Pulcinella, he could be multiplied, or else, like Gioppino, have a son Titta, who is an exact replica of him but is slightly smaller, and a wife Cammela Pagghiazzu, who in female dress replicates the physical characteristics of her husband.[59] These are amongst the few Catanian characters to use dialect.

Peppininu readily took on the various roles of Pulcinella as servant to the hero in plays about the paladins and became central to the opera dei pupi of Catania.[60] His privileged position allowed him to break the dramatic illusion to address the audience, whose voice he could become, expressing their point of view both about the heroic deeds represented and the events and problems of everyday life. In many cases he steered the plot and led to the denouement. For example, the mad Orlando only gets his senses back because Peppininu suggests to Astolfo and the paladins a way of immobilizing him while he passes a rope around his legs and body. Peppininu became the symbolic expression of popular aspirations for natural justice when he punished those guilty of treason by beating them, stoning them, whipping them and carrying out the death penalty.

Like many traditional masks of both West and East (Karagöz, Semar, Pulcinella) Peppininu corresponds to the figure of the trickster, the divine rogue, branded with his ambivalent physical disabilities. Peppininu is a one-eyed limping dwarf. Like Rugantino and often Pulcinella, he has the humpback and is smaller than the other figures. In the Palermitan opera dei pupi his function seems to have been taken over by Virticchiu, a figure of similar small stature, deformed and also usually with only one eye. Virticchiu is often provided with a string to a toe to give him a characteristic kicking movement rather similar to that of Facanapa. He partners the tall 'Nofriu in a classic coupling that allows for much verbal and physical humor. Both have abandoned any hint of the early nineteenth-century servant. They are perceived as contemporary working-class characters and are dressed in modern clothes.[61]

The Palermitan opera dei pupi has left few traces of comic improvisation introduced in the course of the action.[62] However, there was usually a comic introductory scene between 'Nofriu and Virticchiu, who then reappeared before the final act when the "perdomani"

Catanian style cartellone depicting Gano beaten by Peppininu and devils — also Malagigi riding Nacalone. (From Antonio Pasqualino *L'opera dei pupi*. Courtesy Museo Internazionale delle Marionette Antonio Pasqualino. Courtesy and © of Sellerio, Palermo.)

announced the program for the next day and 'Nofriu added his own gloss on it. In the main piece 'Nofriu spoke something approximating standard Italian, but in a concluding farce he, and the other characters, used dialect and here improvisation had completely free reign. In the Canino Theater of Alcamo 'Nofriu and Virticchiu were accompanied by a group of folk characters that included the Neapolitan Testuzza (with a large head), the baron, Lisa and Rusidda.

The ongoing creation of popular characters continued into the twentieth century. The puparo Natale Meli of Reggio Calabria also had a Pulcinella glove-puppet show in which, as well as the familiar figures, there is a character with a very large nose known as Surasonte.[63] Baciccia was used in Liguria and the south of Piedmont and first appeared with the company of Ugo Ponti towards the end of the nineteenth century. He then became the main mask used by Raffaele Pallavicini between 1899 and 1928 and later by his son Gino and was often paired with Gerolamo. Gualberto Niemen created Testafina in the first half of the twentieth century but continued to use Gianduja. Unusually for a glove-puppet, his Gianduja had an opening mouth, a feature found with the Bargnocla of the Ferrari company of Reggio Emilia. Like Arlecchino or Gerolamo, Bargnocla has a bump or "barnacle" of vast dimensions on his forehead, and in addition has moving eyebrows.

Peppino Sarina's Pampalughino, a peasant from the province of Lodi, may have been

'Nofriu and the mad Orlando. Canino Theater. The Orlando figure has a cavity to contain water and can urinate. (From Antonio Pasqualino *L'opera dei pupi*. Courtesy Museo Internazionale delle Marionette Antonio Pasqualino. Courtesy and © of Sellerio, Palermo.)

invented by Sarina's grandfather, Andrea, as a patriotic figure opposed to the Austrians.[64] Clever and opportunistic, fond of wine, and giving blows more frequently than receiving them, Pampalughino resembles Gioppino and Fagiolino, and like them is usually the character who resolves a situation. Between 1875 and 1900 he appeared in every production of the Sarina company. He could be a soldier, page, squire, boatman or jailer. He could chat with St. Joseph in *Gelindo* (the Piedmontese pastoral) or help Napoleon save Tortona from an attack by Barbarossa in *Majno della Spinetta*.[65] Following the popular tendency, Peppino Sarina developed a group of figures around Pampalughino. His Tascone (rather

Pampalughino and Arlecchino, glove-puppets of Peppino Sarina. Typical of the mixture of the older and the newer "masks." (Courtesy Archivio dell'Associazione Peppino Sarina di Tortona [Al]. Photograph Raffaele Vaccari.)

similar to Sandrone) was an illiterate countryman who believed everything that was said to him and was provided with a wife (Gigia), a brother (Fastidio) and an adopted son Bùrtul (sometimes called Burdo).[66] Around 1940 Argentina Burzio adapted Pampalughino as a marionette for the Gambarutti company, where he was known as Pampalugha. They used him for about 15 years, especially outside Piedmont when the dialect of Gianduja, their main mask, could not be understood.[67] Pampalugha performed alongside not only Gianduja and Facanapa, but also Brighella and Tartaglia.

In the early 1900s existing stock characters lost not only their dialects but many of their defining characteristics. So as to speak more directly to children they became younger, and new ones were invented. With Pinocchio Carlo Collodi had created the prototype of the child figure who nonetheless possesses many of the attributes of the zanni of the Commedia dell'Arte.[68] His progress through the book from branch of tree to wooden puppet to real boy, coupled with the experiences he has and the tests and trials through which he passes, are all a recognizable part of the process of growing up. The point of reference remains Collodi's book, but Pinocchio also took on a semi-independent life of his own. Yambo created Ciuffetino, a boy who became immensely popular for some years, while, with television, children's magazines and cartoons, Maria Perego's celebrated mouse, Topo Gigio, is far better known than Pulcinella to today's children and could be called the most important mask of the twentieth century, once more demonstrating the direct rapport between such a character and the audience.

Scripts and Scenarios

The early actors of the Commedia dell'Arte performed scripted plays, the "commedia erudita," and ones where they created the performance on the basis of a plot outline, the "commedia improvvisa." The latter mode of working had largely disappeared from actors' theater by the end of the eighteenth century, but remained a way of working for many puppeteers until at least the middle of the twentieth. Improvisation was a very real skill and worked within tightly controlled parameters depending heavily on the abilities of the performer and audience expectation. The working methods of the Commedia troupes and the performer-centered style can be adapted to virtually any subject matter. A standard scenario employed a number of well-tried formulas and consisted of a collection of instantly familiar stock types and situations. Plot was little more than a convenient peg to hold things together. Actors often had a commonplace book (zibaldone) in which they might record scraps of dialogue, set speeches, and physical or verbal gags or lazzi. Most actors played the same stock roles throughout their career and like their audiences knew exactly how a character might act in a certain situation or respond to a particular verbal or physical stimulus.

The lazzo, as a non-scripted element of the performance, was much used on the puppet stage but it worried régimes sensitive to criticism or over-concerned with morality. In 1753, the papal legate closed down the puppets in the Borgo Nuova of Bologna because of their immoral speech. He took offense at a servant who said that women would avoid making love because her mistress had swallowed an eel which had caused her belly to swell, and that she had been cured in nine months.[69] Filippo Teoli was noted for the double entendre of his improvised sallies and Angelo Cuccoli was still using lazzi that might have been used by Commedia actors 200 years earlier. In one case Fagiolino is about to go to bed and finds his chamber pot missing, so goes to the wing and mimes urinating on it. In *The Doctor and Death* the king's daughter swallows a fishbone that prevents her from speaking. Dr. Balanzone and Fagiolino come to try and cure her. Balanzone sends Fagiolino for "quatèr sold ed sonza" (four sous' worth of lard) and makes the princess lie down on the playboard, facing the front. He pulls up her skirts and greases her buttocks, at which the princess bursts out laughing and exclaims "Ah! Ah! Ah!... Because a bone pricks me in the throat the Dottore lubricates my arse," and her laughter dislodges the fishbone.[70]

Surviving scripts consist of a mixture of carefully written-out texts designed to be read during the performance and of scenarios that simply act as an aide-mémoire, reminding the performers of what happens in each scene. The latter way of working was particularly prevalent on the glove-puppet stages and with the opera dei pupi, both of which perpetuated an oral performing tradition. By the seventeenth century almost anything that was performed by live actors might eventually find its way to the puppet stage. The simpler scenarios usually suited glove-puppets, since here the emphasis was on stock comic characters and situation more than plot. In the nineteenth century marionettes moved closer to the scripted theater of the live actors but their adaptations were generally reductions of the original text and allowed for interpolations by the central comic figure. These were occasionally signposted by the brief phrase "a gusto," indicating that the performer can do as he or she feels appropriate. In most cases it depended on the intuition of the performer to introduce lazzi, or even to make very specific local or topical references. The most heroic action was naturally undermined by the appearance of masks old or new as major players. A Pulcinella, a Gioppino or a Gianduja could transform a piece completely.

When performed by glove-puppets, dramas of the actors' stage repertoire were often reduced to scenarios in which the puppets took over the original plot and used it as a peg on which to hang their performance. Bigio Milesi declared that he could do a play ten times and change it as many times according to the audiences.[71] With the pupi in Palermo the unscripted vastasate that followed the regular episodes of the chivalrous repertoire had only the flimsiest of plot outline and depended entirely on the improvisational ingenuity of the puparo.[72] A prize example of this is *Ladder*, still in the repertoire of the Teatro Arte Cuticchio of Cefalù, which is little more than a comic sketch involving 'Nofriu, Virticchiu and a painter's ladder.

Marionette performances generally occurred in a closed space with an admission charge and a comparatively quiet environment which made possible the development of more complex plots and the use of scripted material. Even here, however, unscripted interpolations remained common. Where glove-puppet shows occurred indoors or slightly away from noisy distractions, they too might develop a fuller, more articulated scenario, as opposed to the series of short episodes and encounters characteristic of the street Pulcinella shows of Rome or Naples.

Some themes lent themselves very well to the manner of working of the Commedia dell'Arte and therefore reappear again and again. The huge diversity of material used and the readiness to borrow from any available source, whether oral folk tradition or written literature, are another reminder that the subject matter existed merely to provide a framework for a performance into which the masked actors or stock characters could step easily. In the puppet theater a part of the audience's delight was in seeing what roles their favorite puppet "masks" might take.

On the glove-puppet stage the working methods and scenarios of the Commedia continued through the twentieth century. Some more creative puppeteers invented new plots, but retained the structures and situations with which audiences were familiar. Romano Danielli's version of *Guerrino Meschino* opens with a long scene between the Dottore, Pantalone, Sandrone and Sganapino, who are planning an elaborate meal. There is much discussion of the menu, making use of comic catalogues and a long tirade by the Dottore (applauded by the audience as a virtuoso set piece). The scene has little to do with the main plot, and is really there as a piece of entertainment for its own sake. Its function is to warm up the audience before they meet Fagiolino, who, of course, plays Guerrino's squire. The dark plot of the nineteenth-century drama *The Crusader* recounts the return from the holy land of Count Alfonso di Savené after an absence of some 20 years only to find his children murdered by his supposed friend, who is about to marry his wife. Cesare Maletti's reduction of this for glove-puppets involved Fagiolino, Sandrone, Apolonia (Polonia) and, briefly, Brighella. Thanks to Fagiolino and Sandrone matters are sorted out as Fagiolino uses his stick, which proves superior to any weapon forged by a smith and reminds us that the (virtuous) man of the people is superior to any (evil) aristocrat.

Cesare Maletti showed how the working methods of the Commedia dell'Arte continued unchanged. In his *As You Sow, So Shall You Reap*; or *Jove, Jove*, which was being performed in the years following the Second World War, Brighella, as a trickster, thinks it funny to tell the gullible Sandrone that if he is hungry he has only to call on Jove with a little rhyme and ask him to strike. Sandrone does this, while Brighella comes up behind him unseen and hits him with his stick. He repeats this, but Fagiolino guesses what has happened and turns the tables. He pretends to fall for Brighella's trick, but keeps turning so that Brighella's approach is interrupted, then, at the last moment he dodges Brighella's stick altogether. He then outwits Brighella and beats him soundly. Finally Fagiolino gives Sandrone an extra bang on the head, just to see how Brighella might have hit him, and they both go off to drink a bottle of Lambrusco.[73]

Working to a scenario as opposed to a full written text remained the primary method for the pupi theaters of western Sicily. These scenarios were not unlike the short synopses that form chapter headings of the prose versions of romances such as *Guerrino Meschino* or those relating to Orlando and Rinaldo. The text of the episode to be performed was broken up into a series of short scenes with a brief indication of what would happen in each. The puparo told a story introducing a great deal of dialogue and taking virtually all the voices. This mode of puppet performance is similar to that of the scriptural shadow shows mentioned by Ottonelli. What it has in common with the Commedia dell'Arte is the working method of using a set of known characters placed in situations that will be resolved according to formulas that are familiar to the audience with large numbers of type scenes recurring from episode to episode. With only the barest plot outline the puppeteer could produce a full performance and maintain a huge number of episodes without having to memorize a script. Where the story-telling mode is uppermost the direct communication with the audience is as much through the voice of the puparo as through the comic figure and this may be another reason why the comic scenes in Palermo are generally specific interludes or a final farce.

Repertoires

The earliest list of the repertoire of an eighteenth-century traveling marionette company is that of Girolamo Renzi. On a bill of 1777 from Prague, he lists 28 pieces, of which 12 have Pulcinella in the title and one has Pantalone.[74] The remaining pieces include *The Great Stone Guest* (Don Juan), in which Pulcinella would have taken the role of the Don's servant, a version of *The Prodigal Son* (the warhorse of the company) and *The Servants' Contest*, described as being in three acts and very funny. The bill mentions new intermezzi, which would have been variety acts and trick puppets, and additionally, in the German language version of the publicity, solo dances by Captain Scaramuzza.

The majority of the pieces presented by Gigli Toscano in Asti in 1779 involved Arlecchino.[75] Plays revolving around the character of Pulcinella or Arlecchino continued into the nineteenth century. When Francesco Rossi brought his company to Asti in 1788 he emphasized the fact that he was bringing theater to Asti and that his burattino show was not like the more vulgar street one.[76] An illustrated bill depicts Arlecchino, Tartaglia, Pantalone and Brighella. The importance of the first two masks is clear from four titles: *The Influence of Saturn against the Amours of Tartaglia* (June 17); *Tartaglia Who Teaches Arlecchino to Behave and Speak Well* (June 18); *Arlecchino Mute from Need, Speaks Out of Necessity* (June 19) and *Arlecchino Supposed Prince* (Monday, June 23). He also presented *Gennaro Turned to Stone by the Evil Magician Norando, Prince of Damascus* (June 22), in which one can recognize Carlo Gozzi's fable, *The Raven*.

Of the countless scenarios of the Commedia dell'Arte that found their way to the puppet stage, the subject of the misfortunes of the central character, who is the victim of a series of practical jokes perpetrated by a trickster figure, is one that crops up in almost every company's repertoire. A conniving audience always feels involved in the plot. The number of misadventures varies, but the commonest are 99 and 33. The minimal plot line is set up mainly to give value to the performance of the trickster and consists of little more than a series of episodes designed to dispose of an inconvenient suitor from the provinces, the gullible Pulcinella, or Arlecchino or, later, Sandrone or Gerolamo. Molière's rather episodic piece, *Monsieur de Pourceaugnac* (1669), is based on this idea and may in turn have influenced some puppet versions. Two scenarios in the Casamarciano collection, *Policinella Driven Mad* and *Policinella Mocked*, have the same theme.[77] Individual puppet showmen often changed titles of well-known works or scenarios that they adapted. Sometimes this was a question of avoiding paying royalties, sometimes just a way of giving a new look to an older piece and putting their own stamp on it. In the early twentieth century Ettore Forni presented the "misfortunes" as *The Return from America and the Shoemaker Count*.[78]

Pulcinella has a hermaphroditic status and is frequently thought of as giving birth to his own young, a theme much used by Bruno Leone in the late twentieth century. Tiepolo picked up a recurrent theme when he depicted Pulcinella hatching from an egg. Subsequently this notion was often transferred from Pulcinella to Arlecchino. *The Birth of Harlequin from an Egg* was performed by Italian companies in London in 1779 and 1780.[79] Hatching eggs producing figures of different sorts are a long-established trick on the puppet stage and survived as a separate variety act right up until the twentieth century. The birth from an egg episode could be inserted into almost any piece. In 1806, Fiando had a comedy: *The Surplus Poor Man and the Ignorant Rich Man with Gerolamo Born from an Egg*. The Colla company had a production in which Famiola hatched from a large egg in the middle of the stage and announced "Je l'ai fam" (I am hungry).[80] *Fasolino Who Dies and Is Born from an Egg* was the title of one of Francesco Campogalliani's pieces.

The inversion of social roles has long been a popular theatrical subject, and this usually relates to a joke or trick in which the audience can share. In Acciajoli's *Il girello* (The Weathercock), adapted for the marionette stage in 1682, a magician makes it possible for a gardener to exchange roles with the king. Apart from the inevitable confusion caused by the apparently contradictory behavior of the "king," there is also a sense of natural justice running through the piece. A Commedia dell'Arte scenario in the Adriani collection of 1730 from Perugia, *Pulcinella Sham Prince* may well have served as a basis for a variety of puppet performances such as Renzi's *Pulcinella Prince by Magic* of 1777 or the Rizzi company's *Famiola Sham Prince*, performed in Asti in 1810.[81] In Sicily the Canino pupo repertoire in the early twentieth century included a *Virticchio Emperor of the Great Mongolia* based on a farce called *Onofrio Sham Emperor of the Great Mongolia*.[82]

The device of a dream (often a trick) is frequently used for role inversion pieces in which a character wakes up to find he is king. *Arlecchino King in a Dream* was a popular Commedia scenario. Angelo Cuccoli and Francesco Campogalliani performed a *Fagiolino Made King in his Sleep*. Théophile Gautier saw the Zane company in *Girolamo Caliph for 24 hours*. *Sandrone, King of the Mammeluks* was popular in Emilia Romagna and also Bologna. Francesco Campogalliani used a version that he claimed to have inherited from his great-grandfather Luigi.[83] It was still being performed by Otello Sarzi and by the Ferrari company in the 1980s.[84] In Sarzi's version Sandrone refuses to let his daughter Lisetta marry Fagiolino. A fairground fortune-teller says that he will become richest when he has lost everything. Sandrone is given some drugged snuff, and when he awakes he is at court as king. On the model of the many misfortunes of Pulcinella and others, he encounters disaster after disaster, until finally the cook (Brighella) persuades him to commit suicide painlessly by taking "poisoned" snuff. He is happy to do this, and when he awakes he is ready to allow Lisetta marry Fagiolino.

The Don Juan theme occurs in virtually every puppet repertoire in Europe.[85] One of the earliest theatrical treatments of the subject, Tirso da Molina's *Il burlador de Sevilla y el convidado di piedra* (The Seducer of Seville or the Stone Guest), dates from before 1630. The subject was already in the repertoire of the Locatelli company performing in Paris before Molière used it for his *Dom Juan*. A mid–seventeenth-century Commedia dell'Arte scenario from the Ciro Monarca collection of manuscripts in the Biblioteca Casanatense in Rome includes a *Convitato di pietra*. The Colla company had a *Don Giovanni the Libertine* (with Famiola) which is surprisingly close to this scenario, but since scripts were copied and adapted again and again, it is not possible to establish when it entered their repertoire.[86]

A puppet version was announced in Prague on the the Renzi bill of 1777, ten years before the première of Mozart's opera in that city.[87] The Incisa diary reveals that the subject was frequently chosen by companies for the last performance of a season that closed with Lent. This familiar piece probably guaranteed a good house and audiences would have enjoyed the grand finale with devils and fireworks. An undated popular edition of the *Gran convitato di pietra* was produced by the printing firm of Tamburrini (active between 1822 and 1840), and in 1862 Giovanni Gussoni published a version specifically designed for the puppet stage. Eugenio Rontini's *Don Giovanni Tenorio or the Great Stone Guest with Stenterello as Pimp, Shipwrecked and a Lucky Man Scared by the Flames of Hell* was printed by Salani in Florence in 1881 and is known to have been much used by puppeteers.[88] In 1927 a scenario was published in Naples, with Coviello and Pulcinella as the servants of Duke Ottavio and Don Giovanni.[89] Six years later Ruggiero Dell'Aquila used this scenario as the basis for his adaptation for the pupi.[90] The dell'Aquila *Don Giovanni Tenorio or Pulcinella Terrified by the Statue of Commander Olloa* concludes with a grand hell scene in which the Don, surrounded by devils, pronounces a moral warning to mankind to learn virtue.

Molière, Goldoni and Gozzi

Molière, Goldoni and Gozzi drew on Commedia scenarios for their plays and in turn were a constant point of reference for puppet companies.[91] An article in the *Corriere delle dame* of 1806 describing the performances at the Gerolamo Theater in Milan commented on the way in which the plots of Molière and Goldoni were well adapted to the marionette stage and always gave the liveliest part to Gerolamo.[92] In 1811, a company at the S. Romano theater, Milan, was also offering pieces derived from Molière and Goldoni, including *L'avaro* (The Miser) and *Tonin buona grazia*.[93] Variants of *Le malade imaginaire* were standard elements of the puppet repertoire. The scene, where the father pretends to be dead to find out his wife's real feelings, goes back to medieval farce. The various *Pulcinella [Arlecchino, Fagiolino, etc.] Doctor in Spite of Himself* recall Molière's *Médecin malgré lui*, but they too follow a much-used scenario.

Goldoni's *Servant of Two Masters* appeared in various marionette repertories as *Arlecchino Servant of Two Masters*. Bigio Milesi had a glove-puppet version of this with Gioppino and Brighella. Goldoni's great aim may have been to lead the Italian theater away from the Commedia dell'Arte and its masks, but puppet companies regularly pulled his plots back into that tradition. A puppet is closer to a mask than to a human actor and does not lend itself easily to realistic psychology. *The Chambermaid* (1751) exists in a Luigi Lupi script copied in 1818 for his marionettes when he was in Parma. It is given the title of *The Venetian Chambermaid* and substantially follows the Goldoni text, cutting a couple of minor characters and changing the name of the main servant from Frangiotto to Arlecchino. The female lead, Corallina, who spoke Italian in the original version of the piece, has her part translated into dialect.[94] In 1919, a poster for Francesco Campogalliani's version of *Sandrone King of the Mameluks* announced that all the Goldoni masks would perform in this show.[95] By this he meant Arlecchino, Brighella, the Dottore and Pantalone.[96]

Carlo Gozzi's dramatic fables, with their Commedia masks and huge element of fantasy and magic, could have been written for the puppet stage. The more serious action is fully scripted, but the intervening comic scenes are merely sketched out as scenarios. After some pruning of the literary and philosophical components, little remained to be done to transfer them to the small stage. *The Blue Monster*, subtitled *An Example of True Faithfulness*, was in the Fiando repertoire in 1815 and became a stock piece in other nineteenth-century repertoires.[97] In 1823 Fiando was offering *Turandot, the Chinese Princess and Enemy of Men*. *The Raven*, *The King Stag* and *The Serpent Woman* are amongst the pieces that remained in repertoires right up to the twentieth century.

A Repertoire for Cassandrino

The Cassandro (or Cassandrino) of the Fiano Theater had the distinction of having a repertoire written for him as well as being fitted into an existing one like the other masks. The sophisticated audiences of the Fiano obviously enjoyed being themselves targets of the satire aimed at Cassandrino. They formed a relatively closed in-group, quick to pick up any ambiguity or innuendo, and connivance between audience and performers contributed to the enjoyment of the show. Much space was left for the improvisations of Teoli and traces of the Commedia tradition are to be found everywhere in the stock types and situations, even if the overall atmosphere is closer to Eugene Scribe and the French Vaudeville than to the Commedia. The Cassandrino repertoire, like those of the major marionette companies, allows for improvised interpolations but is ultimately closer to the "commedia erudita" than to the "commedia improvvisa."

In *Cassandrino, Pupil of a Painter* Cassandrino dresses as elegantly as he can in order to seduce the beautiful daughter of a painter. He declares his passion by singing a cavatina, but the painter, a Byronic figure with huge sideburns, sends him packing and reproaches his daughter, saying "how could you be imprudent enough to allow a tête-à-tête with a man who cannot marry you?" which, observes Stendhal, delighted the audience as an obvious reference to a man of the cloth.[98] Our hero returns disguised as a youthful painter, his gray hair peeping out from under his abundant curly wig and black sideburns. He proposes a secret liaison to the girl, but as he throws himself at her feet he is interrupted by her aunt, to whom he had paid court some 40 years earlier. The painter arrives with a host of students and threatens to undress him and paint him scarlet, since the scarlet (of a cardinal, by implication) has always been his ambition, and to parade him publicly on the Corso. The humiliated Cassandrino agrees to marry the aunt and abandon the scarlet, but at least becomes the uncle of the girl he adores.[99]

The surviving Cassandro scripts all date from the 1830s, possibly after the retirement of Teoli.[100] In these our hero has changed from a relatively respected figure used as a vehicle for satire, into a more ridiculous one. Acute observation and social innuendo have made way for broad farce, often with an exotic setting. In *Cassandro in the Kingdom of the Great Mogul* he is in danger of being impaled, and later of starving to death. There is a deliberate wink at the audience as he announces that he must return to Rome to perform on the puppet stage. In *The Arrival of Cassandro the Singer in the Village of Grotta Gorga*, Cassandro, a singer from the Fiano Theater, has absconded with Vespina to escape his debts. At Grotta Gorga he is mistaken for the bridegroom of the mayor's niece, while the pompous mayor is the main target of satire.[101] In *Bluebeard; or Cassandro Persecuted by Fear* the main joke is the pusillanimity of Cassandro, who, not in love for once, receives an important appointment which in the context of Rome means clerical preferment.[102] Satire on contemporary manners is rife in these plays. The craze for fortune-telling is mocked in *The Treasure with Cassandro the Unfortunate Lotto Speculator*. This genre picture shows Cassandro as an ageing suitor who has ruined himself with the lottery and has turned to trying to foretell the results with cards. In the latter part of the play there is a strange dream sequence where Cassandro is rewarded for his goodness of heart. Fortune and his genius intervene and Cassandro and his beloved are transported in an airborne chariot to a refulgent garden.

The ever-popular nut tree of Benevento figured on the Fiano program in 1812 (the same year as Vigano's ballet) as *The Great Nut Tree of Benevento with Cassandro as the Destroyer of Witches*. It later resurfaced at the Fiano in a more facetious form as *Cassandro Bewitched at the Walnut Tree of Benevento* in 1833–1834. The ever-amorous Cassandro is now placed in the context of a witches' Sabbath. He visits the tree by night in the hopes that this might bring him a wife. Spirits take him to a rocky landscape inhabited by witches, who dance and then transform peasant children into birds. Cassandro, after a ridiculous dance, is transformed into a creature half bird, half goat and ends up on the top of a tree that loses its branches and suddenly opens to drop him onto a large rock. Fortune intervenes, leads him to a beautiful garden and presents him with a beautiful wife. As he sings there is a dance of grotesques. In practice any other of the newer comic masks from Gerolamo to Gianduja or Facanapa could have been dropped into this play. The element of sophisticated social satire was giving way to a spectacular but anodyne children's show with an emphasis on entertainment rather than involvement, and in so doing it was losing one of the elements that made the strength of the Commedia dell'Arte.

CHAPTER 5

Saints, Paladins and Bandits

Ottonelli's distinction between "comedianti pupazzani" and "rappresentanti figurati" has some similarity to Brecht's one between "dramatic" and "epic" theater. In the one case puppets are operated as substitute actors performing a dramatic action; in the other they are an adjunct to story-telling. The latter came to include religious and hagiographic material, elements of folk tale, medieval romance and more contemporary real-life stories of bandits. Most of this was presented in episodic form, whether in a single evening or as a serial. In the pupi theaters of nineteenth-century Rome stories were broken down into 10 or 20 episodes (puntate). By 1860 the pupi companies in Sicily spread serial presentation of long narratives over a complete season of several months, sometimes offering a different episode for virtually every day of the year. The publication of novels in weekly parts also created a huge pool of new material and may itself have contributed to the idea of serial performance. Giulio Preti presented an adaptation of *The Three Musketeers* in 27 episodes, *A Day in the Life of Henry IV* in 27 and *Giuseppe Balsamo, Count of Cagliostro* in 32, while Ponson du Terrail's *Adventures of Rocambole* ran to nearly 100. The marionette theaters of the north rarely went beyond a division into three evenings. In the 1930s the Gambaruttis sometimes divided popular shows such as *The Bridge of Sighs*, *The Bread Peddler* and *Genoveffa* into two episodes, performing the first on Sunday (the most popular day) and the second on Monday, in the hopes of increasing weekday audiences.[1]

Saints' Plays

The medieval church employed articulated wooden statues for quasi-dramatic presentations and used puppets for pedagogic purposes. Ottonelli speaks of secular entertainers using shadow figures to illustrate scriptural material. Virtually all nineteenth-century marionette and pupi companies included religious subjects in their repertoires. These survived longest in rural areas where popular piety remained a strong factor, but lost currency in urban areas and much of Emilia Romagna, where a more lay spirit predominated. Religious pieces often derived from plays for live actors and as late as 1943 the successful film *The Song of Bernadette* inspired the Gambarutti company's *Our Lady of Lourdes*, an interesting example of how film could take the place of popular literature and folk material as a source for puppet shows.

In much of Europe there is a close link between animated cribs and puppet shows.[2] The *Nativity* and the *Passion* were performed by many companies at the appropriate seasons.

Scene from *Our Lady of Lourdes*, Gambarutti marionette company, circa 1950. Based on the film *The Song of Bernadette*. (Courtesy Archivio dell'Associazione Peppino Sarina di Tortona [Al].)

In the later nineteenth century the Sicilian pupi had a Nativity based on Andrea Perucci's drama *La cantata dei pastori* (1698).[3] The birth of Christ is framed in a melodramatic conflict between good and evil, represented by an angel and the devil. The devil does everything he can to stop the event from taking place. He takes the shape of an innkeeper and tries to poison Maria and Giuseppe; then, as a boatman, he attempts to drown them; and finally he attacks them in the form of a serpent. In each case he is thwarted by the angel. The culminating point is the adoration in the stable, but the Herod plot and murder of the Innocents are omitted. The pupi versions emphasize Maria's worry about her purity in the scene of the annunciation. Giuseppe needs a visit from the angel, in his sleep, and the miracle of his staff bursting into flower to help him accept the situation.[4] After the encounter with the serpent, the angel tells Maria that as the omnipotent mother she will trample on the serpent's head — a flight of angels descends, crowns her and hails her as the Immaculate. In the final tableau the "grotto" (stable) was removed to reveal a brightly lit view of paradise with God the Father, rays of sunlight and angels. Perucci introduced a comic Neapolitan figure, Razullo. In Catania this is Pepenninu, accompanied by the beautiful peasant girl, Rosetta, and an ugly and crotchety old woman.[5]

The Piedmontese folk play, *Gelindo Returns*, was in the Fiando repertoire in 1835.[6] Much closer to the folk Herod plays, it centers on the visit of the shepherds and the Magi to the stable. The peasant Gelindo sets off for Bethlehem for the census, but keeps coming home to give instructions to his wife to keep their daughter in while he is away. In the

Razzetti-Rame text the action is framed by the emperor's order to have a census.[7] Domenico Razzetti replaced Gelindo with Gianduja around 1869. An Ajmino script of 1880 used Gerolamo, not Gianduja, but later replaced him with Baciccia, and included Facanapa as his servant. Gianduja gives orders to his family (totally disregarded once his back is turned) and helps the holy family find shelter in a stable. Later he brings his family to worship Christ. The action then shifts to Herod, to his meeting with the magi and their return by another route. The one supernatural element is the appearance of an angel who warns Giuseppe to flee to Egypt. The massacre of the Innocents is a scene without any dialogue and may have been a spectacular piece of pantomime, or simply a painted drop scene depicting the event. A little later there is another such scene depicting the aftermath of the massacre, which was probably a painted cloth too. At the end, Herod stabs himself after discovering that his orders have been carried out so literally that his own son has been slaughtered.

In Sicily at Easter the regular cycles of performances of secular pieces might be interrupted for religious plays. Festing Jones mentions a puppet Passion in Palermo, based on a play for live actors that compressed the events of Holy Week into a single evening. He then gives a detailed account of another Passion presented in Catania by the Grasso family at the Sicilia theater not long after the 1908 earthquake.[8]

The seven episodes were spread over Holy Week. The first, on Palm Sunday, opened with the conspiracy of Annas and Caiphas to destroy Jesus. The Monday performance was cancelled as a meteorite or fireball fell into the sea, creating panic, and there was no audience. The last supper, with a tableau based on Leonardo's fresco, was postponed to Tuesday. Judas was treated as a comic figure, especially in his unsuccessful attempt to return the 30 pieces of silver to the priests. Later in the week he hanged himself. In a dramatic vision a devil came and talked to Pilate's wife, Claudia, justifying Pilate, but was then killed by the archangel Michael. The Good Friday episode of the trial of Christ lasted an hour and included a comic scene of false witnesses, a stupid soldier and a Turk, who constantly contradicted themselves, even admitting they had been bribed. There were a number of Apocryphal elements, as the journey to Calvary with Christ meeting the daughters of Jerusalem and Veronica. The crucifixion was accompanied by an earthquake and the souls in purgatory surrounding the cross and welcoming their Lord. The cycle concluded with a final spectacular scene of the ascension and Christ speaking words of comfort to his mother and telling her it would not be long until she joined him. Jones observed that audience reactions to the Passion were very similar to their reactions to the more regular shows about the paladins and that the structure of the performance was almost identical in its alternation of crowd scenes of court or council and more intimate ones.

The Flood, The Prodigal Son and *Samson* remained popular subjects until well into the twentieth century. In 1814 the Rizzi company was performing its version of Francesco Ringhieri's *Flood*.[9] The Muchetti family had this in their repertoire in the 1860s and it remained there into the second half of the twentieth century.

Jones saw a *Samson* play in Palermo. This was a single evening performance, relatively secular in nature and also based on an existing play.[10] Much of the plot involved amorous rivalry between Samson and a paladin in golden armor (with mobile eyes but few other natural advantages).[11] Companies often used the same puppet is several similar roles. Samson, half naked and with long hair, might well have been used for the mad Orlando, and his violent behavior towards the Philistines probably evoked that hero.

Biblical figures and saints enjoyed a mythological status similar to the heroes of the Middle Ages. Popular piety meant that nearly every region had its own saints' legends, and on certain days of the year these legends disseminated through hagiographic literature became the subject of puppet plays.[12] Popular saints included Rosalia in Palermo,[13] Agata in Catania, Margareta of Cortona, Dorotea and even Genoveffa. In Sicily pieces covering the life of a saint were performed on saint's days for largely female audiences. In the north a religious piece was sometimes given in smaller towns at the request of the female part of the audience — St. John the Baptist being a favorite subject.[14]

The twelfth-century Rosalia belonged to the noble Palermitan Sinibaldo family. She retired from the world to become an anchorite on the Monte Pellegrino, where her remains were found on July 15, 1624, and brought to Palermo. To this was attributed the end of an outbreak of plague and her festival came to be celebrated annually on September 4. By the nineteenth century she was a subject of popular iconography, surrounded by such emblems as a skull (indicating asceticism) and lilies (purity), with, kneeling before her, the figure of Vincenzo Bonelli, who supposedly discovered her remains while hunting on the Monte Pellegrino. Such elements were enough to inspire pupi performances on her festival.[15]

St. George was another popular saint. In one script he struggles against the rather anachronistic demands of the third-century emperor Diocletian that his subjects should worship Mahomet (as well as Apollo), which gives the story a Moors and Christians twist.[16] George's father is executed, but his soul is carried up to heaven in the form of a dove. The magic sword theme popular in heroic legend is here a sword presented to George by an archangel in the Garden of Gethsemane. George, like the archangel Michael, uses the sword to kill the dragon, a scene that in turn evokes classic scenes from the heroic repertoire, such as Ruggiero's rescue of Angelica (*Orlando furioso*, canto X), itself reminiscent of Perseus and Andromeda. The killing of the dragon is followed by the mass baptism of the local population in a lake that appears from nowhere. In a final trial of strength between emperor and saint a statue of Apollo shatters and swords used against George merely bend. In prison and awaiting execution, George has a vision of the crucified Christ and angels and Christ announces that he will join him in glory. A particular piece of popular piety is the death of Paolo, a boy who has helped George. His soul is escorted to paradise by two angels so that he may join the saint.

More marginal in the religious calendar, but vastly popular on the puppet stage, *Genoveffa* appears in many repertoires. Canon Joseph Schmit's retelling of the story was translated into Italian in 1813 and ran through many editions. This edifying tale of wifely patience and fidelity crowned by a saintly death is the legend of Genevieve of Brabant. Her husband, Siegfried of Trier, marches out to defend Christianity against the Saracen hosts, leaving his wife in the charge of Golo, who, failing to seduce her, accuses her of infidelity with Drago, the cook (who is murdered), and arranges for her husband to condemn her to death. She is saved by the fact that her killers are persuaded to leave her in the forest with her newborn child and return to Golo with the tongue and eyes of a dog to prove she is dead. In the forest Genoveffa's child is suckled by a deer. After the passage of seven years Siegfried, hunting, is led by the deer to the cave where she lives. There is the recognition scene, followed by the condemnation of Golo, the rather abrupt death of Genoveffa and the rising of her soul to heaven. A version performed in Puglia in the 1890s by Luigi Luigini's company included a grand (and ad-libbed) battle against the Saracens.[17] In this fully written-out script the hanging of Golo was also an entirely visual scene described as "a soggetto" (improvised). This version developed the relationship between Genoveffa and the jailer's daughter Berta, who has to carry Genoveffa's ten-page letter to Sigefrido (Siegfried), who reads it out in extenso. Much of the action is devoted to discussing the health and death of Genoveffa in preparation for the final funeral tableau, when angels descend with a crown of flowers, an organ plays and electric light is used for special effects. The lying-in-state tableau is a stock one on the marionette stage. In the chivalric repertoire the death of Rinaldo's wife Clarice is treated in a similar manner. Gualberto Niemen in the 1930s presented a glove-puppet *Genoveva di Bramante* [sic] in three episodes, each consisting of two acts, and the grand recognition scene between the duke "Sigifrido di Treveri" and his son Guglielmino was a notable tear-jerker.[18]

Paladins and the Puppet Stage

The paladins, Carlo Magno's 12 peers, were at the center of an enormous repertoire deeply embedded in both folk and literary tradition. Material from Breton and Carolingian cycles was ubiquitous in Europe, but largely derived from French sources such as the twelfth-century *Chanson de Roland*. This formed a rich oral tradition transmitted by bards at a courtly level and disseminated widely by story-tellers at a lower social level. This was the period when the struggle of Christian Europe against the Islamic Moors or Saracens had great immediacy.[19] In the fifteenth century Pulci's *Morgante*, Boiardo's *Orlando innamorato*, Ariosto's *Orlando furioso* and Tasso's *Gerusalemme liberata* gave a new courtly expression to this material.[20] Andrea da Barberino (1370–1431) in his *Reali di Francia* (The Kings of France) introduced cycles of stories that made the French royal line descend from the emperor Constantine. The subject matter also found regular iconographic expression. Philippe le Bon commissioned a vast tapestry in 1382 depicting the battle of Ronceveaux (Roncisvalle) which measured 126 feet by nearly 17.[21] A. Alfano's poem of 1568, *La battaglia celeste di Michele e Lucifero*, mentions stories about the exploits of Rinaldo and Orlando being told on the piazzas.[22]

A carnival song of 1559 by il Lasca (Antonio Francesco Grazzini) includes a comment that actors were turning away from the classics to present the characters of Ruggiero, Gradasso, Marfisa and Orlando. One of the first extant plays to exploit this material was Silvio Fiorillo's *Courtesy of Leone and Ruggiero with the Death of Rodomonte* (Milan, 1614). The Locatelli collection of scenarios of 1617 includes an *Orlando furioso* which reads remarkably like some of the scenarios for the opera dei pupi 300 years later[23]:

Angelica, fleeing, tells how Orlando, her lover, having gone to war for king Carlo, is competing with Rinaldo for her love. The king has promised her to the more valorous of the two. Angelica asks Sacripante, who also loves her, to protect her, and when Rinaldo arrives begs him to flee. Isabella, Odorico, Almonio and Corebo arrive speaking of the sudden rout of the knights. Odorico wants to take Isabella, but Corebo and a crowd of bandits defend her. The sailors tell how Angelica, the daughter of a king, had a sea-god fall in love with her. When her father hid her, the god sent a sea monster to devour everyone until to placate him they tied Angelica, naked, to a rock. Ruggiero saves her by killing the sea monster, which he dazzles with his magic shield. Angelica, when she is free, puts a magic ring in her mouth and becomes invisible. Orlando, Sacripante and Ferraù look for her. When Orlando learns that Angelica has gone with

Medoro, whom she loves, he goes mad. Isabella is delighted to find her beloved Zerbino who, however, is killed when he tries to defend the arms that Orlando has thrown away. She then commits suicide. Astolfo arrives from the sky on the hippogriff with a phial containing Orlando's senses, and when the latter has regained these he goes to join Carlo in Paris.

Apart from the heroic figures, the cast includes a ghost, pirates, sailors, soldiers, countrymen, a hermit, a dwarf, a shepherd, Baiardo, the hippogriff, a sea-monster, as well as the Dottore (Graziano), Pantalone, and a Zanni.[24]

In early seventeenth-century Naples the mountebank Bartolomeo Zito, known for his performances as Graziano, also recited the *Gerusalemme liberata* and the *Orlando furioso* in the hall of S. Giorgio dei Genovesi.[25] The puppet show episode of Cervantes's *Don Quixote* part II (1614) suggests that such material was the staple fare of the Spanish puppet theater by the beginning of the seventeenth century.[26] In 1646 puppets from Castille were brought to Naples for the inauguration of the viceroy Rodriguez Ponce de Leon, Duke of Arcos. It has been speculated that the opera dei pupi may have evolved out of a Spanish type of show. The battle scenes central to the pupi may originally have been of a more epico-religious nature that can be related to the armed dances still to be found in Sicily today in spring festivals of an agricultural and religious nature.[27] Even when secularized these present two easily identifiable groups like cowboys and Indians and the Saracens are invariably the "others."

In April 1791 the Milanese showman Pietro Riva applied for a permit for his "acting company with a magnificent marionette show" to perform in Guastalla, near Parma. One item on the program was "the enchantments of the sorceress Alcina with four dancers turned into four vases of flowers which are then transformed" and another was "the enchantment of Bradamante, who comes out of a mondo novo (machine) and smashes to pieces a figure out of which emerge a devil, a bat, a serpent with its young, and then five Germans who dance the waltz." The mention of Alcina and Bradamante indicates the familiarity of characters from medieval romance to audiences for the marionette theater.[28]

The heroic repertoire was firmly established in the teatrini of Rome by the first half of the nineteenth century. Around 1845 Adone Finardi, who worked for the puppet theater of the Piazza Montanara, wrote a collection of complete playscripts in Italian, with comic scenes in dialect.[29] He converted the *Orlando furioso* into 19 episodes, the *Orlando innamorato* into 13 long parts, and *Morgante Maggiore* into 8 parts, which include the battle of Roncisvalle.[30] He reduced Andrea da Barberino's *Kings of France* into 33 episodes, each comprising three acts.[31]

Many stories deriving from Indo-European folk tale collected around Carlo Magno (Charlemagne). *Big Footed Bertha* tells of his birth in the forest because his mother Bertha had her place as wife to king Pépin taken by her servant Elizabeth of the house of Magonza (Mainz). The young Carlo, disguised as Mainetto, has a number of adventures before gaining his rightful kingdom. Youthful exploits are a popular subject in the opera dei pupi. Carlo's nephew Orlando likewise has early adventures that prepare for his later glorious career. These are related in the *Rolandino* and the *Chanson d'Aspremont* and include the acquisition of the sword Durlindana.[32]

Orlando is the perfect knight and the first of the paladins; his cousin Rinaldo is the second. On the pupi stage he is rather serious and noted for his proud and intense gaze (often indicated by a squint). Apart from his infatuation with Angelica, princess of China,

Orlando shows little interest in women. Rinaldo is known for his amorous escapades and is often the more sympathetic figure. He is regularly the victim of the intrigues of Gano di Magonza, step-father of Orlando and brother-in-law of Carlo, who is only too ready to listen to his lies. Rinaldo is one of the sons of Amone (Aymon). He has fallen foul of Carlo and is even besieged by the emperor in his castle of Monte Albano. Supported by his siblings, notably his warrior sister Bradamante, he is fortunate to posses the miraculous horse Baiardo and to have the help of his magician cousin Malagigi.

Sicilian audiences readily identified familiar characters by emblems and other visual indicators. In Palermo Rinaldo (and his sister Bradamante) could be recognized by a lion crest or a lion embossed on their shields, while Orlando had an eagle. Gano and the other members of the Magonzezi faction had a large M, and the crescent moon was much in evidence with Saracens. Christian heroes wore a vaguely Renaissance armor with short-skirted tunics more reminiscent of seventeenth- and eighteenth-century opera than the Middle Ages while Saracens were distinguished by the wearing of trousers. Characters were divided into armed and unarmed ones.[33] Pages and women, with the exception of female warriors (Bradamante, Marfisa, Rovenza, Clorinda), appeared in court costume. Carlo had armor and sometimes a court costume when off the battlefield. Color symbolism varied. In Palermo Rinaldo wore a red tunic, but in Catania he wore a green one. Orlando's squint, mentioned in many of the literary sources from Barberino to Lo Dico, is usual in Palermo but less in evidence in Catania.[34] The mythical sword, Durlindana, is generally straight in Palermo, but a curved scimitar in Catania. Stage right (left from the audience's position) is associated with the Christians and stage left with the Saracens.

The opera dei pupi is full of magic and enchantment. Malagigi has Merlin's wand instead of a sword and intervenes at moments of danger. Faustlike, he calls on the spirit Nacalone, whom he also uses to transport him from one place to another. Malagigi always uses his magic to defend the "good" (i.e., the Christians). In the Dama Rovenza episode he has a furious duel of magic with the evil magician Tuttofuoco.[35] The magicians transform themselves into a variety of creatures. Malagigi is overpowered, and at the end is saved only by the power of prayer while Tuttofuoco is struck dead.

By 1908 the chivalric repertoire had almost vanished in Rome but continued further south.[36] In Canosa di Puglia Ruggiero Dell'Aquila wrote or adapted some 800 scripts. These included *Count Orlando* (180 episodes), the *Kings of France* (80 episodes) and *Guerin Meschin* (65 episodes). The death of Clorinda in his dramatization of the *Gerusalemme liberata* (32 episodes) was based on canto 12 of the poem. The Saracen Clorinda, disguised in the armor of a Christian knight, is challenged by Tancredi. Only after he has mortally wounded her and baptized her at her own request does he realize she is the woman he loves. In the long final scene Clorinda declares that heaven is opening for her and that she is going there in peace and the episode concludes with a long lament by Tancredi. Video recordings of Anna Dell'Aquila made around 1980 show her using a sing-song type of delivery designed to make the voice carry. She employed the full range of her vocal skills to give this scene extreme dramatic intensity and an elegiac quality and in so doing provided an approximate idea of the style of delivery used in the opera dei pupi of the nineteenth and early twentieth century. Today the performances of Mimmo Cuticchio, influenced by the art of the cantastorie and of Italia Chiesa (Napoli), display similar vocal qualities.

An interesting historical drama written for the pupi by Ruggiero Dell'Aquila is his

Council of Carlo Magno with his paladins. Theater of Francesco Sclafani, Palermo. A typical first scene. Orlando extreme stage right, the emperor left, with Gano di Magonza behind him. (Archival photograph. From Ettore Li Gotti, *Il teatro dei pupi* [Florence: Sansoni, 1957], second edition [Palermo: Flaccovio, 1978].)

version of the celebrated *Challenge of Barletta* about a duel of 13 against 13 that occurred in the early sixteenth century because some French prisoners expressed contempt for the Italians.[37] The Italians then proceeded to beat the French and to kill a Piedmontese mercenary, Claudio Graiano D'Asti, perceived as a traitor for siding with the French. The *Challenge* had local reference (Barletta is close to Canosa) and was even more popular because its patriotic sentiments harmonized with the nationalistic mood of the 1920s.

Chivalric romance also figured in the marionette repertoires in the north of Italy, but most pieces were designed to be performed in a single evening and were as likely to derive from dramas for live actors as from romance narrative. Like Pulcinella, Gerolamo and Gianduja played squire to Orlando. The recurrent battles which were the high spot of the pupi performances were curtailed in the north. Raffaele Pallavicini's most popular repertoire piece was *Pietro of the Keys*, a version of *Beautiful Maghelon*, in which a fight was reduced to four strokes on each side. However, one of his special effects was riders who could dismount and fight.[38] The Pallavicini company had a *Kings of France* which Pallavicini claimed

Opposite: **Anna Dell'Aquila as speaker during the *Death of Clorinda*, 1978. Her son Sante Taccardi is operating the figure. (Courtesy Paolo Comentale, Teatro Casa di Pulcinella, Bari.)**

had nothing to do with Andrea Barberino's work.[39] His *Carlo Magno Emperor of the West*, a spectacular production in four acts, cast Gerolamo as Rinaldo's squire. Scripts passed from one company to another, and this one is remarkably similar to the Lupi's *Paladins of France at the Castle of Montalbano,* a drama in three acts and eight scenes with Arlecchino as squire to Rinaldo. The subject is the treachery of the Magonzesi against Rinaldo and his rehabilitation in the eyes of Carlo Magno.

A *Carlo Magno* in the Ajmino repertoire in 1883 almost certainly derives from a stageplay. Gano and his brother Florante after unsuccessfully attempting to seduce the wife of Rinaldo have plotted his downfall. Orlando defends Rinaldo to the emperor, who has been deceived by the Magonzezi. Finally Clotilde (wife of Rinaldo and usually called Clarice) is vindicated. Gerolamo, squire to Rinaldo, is the comic hero. Speaking dialect, he regularly parodies the heroic genre and rejoices in puns. When Gano is foolish enough to say to him: "Ma non sai che io sono Gano di Magonza" (But don't you know that I am Gano di Magonza), Gerolamo replies: "Se voi sevi l'gall che ai fa mal la panza..." (If you are the cock that causes stomach ache...), and then goes on to make further innuendoes about cocks and hens. The shift towards the comic suggests that audiences in the north now regarded the heroic material as a bit old-fashioned and something that invited parody. A bill for June 1910, included with this script, mentions the Luigi Ajmino company, directed by Bottino Colombo, performing a piece called *The Paladins of France with Gerolamo the Brave Soldier Defending the Castle of Montalbano*. This is described as a highly entertaining comic action in four acts. Unlike Sicily, there would have been little danger here of audiences believing in the reality of the characters and what they stood for, let alone inserting them into the social reality of their daily lives.

Two of the most performed subjects throughout Italy are *Buovo d'Antona* (Bevis of Hampton) and *Guerin [or Guerrino] Meschino*. Buovo's father is murdered by his mother's lover, Duodo di Magonza. She attempts unsuccessfully to poison her son. Later he goes on to have all sorts of exciting adventures. He is also noted for his devotion to Princess Drusiana and his love for his horse Rondello. In the north this provided a single drama of more or less epic structure. A Pallavicini script dated January 17, 1894, *Buovo d'Anton; or Princess Drusiana*, groups the episodes of book 4 of the *Kings of France* into a single play (with Famiola as Buovo's servant). The Lupi script of *Buovo d'Antona* consists of four acts and 11 scenes, as opposed to the ten parts of Finardi's Roman version for the Montanara. Belli commented specifically on the popularity of Buovo d'Antona at the Ornani Theater in Rome.[40] The much-loved story of Buovo often stood alone, but in Sicily this mini-cycle ran to a very large number of episodes with the Canino family. The unsympathetic role of the Magonza family made it easy to attach the story of Buovo to heroic cycles concerning Orlando and Rinaldo and thus to incorporate it into the grand sweep of the history of the kings of France and the paladins.

Guerin Meschino (Guerin the Wretched) was a romance by Andrea Barberino, but by the late nineteenth century the main source for the opera dei pupi was less Barberino than Giuseppe Leggio's popular edition of the story. This draws on a variety of sources, combining knightly deeds with religion, enchantment and prophecy, but has little historical basis. Son of King Milone and his wife Fenisia, Guerin is separated from his parents as a baby, acquired by pirates and sold to a rich man in Constantinople. He grows up at court and distinguishes himself as a knight, but his unknown origins are a problem. He embarks on a quest to find out who he is and who his parents are. This takes him via Africa to the eastern end of the known world to the trees of the sun and the moon. Back in Italy he visits the Sibyll, who sometimes becomes the sorceress Alcina on the puppet stage. She keeps him a long time and attempts unsuccessfully to seduce him. Later his search takes him to the underworld of purgatory via St. Patrick's cave in Ireland. Eventually he finds and rescues his parents, who have been imprisoned for years in the castle of Durazzo in Albania. The

Pulicane. Catania, circa 1880. The dog-headed Pulicane is a secondary hero in *Buovo d'Antono.* This trick figure has a string that releases blood and guts when he is mauled by the lion. (Pulicane belonging to the Marionettistica dei Fratelli Napoli. Courtesy the Marionettistica dei Fratelli Napoli. Photograph Davide Napoli.)

adventures continue, but these are the episodes most often exploited on the puppet stage, especially in single-evening dramas.[41] The multi-episode versions presented by the pupi follow the entire life of Guerin, from his childhood and early exploits to his death, and miss no opportunity to show his fights against giants, monsters and, of course, Turks.

Ernesto Puzzo's version of *Guerin Known as the Wretched* focused on the magical elements and the fairy Alcina, with spectacular transformations of both scenery and puppets. One figure turned into five dancers and a serpent. There was a dance of 16 warriors and then one of 16 devils. Thirteen seats became baskets of flowers and a fountain and 24 ballerinas turned into ghosts.

The Gambarutti company used a rather literary text in verse. Franco Gambarutti remembered his father performing this in the suburbs of Milan, where his audience forced him to make an impromptu translation into popular prose.[42] The Colla family had a modern version, as did Vittorio Podrecca, whose *Guerin Meschino at the Trees of the Sun* (1919) was a "heroic-comic legend" in three acts by Giovanni Cavicchioli with musical comments by Adriano Lualdi and sets by Bruno Angoletta.

Medieval romance figured in various glove-puppet repertoires. In the early 1800s Carlo Cuniberto advertised performances of *Beautiful Maghelona* based on the story of Pierre de Provence, who loved the daughter of the king of

The Death of Pulicane, **cartellone by Natale Napoli, circa 1936. (Tempera on wrapping paper. Courtesy the Marionettistica dei Fratelli Napoli. Photograph Alessandro Napoli.)**

Naples. Pierre was kidnapped by Saracen pirates, Maghelona entered a convent, and many years later the two were reunited. Angelo Cuccoli in his *Book of Plays* (1860) mentions a *Guerrino* in six parts and the episodes seem similar to those selected for the marionette versions, but allow much space for Fagiolino and the other masks.[43] In the Lodigiana glove-puppeteers specialized in the cycles taken from the *Kings of France* and from *Guerrino il Meschino.* Peppino Sarina had a *Kings of France* (including *Buovo d'Antona*) in 35 episodes, a *Paladins of France* in 100 episodes and a *Guerrino Meschino* with 15 (with a sequel, *The Children of Guerrino,* in 10 episodes). Manzella Costantino (1892–1960) had a *Paladins of France* in 15 episodes, a *Guerin Meschino* in 8 and a *Kings of France* in 15.

In Bergamo Bigio Milesi performed a *Guerin Meschino.* He claimed that he had never read the story and that his version was based on what he had picked up from other puppeteers, which is an interesting example of oral transmission. His Gioppino was Guerin's squire and Gioppino's stout stick counterpointed Guerin's sword in a way that shifted the tone from the heroic to the comic. It must also be admitted that a glove-puppet clutching a sword held horizontally has some difficulty in maintaining heroic dignity.[44] Romano Danielli set the tone of his version of the story with a prologue in which Tartaglia appears as factotum to the emperor of Constantinople and where both comic tirade and lazzi are employed to the full. Fagiolino accompanies Guerin and the regular swinging of the long

Top: Guerrino at the trees of the sun and moon. Guerrino consults the oracle in his search for his parents. Illustration from G. Leggio's retelling of the story, circa 1900. (Courtesy Museo Internazionale delle Marionette Antonio Pasqualino.) *Above:* 50 Astolfo, Pampalughino and the horse Baiardo in a performance by Peppino Sarina, Broni, 1923. (Courtesy Archivio dell'Associazione Peppino Sarina di Tortona [Al].)

tassel at the end of his cap punctuates and lends emphasis to what he is saying. He chats up Alcina's maid. When he goes as ambassador to see the tyrant who has imprisoned Guerin's parents, he explains that he is the "scudiero" (squire) and then adds a rhyming tag: "tra la la la liero." Guerin kills the tyrant in a final sword fight and Fagiolino, in classic glove-puppet fashion, disposes of the body on the end of his stick.

Story-telling and Puppet Performance

The high level of illiteracy in the south of Italy ensured the ongoing importance of the story-teller.[45] The oral transmission of literature through story-telling usually has an ultimate reference to a written source. In Naples the story-tellers or "cantastorie" were known as "rinaldi" after the popular hero Rinaldo and are often depicted with a text in their hands.[46] Sicilian scholars make a distinction between the "cantastorie" who usually sang or read metrical versions of stories and the "contastorie" who spoke in prose, retelling the story in their own words, accompanying it with lively gestures and frequently improvising or developing episodes in an extremely dramatic manner.

An early contastorie in Palermo was Maestro Pasquale, who performed on the piano S. Oliva, and whose repertoire included the entry of Roger the Norman into Palermo and the revolution of Giuseppe Alessi.[47] The original historical references of the stories were long forgotten, but the material had a particular resonance in Sicily, which had been under both Spanish and Arab domination and had repeatedly suffered attacks from the Turks and from pirates from North Africa. When Giovanni Grasso arrived in Sicily with his version of the *History of Orlando*, audiences saw this evocation of a heroic past in contemporary terms. The arrival of Garibaldi and the departure of the Bourbons fuelled the fire of Sicilian nationalism. For about 40 years after unification, the popular imagination, through the puppet theaters, returned to a sort of feudal tribalism and natural justice was a recurrent theme. By 1900 the focus began to shift to the entertainment value of the opera, with the pupari concentrating on technical improvements, including the careful crafting of the armor.

In the mid–nineteenth century serial publications of medieval romance were popular in various parts of Europe. In Sicily Giusto Lo Dico, a primary school teacher with little formal education or real erudition, produced his 3,000-page *History of the Paladins of France* (1858–1862), which assembled material that was being transmitted by public story-tellers. It became a specific point of reference for both "contastorie" and puparo alike. Lo Dico's work was as much an effect as a cause of the flowering of interest in chivalric material.[48] Pitrè found examples of story-tellers apparently reciting whole pages of Lo Dico's *History of the Paladins of France*. In fact they had never read it but were returning to the same oral sources.[49] Lo Dico's heroic values and emphasis on codes of honor struck a particular chord with popular audiences around 1860. His version subscribes heavily to popular superstition, especially in the more miraculous or magic elements of the story. Many pupari used the résumés at the beginning of each chapter of Lo Dico as a scenario upon which to embroider, and retellings of romance by G. Leggio were treated in the same way. Unfortunately the publication of an easily accessible fixed text resulted in a concomitant impoverishment of the material.

The numerous contastorie in nineteenth-century Palermo and Catania performed like

Canta storie detto Rinaldo.   *Chanteur de la Jerusalem.*

A "Rinaldo" performing in Naples. Nineteenth-century print. ("Canta storie detto Rinaldo." Courtesy Istituto per i Beni Marionettistici e il Teatro Popolare.)

the pupi theaters on daily basis. Each episode lasted a couple of hours and the telling of the entire cycle of the paladins could take two years.[50] They also told stories of saints such as Genoveffa and some had a version of the tragic local story of the baroness of Carini, executed by her father as an adulteress. The regular audiences sat on three or four benches, for which they paid a small fee, while the rest stood around and usually made a small contribution. The Palermitan story-teller, unlike his counterparts in other parts of Italy or Spain, did not rely on a painted cloth with episodes that could be pointed to. Armed with a stick or wooden sword, he performed episodes from the chivalric cycles, always stopping at a point where the audience would be bound to return the following day. As on the pupi stage the sword could be waved in moulinets in the air, used for Ruggiero to chop off Rodomonte's head, or held in both hands for Rinaldo to split Angolante from stem to stern. Orlando could thrust it violently into the stomach of the giant Ferraù, piercing the seven plates of armor protecting his one vulnerable point.[51] The contastorie did not disappear from the streets of Palermo until the 1960s. One of the last was Roberto Genovese, who divided the cycle of the *Kings of France* into 340 two-hour episodes backed up with a vast repertoire of voices and gestures.

The serial presentation of chivalric material by the earlier contastorie had its impact on the puppet theaters but by the later nineteenth century many story-tellers were drawing their material from the opera dei pupi. A number of contastorie, or "cuntisti" (as they were also called) ran puppet theaters or worked in them. Giuseppe (Peppino) Celano (1903–1973) as an adolescent accompanied his father to both the cinema and to Franco Russo's "opra" in the via Gesù e Maria in Palermo (admission 10 centesmi, accompanied children free). He later helped in a puppet theater and during his military service regaled his comrades with stories of the paladins. By 1925 he was an actor and in the winter worked for the opera dei pupi. Back in uniform in 1936 in East Africa he developed his storytelling talents and in 1938 he met the Greco brothers at the Quattro Fontane theater in Rome. Demobilized that year, he opened a teatrino in Palermo (rione di S. Pietro), but with the

The cantastori (and puparo) Giuseppe Celano of Palermo, performing the cuntu, 1950s. Archival photograph. (From E. Li Gotti, *Il teatro dei pupi* [Florence: Sansoni, 1957], second edition [Palermo: Flaccovio, 1978].)

war he was mobilized again. After the war he reopened his theater in Palermo. He performed with puppets during the winter, but in summer returned to the open air as a contastorie. In Celano's last years Mimmo Cuticchio came to him to learn his art, which he had by then developed into a particular blend of story-telling and puppetry.

The Opera dei Pupi and Religion

A final apotheosis with the ascent of the soul to heaven was one of the topoi of the marionette stage of the nineteenth century. In Piedmont, Romeo and Juliet, after their suicide, were to be seen surrounded by clouds and cherubs, while similar endings were sometimes provided for *The Poor Baker of Venice*, *Giovanna d'Arco* (Joan of Arc) and *San Rocco*.[52] The opera dei pupi is infused with popular piety and this affects the entire heroic repertoire. The "cartelloni" depict countless death scenes with angels bearing aloft the soul of a deceased Christian. This derives from religious iconography. Some performances of the medieval church included machines in the shape of a mandorla containing the soul of the deceased that was designed to be drawn up to the church roof supported by angels.[53] Lo Dico's work is full of references to apotheoses and these readily transferred to the pupi stage. Every company had angels amongst the basic stock of figures. Usually one or two would fly in and a painted cloth depicting the naked soul of the hero surrounded by a little flight of cherubs was dragged up from behind the body. To enhance the effect still further, this cloth was often replaced by one showing God the Father waiting to receive the soul of the hero in paradise.

Orlando was implicitly compared with Christ and parallels could be found between the battle of Roncisvalle and the Passion of Christ. At Orlando's death audiences were totally hushed, hats were taken off and people even crossed themselves. In western Sicily the music was often that used for religious processions on Good Friday in Trapani. In Palermo, where most of the voices were provided by the puparo, a child of the family spoke for the angel:

> Orlando, Orlando, you are dead according to the will of God. Light your pallid face with a smile and we shall carry your soul aloft to the celestial paradise.[54]

Orlando does not die of his injuries. His death has a mystic quality about it. Blood suddenly gushes forth from his eyes as he surveys the slaughter of all the paladins. His horse Vegliantino expires and his attempt to break his sword Durlindana is unsuccessful. He dies, but resurrects briefly to present Durlindana to the emperor before angels come for his soul.

A defeated, but baptized, pagan warrior could receive an apotheosis, while devils might remove the soul of an unbaptized pagan or enemy of Christendom. Loyalty and disloyalty provide the Manichean opposites for the opera dei pupi in both political and religious terms, and this explains the very real hatred that audiences often expressed for Gano di Magonza.[55] A part of the mythology of the puppet theater is stories of audience members confusing illusion and reality and attacking Gano di Magonza onstage, or even attempting to obtain the puppet to wreak vengeance on it. Gano, who betrays Orlando, was viewed in much the same light as Judas.[56] He received comic treatment, but at his death a little black soul often emerged from his mouth, only to be snatched away by the devil.[57]

The key episode of the cycle of the paladins is the battle of Roncisvalle, whose main source is the *Morgante* of Pulci, who weaves in the story of Rinaldo and Riccardetto.[58] Following the death of his wife Clarice, Rinaldo leaves the world and becomes a hermit. Riccardetto, his brother, seeks him out and persuades him to return to save Carlo and the paladins, and an angel appears, bringing back his armor. They reach Roncisvalle too late for the paladins, but are at least able to save the emperor and avenge the treason. The first section of one nineteenth-century cartellone shows the angel bringing Rinaldo his armor, and the final one depicts Rinaldo's death and apotheosis. The other episodes represented here are the treacherous plot hatched by Gano and the Spanish brothers under the carob tree (which rains blood), the paladins riding into ambush, a series of battle scenes, including Orlando blowing his horn, his brief resurrection to hand over Durlindana to Carlo Magno, and the final quartering of Gano, tied between four horses, with two small devils awaiting his soul.[59]

Expansion of Heroic Material

The stories of the paladins were inserted into an ever-growing chronological context, just as successful films today breed sequels. The paladins had a slender basis in reality

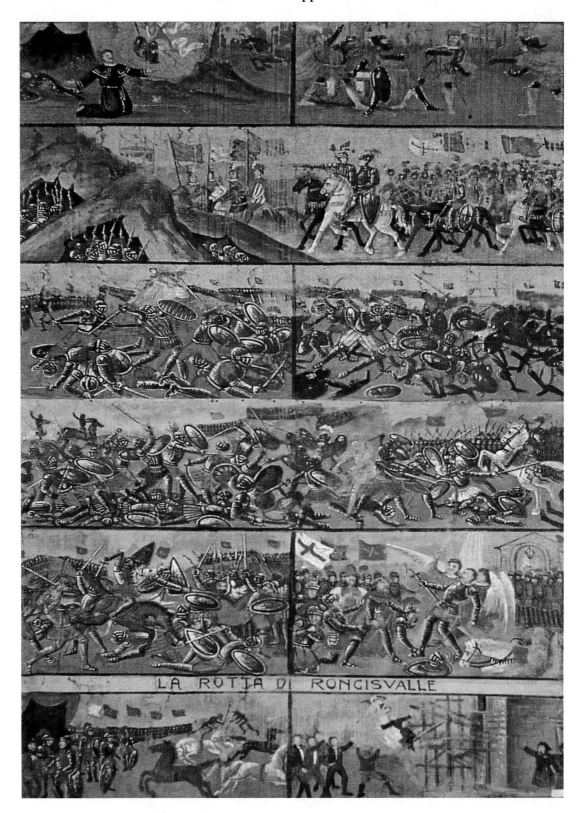

but the last years of the nineteenth century saw the invention of totally new material, re-utilizing familiar topoi and structures. In Catania Gaetano Crimi's *Greek History* traced Carlo Magno's ancestry back to the Trojan war and made him descend from Hector. The Trojans were the "goodies" and the Greeks the "baddies."[60] The highly popular *Erminio of the Golden Star and Gemma of the Flame and Medieval Adventures* and its sequel *Tigreleone* were probably created directly for the pupi of Grasso's Machiavelli Theater in 1887.[61] The complicated plot retains the struggle between Christian and Saracen and the emphasis on family honor. Like the heroic cycles (and many melodramas) it moves from one generation to the next, with lost children brought up apart from their parents and subsequently reunited after a grand recognition scene. Children of Christian origin have often been brought up as Saracens and have to be baptized. Erminio is the offspring of the king and queen of Morocco, forced into exile before his birth, and the action ranges across Russia, China, France, Poland and Constantinople, sometimes with echoes of more contemporary issues such as the Russo-German war. Many of the situations are borrowed directly from the *Kings of France* and little is changed beyond the names of the persons concerned. In this way puppeteers worked their way through these immense and multi-episode narratives with type scenes following patterns familiar both to performers and audiences. Erminio acquires the sword Fede, an equivalent of Orlando's Durlindana. Like Ruggiero with Rinaldo's sister Bradamante, he falls in love with the Saracen warrior princess, Gemma. He then becomes involved in a war between the Russian emperor and the Chinese one Benares, caused by the arrest of the Russian prince Soranzo in Beijing. Having been separated by pirates and other adventures, Erminio and Gemma eventually return to Europe, where she is baptized and they marry, producing a son Tigreleone. Like the young Carlo Magno, the ten-year-old Tigreleone performs a number of exploits. Most striking is the rescue of the captive Christian princess Sciura from the hands of the Saracen tyrant Diamante, who is about to murder her for spurning his advances. Tigrelone does this single-handed, slaughtering a host of Saracens and decapitating Diamante as he is about to slay Sciura. Later Tigreleone takes on many of the characteristics of Rinaldo, especially the more amorous ones, and Catanese puppeteers often used the Rinaldo puppet for the adult Tigreleone.[62] Tigreleone is balanced by the noble savage, Ideo of Syria, in an adversarial relationship similar to that of Rinaldo and Orlando. Ideo meets his death in a final single combat, but first he is baptized by Evangelina (a nun who has exchanged her habit for a suit of armor). Religion is important here, but the specific opposition of Christian and Saracen is less prominent than in the paladin pieces.

The saintly knight Guido Santo (a descendant of Carlo Magno) was already the subject of a pupi cycle. Costantino Catanzaro provided a sequel to this with three novels on the subject of Guido di Santa Croce.[63] Despite a medieval setting, the most obvious influence is the serial novel, most notably Alexandre Dumas's *Count of Monte Cristo*. An escape scene mirrors that of Edmond Dantès from the Château d'If and the vengeance theme is also very similar.[64] The love interest, already more obvious in *Erminio*, is greater than in the chivalric repertoire. The wicked king Roget of Constantinople is a stock villain of the melodrama

Opposite: **Palermitan cartellone of the battle of Roncisvalle. (In Museo Pitré. From Marcella Croce,** ***Pupi, carretti, contastorie — aspetti della tradizione cavalleresca nelle tradizioni popolari siciliane*** **[Palermo: Flaccovio, 1999].)**

stage and the theme of children separated from their parents evokes melodrama more than heroic romance. Guido, as the knight of the Red Cross, remains incognito for much of the action. Once he has killed Roget, like Rinaldo, he abandons arms for a tonsure and a life of penitence, but like Rinaldo is also called back into the action (on several occasions). He dies surrounded by his children and grand-children and is provided with an apotheosis.

In Catania Raffaele Trombetta created a local hero almost as important as Orlando with *Uzeta il Catanese*, which opened the Mazzini theater. This completely invented serialized piece in the heroic style had a local and patriotic theme. Uzeta is rich in virtue, but of a humble background. He saves the city of Catania from the Moors and then marries the princess who has earlier rejected him.

Uzeta il Catanese. **Cartellone, Rosario Napoli. (Courtesy the Marionettistica dei Fratelli Napoli. Photograph Salvatore Napoli.)**

Opposite, top: **The death of Diamante di Spagna. Catanian cartellone for *Erminio della Stella d'Oro*, Rosario Napoli, 1929–1930. (Courtesy the Marionettistica dei Fratelli Napoli. Photograph Salvatore Napoli.)** *Bottom:* **The death of Guido di Santa Croce. Catanian cartellone, Sebastiano Zappalà. (Courtesy the Marionettistica dei Fratelli Napoli. Photograph Melo Minnella.)**

Brigand Plays

Italy has a centuries-old history of banditry. In a country racked by endemic poverty and recurrent famines there were many cases of impoverished peasants who resorted to part-time banditry. In the Apennines bandits posed a constant threat to dwellers of the Po valley in the area around Bologna, Ferrara and the Romagna until about 1890.[65] After 1861 there was a marked rise in banditry in the south, especially in Calabria, Basilicata and Sicily. Bandits thrived in the vacuum created by almost complete lawlessness and the absence of a strong central government, and ordinary people often felt that a local bandit was closer to them than some rather remote authorities. The Sicilian Turriciano (Pasquale Torregiani) began his career because of his refusal to be drafted into the "Piedmontese" army. When he was finally captured in 1868 a further 121 members of his gang were also caught, while 24 escaped.[66] In the administratively hopeless situation of post–Garibaldian Sicily the Mafia was a positive force, providing meaningful structures and some semblance of alternative government. It even received a degree of legitimation from the Church.[67] The codes of honor of the Mafia and the devotion to the Church translated to the stage of the pupi and blended easily with the presentation of chivalric material. Audiences acquired a special interest in the character of Rinaldo, who combined the high ideals of the Mafia with the appeal of the social bandit, helping the weak and standing up to the strong.[68] His revolt against his overlord Carlo was prompted by a sense of unjust treatment and with his group of followers he became a Robin Hood figure — an outlaw, but never failing in his loyalty to Christendom and the ideal of the emperor. The same was true of Garibaldi, who became a popular figure on the puppet stage and absorbed much of the mythology of the social bandit, ready to right wrongs, help the poor and combat injustice. As a popular hero he confronted the Austrians in much the same way that Orlando or Rinaldo stood up against the Saracens.

Puppet brigands and bandits are found from one end of Italy to the other. The highest density was in Sicily, where every company had one or more brigand plays in the repertoire. The bandit became as much a stock type as Arlecchino or Gerolamo and it was quite common for a single figure to be re-utilized as different individual bandits. The publisher Piazza in Palermo, editor of Lo Dico and Leggio, produced a stream of stories about famous bandits, which the pupari and story-tellers absorbed and diffused throughout the island.[69] Favorite bandits were Antonio Testalonga, Leone, Rinaldi, Salomone and Pasquale Bruno and pieces about them remained popular with audiences until about 1940.

The bandit play was based on the life and career of the "hero" and had an epic rather than a dramatic structure, even when the events were grouped into a single evening. It usually started with an offence or injustice and then proceeded through a series of symbolic events and escapes before the final killing or arrest. The classic myth was that of good men suffering from an act of social injustice or a crime that required avenging, who therefore left their villages and collected together a band of men as desperate as themselves and committed robberies and murders. There were always safe houses to which they could go, and the liberality with which they redistributed amongst the poor the riches they had acquired assured them both popularity and a considerable degree of safety. The transformation of a brigand into the hero of a puppet play depended not on his real activities but on the way in which the popular imagination turned him into an iconic figure. A small number were perceived as criminals, but most were seen as agents of popular justice and historical fact was amended accordingly. Most were depicted in the context of the family, as good sons or brothers. They were almost inevitably pursued by the carabinieri (military police), from whom they had some exciting escapes, and many ended their careers as a result of betrayal (often by a close associate) but met a "heroic" end. The essence of these pieces was populist and the portrayal of the authorities as unjust, incompetent or actually oppressive gave a distinctly subversive twist, which explains why performances could be liable to police intervention. In Sicily in the later nineteenth century, the police forbade performances of brigand plays at the opera dei pupi and Pitrè found it necessary to intervene to defend the puppeteers.[70] In Barletta in 1906 Michele Immesi announced a piece about the bandit Nicola Morra (still alive at the time), but this was banned on the grounds that it might lead to disturbances.

Antonino Blasi, known as Testalonga, ranged through Sicily with his band, spreading terror until he was finally arrested and hung in 1766, as was his contemporary Giuseppe Guarnaccia.[71] Luigi Canino had a five-act Testalonga play with 16 different scenes ranging from cottage interiors, landscapes and forests to a large farmhouse, a room in the prince of Trabia's castle and a garden. The action is triggered by a brutal attempt by the prince's overseer to evict Blasi's mother. Blasi arrives in the nick of time and kills him, thus becoming an outlaw. From the rather sinister life of this brigand was created a myth that presented him in the favorable light of the social bandit. His "beneficent" acts include saving the daughter of an old man and providing money for a poor peasant to pay the priest to bury his wife (Blasi subsequently robs this back from the greedy priest). The less pleasant episode of the disfigurement of the servant of the prince of Trabia and the shooting of a soldier urinating through a crack in the cave in which the bandit is hiding are "justified" by the situation. In the final combat Testalonga and his associate Antonino Romano run out of ammunition, so they say their prayers and kill themselves.[72] This contributes to their "heroic" status and also means that they escape hanging, the ignoble fate of their comrades.

Pasquale Bruno (executed in 1805), another victim of social injustice turned bandit, provided material for a story by Alexandre Dumas. Popular publishers such as Piazza took it up and pupari seized on it. Bruno's father Antonio Pasquale had been executed for trying to avenge the rape of his wife by the count of Castelnovo and his head had been displayed in cage outside the count's castle. Bruno shot down the cage. Later, the count's daughter, the princess of Carini, vindictively prevented Pasquale's marriage and he became an outlaw with a private vendetta against the family. A legend grew that he could not be killed with a sword or bullets. The Canino family had a version in three three-act parts dating from the middle of the nineteenth century, and a later five-act one to be performed on a single evening.[73]

Paci Paciana (Vincenzo Pacchiana) was born in 1773 and married in 1794.[74] By 1806 there was a price on his head (100 zecchnini for him alive, 60 for him dead). He was murdered by an associate and his head was exhibited on the guillotine in Bergamo. As a smuggler who terrorized the Val Brembana, murder and robbery were natural to him, but this did not alter the perception of him as a sort of Robin Hood. In a roughly contemporary poem Gioppino refers to Ciapì (a nickname for Paciana), which indicates how rapidly he passed to the puppet stage. Bigio Milesi remembered his father giving him 10 centesimi as a child, with which he went to see the puppeteer Colombo perform a Paciana piece spread

Painted publicity for the bandit piece *Paci Paciana*, with episodes of Paciana's life. Luigi Cristini repertoire, Bergamo. (Courtesy Collezione Fratelli Cristini, Bergamo. Photograph Domenico Lucchetti. Published in Pino Capellini, "Baracca e burattini" [Bergamo: Grafica Gutemberg Gorle Editrice, 1977 e 1997]. Photograph Domenico Lucchetti. Courtesy Archivio Privato Famiglia Domenico Lucchetti.)

over two evenings.[75] Later, he too had a two-episode version in which Gioppino appeared as a poor man who gives food to Paci Paciana.

Stefano Pelloni (1824–1851), better known as Il Passatore (the ferryman), was one of the most feared brigands of Romagna. Like many of his kind, his active career was brief (1849–1851). Since the authorities were either the papal ones or the Austrian police, he was automatically consecrated as a popular hero and thought of as a gentleman bandit who robbed the rich to give to the poor. His mythical status was such that he was soon found in many puppet repertoires, although the subject could not be staged in Bologna before

Mayno della Spinetta and his band. Group of figures from the Pallavicini company. Piedmont.
(Arrangement of marionettes of the Pallavicini company for the exhibition Napoleone e Mayno:
L'Età di Marengo nel Teatro di Burattini e Marionette, Alessandria, June 2000. Courtesy Archivio
dell'Associazione Peppino Sarina di Tortona [Al]. Photograph Angelo Anétra.)

1860, when the city ceased to belong to the papal states. Popular novels were written about Il Passatore and in 1947 he became the subject of a film.

Mayno della Spinetta (also spelled Majno or Maino) operated during the Napoleonic period in the region around Alessandria. As a parody of Napoleon, emperor of France and also king of Italy, he was known as King of Marengo and Emperor of the Alps. His career lasted from around 1802 until his betrayal and shooting in 1806. He probably became an outlaw to evade conscription (and almost certain death) in the Napoleonic armies and his hostility to the French occupation made him a sort of Piedmontese national hero. Mayno was celebrated for the ingenuity of his disguises, the way in which he constantly evaded capture, and for the famous exploit of the robbery of the pope on the occasion of the latter's visit to Napoleon. Mayno was in the repertoire of the Gerolamo Theater by 1841.[76] Magnin mentions the comic interventions of Gerolamo in what he calls *The Terrible Majno, Bandit Chief,* a "melodrama in five acts with daggers, faintings and pistol shots."[77] The piece generally required two or even three evenings; Peppino Sarina's version grew to over 40 episodes.[78] In the 1940s and 1950s Mayno became equated with the partisans in the minds of audiences.

Giuseppe Musolino, who spent 54 years in prison before his final release in 1949, was

Mayno stabs a French soldier. Painted publicity (tempera on cloth), early 20th century, for Peppino Sarina's *Mayno della Spinetta*. As in Catania, each episode of this lengthy cycle had its own cartellone hand-painted by Sarina. (Courtesy Archivio dell'Associazione Peppino Sarina di Tortona [Al]. Photograph Raffaele Vaccari.)

the subject of plays from Sicily to Lombardy. The Gambarutti family had a *Musolino* piece written by Cesira Burzio when the bandit himself was still active.[79] Musolino was as prevalent on the glove-puppet stage as on the marionette one. Some showmen grouped the events into a single evening, others spread it over several performances. Antonio Sarzi divided the story into four evenings of three acts each while Oreste Salici used a five-act glove-puppet version.[80] The major focus is on Musolino's unjust imprisonment, on false evidence, and his horrendous revenge on those who caused it. Key episodes of the Musolino legend include his escape from prison and subsequent disguise as a priest, riding a donkey, who talks to

Arrest of Musolino from the cycle *Musolino the Calabrian Bandit,* performed by Peppino Sarina, whose face can be seen under the puppet carabiniere on the right. Courtesy Archivio dell'Associazione Peppino Sarina di Tortona [Al].)

the soldiers sent to rearrest him and who fail to recognize him. In the fifth act he is given a huge soliloquy in which he complains of the injustice of his lot. He mentions that the newspapers refer to him as "bloody," whereas all he really wanted to do was to get married and raise a family. In a final speech, after his arrest, he stresses that he was pushed into a career of banditry so as to achieve revenge, since in his native Calabria human justice was not fulfilling its duty. He declares that "the people have more elevated thoughts, ideals of peace and brotherhood. I have made myself the executor of the vendetta to which innocence must have recourse." A very popular piece during the Fascist period, *Musolino* was a direct challenge to those who were considered to abuse power.

Luigi Natoli's best-seller serial novel, *I Beati Paoli* (1909–1910), has an avenger theme that gave rise to many puppet plays in Sicily. It harks back to Eugène Sue's *Mystères de Paris* and Alexandre Dumas's *Monte Cristo* with its theme of a pre–Mafia secret society existing to right wrongs. Its leader, the aristocratic Coriolano della Floresta, an equivalent to Sue's Prince Rodolpho, but also to the social bandit, administers a form of popular justice in eighteenth-century Palermo and helps the hero, Blasco di Castiglione, despite constant persecution, to achieve the highest social elevation.

Guappi and Camorra

Naples was one of the poorest and most populous cities in Europe. A specific type of puppet show evolved that had aspects of both the chivalric play and the bandit one, but related directly to the criminal underworld of the city. Known as "storie borghesi," these pieces involved contemporary urban life strongly injected with an element of "verismo" as opposed to medieval romance and characters were in modern dress rather than armor. They spoke Neapolitan dialect, unlike the more literary Italian of the paladins. Audiences were familiar with this jargon and instantly warmed to terms such as "zumpata" (a duel with knives) and "sfregio" (a slashing of the face with a razor or sharpened coin as a punishment). Central to this was the Camorra, a secret society originating in Spain in the fifteenth century and spreading from there to Naples. Their main activity was protection rackets, levying a percentage on almost every activity from gambling houses to small traders. One of the earliest plays of the borghesi repertoire was *Naples 1799; or the Foundation of the Camorra.*

Prior to unification Naples was virtually ungoverned and this gave the Camorra extraordinary power. In 1820 they redefined themselves as the Bella Società Riformata. Rather like the Mafia they emphasized values of loyalty to other members, to the family and the Church.[81] In 1860 the Neapolitan minister Liborio Romano used the Camorra as police under Salvatore De Crescenzo, known as Tore 'e Crescienzo. They operated in the interregnum following the departure of King Francesco and for a time were all-powerful. They remained a sort of unofficial police force until the end of the century. In 1862 another society, the "guappi," was set up to help combat the dominance of the Camorra in the social order. The guappi were of more middle-class origin and aimed to defend the weak and protect society against the Camorra. Gradually the guappi and the Camorra merged in the popular imagination. Puppet shows using this material were referred to as "storie dei guappi" and popular audiences identified with the guappi as positive heroes. There were good guappi

Garibaldi saves Tore 'e Crescienzo from execution. Neapolitan cartellone, 1920–1930. (Courtesy Collezione Maria Signorelli. Photograph Maristella Campolunghi.)

and bad ones, a distinction rather similar to that between the social bandit and the purely criminal one. A guappo of special importance was Nicola Ajossa, who confronted and beat (but did not kill) Tore 'e Crescienzo in a famous zumpata. As a puppet, Tore 'e Crescienzo became as important in Naples as Rinaldo or Orlando and this duel was the central episode when the *Tore 'e Crescienzo* cycle was presented by the Neapolitan pupi. A scene that always attracted audiences was one announcing "morte a sangue vero" — death with real blood that stained the shirt.[82] Vincenzo Corelli created the very popular *Story of Marco Spada; or the Lion of Calabria*, which provided a prehistory for *Tore 'e Crescienzo*, beginning in Napoleonic times and blending fiction with recognizably real events and people. The "borghese" repertoire was often referred to as the *History of Old Naples* or as *The Mysteries of Naples*.

Rinaldo and the paladins made way for these urban street heroes with their strong personal sartorial style, supposedly inspired by Tore 'e Crescienzo. This consisted of flared trousers and jackets trimmed with fur and decorated with extravagant buttons and elements of jewelry, the whole topped with a magnificent cap. The guappi repertoire, also known as "patuti" was immensely popular with the poorest classes, especially in the suburbs. Ciro Perna specialized in this repertoire, but interest in it did not extend far beyond the poorer areas of the city and suburbs. Corelli relates that he adapted the show to where he was performing and wove real-life characters into the story to give yet further immediacy.[83] He too found that when performing for more middle-class audiences or traveling in Puglia he had to revert to the heroic repertoire.

With the heroic repertoire the pupi performer saw himself as transmitting a significant form of literature. The paladins existed in an idealized world governed by codes of honor. Audiences gave this idealized world immediacy in terms of their own experience of life. The verismo of the guappi repertoire with its direct reference to the Camorra was already far closer to the day-to-day experience of the audience and as such belonged to the domain of popular literature, but for this reason suffered more direct competition from the cinema and became out of date far more easily. During the Fascist period the guappi repertoire was strongly discouraged, but by now many performers had already lost touch with the heroic one and this may help explain why the latter declined rapidly in Naples, but continued to flourish in Sicily.

CHAPTER 6

The Creation of New Repertoires

Puppets and the Theater Industry

La Baldassara is one of the earliest stage plays known to have been performed also by marionettes. Acciajoli reached the marionette stage by the end of the seventeenth century and was followed later by Metastasio, Molière, Gozzi and Goldoni. The Bolognese showman who visited Asti in 1780 and 1783 had over 40 pieces in his repertoire and their titles echo the theatrical repertoire of the time: *The True Friend, The Fable of the Water Snake, The Life, Enchantments, Conversion and Death of Pietro Bailardo* (Abelard). There is also a hint of the religious repertoire with *The Tyrant Struck Down and Piety Triumphant.* Two pieces that became very popular on the marionette stage were *The Great Dragon of Transylvania* and *The Fable of the Three Brancafero Dogs.* Arlecchino, the comic figure of the company, appeared in scenarios such as *Arlecchino and Brighella Thieves* and also in reductions or adaptations of plays already familiar in the actors' theater. One script, *The Fall of Abdalach by the Magic of Arlecchino,* survived in a rare Lupi script, *The Birth of Arlecchino from an Egg,* dating probably from 1781 and subtitled *The Fall of Abdalach, Tyrant and Usurper of Bassalora.*[1] This script demonstrates how a play for actors' theater might be adapted for marionettes. There is a vague melodramatic plot about the saving and reinstatement of the widow and son of a murdered king but also a reversion to Commedia masks. Two of the characters are replaced by Tartaglia and Pantalone while Arlecchino has the central role and sometimes acts like a master of ceremonies.[2] In the most developed of the four scenes the magician Vermanduff meets the ghost of the king in a forest by night (accompanied by thunder and lightning), promises to help him and calls up a couple of devils who arrive with an egg. To the accompaniment of music the magician, Faustlike, calls on Lucifer, Asmodeus, Astaroth and Beelzebub. The shell breaks and a baby Arlecchino emerges calling out "pappa, pappa." Vermanduff touches Arlecchino with his wand, baptizes him and endows him with magical powers. Arlecchino passes rapidly from babyhood to manhood, and then departs for the court in a cloud chariot accompanied by the young prince and his faithful servant. In the final scene the impenitent tyrant, Abdalach, like Don Giovanni, is swallowed up in flames, and this is followed by a grand transformation scene.

By the end of the eighteenth century traveling puppet companies were visiting smaller towns and villages as well as urban centers. In many cases they were the only purveyors of theatrical fare to a large section of the population which either could not afford to go to the theaters in the larger towns, or simply lived too far from them. A distinction between high culture and popular culture was becoming more evident and showmen intent on earning a living were conscious of a growing market in the latter field. The birth of a new theater-going public was a cultural phenomenon of nineteenth-century Europe and a repertoire with an ethos deriving from the French melodrama was created to satisfy a new and insatiable demand.

The most popular subjects for the puppet stage were not always the ones that were attracting large urban audiences. There is however a close parallel between the repertoires of the traveling marionette theaters and those of the strolling players or "guitti" and right up to the twentieth century entertainers moved between puppets and live acting.[3] In aesthetic terms the passage from flesh and blood actors to wooden ones has an impact on the nature of the performance and on the audience's reception of it, but this was probably missed by those whose main concern was to spend a couple of hours witnessing an enactment of a fictitious narrative. Guitti and puppeteers performed to audiences in villages and small towns, using parish halls, stables and sometimes the local theater. They had direct access to popular audiences eager for distraction and totally unconcerned with the literary merits of the piece and they built up large enough repertoires to allow them to stay in a town or village for a month, and offer, if necessary, a different show every night. Older plays lingered on in this context long after they had been forgotten elsewhere.

As theater became one of the mass media, audiences were eager to identify with the dramatic fare offered. Historical figures, however legendary, were seen as real and even contemporaneous, and there was a readiness to accept theatrical fiction as truth. Melodrama, which its strong populist slant, simplified issues to a conflict between good and bad, with the ultimate triumph of the former. The generic distinctions of the more literary theater meant little and audiences were happy to pass from serious action to comedy. Theater became steadily more and more spectacular, with a new emphasis on staging and scenery. Many of the successes of the French popular theaters reappeared with the bigger marionette companies of the latter part of the century: *The Three Musketeers* and *The Count of Monte Cristo* (Alexandre Dumas), *The Two Orphans* (Adolphe Dennery and Eugène Cormon) and adaptations of Jules Verne's novels *20,000 Leagues under the Sea* and *Around the World in Eighty Days*.

The luxurious productions of the Lupis in their permanent theater made a nightly change of program impractical and resulted in a tendency to run a production more continuously over a certain time. After the hugely successful visits of the Holdens in the 1880s the larger companies shifted towards operetta and variety. The establishment of cinema meant that there was little renewal of the popular theatrical repertoire and puppet companies either had to fall back on a slightly old-fashioned one (which many of the traveling ones did) or create pieces of their own.

Puppet Actors and Scripts

The traveling marionette companies treated their puppets as substitute actors and changed their costumes daily for the roles to be played that night. Most popular plays of the nineteenth century were constructed along the same familiar lines and used similar type roles (hero, villain, leading lady, ingénue, etc.). When these were adapted to the puppet stage they could easily be performed with the company's basic set or "muta" of figures.

Scripts were regarded as a part of the capital of a puppet company. Showpeople were unwilling to communicate them to people outside the profession.[4] Scripts were jealously guarded but might be exchanged or passed on to other companies for copying. This was often carried out by a professional copyist and, coupled with the cost of paper, could represent a real financial outlay for an impoverished traveling company.[5] Many scripts carry an indication of the date and place of copying, and sometimes of ownership. A note of a name on a text preceded by "di" or "proprietà di" was an indication of ownership rather than authorship.[6] Where the script was a complete play text it was generally written in large format exercise books generously spaced, so that it could be read during the performance. Except in situations where there were separate speakers, performers had to read a script propped up in front of them as well as manipulate. The bottom right-hand corners of the pages of a much performed piece were black with much thumbing and turning. A script used over a period of years might have numerous additions and corrections marked on it. There were few stage directions, but exits were generally marked by the word "via" (s/he leaves) or "viano" (they leave). Characters were listed on the front page, often with an indication as to the side of the stage from which they might enter. It is quite common for a script to have one or more police stamps authorizing performance. These generally mention a place and are dated, which helps trace the movements of a company. Sometimes a showman might write a comment about the size (lack) of audience, the weather or other extraneous events.

It was very rare for any credit to be given to the author in a company's publicity, and pieces were chosen either because of exciting plots or because of the possible familiarity of their titles to potential audiences, but even the titles were seldom fixed and might be changed or modified. A less successful piece might be dished up with a new title, or a subtitle might become the main one. In 1882 the Italian Society of Authors, later to become the S.I.A.E., was created to protect authors' rights. Puppet companies began to deposit their scripts with the S.I.A.E. in an attempt to protect their copyright and perhaps receive a small additional income. It is quite difficult to understand how this worked, since so many of the scripts had already been passed from family to family and many of the themes were simply variants of well-known pieces already in the repertoires of numerous companies and for all intents and purposes in the public domain.

Puppet companies found that they too had to pay royalties for the performance of plays from the repertoire of the actors' theater. To be in compliance with legislation the more important ones paid a fee on a regular basis to the S.I.A.E. Some avoided this by resorting to expedients such as changing the title of a well-known piece, or giving it only as an alternative one. Franco Gambarutti mentions the family company presenting the immensely popular French melodrama *Les deux orphelines* (The Two Orphans) under the title of *The Blind Girl and the Cripple*, with "The Two Orphans" given only as a subtitle and in small print.

A pre-existing or even published script did not necessarily mean that this is what the audiences actually saw performed on the marionette stage. There were the necessary cuts and adaptations, but also space was made for improvisation, especially with the comic character. The extensive repertoires that showmen had to carry in their heads, like the long and complicated narratives of the opera dei pupi, were simplified and often managed by recourse to type scenes and situations familiar to both audience and performer.

Many companies worked from a collection of scenarios rather than fully written scripts.

These served as an aide-mémoire for a performer, who in many cases might be only semi-literate. Spoken dialogue was commonly transmitted orally from one generation to another. Sometimes a set speech to suit either a general situation or a specific one in a particular play might be written out in full.[7] Some showmen worked from a complete script, but this did not prevent improvised interpolations. In Emilia Romagna glove-puppet showmen made very free adaptations of the successes of the live theater of the day. The Cuccoli repertoire contained the titles of a huge number of plays, but no fully-written scripts as such.[8] When a company spent a long period on the same pitch performing to the same audiences, up to a hundred different shows could be presented in one season, and the following season there would be a new repertoire.[9] For the glove-puppet performer the original play was usually little more than a subject to be embroidered upon. It provided a framework of a series of situations into which Fagiolino, Gioppino, Arlecchino, Gerolamo and others could easily be inserted, and the "script" itself consisted of a list of scenes, props, sound effects and characters which was pinned up backstage.

Popular Publications

By the later eighteenth century popular literature was beginning to appear in cheap editions that were sold by itinerant peddlers. Many were hawked by sellers of religious articles and designed for amateur theatricals, but were also bought by professional entertainers.[10] The publishing company Serafino Majocchi of Milan, active from the beginning of the nineteenth century until 1980, even included a specific range of plays based on scripts of glove-puppet and marionette plays.

The "Romantic" nineteenth century was obsessed with the world of the Middle Ages. This resurfaced in cheap popular editions by such publishers as Natale Tommasi of Milan and also provided fodder for the theaters. It found its way into the repertoire of the puppet theaters in ever-increasing numbers from the 1830s onwards. In Rome, Naples and Sicily, although this is often forgotten today, it became a staple of the opera dei pupi. *The Poor Baker of Venice, Alvaros of the Bloody Hands, Francesca da Rimini, Ginevra degli Almieri,* and *Ginevra di Scozia* were lapped up by marionette companies. *Ginevra di Scozia* (on which Handel's *Ariodante* is based) figured in many marionette repertoires. It involves the paladin Rinaldo but is a self-contained story based on a tale contained in cantos IV and V of the *Orlando furioso*. Ginevra degli Almieri is the heroine of the sixteenth-century Florentine story. She supposedly died of the plague and was buried, but in fact recovered and escaped from the tomb. Her husband, believing she was a ghost, chased her away, and she found refuge with a young man who was in love with her and whom she then married. This was much performed on the nineteenth-century stage and transferred to the puppet theaters. A script for performances in Rome in the 1820s was titled *Ginevra degli Almierei with Pulcinella Frightened by the Dead*.[11] In this version the husband Ramiro remarries a woman with a good dowry, and there is a reference to a previous wealthy wife who had escaped him by pretending to be dead. At one point the servant Paolino suggests to Pulcinella that they should steal Ginevra's ring from her corpse in the tomb, and this gives rise to considerable comedy. A final court scene attempts to sort out the matrimonial tangle, and there is further comedy with Pulcinella dressed as an American lawyer.

The second half of the nineteenth century was characterized by adaptations of classic texts and abbreviated versions of well-known stories in popular editions, and these were mopped up by an increasingly literate population of the less well-off. Publishers sprang up to meet this expanding market. In Milan, Natale Tommasi brought out a catalogue of "Historical and Popular Novels" that included *Hamlet of Denmark, Ernani the Bandit, Lohengrin, Ruy Blas, Mignon, Masaniello, The Bandiera Brothers, Boccaccio, Messalina, Il Passatore, Antonio Schiavone, Monti e Tognetti, Pia di Tolomei, Rinaldo in Love, Pietro Micca, Count Ugolino, The Two Foscari, The Battle of Legnano, Giuseppe Garibaldi, Giordano Bruno* and *Giulietta e Romeo.*[12] In a prose narrative based on the libretto of *Aida* the publishers Figli di Angelo Bietti presented the love of Aida and Rhadames as if it were historical fact.[13] Other important publishers were Sanzogno and Cesare Cioffi, both of Milan. Cioffi had a series on famous brigands, and another based on the novels of Xavier de Montépin, whose *Porteuse de pain* (Bread Peddler) probably reached the Italian puppet stage by this route. A number of more humble printers such as Francesco Sanvito of Milan or the bookshop All' Insegna del Tasso in Naples also produced play texts. Puppet showmen drew extensively on this abundant printed material and attempted to convey the impression that the fictional events narrated were real.[14]

Il povero fornaretto di Venezia *and* I promessi sposi

Francesco Dall'Ongaro's frequently reprinted drama *Il povero fornaretto di Venezia* (The Poor Baker of Venice), together with adaptations of Manzoni's novel *I promessi sposi* (The Betrothed) and *Genoveffa* was amongst the most popular pieces for the marionette stage in the second half of the nineteenth century and for much of the twentieth. *The Poor Baker*, with its sixteenth-century subject of a terrible miscarriage of justice, is a strongly political piece and as such belongs to the revolutionary years of the 1840s. A nobleman has killed his wife's lover and the corpse is found by a hapless young baker, Pietro Tasca, who is accused of the murder, tried and executed entirely on the basis of circumstantial evidence.[15] This intensely populist play in which a poor young man is sacrificed to conceal aristocratic adultery remained a standard piece for the marionette stage long after it had been dropped by live actors.[16] *The Poor Baker* was in the Lupi repertoire in 1855.[17] It was also one of the pieces regularly performed by the Pallavicini family until at least the early 1930s.[18]

The reduction of the text for the puppet stage resulted in the omission of the more psychological elements in favor of anything that would drive the plot forward. Characters of lesser importance disappeared or were conflated with others and in some cases most of the members of Venice's Council of Ten ended up painted on the backcloth, or reduced to a cut-out silhouette. Popular figures were introduced to play minor roles and give color to basic utility scenes, but this changed the entire nature of the piece. Fagiolino, Baciccia, Gianduja and Tartaglia all appeared in *The Poor Baker* and this allowed performers to fall back on stock scenes.[19] The Reccardini script gave a special role to Arlecchino and Facanapa as keepers of the madhouse (a scene absent from the original drama). In a Pallavicini script that had belonged to Ugo Ponti, Gianduja appears as a seller of malmsey wine and Baciccia as a gondolier. This heavily cut version omits an important scene that explains motivations for behavior and also the ball which the murderer husband forces his wife to attend,

The Council of Ten and the hanging of the baker, scene from *Il fornaretto di Venezia*, performed by the Perozzi-Burzio company (Segnano, October 14, 1951). Some members of Council are painted on the backcloth. The discovery space, center, was used for the execution. (Courtesy Associazione Peppino Sarina di Tortona [Al].)

fully aware that he has killed her lover. Added is a final tableau of the hanging of Pietro.[20] Another script belonging to the Pallavicini family, and later to the Zaffardi company, uses Facanapa as a jailer and Baciccia as the gondolier. The final tableau shows Piero (Pietro), hung, with a kneeling monk presenting a crucifix. His innocence is proclaimed and the piece ends on a pathetic rather than a revolutionary note as Marco, his father, enters mad and singing a ditty about a bold and noble Venetian gondolier, after which he cries out "who will give me back my son, my poor Piero" and collapses.[21] Another Zaffardi script has Gerolamo as the gondolier and Facanapa as a baker's assistant. A note indicates that some performers show the initial murder using music and dumbshow (as in Dall'Ongaro's play), while others make a short scene out of it. This scene is included here and provides a good example of how the marionette performer often aimed for greater clarity and simplification.[22] In the final spectacular hanging tableau, Marco appears and curses the Council of Ten, but the original political significance is weakened by giving the last line to the cuckolded husband, who addresses his errant wife: "You with a kiss and I with a dagger have killed two victims."

A Burzio version still used by the Gambaruttis in the later 1950s draws on a less-known treatment of the subject by Giuseppe Gandolini, published in 1846. This removes the jealousy plot and emphasizes the miscarriage of justice, but it also omits the strong element of class conflict. The piece becomes less a political drama than the personal tragedy of Pietro. In the prison scene he is given a long monologue and is also shown being tortured. The ball is retained as a spectacular visual scene but is drained of all dramatic content.

The Poor Baker went through further transformations on the glove-puppet stage. The plot outline of Filippo Cuccoli's version is noted in the *Book of Plays*, assembled by Angelo Cuccoli in 1860. Pietro Tasca, the baker, is the only character in the much reduced cast to retain a name from Dall'Ongaro. Fagiolino plays the tragic role of Marco and the Dottore appears as a confidant to the "podesta," the equivalent of the rather abstract masked figure of the original play.[23] Giovanni Bresciani (1882–1952) worked from a fully written script, although this was less than half the length of the original. He introduced an apotheosis for Pietro after his execution. The lesser roles were played by Pantalone, Fasolino Gioppino, Brighella and Sandrone. In the 1980s the piece was still in the repertoire of Romano Danielli, with emphasis on Sandrone as a good-hearted jailer and Fagiolino as a gondolier anxious to help the escape of Pietro.[24]

Alessandro Manzoni's masterpiece, *I promessi sposi* (1827), is inherently theatrical with its extensive use of dialogue, sharply defined characters, central theme of virtue in danger and eventual happy end. Reduced versions of the novel were published as popular literature, and these were drawn on by puppet companies whose practice was to take passages of dialogue verbatim and to omit descriptive passages except where they could be incorporated into the staging. *I promessi sposi* first reached the stage in 1827 and by 1835 a version was in the Colla repertoire. In the early 1900s *I promessi sposi* was still being regularly performed as a drama by marionette companies in Piedmont and Lombardy and it remained with some until the 1950s. Of the nine operatic versions the most significant are two by Amilcare Ponchielli (1856 and 1872) and one by Petrella (1869) with a libretto by Antonio Ghislanzoni. Ghislanzoni tried to follow the novel faithfully, using whole chunks of Manzoni's dialogue, and his version became an important source for subsequent marionette adaptations.[25] He retained the general atmosphere of the novel, included realistic and colloquial dialogue, and developed the comic role of the pusillanimous priest Don Abbondio (usually given to Gerolamo).[26] His last act focuses on the villain, Don Rodrigo, in his castle, where he has contracted the plague, and then passes to the celebrated lazar-house scene, where Renzo and Lucia, the betrothed of the title, are reunited and where Renzo forgives the dying Rodrigo. A pious final tableau shows the dying Padre Cristoforo with his hand raised to heaven. The moral tone of Manzoni's novel and the theme of the feudal lord abusing his "droit du seigneur" fitted easily into a notion of the poor being victims of the rich and struck an immediate chord with many at a time when the socialist ideas of Mazzini and others were in the air. The Spanish domination of the Duchy of Milan and the mountainous regions of Lombardy in the seventeenth century seemed easily comparable to the situation of Lombardy as an Austrian province after 1815, and audiences readily identified with the notion of oppression and foreign occupation. When Podrecca staged it in 1918, and the Colla company revived it for the centenary of the novel in 1927, they were staging it as opera and this represented a more consciously artistic approach.

Spoken Opera

The repertoires of all companies contain titles reflecting the popular operatic successes of the century. These included *Robert the Devil*, *Hernani the Bandit*, *Pia di Tolomei*, *The Two Foscari*, *Masaniello*, *Ugo and Parisina* and *Giulietta and Romeo*. Apart from the usual incidental music, audiences did not expect a musical entertainment. Some companies used the libretto directly, simply turning recitative into dialogue and getting rid of the arias. Popular operas (and the sources from which they derived their libretti) gave rise to cheaply printed fiction frequently used by puppet companies. Many came from the press of Natale Tommasi, and were usually labelled "romanzo popolare" or "storico popolare."[27] They were chosen for their dramatic potential, but there was not an exact correlation between the popularity of a work on the operatic stage and on the puppet one. Some of Verdi's earliest and now almost forgotten titles received more attention on the marionette stage than on the operatic one. Rossini's *William Tell*, with its anti–Austrian overtones, was heavily cut at Turin's Teatro Regio for political reasons and little performed but remained in the Lupi repertoire for a long time.[28]

Ugo and Parisina, from a sixteenth-century tale by Bandello, is the subject of Donizetti's opera *Parisina*. The original story concerns a fifteenth-century ruler of Ferrara, Modena, Reggio and Parma who had his young wife and his son put to death for their adulterous affair in 1425. Pirro Gozzi performed this with glove-puppets in the early 1900s but removed the incest motif. In his version Ugo is son of the duke by an earlier marriage. Ugo and Parisina have long been in love, but the tyrannous and womanizing Nicolò III d'Este takes her as his wife with inevitable tragic results.[29] Leonello, a scheming courtier, also illegitimate son of the duke, informs the latter of a meeting between Parisina and Ugo and implies a sexual relationship. The young people are condemned to death, but no sooner has the death knell rung than the duke repents, realizes his error and cries out for the execution to be stopped, but too late, and the final words are pronounced by the priest who has attended the unfortunate pair: "Wait, o duke, shortly you will taste the fruits of your crime from the avenging hand of God."

The simple linear plot follows its inexorable path without the slightest turn in the action or glimmer of hope for the doomed pair, and is not lightened by any of the usual comic characters. It is atypical of the nineteenth-century melodrama which usually involved a happy end or at least the triumph of good over evil. Marionette performances based on opera libretti or popular romances adapted from tragic operas tended to have happy-end versions. *La traviata*, *Il trovatore* and *Aida* are cases in point.[30] The Reccardini version of *Aida* retained little more than Verdi's plot outline and a spectacular scene of the grand march of the priests. It was framed by a scene between the poet and the call-boy of the theater and ended with Facanapa rescuing the lovers and a grotesque dance in the garden of delights.[31]

French opera was another source of good plots. In Meyerbeer's *Robert the Devil* (1831) the hero is the son of the devil, who follows him round as his mentor, Bertram. Thanks to Alice, his love, Robert finally escapes damnation and in the final scene in Palermo cathedral his soul is drawn to heaven by a celestial choir.[32] This treatment has echoes of Goethe's *Faust* (1808/1823). The traditional *Faust* play was a mainstay of the Germanic repertoires and certainly known to Italian puppeteers. With *Faust Mefistofeliz* Ruggiero Dell'Aquila combined various sources, including Gounod's *Faust* (1859), for the Aurora Theater in 1922.[33] *Faust Mefistofeliz* focuses on the Marguerita (Ghita) plot, and there is no question of Faust's magic tricks or use of his wealth. Both the jewel scene and the Walpurgis Night one are omitted. The prologue in hell with the plan to ensnare Faust is retained. Charon presents a procession of damned souls to Pluto. These include a dishonest and stupid politician who has deceived his electors, enriched himself, acquired every honor and seduced half a dozen girls. A witch transforms Faust into a young man. In a very brief scene Mefistofeliz sees Ghita go into a church, but cannot follow. At the end Ghita is imprisoned by the Inquisition for the death of her brother Valentino and for murdering her mother with a sleeping draft provided by Mefistofeliz. She prefers to face death rather than escape. Faust discovers that his time is up and is taken by Mefistofeliz, after which the scene changes to paradise for Ghita's apotheosis (accompanied by Bengal fire).

Shakespeare Reduced

The Romantic period "discovered" Shakespeare.[34] Audiences wanted exciting plots, and his plays provided raw material out of which a performance was created. Puppeteers selected strong scenes and striking situations, then cobbled together some elements of the plot and added material of their own. Sometimes a source of a puppet production could be a translation of the play, but here too a more usual source was operatic libretti reconverted into popular retellings of the story. Rossini's *Otello* (libretto F.B. Salsi) dates from 1816, Mercadante's *Amleto* (libretto by Romani) reached La Scala, Milan, in 1822 and Arrigo Boito adapted *Hamlet* for Franco Faccio's operatic version in 1865. Verdi's *Macbeth* (libretto F.M. Piave and A. Maffei) was performed in Florence in 1847.

Hamlet could easily be reduced to a revenge melodrama. The Lupi script dating to around 1868 and performed at the San Martiniano theater derives most directly from a translation of the play.[35] It gives a good idea of the process of adaptation and cutting that showmen practiced. "To be or not to be" (placed directly after the scene between Hamlet and the players) is abbreviated to the first 17 lines and ends with the reference to "the pangs of despised love," the cue for the entrance of Ofelia. Claudio is given no remorse, Polonius is little more than his sidekick and Rosencranz and Guildenstern disappear (the latter's name survives as Guilden, a nonspeaking page to the king). The play within the play is performed by smaller duplicate figures of the players on a stage with its own curtains and Arlecchino appears as the leader of the company. The last two acts are highly condensed. In act 3 the king arranges with Laerte for a duel with Amleto using a poisoned sword. The queen brings the news of the death of Ofelia, and the scene changes to show a moonlit lake with her body amongst the reeds and the entrance of Amleto, who throws himself on his knees in despair. Next comes the cemetery (by moonlight) and the scene with the grave-diggers, retaining "alas, poor Yorick." In the best marionette tradition, there is a funeral procession, complete with horsemen, monks and the court. Then Amleto and Laerte confront each other with their swords. The ghost appears and tells them that the king is guilty and has poisoned the sword. Amleto disarms Laerte, then runs the king through, calling him a poisonous reptile and consigning his soul to hell, and there is a final effect of the ghost illuminated by a beam of light.

Macbeth, with its witches, battles and generally gothic atmosphere, has always lent itself to adaptation for popular entertainment. Verdi's opera of 1847 contributed to the theatrical currency of the subject in Italy, although as a drama it did not reach the stage until 1858. Ariodante Monticelli's classic marionette version, subtitled *The Assassination of Duncano*, is described as an extraordinary and fantastic drama and ballet.[36] Famiola has a major role as

Macbeth's servant but makes little use of dialect beyond a few solecisms, mainly with reference to the name of Macbeth. He is scared of spirits and the supernatural and his account of an unfortunate encounter with four devils that use him as a football counterpoints the much more serious encounter of Macbeth and Banco with the witches. Act 4 is given over entirely to the latter. The smells emanating from their large caldron appeal to Famiola, who has an encounter with an amorous elderly witch who loses her arms and head and is transformed into a vase of flowers, which becomes a little devil, who turns out to be an extending long-short figure. To conclude the act the caldron turns into a horrible winged dragon, the rocks become devils, snakes and monsters, and the cave itself is transformed into a full-scale hell scene. Macbeth, having been shown the various (Shakespearian) apparitions, finds himself in the middle of a ballet of spirits and dancers reminiscent of Davenant's seventeenth-century musical version of the play. When he finally dies, two devils come up through the ground and, like Don Giovanni or Gano di Magonza, he is carried off to hell.

Utterly different from the Monticelli *Macbeth* is a Sicilian scenario in the Canino repertoire apparently adapted directly from a live stage performance of the play and not from a written source.[37] Lady Macbeth's name is picked up as Ladeu, Malcolm's as Lalcolmin. Don Liberto Canino reduced the piece to the standard three acts of a single-episode pupi piece. The simplified plot, devoid of any comic scenes, presents the plotting and carrying out of the assassination, by Ladeu, not Macbeth, and the eventual avenging of the king's death in a final grand combat when the "city" of Scotland is retaken by Lalcolmin. Macduff barely features in the action. The sleep-walking scene is retained, but the death of Ladeu and the approach of Birnham Wood are both omitted. Witches and devils appear in the first scene, and again at the start of act 3, when they drop serpents, monkeys and other animals into the cauldron. There is no specific mention of the prophecies apart from a laconic indication at the end of the scene that the spirits begin to appear. A similar stage direction is used in the banquet scene for the ghost of Banco and probably Fleozio (Fleance).

When the Napoli family staged *Macbeth* in 1976, the intention was to explore how far the plays of Shakespeare could be interpreted by the pupi. The adaptation allowed the piece to be handled by four operators and the plot was reduced to three acts. The first focused on the murder, the second on the tyranny of the Macbeths, and the third on the liberation of Scotland. This format was the familiar one of the opera dei pupi and the characters were simplified so as to iron out ambiguities and give greater emphasis to the more positive heroes. Where Shakespeare created the opening battle through language, the Napolis presented it with its heap of corpses.[38] The murder of Duncan was shown, not recounted, and immediately suggested that of Ruggiero in the Orlando cycle. Macbeth was reminiscent of the treacherous Magonzesi and witch scenes evoked familiar Malagigi scenes and their diabolical setting.

Othello was in the repertoire of the Petrelli company of Bologna in 1831, making it the earliest recorded Shakespeare production on the glove-puppet stage.[39] Othello was played by Tommaso Salvini in 1856, and that alone may have been enough to encourage marionette companies to present their own interpretation of the piece. It was staged by the Lupis in 1865 and was in the Ajmino repertoire in the late 1880s. The Mazzatortas were traveling with an *Otello* in 1900 and around this date, the Preti family had a glove-puppet version based on a piece of popular fiction by Mario Mariani, itself adapted from the libretto of Verdi's opera.[40]

The most popular story with Shakespearean associations was that of Romeo and Juliet.

Giulietta e Romeo was the subject of two ballets in the 1780s and provided the plot for Zingarelli's opera of 1796 (libretto by G.M. Foppa). The most direct sources were Italian. An adaptation of Shakespeare's play was made by Luigi Savola in 1818 and provided a partial source for Felice Romani's libretto for Vaccai's *Giulietta e Romeo* (1825), itself a significant precursor of the better-known Bellini opera *I Capuleti e i Montecchi* (1830), also with a libretto by Romani. Opera libretti were the source of marionette versions of *Giulietta e Romeo* for most of the nineteenth century. The first of these was *Le tombe di Verona* (Milan, 1821), in the repertoire of Antonio Macchi, and it was probably based on the ballet with this title performed at La Scala in 1820.[41] By 1834 the Lupis were staging their *Giulietta e Romeo* at the San Martiniano and for years this was one of their most popular productions. Apart from the libretto of Bellini's *I Capuleti e i Montecchi*, a major source in Sicily was probably a cheaply produced serial novel printed by Piazza of Palermo. In the Canino family's four-act scenario of *Giulietta e Romeo* the main characters are Romeo, Lorenzo, Capoletto, Tibaldeo, Giulietta, Giustina (nurse), Paride (Paris), and an incidental character called Enrico, who serves as a messenger.[42] Unlike the opera, Paride, and not Tibaldeo, has been selected to marry Giulietta. As in the opera, Lorenzo is not a friar; his role is like Shakespeare's Benvolio, but he is also responsible for Giulietta's sleeping draft. The piece opens with a night scene in a garden in which Romeo speaks of his love to Giulietta. There is no ball scene. In act 2 Romeo has to kill Tibaldeo, who has intercepted him climbing over a wall at midnight to see Giulietta. However Giulietta refuses to run away with Romeo and they are never married. In act 4 Romeo and Paride have a sword fight reminiscent of many other productions of the opera dei pupi, but this is interrupted, as in Bellini's opera, by the passing of the funeral procession, which causes them both to drop their swords. The opera allows for a final grand scene between the lovers in the tomb, but the pupi version is relatively perfunctory. Romeo simply poisons himself and Giulietta kills herself with a dagger.[43]

A late nineteenth-century cartellone by Francesco Rinaldi for a Palermitan performance of *Giulietta e Romeo* divides the action into five separate scenes. It shows how closely the story was reconceived in terms of the Sicilian pupi for audiences familiar with the chivalric repertoire. The first scene depicts a single combat between Capulets and Montagues in front of the seated duke of Verona and the second a battle in full armor between Capulets and Montagues (historically Guelphs and Ghibellines) in which Romeo kills Giulietta's brother.[44] After this comes the feast where Romeo is discovered and has a sword fight with Tebaldeo, observed by Capulet, Giulietta and a group of other figures. A scene in Giulietta's bedroom shows her fainting in the arms of her father as she hears of the death of her brother and Tebaldeo and others rush in. Next is the duel between Romeo and Tebaldeo at the gates of the town, interrupted by the passing of the funeral procession of Giulietta. The final two sections have the arrival of Romeo at the tomb, with two friends, who lift up the cover, while he swallows poison, and also the suicide of Giulietta. Her father and his followers rush in, too late, while, surrounded by cherubs, the souls of the embracing lovers mount to heaven in a final apotheosis.

Topicality

Fights have always had a significant place in puppet repertories, whether in the case of two glove-puppets battering each other with clubs, of pupi clashing swords and shields, or of grandiose battle scenes performed by marionettes. When Story visited the Roman pupi theaters he was told that the program always involved battles ("sempre battaglia"). Gregorovius describes the great fight in a *Christopher Columbus* then playing with great success (three times a day):

> The shooting, the drums, the blowing of horns and the clashing of the puppets together and the shouts of enthusiasm from the audience produced the most perfect din of battle that has ever been heard on a stage.[45]

The traveling marionette theaters of the nineteenth century carried one or more pieces inspired by Epinal illustrations of Napoleonic battles or by later ones against the Austrians. Like the panoramas and optical shows, these were selected for their overall spectacular nature rather than for the excitement of the hand-to-hand fighting that is the hallmark of the pupi. Pyrotechnics and realistic firearms were popular.[46] Towards the mid-century one of the functions of the puppet stage, and especially the marionette one, was to recreate in visual form the battles that people could only read about. Shortly after the actual event, the Fiando presented the capture of Algiers by the French in 1830. The taking of Constantine (Algeria) in October 1837 resulted in a highly successful piece that ran for 115 performances between December 1838 and March 1839.[47] Major disasters could also be presented by marionettes. The floods of the Danube in 1838 inspired a production whose takings were forwarded to some of the victims in Buda and Pest. There was a certain element of living newspaper about this that was similar to the Pathé news that was shown in cinemas in the twentieth century.

Marionette companies exploited the Napoleonic battles of Lodi and Rivoli. Giacomo Colla still had *Napoleon at the Great Battle of Austerlitz with Famiola as a Conscript and Officer* in the early years of the twentieth century. In 1849 the Lupis staged the recent victory of the Piedmontese over the Austrians at the battle of Goito. In 1859 Giuseppe Colla was in Palestra when the Piedmontese defeated the Austrians and this immediately provided a subject for an immensely popular marionette show. In the same year the French beat the Austrians at Magenta and at Solferino (near Mantua) and a *Solferino* still featured in the Muchetti repertoire in the 1880s. An anecdote about Antonio Reccardini, in Venice in 1859, mentions how a number of Austrian officials in his audience were disturbing the show, so he made Facanapa turn to Arlecchino, complaining about the noise and asking him for a "Solferino" to light his pipe (a play on the word "zolfanello," a sulphur match). This resulted in a visit to prison.[48] The siege of Paris in 1870 reached the Gerolamo Theater in 1873. In March 1886 Antonio Colla announced a piece based on the colonial disaster of Dogali, in which 600 Italian soldiers had been wiped out. The authorities stepped in and stopped performances. Colonial policy was a sensitive issue and they were afraid of riots.[49] *Dogali* was eventually performed with much success in 1888. Italian colonial expansion was also reflected in Rinaldo Zane's production of *The Italians at Massaua* at the Gerolamo in January 1893. The execution of Caserio, the funeral of King Umberto or the earthquake in Calabria are all examples of events rapidly converted into marionette shows. In 1916, Giacomo Colla presented a patriotic and topical piece, *The Taking of Gorizia, with Famiola Sergeant of the Alpine Troops*, recalling the Austro-Italian fighting there at the period.

The growing sense of a nation and the revolutionary movements of the 1840s found a reflection in the repertoires. The extirpation of foreign rule, especially French and Austrian,

The Battle of Solferino, **Muchetti company, Adro. Archival photograph (set up in open air —
note grass). (Muchetti company. Courtesy Bruno Poieri.)**

together with the removal of the Bourbons in the south and of the papal authority over its
former territories, generated a climate of patriotism. The risings of 1848, from Palermo's
revolution to Milan's five-day one, found their way onto the puppet stage. The Piedmontese Famiola, with his red, white and green costume, epitomized the new patriotic spirit.
After 1860 the puppet repertoire was most affected by pieces which made Garibaldi the hero
and in which Vittorio Emanuele figured as king of Italy.[50]

The popular imagination has a tendency to translate everything into terms of the present and to ignore notions of historical perspective. The opera dei pupi showed how the past
could have contemporary relevance, but in many cases audiences also wanted novelty. Popular theater audiences of the nineteenth century developed an increasing desire to see the
everyday reality of their lives on the stage and this led showmen to blur the gap between
fiction and reality. In 1819 the first bicycles were being demonstrated, so the Fiando Theater promptly staged *The Bicycle Race*; a century later the Gambarutti family put motor cars
and television onto the puppet stage. When the first railway line opened between Monza
and Milan in 1840, Gerolamo was the eponymous hero of a piece celebrating the event.[51]
From the 1870s the Gianduja and Gerolamo theaters began to stage major end-of-year
reviews. The Lupis became noted for such shows, which mentioned almost everything of
note during the year and presented events in an entertaining and spectacular manner. In
Milan in 1879 signora Fiando staged her *Review of 1878* with Meneghino and Gerolamo as
airborne travelers.

Garibaldi and a friar, from *The Revolution of Palermo* in the repertoire of Luigi Cristini, Bergamo. (Published in Pino Capellini, *Baracca e burattini* [Bergamo: Grafica Gutemberg Gorle Editrice, 1977 e 1997]. Photograph Domenico Lucchetti. Courtesy Archivio Privato Famiglia Domenico Lucchetti.)

Popular audiences readily assumed that events portrayed on the puppet stage were true, and most showmen encouraged this belief. After 1860 newspapers began to provide a regular source of material to be transposed and text for some scenes was lifted directly from them. Horrific crimes gave rise to such sensational pieces as the Piedmontese *Hyena of San Giorgio*, a Sweeney Todd–style piece with murder and cannibalism.[52] Bigio Milesi, in Bergamo, entertained audiences with the story of Vincenzo Verzeni, a serial killer of women (supposedly he sucked their blood). The post–World War II history of Italy was a dark period. The Gambarutti company reflected this in their production of *Il bandito Giuliano*, based on the life and murder of Salvatore Giuliano in 1950, attributed to the right wing and the Mafia. In a lighter and more fictional vein they reflected the struggle between Communism and the Church when they brought Guareschi's unconventional priest Don Camillo to the marionette stage.

Garibaldi's entrance to Naples. Scene from a production by Carlo Colla e Figli. Archival photograph. (Courtesy Compagnia Carlo Colla e Figli.)

From Alcina to Pinocchio

Fantastic spectacle can be found in medieval religious drama, with its depiction of hell and devils, and in the later extravagant intermezzi of the sixteenth century. The baroque theater emphasized the marvelous. Once elements of this percolated down to the puppet theater, depiction of magic and the supernatural proved to be a form of entertainment that delighted audiences. In almost every guarattella performance the devil arrives to take Pulcinella away (and usually fails). Devils and magicians, appearing and disappearing in a burst of flame, are a regular element of the glove-puppet stage, where the symbolism of coming out of the ground is most appropriate. A central figure in the pupi theater is the enchantress Alcina, who can change from beautiful woman to old hag to death. Malagigi, with his tame devil Nacalone, has regular recourse to "good" magic and Nacalone can also transport him through the air as the hippogriff transports Astolfo. Flight is natural to marionettes, but at a more profound psychological level it carries with it a sense of freedom from the constraints of the everyday.

The fascination with Faust on the German puppet stage had an equivalent in Italy with the walnut tree of Benevento, a pre–Christian place of cult subsequently associated with a witches' coven in Italian folklore. Filippo Acciajoli had a play on the subject and Salvatore Vigano's ballet of 1812 was subsequently staged at the Teatro Re in Milan (probably with marionettes) and adapted for the Borromeo marionettes in 1823.[53] The subject of the nut tree of Benevento illustrates the passage from folk material to fairy-tale. The 1851 Emiliani production of *The Great Demogorgone; or The Walnut Tree of Benevento* was a children's show.[54] In the atmospheric opening the powerful wizard Demogorgone was shown sitting beneath the famous tree, whose branches were occupied by various dark genii with torches. As well as bad fairies, devils and other evil genii, the audience was treated to lightning and subterranean rumbles and the disappearance of Demogorgone in a ball of fire.[55] In the last part Rugantino has to climb the sinister tree and throw down some nuts to defeat the power of evil, whereupon the scene transforms to a temple of happiness. The loving married couple Gualtieri and Aigenide, earlier separated by the witches, is now reunited and the latter

The three faces of Alcina. Canino Theater. Alcina as beautiful young woman, old sorceress and death. The head is designed to rotate. (Courtesy Museo Internazionale delle Marionette Antonio Pasqualino.)

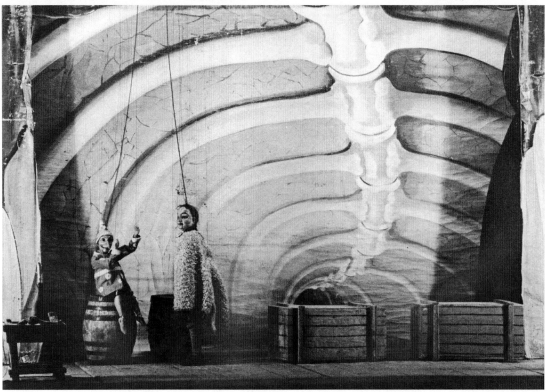

Opposite and above: Pinocchio with the cat and fox; Pinocchio in the whale; the trial of Pinocchio. Lupi, early 20th century. Gepetto is played by Gianduja (see scene in the whale). These photographs probably reflect the original Lupi production of Pinocchio. (Archival photographs. Courtesy Teatro Gianduja — Museo della Marionetta di Torino.)

depart, cursing, before the grand finale. In one self-referential scene Rugantino informed the fairy Lirina that he knew who she was because he had seen her so many times in the puppet theater of the Piazza Navona. The sorceress Alcina, perhaps because of sexual overtones, remained tied to the more adult repertoire of the pupi, but elsewhere the fairy play with witches and magic became something to delight more juvenile audiences.

Gozzi's fables blended the eighteenth-century vogue for the fairy-tale with a philosophical theme. The main plots easily passed from the adult to the juvenile audience, joining pieces derived from Perrault such as *Puss in Boots* and *Sleeping Beauty*. The juvenile market was firmly established by the mid–nineteenth century and by the early 1900s showmen began to look more attentively at this as a means of ensuring their subsistence. Many shows previously performed to a general or adult audience were now reshaped in terms of the younger spectator, and a new repertoire began to emerge that was not necessarily based on actors' theater. The Lupi's Gianduja Theater and, after 1911, the Colla's Gerolamo Theater were seen as children's theaters.

From a modern perspective, the great classic of the children's puppet theater is *Pinocchio*, which has held the stage long after the disappearance of much of the nineteenth-century puppet repertoire. Collodi's novel was published in weekly parts in the children's newspaper, the *Giornale dei bambini*, in the 1880s.[56] As an allegory of Italy at the period it could be read equally by adults or children. With its intensely theatrical conception and considerable use of dialogue, dramatic situations and instantly recognizable character types, it did not take long for it to reach the puppet stage. The extraordinary and ongoing popularity of *Pinocchio* may be explained by its self-reflexive nature. It is a profoundly theatrical piece, playing on the Romantic idea of the nature of the puppet and its relationship to a living person, and as such is completely in tune with the movement in twentieth-century theater that turned its back on naturalism. The earliest adaptation was made by the Lupis in 1890. They followed the Collodi text closely, omitting two violent scenes, the killing of the cricket and the hanging of Pinocchio, and used Gianduja as Gepetto. The allegorical element of *Pinocchio* was less evident in their production, which focused on talking animals, the fairy and magic. Like *Puss in Boots*, *Pinocchio* looked forward to the period when animals provided with speech and other human attributes would become central characters in pieces for children.

Puppet showman also offering card tricks, Venice, 18th century. Giovanni Grevembroch. The showman's apron has two large pockets to hold puppets when performing. ("Giuocatore di Buratini," Grevembroch — M24183 — dis. G. Costumi — Vol III tav 164. Courtesy Fondazione Musei Civici di Venezia.)

Pietro Longhi. The stage (and probably a portrait) of Alberto Borgogna, Venice, circa 1760. Puppet Pulcinella is accompanied by a live dog. ("Il casotto del Borgogna." Pietro Longhi (Pietro Falca), Venice 1702–1785. Oil on canvas, 55.2 by 72.6 cms. Vicenza, Gallerie di Palazzo Leoni Montanari. Courtesy Collezione Intesa San Paolo.)

Opposite: Late 18th-century stage with a group of figures of varying sizes and probably from more than one set. Extending trick figures are on either side of the stage. Dottore is center, and on his right Arlecchino, Colombina Brighella, Pantalone. Another Arlecchino rides a devil. (Marionette theater. Courtesy Museo Davia Bargellini, Bologna.)

Top: Watercolor by Achille Pinelli, 1833. This probably depicts Ghetanaccio's show with the characters of Colombina, Pulcinella, Rugantino and a devil. ("Chiesa dei Santi Quirico e Giulitta con popolani e palco con burattini." Courtesy and © of Comune Di Roma — Sovraintendenza Beni Culturali — Museo di Roma.) *Bottom:* Pulcinella in Rome. Bartolomeo Pinelli, 1817. (Author's collection.)

Poster for *Saint Rosalia* painted by Pina Patti Cuticchio: battle between Arabs and Normans; Baldovino asks for the hand of Rosalia; Jesus appears to Rosalia; Rosalia leaves the palace to become a hermit; Baldovino meets a lion; temptation of Rosalia; death of Rosalia; Rosalia appears to the hunter; confession of the hunter; Saint Rosalia saves Palermo from the plague. (Courtesy Associazione Figli d'Arte Cuticchio.)

Top: Bibiena-style scene painted with per angolo perspective, approx. 82 by 172 cms. Antonio Galli-Bibiena or his school. (Museo Davia Bargellini, Bologna.) *Bottom:* Scenery, possibly from a marionette theater in a convent in Jesi, late 18th or early 19th century: 1 backcloth (120 cms wide by 168 cms high), 1 cut-cloth or "principale" (120 by 168 cms), 6 wings (30 by 114.5 cms). The two center arches are cut out, showing a cloth behind continuing and reducing the per angolo perspective. (Tempera on cloth. Courtyard n. 12. Mereghi collection, Jesi. Courtesy Pinacoteca Civica di Jesi.)

Opposite, top: Catanian cartellone of the battle of Roncisvalle depicting the death of Orlando's companion, Oliviero. Natale Napoli, 1960. Saracens are indicated by crescent moons on their helmets. Tempera on wrapping paper. (Courtesy the Marionettistica dei Fratelli Napoli. Photograph Salvatore Napoli.)

Opposite, bottom: Group of Neapolitan "guappi." Noticeable is the emphasis on showy masculine costumes. (Courtesy Museo Internazionale delle Marionette Antonio Pasqualino.)

Top: Scenery from Jesi. Grotto consisting of 2 backcloths (120 by 168 cms), 1 cut-cloth or "principale" (120 by 168 cms), 6 wings (29 by 100 cms). Tempera on cloth. (Mereghi collection, Jesi. Courtesy Pinacoteca Civica di Jesi.) *Bottom: The Nut-tree of Benevento.* Hell scene with figures, Borromeo theater, Isola Bella, 1828, by Alessandro Sanquirico (now on the Isola Madre). ("Isola Madre — Lago Maggiore — Palazzo Borromeo — il teatrino." Courtesy Grafiche Reggiori srl — Cittiglio [Va].)

Top: Neo-classical palace scene with figures. Early 19th century. Painted in the style of Alessandro Sanquirico. Possibly used by the traveling company of Onofrio Samoggia. Rissone collection. (From *Il teatrino Rissone* [Modena: Panini, 1985]. Courtesy Museo-Biblioteca dell'Attore, Genoa.) *Bottom:* Inn yard. Early 19th century. Possibly used by the traveling company of Onofrio Samoggia. Rissone collection. (From *Il teatrino Rissone* [Modena: Panini, 1985]. Courtesy Museo-Biblioteca dell'Attore, Genoa.)

Top: Backcloth of forest by Nicolo Rinaldi (Faraone). Palermo, late 19th century. Tempera on canvas. *Bottom:* Backcloth (or painted curtain) of scene of Saracens disembarking by Nicolo Rinaldi (Faraone). Palermo, late 19th century. Courtesy Museo Internazionale delle Marionette Antonio Pasqualino.)

The lazaretto of Milan scene from *I promessi sposi* (The Betrothed) performed by Carlo Colla e Figli company. The scene is based on illustrations by Francesco Gonin for the original edition of Manzoni's novel. (From *Ricordi della vecchia Milano — storia e arte della Compagnia Carlo Colla e Figli*, a cura della Società Fiscambi, Ente Editoriale dell'Università Cattolica del Sacro Cuore, Milan, 1966. Courtesy Compagnia Carlo Colla e Figli. Photograph Giovanni Bonicelli.)

Top: The Flood, back scene with tableau including figures ("comodino"). Tempera on paper. Muchetti company, Adro. (Courtesy Bruno Poieri.)

Top: Morgari — backcloth for the Temple of Neptune. The transparency is lightable from the back for special effects. Probably used by the Lupis at the San Martiniano Theater in the early 1840s. (Giuseppe Maria Morgari [1788–1847]. Backcloth on cloth of varying thicknesses. inv. 406/D. Courtesy Fondazione Torino Musei. From Mercedes Viale Ferrero, *Scene per un teatrini di marionette nella vita di Torino ottocentesca* [Turin, 1983].) *Bottom:* Backcloth or curtain depicting the interior of the San Martiniano Theater, 1882. (Backcloth [no. 93, 12]. Courtesy Teatro Gianduja — Museo della Marionetta di Torino. Photograph Roberto Parodi.)

Top: View of Piazza Vecchia of Bergamo. Painted scene or front curtain for the stage of Arturo Marziali. Puppet shows often occurred under the arcades in the background. (On loan to the Fondazione Bergamo nella Storia — Museo Storico di Bergamo. Courtesy the Scuri family, Bergamo. Photograph Domenico Lucchetti. Courtesy Archivio Privato Famiglia Domenico Lucchetti.) *Bottom: Ballo Excelsior*, revival. Carlo Colla e Figli company. The figures in the center each have the classic rod to the head and lower back. (Courtesy Compagnia Carlo Colla e Figli.)

Top: Bruno Angoletta, design for *The Tempest*, Teatro dei Piccoli, 1921, 14 by 25 cms. This illustrates the new painterly approach to stage design embraced by Vittorio Podrecca. (Courtesy Collezione Maria Signorelli. Photograph Maristella Campolunghi.) *Bottom:* Fortunato Depero. Reconstruction of the *Balli plastici* (1982). This is a group of figures for exhibition, not a scene. Note the Depero poster in the background. ("La rivista delle marionette, 1918," Fortunato Depero. Courtesy MART — Museo di Arte Moderna e Contemporanea — Rovereto [Tn].)

Waltzers. Soft-sculpture rod puppets by Maria Signorelli for the Opera dei Burattini. Music F. Chopin, choreography L. Mian, Rome, 1954. (Courtesy Collezione Maria Signorelli. Photograph Maristella Campolunghi.)

Pulcinella Paladino. The puppet used by Paolo Comentale and designed by Emanuele Luzzati, who has transformed the classical figure of Pulcinella. (Courtesy Paolo Comentale, Teatro Casa di Pulcinella Bari.)

Giacomina e il popolo di legno. Is Mascareddas company. Giacomina meets the old women. Highly simplified and stylized puppets evoking toys of the 1930s. (Courtesy Is Mascareddas company, Cagliari.)

Topo Gigio. Maria Perego's internationally famous television puppet. (© Maria Perego.)

CHAPTER 7

Music and Spectacle

"Burattini in Musica"

In Europe of the seventeenth and eighteenth centuries a distinction between word-based theater and a theater depending for its effect on spectacle and music was fundamental. Puppet theater falls into both categories. Music and puppets belong together, whether it is a bagpiper in the street with a jigging doll, the solo musician accompanying a guarattella show, which almost invariably winds up with a dance, or singers and a small orchestra for marionette opera. When Domenico Segala applied for a permit to perform in Reggio Emilia in November 1660, he indicated that he wished to perform with little wooden figures and let people hear certain instruments.[1]

The idea of substituting puppets for human performers offered new possibilities for private theatrical activities. Such productions came to be known as "burattini in musica." Some operas were written directly for the puppet stage, others were adapted. In Paris in 1647, Cardinal Mazarin commissioned an *Orfeo* from the leading Roman composer Luigi Rossi with a libretto by Francesco Buti. This "tragedia-comedia," one of the most magnificent spectacles of the first half of the century, was performed for the nine-year-old King Louis XIV and the court at the Palais Royal Theater, where Giacomo Torelli was responsible for the staging. The enormous cost of the production, coupled with the fact that it was sung in Italian and involved many Italians, led to a xenophobic outcry and the Italian musicians had to leave Paris for the time being. Puppets surrounded by the marvels of the baroque stage did not remain restricted to the court for long. Only a few months after the performance at the Palais Royal two puppeteers were offering public performances of *Orfeo*.[2]

When La Grille's troupe from Italy performed at the Marais du Temple as the Théâtre des Pygmées in 1676, the printed libretto indicated:

> Something that has never been seen before: numerous richly dressed human figures four feet high on a vast and magnificent stage performing five-act plays with music, ballets, flying machines of a completely new invention, and scene changes. These figures recite, walk and move like living people in a most agreeable way, and without being suspended from above.[3]

The comment that the figures were not "suspended" indicates that they were not operated from above by strings or rods, but almost certainly from underneath, moving in channels according to the system associated with Bartolomeo Neri. In opera and tragedy of the time movement was relatively slight. Stage attitudes and gestures were highly coded, limited in number and derived more from rhetoric than the realistic imitation of human behavior. It was easy for puppets to imitate them. The Abbé du Bos, writing in 1719, also described the Pygmées, adding that the voice was provided by a musician under the stage, and that he had seen this sort of thing in Italy, in the operas performed for an "illustrious cardinal," using puppets about four feet high, which no one had found ridiculous.[4]

In Italy many operatic pieces initially conceived for live performers transferred to the marionette stage. Giulio Rospigliosi's *La Baldassara, the Actress of Heaven* (music by Anton Maria Abbatini) was performed in Rome with live performers during the Carnival of 1668, and with puppets the same year. Filippo Acciajoli's operatic performances seem to have been written for live actors first but then probably transferred to the puppet stage he created in Rome.

The first recorded case of puppet opera in a public and paying theater was found in Venice in 1680. A private theater in the Zattere presented *Leandro*, a "dramma per musica" by Count Camillo Badovero (Badoer) with music by Francesco Antonio Pistocchino. The story of the ill-fated love of Hero and Leander was performed by "wooden figures," with singers hidden backstage. The venture was successful and, re-titled *Gli amori fatali* (The Ill-Fated Loves), it transferred to the San Moïsè Theater, which had become available.[5] The rest of the repertoire consisted of pieces by Acciajoli: *Damira placata* (appeased), with music by Marc Antonio Ziani; *Ulisse in Feaccia,* with music by Antonio del Gaudio and *Il Girello* with music by Pistocchino. Considering the use of his libretti and his fondness for machines and scenic inventions, it is almost certain that Acciajoli was involved with these productions. The libretti were published in small volumes which were distributed to the spectators. That of *Damira placata* is prefaced by a short poem in which the audience is told they will be astonished by the force of human ingenuity in giving silent gestures to a piece of wood, while the introduction to *Ulisse in Feaccia* (1681) refers to the skillful expression of human attitudes with a piece of wood or figures made of wax. It is generally assumed that these figures were marionettes, and Acciajoli may well have come into contact with a marionette company. However, it is possible that the whole set-up was similar to the earlier puppet theater developed by Acciajoli.

In *Damira placata* the scheming Fillide usurps the place of the queen, whom she has attempted to have murdered.[6] At the end of the highly complicated and exciting romantic plot Damira and her husband are successfully reunited. Exotic spectacle is provided by an Egyptian setting and dance interludes. The Acciajoli libretti contain comedy and comic figures that are specially appropriate for the puppet stage. In *Damira* there is Nerillo, a eunuch, who also acts as a commentator. In *Ulisse in Feaccia* Ulisse's ridiculous humpback servant, Delfo Gobbo, has this function. Ulisse (Ulysses) and Delfo are shipwrecked on the shore of Traccia. Ulisse has a flirtation with the two daughters of the king but Minerva appears to him in a vision and he decides to go back to his wife Penelope. As they leave by ship at the end, Delfo, like the classic zanni, rails against fate which wants him to perish in water, when he is longing to drown in wine.

Acciajoli's most successful comedy, *Il Girello*, was adapted for puppets at the San Moïsè in 1682. Girello, a gardener, thanks to a magician, is able to take on the appearance, and therefore function, of the king. This variant of the "king for a day" motif leads to endless confusion as the roles switch back and forth. A supernatural scene with spirits and magic made it ideal for marionette stage.

Pieces sometimes passed from the marionette stage to the live one. Tommaso Stanzani's *La Bernarda*, a rustic drama for music in Bolognese dialect, was presented with puppets at the Teatro Pubblico in Bologna in 1694, but later the same year it was done by live actors at the Teatro Formigliari.[7]

The three short seasons of opera that the abbé Labia offered his acquaintances in the 1740s are relatively well documented and provide valuable information.[8] *Il cajetto*, a "dramma per musica" in three acts by Antonio Gori with music by Ferdinando Bertoni, was staged in 1746. The printed libretto distributed to the guests, unlike plays published at the period, is virtually an acting edition: "kneeling to Cajetto," "distancing himself from him as about to depart," "takes a few steps, stops, turns back." This suggests that the figure-workers were amateurs or possibly servants. Audiences could admire the beautifully made "fantocci" (puppets), but the singers (hired for the occasion) were hidden and remained incognito. The puppet performers rejoiced in such evocative names as Il Signor Antonio Bamboccio, La Signorina Margherita Pua, La Signora Maddalena Statuina, Il Signor Alessandro Burattini, Il Signor Francesco Figurina, Il Signor Bernardo Ordigni and Il Signor Carlo Piavolo.[9] Set against the background of the Roman siege of Faleria, the plot is an intricate mesh of teenage amours. The idea of a largely juvenile cast played by puppets added to the enjoyment, as did the eighteenth-century emphasis on the spirit of generosity. Spectacular scenic effects included a cloud machine for Diana and a final grand transformation of a gloomy prison into the palace of Apollo.[10]

Piero Metastasio's three-act *Didone abbandonata* (Dido Abandoned) received its first performance in Naples in 1724, with music by Domenico Sarro. When the piece was presented with puppets at Labia's Teatro (nuovo) S, Girolamo in 1747, it was with music by Andrea Adolfati, and a year later with music by Ferdinando Bertoni. *Didone* has echoes of Racine's *Bérénice*, when Enea (Aeneas), like the emperor Titus, has to choose between duty and love. Enea is presented as a proto–Christian, and the African forces under Iarba are referred to as the "mori" (Moors) and this, of course, gives an opportunity for fight sequences evoking battles between Christians and Saracens. The grand spectacular ending has the burning of Carthage, Didone throwing herself into the flames and a full-scale conflagration quenched only by a violent sea storm, the restoration of calm and the kingdom of Neptune rising out of the waves, riding a shell drawn by marine monsters and surrounded by festive hosts of nymphs and sirens.

The nineteenth-century "melodramma" was as much a visual as a musical experience, as the baroque opera had been, and the foremost scene-painters of the day were often employed to make sure that this was the case. The larger marionette companies often included opera in their repertoire. Louis Peisse in 1835 wrote to Charles Magnin describing how marionettes in Rome (probably at the Fiano) were presenting serious operas such as *Otello* and *Semiramide*, complete with ballet, singing and an orchestra of five or six instruments. He added that he was both amused and moved by the show as he would have been at the San Carlo or the Paris Opera and that the limited movements and gestures of the puppets were strong and expressive even in pathetic and tragic situations.[11]

Opera Buffa to Modern Opera

Eighteenth-century opera seria invites the mock-heroic, and puppet interpretations almost inevitably included a comic figure with which audiences could readily identify. The more intimate opera buffa easily became preferable to opera seria and found a particular niche on the nineteenth-century marionette stage. The Fiano staged *L'Italiano [sic] in Algeri in 1833* when Rossini's opera was on the program of the Argentina Theater. What the audiences experienced was a spoken version of Rossini's work with a small number of sung passages.[12] The subtitle "Il pampaluco[13] con Cassandro Kaimakan" shifts the emphasis to the comic character Cassandro (Taddeo), the elderly gallant who accompanies Isabella and is wrecked with her in Algiers.[14] The script indicates that this was a scenically splendid production.[15] The censor imposed certain changes, such as replacing the Italian word "mezzano" (procurer) with the neutral "Kaimakan," but for an audience in the know this only increased the enjoyment, and Teoli certainly was able to wring every possible sexual innuendo out of the libretto. At the end Cassandro discovers that Isabella has only been flirting with him. She finds her lover Lindoro and all Cassandro can do is comment that he is left with empty hands.

Opera buffa with its very singable tunes appealed to the socially more mixed audiences of the nineteenth century and was within the range of capabilities of many marionette companies. Late eighteenth-century and early nineteenth-century pieces with small casts such as *La serva padrona* became a regular part of the repertoire of certain companies.

Another popular genre was the French vaudeville, a light comedy in which most scenes were rounded off with the singing of a verse or two. One of the favorite vaudevilles to find its way into the repertoires of Italian marionette companies was *La pianella perduta* (The Lost Slipper).[16] This is set in a village community and has a distinct rustic flavor. Like most vaudevilles, everything hinges on a basic misunderstanding and centers on two young lovers who are able to get married at the end despite earlier obstacles. When Gustave Flaubert visited the Fiando in 1845 he commented, possibly prematurely, on the lack of audience interest in the drama and described this as a dying genre on the marionette stage. The middle-class urban audience preferred to see Donizetti and Scribe and had a marked fondness for ballets.[17] By the end of the century operetta spread to the marionette stage and immensely popular works such as *La Gran Via* and *The Geisha* were given lavish productions.

In the final years of the century the traveling theaters still had their repertoire of dramas, but opera and musical entertainments were more in demand in cities such as Milan and Turin. *L'elisir d'amore* was in the Zane repertoire during their season at the Gerolamo in 1895.[18] In 1897 Rinaldo Zane presented Serafino (Amadeo) De Ferrari's *Pipelet; or The Doorkeeper of Paris*. Zane's 1898 *La bohème* used music from both the Puccini version and the less well-known Leoncavallo one, and in 1899 he staged Errico Petrella's *Promessi sposi*. These were publicized as being performed by "singing marionettes," which suggests that the Zane company was using marionettes with opening mouths for operatic performance. Today, the revived Colla company of Eugenio Monti Colla uses figures with moving mouths to "sing" opera and great attention is paid to lip-synchronization.

With the twentieth century marionette theater began to be reconsidered for its artistic potential. The gramophone placed opera performance within the scope of traveling marionette companies, since they did not need to pay for either an orchestra or singers. They presented curtailed versions of real operas using selected arias and music, but converted recitative into spoken dialogue. Franco Gambarutti speaks of performing *Aida, Tosca, The Force of Destiny* and *Il trovatore* in this way.[19] The revived Carlo Colla company went rather further and a major model was the Salzburger Marionettentheater. Giancarlo Menotti first invited them to the Spoleto festival in 1970 (where they presented *Excelsior*). On subsequent visits their offerings included *Aida*, *Il trovatore* and *Nabucco* as reduced versions of the Verdian "melodramma." The production evoked the operatic stage of the nineteenth century and the use of high-quality recordings created an experience very different from that of a nineteenth-century marionette theater with a small band and its own singers.

Vittorio Podrecca with his Teatro dei Piccoli set out to present marionette opera in the contemporary sense of bringing together different art forms and restoring the centrality of the music. Early seasons of the Piccoli involved a small orchestra and three singers in the wings, forming a chamber opera company.[20] By the time of the great tours in the 1920s there were eight singers. The 1914-1915 season opened with a three-act comic opera already in the repertoire of the Gorno company, *Crispino e la comare* (Crispin and the Gossip) by Francesco Maria Piave with music by Luigi and Federicco Ricci (1850). This was provided with new sets and costumes designed by Pierretto Bianco.[21] The Gorno's Facanapa played the part of Crispino and Miss Legnetti, a singer created by them, that of Annetta. Massenet's *La Cenerentola* (Cinderella) joined the repertoire in 1916 and a reduced version of Petrella's *Promessi sposi* in 1918.[22] Rossini was represented in 1916 with *Opportunity Makes the Thief; or The Exchange of Suitcases* and in 1921 with *The Thieving Magpie*. In the latter there was particular applause for a ballerina who danced on her points and who later became one of the special numbers of the company.

Other lighter musical pieces performed in these years included Giovanni Bottesini's fantastic opera *Ali Baba* and two zarzuelas, Valverde's *La Gran Via* and Antonio Vives's *King Farfan's Tooth*. Podrecca also commissioned new music for the puppet theater. This included scores for Carlo Gozzi's *Love of Three Oranges*, *L'Augellin Belvedere* and *Pinocchio*, composed respectively by Francesco Ticciati, Ferdinando Luizzi and Giovanni Giannetti. The most important piece to be commissioned by Podrecca was a new three-act opera of *Sleeping Beauty* by Ottorino Respighi.[23] Within a few years this work achieved more than 1,000 performances. Giovanni Giannetti wrote music for a short modern "scena lirica," *Pierrot e la luna*. Depero's *Balli plastici per marionette* had music by Alfredo Casella, Gerard Tyrwhitt, Malpiero and Chemenov (Béla Bartók).

Throughout his life Podrecca was committed to the idea of marionettes and music. Shortly before his death he declared:

> Marionettes are made of the same stuff as music, of the rhythm of life and art which emanates from them when they are created and presented not showing their banal and distorted aspect which is either boring and crude or cerebral, sophisticated and hermetic, but in a limpid, noble, fascinating and distinguished form.... Marionettes also, because they are operated by strings, resembling musical instruments, are themselves musical instruments, are interwoven with music of melodic and symphonic essence.[24]

"Melodramma" and "Melodrama"

The programs of the marionette companies of the nineteenth and early twentieth century might give the impression that opera was everywhere. Opera titles were used as a point of reference and the libretti provided a ready supply of plots. Repertoires list titles of Rossini, Bellini, Donizetti and Verdi operas, but what the audiences for marionettes and even glove-puppets witnessed was something quite different. The opera, or "melodramma," was

Vittorio Podrecca and puppets for Ottorino Respighi's *La bella addormentata nel bosco* (Sleeping Beauty). (Courtesy Teatro Stabile Friuli-Venezia Giulia.)

immensely popular in nineteenth-century Italy.[25] The Italian "melodramma" was a drama in music that embraced the content and sentiments of the English and French melodrama. In place of the classical myths and heroic ideals of opera seria here was a world of the Middle Ages, full of thrills, pathos and visual excitement with the inevitable triumph of good over evil. Proprietors of marionette shows required good stories with known titles and often took the libretti of operas and rewrote them for their own purposes. Even the music they used was not necessarily that of the original composers. In form what was presented on the marionette stage was much closer to the melodrama than the "melodramma." It was a spoken drama with incidental and atmospheric music that heightened the dramatic impact and created a mood, but was often as invisible as cinema music. By the early twentieth century the Rame family had their version of *Lohengrin* as a drama, thanks to a prose romance version of the plot, and used gramophone records of Wagner for incidental music.

Opera music was picked up by military bands and amateur orchestras and thus became part of popular music. Local musicians were often engaged by traveling marionette companies and by this route well-known operatic music reached the marionette stage.[26] The size of a band varied from a single instrument to a group of about a dozen musicians and payment might range from an actual fee to free drinks. Only a few companies with fixed theaters, such as Lupi or Fiando, could have the luxury of their own band. The Carlo Colla company prior to its establishment at the Gerolamo (Fiando) in 1911 employed local musicians wherever it stopped. At the Gerolamo they had an orchestra that numbered about a dozen.[27] Usually the orchestra was conducted from the keyboard, or else by the lead violin, and this individual was responsible for the selection, adaptation and orchestration of pieces of music, and for the copying of the necessary parts for the other musicians. The Fiando orchestra in the early years was directed by the celebrated violinist Giovanni Ricordi (1785–1853). The rest of the band consisted of a pianoforte, four or five stringed instruments and almost certainly some wind ones.[28]

Names of composers were rarely given on bills, and music might be taken from a variety of sources.[29] The intensely dramatic and exciting nature of Verdi's work made him one of the most popular composers to pillage for incidental music, but his operas themselves seldom appeared in anything like their original form. When an opera subject transferred to the marionette stage, the original music was selected in terms of its dramatic usefulness or expressiveness. Although omnipresent, it was limited to what was necessary for a scene or situation, and a few bars (rather than a complete piece) usually sufficed. Apart from the overture, the function of music was to link scenes, create atmosphere, introduce characters or provide a musical leitmotif for them, underscore a particularly significant speech and give extra strength to a frozen moment or tableau.

In 1879 the Colla company presented *I promessi sposi*, inspired more by the Petrella opera than by Manzoni's novel. Some of the incidental music was by Petrella, including a polka for the happy end, although this was later replaced with a march from Gounod's *Queen of Sheba*.[30] By 1911 some sung passages had been reintroduced. Petrella's music was very heavily edited, in some cases with modification of the tempo or key. A note on the cover of the script indicates "appropriate music."[31] The prelude to the rise of the curtain in the opera consisted of 119 bars, but at the Gerolamo this was reduced to 14 followed by a pause and another 4.[32] Only one piece of music was used in its entirety and this was to cover a long procession at the end of the third act when Lucia is returned to her mother. A stage direction "processione ad libitum," left the company free for one of its long and spectacular parades of figures across the stage.

The glove-puppet companies of Emilia Romagna in the nineteenth and early twentieth centuries worked in a similar way to the marionette ones but gave greater prominence to the comic characters. In a *Lohengrin* staged by Raffaele Ragazzi, Sganapino played Lohengrin's squire and, as the swan departed, he called after it "you're going away and I'm stay-

The Sarina family as musicians in front of the stage, circa 1900. (Archival photograph. Courtesy Associazione Peppino Sarina di Tortona [Al].)

ing here."[33] In Bologna *Il trovatore, William Tell, The Force of Destiny* (with Sganapino as Frate Melitone), *Aida, Tosca, Robert the Devil, Ernani, L'elisir d'amore, L'Africaine, La Gioconda; or The Tyrant of Padua, Lohengrin* and *Rigoletto* could all be found on the glove-puppet stage. Many contained sung numbers but the "orchestra" was most likely to consist of mandolins, guitars and accordions.[34]

"Far Ballare i Burattini"

The jigging doll or the planchette figure in the street attracts attention because of its movement in time to music or percussive rhythm. The physical movement of a puppet draws attention as an animated figure and encourages the spectator to believe that a voice produced by a concealed speaker or singer is emitted by it. Seventeenth-century requests for permits use either the word "ballare" (dance) or "giocare" (play) to indicate performance with puppets. When the Frenchman Antonio Ventade visited Reggio Emilia in 1664 he indicated that he wished to "far ballare" a number of small figures and execute ballets and other French entertainments with them.[35] By the eighteenth century "far ballare i burattini" was a common term to express the general idea of giving a performance with puppets.

The word "ballo" in the context of the puppet stage can cover almost anything from a solo dance to a variety act and from a full-length ballet to a musical extravaganza (with or without words). The earliest examples of puppet ballet are to be found in the dance entries of early opera that had transferred to the marionette stage. At the end of act 1 of Acciajoli's *Damira placata* a group of Armenian merchants dance. At the end of the second act, when the heroine is feigning madness, a group of madmen perform their grotesque "ballo." The final scene of the first act of *Ulisse in Feaccia* is in a "delightful garden" and a dance is executed by a group of gardeners, male and female, presumably equipped with such props as rakes and baskets. In *Il Girello* no specific "ballo" is mentioned, but Girello's encounter with the sorcerer in act 1 almost certainly provided an opportunity for a relevant dance entry by the spirits conjured up.

Until the end of the eighteenth century ballet had consisted of dance interludes with a theme. This changed with the "ballet d'action" of Jean Noverre (1727–1821), which told a story through music, dance, pantomime and spectacle, and this genre lent itself to the puppet stage. In Italy the "ballet d'action" was developed further by Salvatore Vigano (1769–1821), who devised a number of pieces for La Scala. His popular *Prometeo* (Prometheus), first staged in 1813, had reached the Fiando Theater by 1814.[36] The Maggi company presented it in Bologna in 1819 and Ireneo Nocchi also had a grand production of it. The Fiando version of 1844 was visually splendid and had Gerolamo as the central figure. The music for *Prometeo* was taken from Beethoven's "Die Geschöpfte des Prometeus" and Haydn's "Creation." On the marionette stage this was reduced to incidental music for dance interludes and an element of dialogue was introduced.

In 1801 the writer of an article on the Fiando theater compared marionette dancers more than favorably to live ones, observing that they could perform caprioles and entrechats, execute steps in harmony and move their arms and bodies with speed and grace. He also commented on a "grotesco" (a character or comic dancer) who could leap higher and open his legs wider than the dancers of La Scala, without creating any worries about his safety. Perhaps anticipating Kleist's essay on the marionette, the writer also observed how much the marionette dancers defied gravity, as opposed to the more earth-bound human ones.[37]

When Stendhal visited the Fiano Theater in Rome in 1817 he was full of admiration for the ballet *The Enchanted Well*,[38] which was based on the *Thousand and One Nights*. He commented on the naturalness and grace of the dancers. Marionette ballet dancers fascinated visitors from Stendhal to Dickens. Auguste Jal, in his *De Paris à Naples*, after a visit to the Fiando in 1834, compared their Taglionis and Pierrots of wood to the main dancers of the opera in Naples, London and Paris, which he felt they even surpassed occasionally. He was impressed by the number of specific steps they could execute, and by the way in which a ballerina could re-enter for a bow with her hand on her heart. Enrico Cecchetti (1850–1928), the celebrated ballet master for Diaghilev and later La Scala, who also trained Pavlova and Nijinsky, had a collection of some 200 marionettes which he used for demonstration when training his students in Saint Petersburg.[39]

Ballet dancers had a rather special design which allowed them to emulate the great exponents of the Romantic ballet. Like the Commedia masks, many had bodies in two pieces linked by strips of leather, a tube of fabric, or even interlocking staples, which gave flexibility. Ankle joints and freer-moving hip joints allowed for a greater range of physical movement that might itself be comic or grotesque. Classical ballet positions are largely designed for frontal viewing, with a major emphasis on movements and attitudes parallel to the footlights. Many marionette dancers had a hip joint that articulated laterally rather than from front to back. Strings drawing the foot against the calf were used for battus and fouettés, and the insertion of a clock-spring into the knee joint allowed for a realistic quivering movement. Surviving dancers in the Colla and Lupi collections have a rod to the back of the pelvis as the main support, and one to the head which is used to produce head movements and, played against the back rod, allows the body to take a surprising variety of attitudes, as well as helping leaps and arabesques. The celebrated ballerina of the Teatro dei Piccoli has no rods. Two strings attached to her hips, with a separate control bar, give an amazing fluttering movement to her point work. The arms are also provided with their own control bars with three strings. Each bar has a separate manipulator which creates a particularly entrancing fluidity for a performance of Saint Saëns's "Dying Swan." This is a case where the Holden "trick" of more than one manipulator for a figure produces a stunning effect.

Ballerina. Teatro dei Piccoli. Possibly inspired by Pavlova, the ballerina danced to the music of Camille Saint-Saens's "Dying Swan." A flexible body and additional arm strings ensure a fluid movement very different from the precise choreography of the classical marionette dancers. (Courtesy Teatro Stabile Friuli-Venezia Giulia.)

The repertoire of the Fiano included a number of "balli." Some had classical subjects similar to those of the bigger theaters: *Castor and Pollux, Diana and Endymion, Dido Abandoned, Cupid and Psyche.*[40] Other popular titles were *Alonso and Cora* and *Don Giovanni; or The Stone Guest,* together with many comic ones with Arlecchino. The "balli" included speech and were similar to the pantomime with dialogue popular in France in the late eighteenth century. In 1829 the *Gazzetta teatrale* referred to them as "spoken and sung ballets."[41] By 1816 Cassandro was a central figure at the Fiano and in 1817 he appeared in at least 9 of the 19 "balli" performed that year. In 1826 he was the hapless "hero" of *The 99 Misfortunes of Cassandrino,* and in the 1830s he appeared in *Grand Ballet of Cassandro in the Kingdom of the Great Mogul.*[42]

The "ballo" was the standard afterpiece of the nineteenth-century marionette theater.

Rather like the pantomime in England, the spectacular "ballo" gradually developed into a main attraction and could often involve over a hundred figures. The Lupi company began to reduce the first part of the program to a short farce which changed more often than the "ballo" which eventually became the complete program. The Lupis staged *Aida* as a "ballo" in 1872, a few months after the opera's première in Cairo on December 24, 1871, but barely a month after that of La Scala.[43] When it opened at the San Martiniano Theater, none of the music was by Verdi — but the script carried a note expressing the hope that the music would arrive the following week. Once the music arrived, the triumphal march was used, but this was alongside music from Hervé's *Chilpéric* and Verdi's *Macbeth*. As the years went by more of Verdi's music was introduced, and in a recent revival, well-known parts of the opera accompanied the pantomimed action. Subtitled "The Invention of Gunpowder," the Lupi's *Aida*, described as a "tenebrous anti-historical chemical Egyptian action," introduces the "ballo" with a three-act farce in which Gerolamo is the mayor of a small town which has a new theater.[44] A down-at-heel traveling company is engaged by him to open the theater with a performance of *Aida*, the new triumph from Milan. He tells them to leave out the singing and concentrate on the dancing and spectacle and he falls for a transvestite Venetian ballerina (the only other character to use dialect). Once the casting has been done the "ballo" goes ahead. Parody might be anticipated, but the story is presented straight, except that a spectacular happy end is provided to satisfy Gerolamo. Aïda and Rhadames scrape saltpeter off the walls, manufacture gunpowder and blow their way out of their tomb in a grand finale reminiscent of what the mayor insists on calling "Solomon and the Philistines."

Luigi Manzotti's hugely successful *Ballo Excelsior*, with music by Romualdo Marenco, was first staged at La Scala in 1881, and subsequently in many of the opera houses of Europe. This visually and musically exciting show had a particular resonance in Italy because of the decline of the temporal power of the Church following unification. Clerical obscurantism was perceived as an obstacle to progress and *Excelsior* offered the possibility of attacking it without danger of reprisal. The main action was the battle of darkness against light. The Church represented darkness, while the genius of light and progress was symbolized by Volta's experiments and Edison's electric filament lamp. In Milan the Zane and Antonio Colla companies presented *Excelsior* in 1884 and Carlo Colla II did so the following year. In 1888 Antonio Colla brought *Excelsior* to London, where one reviewer admired the quality of manipulation, especially of the dancer, and found it "a very faithful and accurate imitation of the real thing," but a little dull.[45] At almost the same time the Prandi company visited London, and also performed *Excelsior*, but had a far warmer reception.

Variety Turns

The "ballo" was sometimes no more than a few variety turns at the end of a show or even a brief and usually bucolic dance to wind up a glove-puppet performance. Variety marionettes were designed to evoke amazement and delight by the acts performed and by the virtuosity of the puppeteer. Accounts of Italian marionette companies visiting England in the late eighteenth century emphasize specialty numbers with a simple pantomime action

The Fantocci Lirici of the Fratelli Salici in a variety show with a puppet orchestra. (Fratelli Salici "Varietà." Archival photograph. Courtesy Eugenio Monti Colla.)

or various tricks and transformations, and the Italian "fantoccini" that could be seen in the streets of London in the first part of the nineteenth century presented a reduced version of this sort of program. The Borromeo collection includes a group of producer puppets and trick figures, such as a sedan chair that opens up and disappears beneath the skirts of the lady who emerges from it, or a Pulcinella who can dismember to produce a number of little Pulcinelli. The vastly successful tours of Holden's in the 1880s combined with the rise of the music hall prompted Italian companies to develop variety numbers. The Lupis placed a music-hall stage (the Bijou) complete with puppet orchestra on the stage of the Teatro d'Angennes. This device may also have provided an opportunity to continue to use the rather smaller marionettes and scenery from the San Martiniano Theater which they had recently vacated.[46]

In the south of Italy by the early twentieth century, most showmen had a few all-string figures for specialty acts. Luigi Di Giovanni of Naples, with his Grande Compagnia Italiana dei Fantocci, switched to virtuoso variety marionette acts. Jones mentions a "ballo fantastico" performed one night after an episode of *Guido Santo* in Palermo.[47] This included a skillfully manipulated rope-dancer and the classic "Grand Turk" act, not very different from one shown by Carlo Perico in London in the 1770s:

It was done by a heavy Turk who danced cumbrously; presently his arms detached themselves and became transformed into devils who danced separately; then his legs followed their example; then his head descended from his trunk and, on reaching the stage, became transformed into a dancing wizard carrying a rod of magic and beating time to the music; then, while the body was dancing by itself, various devils came out of it followed by several serpents that floated among the devils; after which it developed a head, a neck, wings and a tail, so that it became transformed into a complete dragon, and the wizard mounted upon its back and rode about wizarding all the other creatures. Altogether the original Turk became transformed into sixteen different marionettes.

The Opera dei Pupi

The title "opera dei pupi" was a jovial reference to the idea of "big" theater being performed by puppets. It often had the grandiose quality of opera seria, but singing was not a feature of this type of entertainment, although music was. A violin was probably the commonest instrument in use. A horn (often a conch shell) provided the sound of Orlando's horn as a special effect. When Michele Immesi opened his teatrino in 1890 he had a small orchestra consisting of a violin, a guitar and a double bass, though in his later years these were abandoned for gramophone records.[48] In the larger theaters of Catania a small orchestra was not uncommon. In western Sicily the most familiar instrument was the "pianino," a small cylinder piano. Unlike the barrel-organ, the cylinder piano was a box containing strings that were hit by little hammers set in motion by the metal projections on the surface of a cylinder. Many were constructed by Fasoni of Naples and according to tradition Alberto Canino initially earned his living with such an instrument, later using it for interval music in puppet shows. A pianino could be set up with about a dozen tunes. The musician was often a young member of the puppeteer's family, and much depended upon the speed at which the pianino handle was turned. Many of the tunes were airs from popular operas and these filled gaps between the scenes, underlined speeches or actions and generally set the mood.[49]

In battle scenes the puparo put on a clog, or "zoccolo," that produced a

Mechanical cylinder piano or "pianino." This often replaced other musical instruments and could be played by a younger member of the family. (Courtesy Associazione Figli d'Arte Cuticchio.)

Battle music (violin) for the opera dei pupi. Published by G. Pitrè in 1889. (From Giuseppe Pitrè, *Usi e costumi credenze e pregiudizi del popolo siciliano*, vol 1. Courtesy the Pitrè family and Edizioni Brancato.)

loud noise when stamped on the ground and created a rhythm to accompany the fight. A drum added to the excitement. Immesi used a "zinzenné," a length of wire with a collection of pieces of metal threaded onto it that rattled when shaken. The clattering of the swords of the puppets, as they met each other or banged shields or armor, also gave a strong rhythmic structure to these scenes.

The battles were to the opera dei pupi what the ballet interludes were to other marionette theaters. Carefully choreographed with an emphasis on rhythm, they started with a

Combat between Orlando and Rinaldo (demonstration). Jealousy over Angelica is the cause of this frequently performed fight whose choreography displays the skill of the puparos. (Francesco Sclafani [1911–1991]. Archival photograph. Courtesy Museo Internazionale delle Marionette Antonio Pasqualino.)

series of brief encounters between a major figure on one side and a series of ordinary soldiers on the opposing (Saracen) one. The puppets advanced towards each other and retreated a few times. Then the unfortunate common soldier was killed and the control rod dropped to the ground. The combats between armed knights were of a highly formalized nature, and it is here that the element of choreography becomes most evident. The Sicilian pupo stands firmly on the ground in a position dictated by its own weight and the control rod serves to change attitude. This means that the strength of the puparo's arm is directly behind every movement and lends a precision to each step that, in turn, has its own percussive effect.

Rhythm and repetition are the two key elements. The prelude to a combat is often the lowering of the visor, the drawing of a sword and the taking up of opposing positions. A knight may also rub or tap his sword against his leg to show anger or impatience and give a further audio clue that conflict is about to happen. Initially the characters keep their distance. The sword tips engage to a relatively slow rhythm and the puppets themselves remain in one spot, swiveling slightly on one leg while the other swings. As the rhythm increases they take up positions one slightly upstage of the other, turning their bodies into and away from the fight. A strongly marked scissors movement of the legs is used to punctuate the rhythm.[50] The percussive effect of metal striking metal and the crashing of the performers' clogs become more evident; the pianino starts to play faster. The ta ta ta ta tá rhythm makes way for a movement that brings the two characters together, their bodies literally clashing, and this is repeated half a dozen times. Any semblance of realism is now abandoned. Their feet leave the ground and they are swung towards each other. Sometimes this concludes with a great clinch and one of the characters is killed. On other occasions the protagonists pull back and repeat the sparring of earlier at an accelerated rhythm before a final encounter, which generally leaves one of them on the ground. Battle scenes were carefully watched and appreciated by audiences, and the skill of the puppeteers was judged by their execution.

A choreography making use of percussive effects can also be observed on the glove-puppet stage. The direct control of the glove-puppet, like the pupo, makes for a similar precision of movement. Pulcinella's or Gioppino's stick bangs the playboard, the side of the stage, or an opponent's wooden head in a particularly rhythmic way that is woven into the dialogue, creating a pattern of articulated sound and percussion. This is often reinforced by the head of the figure banging either the side of the stage or the playboard. Here too the choreography of a fight is a measure of the performer's skill.[51]

Mimmo Cuttichio's teatrino with about 100 seats is only yards from the colossal Teatro Massimo of Palermo. In the last years of the twentieth century he began to explore the idea of the pupi presenting opera. His *Don Giovanni all'opera dei pupi* (2003) brought the performance outside his own teatrino to larger spaces and was not a straightforward opera dei pupi production. It took the Da Ponte–Mozart opera and invited the audience to perceive it through the eyes of Leporello, transformed into a Palermitan street boy and operated by a visible puppeteer. Behind him was a pupi stage where scenes from Mozart's opera, performed to a Deutschegramophon recording, were placed as a background to the lively action of Leporello.[52] Spectators were visually reminded that the pupi are rod marionettes, and as such are not necessarily very different from the rod marionettes that have performed opera in other parts of Italy. At the same time most audience members would have carried with them some idea of the context of the opera dei pupi and the associations of the pupi with the heroic cycles. They would also have been familiar with *Don Giovanni* and there was therefore an element of post-modern quotation in the presentation of it in this manner.

Cuticchio continued exploration of opera when he used the pupi to present a new and specially commissioned work, Salvatore Sciarrino's *Terrible and Horrifying Story of the Prince of Venosa*, which concerns the cruelty with which this late Renaissance musician prince put his adulterous wife to death. This is a modern opera, but in violence and tone is not very different from what audiences of the pupi theaters might expect and has many thematic similarities to such pieces as the *Baronessa di Carini*.

Where Cuticchio's work really differs in emphasis from that of the Carlo Colla e Figli company is that the Colla's aim is fairly close to the tradition of miniaturized opera, whereas his is to explore the very nature of opera through the pupi.

The Box of Illusions

Theater often requires the suspension of the critical faculty so that the identity of the human actor may be subsumed by the stage character. The puppet being made of wood, paint, paper and fabric fits more easily into the artificial environment of the theater of which it is already a part. Some marionettes look so human that we may be deceived into thinking them such, and some showmen have done their utmost to give them movements evoking the human. Glove-puppets, despite their anatomically incorrect bodies, can also persuade us of their reality. In the final issue it is less the physical appearance of the figure than the energy that the performer transmits via voice and movement that creates a sense of reality and leads the spectators into perceiving it as alive.

A puppet stage is a structure designed to conceal the performer and allow for focus on the figures. The simplest form is a screen. The medieval *Roman d'Alexandre* drawing shows a glove-puppet stage, turreted to look like a castle, with the puppets behind the battlements. The "simulated castle of cloth behind which the performer hides" evoked by Ottonelli is very similar.[53] The word "castello" for a glove-puppet stage has survived today in both French (castelet) and Italian and evokes the idea of a vertical structure with the puppets looking over the "ramparts."

The classic glove-puppet stage consists of four uprights enclosed in cloth with a square opening at head height. At the base of this opening is a shelf or "play board" behind which the puppets appear. This serves as a "floor" on which properties can be placed. For greater immediacy of contact and because of sightlines, glove-puppets generally perform close to the front of the stage. Below are two vertical slits or holes covered by a flap of cloth. These allow puppets to appear outside the main frame of the opening and are also used by the performer to poke his head out to address the audience or exchange dialogue with a puppet. Many shows depend on a single operator, playing all the parts and speaking for all the characters. To present complete plays usually required a larger booth to accommodate scenery, additional figures and manipulators. Antonio Sarzi's booth, as described by his son Francesco, consisted of four uprights measuring 2.5 meters. These were locked together by crosspieces. The stage was equipped with curtains and three sets of wings, the narrowest in the front and the widest at the back. Back scenes were pulled up and down with lines and the lighting was mounted on two bars across the top of the frame. All around the inside were hooks on which the puppets could be hung. At about waist-height below the play board was a bar on which the puppets used in the show were hung upside down.[54] Aldo Rizzoli (1885–1968) of Bologna had a stage opening about three meters wide, and could have up to ten characters on the stage at once.[55] When such a stage was set up in a hall or theater, it was common practice to extend the front laterally with panels to fill space and focus attention in on the action.

Ottonelli does not describe the rather grander marionette stages that came into existence in the seventeenth century and adapted themselves to the scenic wonders of the baroque stage, but he has left a valuable description of a marionette stage used for street

Nino Insanguine and two of his sons. Catanian manner of operation. Archival photograph. (Courtesy Museo Internazionale delle Marionette Antonio Pasqualino.)

performances. He speaks of a stage about the height of a man's chest, with an opening two palms high (about 45 cms), a stage of the same depth, and a width of two "braccia" (something between 1.5 and 2 meters). Such a stage implies small puppets, probably around 30 centimeters high.[56] Ottonelli also mentions a multitude of little lights, above and below, an indication of evening performances, and a wire mesh screen in front.[57]

The classic marionette stage is a scaled-down version of the actors' theater modified to allow for the operation of figures. Most commonly the operator stands behind the back-cloth on a raised area known as a bridge. This includes a bar on which the arm can be supported or the puppeteer can lean and varies in height. By the nineteenth century the larger marionette theaters had developed bridges that were about six feet above the stage floor. With the use of longer rods and strings this allowed for more elaborate staging. Emanuele Macri, in Acireale, introduced such a bridge for his pupi, as did the Puzzo brothers at their Eden theater in Siracusa in the 1920s. In Catania the bridge behind the backcloth was known as "'u scannapoggiu." Most commonly the bridge is about three feet above the stage floor and supports the scenery. Sometimes figures can be worked from both sides of it, thus providing a much greater usable stage depth. This happened in Naples, where it was called the "scanno."[58] When Nino Gambarutti and Argentina Burzio staged a battle scene in *Guerrino Meschino* they used the space behind the bridge for combats on horseback while the battle between the foot-soldiers continued in front.[59]

The positioning of the puppets on the stage depends on how far the operators can reach from the bridge. A small company might use only the back part of the stage, with all the action occurring between the backcloth and the back set of wings even when a sense of perspective was given by using further sets of wings in front. Big companies used an additional bridge placed directly behind the proscenium arch and the operators stood with their backs to the audience. This allowed marionettes to occupy the downstage area. The big marionette companies created an extra effect of perspective by using smaller figures to cross the back of the stage, larger ones for the middle-distance and full-size ones for foreground.[60] In such scenes there might occasionally be a third bridge behind the more distant back scene.

In Palermo and western Sicily there is no bridge. The operators stand directly on the stage floor behind each set of wings and the width of the stage is determined by their ability to move a puppet across to an operator on the opposite side. This is a practical solution to the spatial limitations of tiny teatrini with little width or headroom, and may have been a more widespread practice in the past.[61] Gaspare Canino's theater in Alcamo had a stagefront 4 meters wide and 2.4 meters high. His stage was 2.3 meters wide and 3.5 meters deep. Thirty centimeters behind the opening was a false proscenium, which scaled down the stage width. Between this and the first set of wings was a space of 28 centimeters and between this and the second wing, and between the second wing and the backcloth were spaces of 80 centimeters where operators stood. This was a fairly standard arrangement, though Canino could use a depth of up to six wings if required.[62] In the chivalric cycles, one of the most celebrated and technically difficult episodes is the battle of three against three on the island of Lampedusa, which involves three pairs of figures executing single combats at different levels of the depth of the stage and requiring six operators.

The Scenic Stage

The European stage from the sixteenth to the nineteenth centuries was obsessed with perspective and the idea of creating three-dimensional space while painting on flat surfaces. The idea of combining opera with moving figures may derive from the scenographic experiments of Sebastiano Serlio, who advocated flat figures at the back of his stage to scale down

Enzo Mancuso operating from the wings in the Palermitan manner. Nino Mancuso behind. (Courtesy Museo Internazionale delle Marionette Antonio Pasqualino. Photograph Rosario Perricone.)

size from the human actor and to avoid dwarfing the scenery.[63] He suggested that when the actors were absent, pasteboard figures of a size proportionate to the architectural elements represented by the scenery might be pushed across the stage on laths running in grooves, rather like a precursor of the paper theaters popular in the nineteenth century. Baroque opera was primarily a visual entertainment supported by music, singing and dancing. It was a highly artificial genre, and its flying machines, apparitions and transformations all belong to the ideal world of the marionette.[64] Private theaters provided an opportunity for the display of spectacular staging on a relatively small scale, and this was significant in terms of cost, as well as in terms of the space in which the performance might be given. Lighting effects that might have been difficult on a large stage were far more manageable on a small stage whose restricted space allowed for the throw of the comparatively weak lighting of oil wicks and candles.

Scipione Maffei said of Cardinal Ottoboni's theater that "there were never seen more admirable and more ingenious scenery, perspectives and stage effects in such a small space."[65] The considerable height of the proscenium opening, in the region of 30 palms (6 meters), suggests that the cardinal's "popazzi" were not marionettes but figures moving in grooves, like those of Acciajoli or the Pygmées. In 1712, the Chevalier Chappe, in a letter to the Marquis de Torcy, described a performance of *Ciro* in Ottoboni's theater and commented that "the actors have the finest voices in Italy."[66] By "actors" he meant the singers. He is not referring to the figures, whose operators were probably members of the cardinal's staff (as in the 1690s). A late seventeenth-century Piedmontese showman, Francesco Mazzetti, boasted that his theater had the richest of figures and the best of performers.[67] He uses the word "recitanti" for the latter, making quite clear that they were speakers or singers. He comments on the richness of the figures, but the operators were mere mechanics and not seen as worth mentioning.

Scenic Elements

Within the physical frame of the proscenium arch, scenery creates a picture brought to life by the presence of the puppet. It may produce a complete environment and give an illusion of space or simply be a conventionalized shorthand indication of the place of the action. In the latter case its value is more symbolic than realistic. In the sixteenth or seventeenth century the average street glove-puppet stage probably had only the most rudimentary scenery. Garzoni speaks of a troupe of Commedia players who simply set up their platform and "a scene sketched in charcoal without the slightest degree of taste."[68] Where scenery was used at all on the glove-puppet stage, it was almost certainly roughly delineated in this way. Finardi's *Buovo d'Antona*, staged at the Montanara Theater, Rome, required only two backcloths for the two acts of part 11, and these alternate between a room in a castle and a landscape. Part 1 of his *Orlando furioso* requires four different landscapes to indicate shifts in place and time. The only specific detail is that one includes the river in which Ferraù searches for his helmet.

The classical puppet theaters used the same terminology as the live theater for scenic elements. Some limited themselves to a back scene, known as the "fondale," which was either painted on cloth or on paper reinforced at the folds with strips of cloth.

On the marionette stage the "fondale" sometimes had cutout elements (door, window, arch), behind which a smaller element of scenery, the "fondino," would be placed to complete the scene. A special effect was a fondale consisting of two layers of cloth, one of which had elements cut away to let light through. Known as a "transparente," this could be back-lit for night scenes, volcanic eruptions and conflagrations.[69] The earliest known surviving transparente is one used by the Lupi company at the San Martiniano Theater in the 1840s in a scene of the Temple of Neptune by Giuseppe Morgari (1788–1847).[70]

"Fondali" were commonly attached to a batten of wood on the top and bottom and hung one in front of the other. Sometimes they were removed manually, but the preferred method of scene-changing by the nineteenth century was a system with a roller, which can still be observed with the Sicilian pupi and on the Lupi stage. Later a few companies with permanent theaters such as Lupi or Colla introduced a flying system. When the Lupi company moved from the San Martiniano Theater to the bigger Teatro d'Angennes they had to add pieces to a number of their cloths. Around 1900 the Carlo Colla company had to do the same. Scenes for *Around the World in 80 Days* were enlarged from 3.87 meters to a standard 5.7 meters and the height increased from 1.83 to 2 meters.

The average pupi performance required about a dozen scene changes which contributed to the rhythm of the action, and in some cases change of location indicated passing to events happening simultaneously. As in the actors' theater scenery was frequently announced in the publicity. A few glove-puppet companies emulated the marionette theaters in this. Rossi at the end of the eighteenth century and Peppino Sarina in the twentieth both emphasized the scenic importance of their shows. Where a glove-puppet performance was a three-act farce, a change of scene for each act usually sufficed.

The fondale was framed by borders ("soffitti") and two or three pairs of wings ("quinte"). These masked the offstage area, gave a sense of perspective and scaled down the scene to the proportions of the puppets. On the pupi stage and many glove-puppet ones the emphasis was on a back scene while wings and borders often remained unchanged. Some were fixed or even architectural elements, especially the first set, which often took the form of a false proscenium and might be decorated with large formalized vases of flowers or swags of drapery.

Wings and borders were often made in a single piece that could be set or removed in a single maneuver. Another popular framing device was a cut cloth, known as a "principale." This was usually placed near the back of the stage. With one or more openings onto a back scene sometimes placed behind the bridge, it allowed for a dwindling perspective that evoked a huge sense of distance. The Colla and Lupi companies frequently used a series of "principali" to striking visual effect. In an age of oil and candle lighting the "principale" provided an opportunity for more spectacular lighting effects and really came into its own in nineteenth century stage design when a strong foreground contrasted with the apparently limitless spaces evoked by the more lightly painted fondale beyond.

The transparent gauze was a popular element of Romantic staging that also transferred to the marionette stage. When the Carlo Colla company staged *La serenata di Pierrot* in 1900, they had an attractive undersea scene made up of a front gauze, three cut cloths and a backdrop.

Most marionette companies possessed a number of free-standing scenic elements in the form of flat cutouts in pasteboard with trompe l'oeil painting. The most common were the "rompimento" (a ground-row, an urn or a kiosk), the "terrazzino" (a more substantial ground-row, such as a town wall) and the "spezzato" (a rock, tree or architectural element that could serve as a wing, but was not usually the full height of the stage). For the Grasso presentation of the spectacular entry of Christ into Jerusalem at the Sicilia theater in Catania in the early 1900s the bridge and backcloth were removed to reveal a set tableau of cutout pieces with the figure of Christ on the ass surrounded by apostles carrying palms.[71]

The "cartonaggi" were similar to cutout pieces of scenery and were often used to provide set groups of figures or additional individual ones. Sanquirico designed a number for the Borromeo theater; the Puglisi family in Sortino made extensive use of the technique for extra figures; the Mucchettis of Adro employed them in *The Flood* for the Ark and numerous animals, and in their production of *I promessi sposi* (1870) had a variety of processions that were later mounted on a moving band that made them pass across the back of the stage.[72] Giordano Ferrari used painted card silhouettes for crowd scenes on the glove-puppet stage.

In the eighteenth and nineteenth centuries the theatrical terms "scena lunga" and "scena corta" occur in some marionette scripts (Filippo Juvarra also used them in his notebooks). The scena lunga was a spectacular scene that used the depth of the stage and involved a larger number of characters. The scena corta was a shallow scene, often no more than a painted cloth without wings placed relatively well downstage, and was used for more intimate scenes. It also functioned as a carpenter's scene, allowing a more complex one to be prepared behind. The practice of alternating between a scena lunga and a scena corta was sometimes used on the glove-puppet stage too.

"Cartonaggio" used by Muchetti company. Flat pasteboard group of figures. This mode of creating a "crowd" scene was common to many puppet companies. (Muchetti company. Courtesy Bruno Poieri.)

Front curtain painted by Peppino Sarina with an allegorical representation of the different genres presented. (Courtesy Archivio dell'Associazione Peppino Sarina di Tortona [Al].)

The classic guaratella stage is seldom provided with any sort of front curtain, but otherwise puppet theaters employed a variety of curtains and drops. The "sipario," or front curtain, rose to signal the start of the show and remained raised until the end. This was painted with an allegorical scene or one evoking the repertoire of the theater.[73] Behind the sipario was the "siparietto," whose function was that of an act drop. It was used only to punctuate the ends of acts and not usually to hide a scene change, which was done in full view of the audience. Like the sipario, it was painted, sometimes with a subject specific to the production. With the Sicilian pupi the siparietto also provided a background for a short comic interlude or for the "perdomani's" announcement of the show for the next day.[74] The "comodino" was a painted drop lowered to create a fixed tableau illustrating a key moment of the show. This could have the effect of a cinematic long shot. It often had a crowd of people painted on it and was a rapid way of achieving a spectacular effect. In the Colla revival of *I promessi sposi* in 1927 the lazar-house scene of the denouement was hidden by the dropping of a cloth that depicted the lovers being received at the door of the church by Don Abbondio. This then rose for a tableau of the wedding itself. The Razzetti-Rame script for *The Battle of Solferino* requires a "view of Solferino" which depicts the battle. Soldiers appear in the foreground and the atmosphere is heightened with flashes and the sound of guns. Antonio Colla employed the comodino for an allegorical representation of the "Cinque Giornate" (during the revolution of 1848 in Milan) and for the entrance to Milan of Napoleon III and Vittorio Emanuele II. In the opera dei pupi a comodino showing God surrounded by angels could be dropped for the apotheosis of a good character.

Act drop ("siparietto") painted by Pina Patti Cuticchio depicting the rescue of Angelica by Ruggiero on the hippogriff. In front are Virticchiu (double expression) and 'Nofriu in a prologue. (Courtesy Associazione Figli d'Arte Cuticchio.)

Stock Scenery

The classical puppet theater used stock scenery deriving from the idealized settings of the Renaissance which were classified as type scenes to be used as appropriate and not thought of as realistic or specific environments. The Serlian vocabulary of tragic, comic and pastoral by the eighteenth century had been amplified to include palaces, forests, rocky caves, rustic interiors, prisons, oriental scenes, etc., which could be employed according to the general requirements of any piece. The great concern of the scenic artists was the use of paint to create a sense of space, with vistas and perspectives. The nineteenth century was the golden age of scene painting, but the idea of scenery being designed exclusively for a single production did not evolve until the twentieth. The principle of stock scenery still survives with the opera dei pupi. In episode after episode it is possible to see combinations of Carlo Magno's palace, Christian and Saracen camps, forest scenes, open landscapes, walls of towns (for battles), beautiful gardens, seaside scenes, bedchambers (for murders and dreams), rocky caves (for scenes with devils, magic or bandits) and prisons.[75] On the glove-puppet stage a similar repertoire of stock scenes existed, with a particular fondness for cemeteries, hell scenes and rustic interiors.

Local topographical scenes were hugely popular. Gioppino regularly appeared in front of the Piazza Vecchia in Bergamo. St. Mark's square was de rigueur for a Venetian company, as was the bay of Naples and Vesuvius for a Neapolitan one. Spectacular views of

Cave. Glove-puppet backcloth used by Arturo Marziali, Bergamo. One of the stock scenes for sorcerers, brigands and devils. (On loan to the Fondazione Bergamo nella Storia — Museo Storico di Bergamo. Courtesy the Scuri family, Bergamo. Published in Pino Capellini, *Baracca e burattini* [Bergamo: Grafica Gutemberg Gorle Editrice, 1977 and 1997]. Photograph Domenico Lucchetti. Courtesy Archivio Privato Famiglia Domenico Lucchetti.)

Turin still subsist on Lupi backcloths.[76] A review of a Zane production at the Fiando in 1882 commented on the growing tendency of the big marionette companies to present productions reflecting the big theaters.[77] A major new production might involve the painting of some new scenes but stock scenery regularly turned up also. Adaptations of Jules Verne novels added to the scenic vocabulary with under-sea environments, a trip to the moon and a variety of novel geographic locations. The more ambitious companies were in touch with the latest developments in the art of scene painting and leapt on the predominant mode of realism in the spectacular theater. A fascination with low life led to naturalistic presentations of the life of the under-classes in adaptations of Emile Zola's *Assommoir* (The Dram Shop) or Xavier de Montépin's *The Bread-Peddler*. The Lupi production of the former was apparently almost as naturalistic as the live one.

Generally the puppet stage, like the ballet one, remained uncluttered by furniture, most of which was simply painted on the scenery. Furniture remained purely functional. A bed was used for dying, being murdered, or simply having a dream or vision, and chairs, tables and so on were also only on stage if the action demanded. The Lupi company was exceptional for the emphasis it placed on the furnishing of the stage and in this it followed the lead of the domestic drama of the actors' theaters.

Scene Painters and the Puppet Stage

Scene painting for the puppet stage ranges from work by the finest of artists and scene painters to folk art. The Bibiena family revolutionized stage design at the end of the seventeenth century. Ferdinando (1657–1743) broke with the idea of a central vanishing point and introduced that of the "per angolo" perspective, where the painting on the backcloth led the eye diagonally towards a corner of the stage and beyond, an effect heightened by the arrangement of the wings, which were no longer always arranged in symmetrical pairs. The vanishing point was no longer within a potential line of vision and the spectator was left with a feeling of looking at a part of a scene that continued offstage, rather than one that was artificially assembled according to the laws of perspective. By increasing the scale of the foreground elements in relation to both the performer and the spectator it was possible to suggest that there was an immense scene extending well beyond the frame of the proscenium arch and that what was visible was only a small part of the "reality" represented. The audience might see only the lower part of a huge column that continued out of sight and the sense of space was further enhanced by the visual trick of raising the horizon line.

There no evidence of direct involvement of the Bibiena family with design for the marionette stage, apart from a tantalizing reference to scenery for an Italian marionette theater brought to London in 1780 as having been painted by Antonio Bibiena, who is best known as architect of the Teatro Comunale of Bologna and the Teatro Scientifico of Mantua.[78] A marionette stage, now in the Davia Bargellini museum in Bologna, also shows clear links to the Bibiena sphere of influence.[79] Five backcloths depict a magnificent palace, the courtyard of a palace, a garden, a hall and a pavilion, each with two sets of wings.[80]

In his designs for Ottoboni's "popazzi" Filippo Juvarra moved away from the symmetry of baroque scene design and created unexpected vistas with "per angolo" perspective. The architectural concepts he invented became more and more fantastic, creating a self-contained stage world that was a foretaste of the buildings he would later design for the Savoy family in Turin. In practice the settings are far too complicated to be imitated by a working marionette theater, but could be used for one with figures moving in grooves.[81] The printed libretti of three of the works performed in the Ottoboni theater, *Costantino Pio*, *Teodosio il Giovane* and *Ciro*, were accompanied by engravings which can be compared with Juvarra's original pen and wash drawings.[82] Juvarra's designs include a camp, a port with ships, numerous architectural scenes described as cabinets or courts, public squares with monuments, gardens, monumental staircases, royal apartments, woods, temples, views of palaces, rustic scenes, prisons and even a landscape with a bridge that seems to prefigure a favorite pre–Romantic image. He also anticipates Romanticism in his use of chiaroscuro painting to suggesting light falling from one side of the stage.

A collection of scenery similar to that in the Davia Bargellini museum is to be found in the diocesan museum of Jesi (Marche). This dates from the end of the eighteenth century and the start of the nineteenth and is thought to have been painted by Lorenzo Daretti (1724–1809) or his son Scipione (1756–1792).[83] Lorenzo Daretti studied in Bologna under the Bibienas and this scenery, with its diagonal perspectives and combinations of columns, arches and other architectural elements, shows their influence. It is simplified into a combination of backcloths, cut cloths and wings suitable for a marionette stage and is a masterly example of trompe l'oeil painting creating a huge sense of space and depth and making full use of chiaroscuro. The Jesi scenery may have been used for performances in the convent of St. Anna, which was noted for its concerts. Marionettes would have allowed the pupils to give theatrical performances while remaining unseen themselves. The backcloths

are 1.2 meters high and 1.68 meters wide, as compared to 82 centimeters by 1.72 meters of the Davia Bargellini ones. The slightly higher backcloths, combined with considerably lower wings (of which there are often three sets), suggest that the manipulation was from the sides, as in Palermo.

The Romantics emphasized local color and historical and social detail. The play of light and shadow became a major factor in scene painting, which now stretched to the limit the depiction of three-dimensional space on a flat surface. This was the great age of the backcloth. A sense of perspective was achieved less by a series of wings than by a progression from a relatively dark and strongly painted foreground to an almost evanescent distance, which made it harder for the eye to focus on a vanishing point. The vistas and perspective tricks of the Bibienas made way for wide expanses extending beyond the stage picture and the main function of the wings was to mask the extremities of the backcloth.

The scenery of the Rissone collection has been heavily restored, but its 30 backcloths, 76 wings and 8 cut cloths give a remarkable impression of the working material of a traveling puppet theater in the first half of the nineteenth century. The backdrops, painted on both sides in tempera on thick paper mounted on cloth, originally measured 1.17 meters high by 1.7 meters wide, but later had an extra 20 centimeters added at each side to fit a larger stage.[84] A few backcloths have echoes of the Bibiena style and a number retain the diagonal perspective. The neo-classicism of Alessandro Sanquirico of La Scala is another obvious point of reference.[85] Shadow and perspective are not always very skillfully handled and this is a useful indication of the way in which puppet companies might employ a lesser artist to imitate what was happening in the big theaters. The landscapes framed by a darker cut cloth have a distinct early Romantic flavor, as do the wilder scenes of caverns and precipices, while the contemporary rage for the medieval is expressed in gothic palaces. There are excellent rustic interiors with a degree of realistic detail and one domestic interior evokes an ordinary bourgeois salon of the earlier nineteenth century.

No scenery or designs survive for the Fiano Theater, but descriptions in some of the scripts indicate a fully equipped marionette stage.[86] The first act of *Bluebeard*, "a spectacular, tragic and melodramatic action" (1833–1834), starts in a wooded landscape outside the palace of Adramalech (Bluebeard) and ends in the best baroque tradition as the stage is covered by a thick cloud, accompanied by thunder and lightning. This *scena corta* is followed by an elaborate throne room and a ballet interlude. "Long" and "short" scenes alternate up to a spectacular battle in the last act. This starts in the open countryside and after the heroine Zulima stabs the tyrant, his palace, seen in the distance, is set on fire. The countryside is transformed into a grand gallery for a wedding scene, complete with ballet entries and unspecified "tableaux." Scenery has a direct role in the action and includes a number of practicable elements such as steps, doors that open and even a sign that lights up and tells Zulima to avenge the innocent blood of her cousin (a previous wife).

Viale Ferrero published a volume on a collection of scenery now in Turin's Palazzo Madama. This is the work of a number of scene painters active at the Teatro Regio and was

Opposite: **Filippo Juvarra, design for courtyard. Scene 5 from *Costantino Pio*. Pen and wash. Rome, Teatro Ottoboni, 1710. (Filippo Juvarra, design for courtyard. Turin, Biblioteca Nazionale/Ris. 59, 4 f. 109 [2]. Courtesy Ministero per i Beni e le Attività Culturali, Biblioteca Nazionale Universitaria di Torino. Photograph Roberto Parodi and Roberta Bueno.)**

apparently for the Lupi's San Martiniano Theater of the 1840s. All the backdrops are painted in tempera on cloth. They measure 1.6 by 2.3 meters, and some are accompanied by cut cloths as well. Giovanni Venere, who was part of the team of Luigi Vacca and Fabrizio Sevesti at the Regio in 1825, was working for the San Martiniano together with Giuseppe Morgari in 1840. Venere's scenes include a pavilion, a medieval arcaded porch with a view of a garden, probably used for *Il Templario* (the Lupi version of Scott's *Ivanhoe*), a vaguely Roman palace, and an Egyptian palace, perhaps for *Nuovo Moisè in Egitto* and *Cesare in Egitto*. Giuseppe Bertoja (1808–1873) painted a baroque hall for a ballet of the *Siege of Leiden*, which had been staged at the Teatro Regio of Turin in 1844. He later developed this for his act 1 setting for Verdi's *La traviata* at Venice's La Fenice in 1853.[87] All these scenes evoke the spectacular productions of the Teatro Regio, but the practical arrangement was simplified for the marionette stage, often with an extensive use of the cut cloth. Marionette scenery was conditioned by the practical requirements of the medium and the aim was to create or approximate the visual effects of the live theater, but not to be a scale model of it.

The Borromeo family with their private marionette theaters employed the best scene painters of the day. In 1823 Alessandro Sanquirico re-created for the Borromeo marionettes a piece based on Vigano's ballet *The Walnut Tree of Benevento*. He also painted some scenery for Carlo Gozzi' s *Blue Monster*. His great work for the Borromeo family was his decoration of the little theater of the Isola Bella in 1828 for a visit of the king and queen. In 1831 he converted it into a more permanent marionette theater, prolonging the neo-classical architecture of the auditorium and scaling it down with two further false proscenia painted in perspective with architectural motifs and swags of drapery. The stage had four sets of wings and a back scene, with a potential discovery space beyond.[88] In 1830 Sanquirico painted a set of stock scenes for the Borromeo's Milan theater — a garden, a study, a room with a bed alcove and the appropriate side wings and borders. He also provided a curtain with silver stars. Carlo Fontana, who worked at both Turin's Teatro Regio and La Scala, carried out work for the Borromeo theaters between 1833 and 1842.[89] He provided a number of scenes for the Lupi theater also. Sanquirico looked back to neo-classicism and idealized settings, but Fontana represented a more full-blooded Romanticism with a growing touch of naturalism.

Throughout the nineteenth century the scenery and spectacular effects were the great attractions of the marionette theater. When Lupi and Franco first presented Vigano's *The Vestal* in 1828, they boasted that they had complicated machinery and scenery similar to that painted by Sanquirico for the original production at La Scala in 1818. When the Fiando Theater staged *The Burning of Saronno*, also in 1828, the scenic effects had audiences returning again and again.[90] In January 1841 the traveling marionette showman Michele Bergante announced in the *Gazzetta Piemontese* that his show was decorated with a quantity of scenery by famous theater scene painters.[91] A bill for 1880 for the Reccardini company's *Aida* indicates the scenery as having been painted by the scene painter of the Teatro Comunale of Trieste.

By the 1880s scenery for the Collas was being produced by Faggiani of Turin and the painter Leone Mens. In 1885 Mens was one of a group of painters who designed *Excelsior* for Carlo Colla II and placed modern scientific life firmly on the marionette stage with trams, bicycles and steamers. For *The Three Hunchbacks of Damascus* some scenes originally painted by Mens were touched up by Lualdi, who also contributed some new scenes. Lualdi and

Botazzi painted the Colla scenery between 1911 and 1935. When *Guerrin Meschino* was revived at the Gerolamo, the scenery was a mixture of old Mens ones touched up, and new ones by Lualdi, Botazzi, and Gotti. They included the Byzantine court, a forest, an Indian valley, a cavern, a beautiful garden with a series of swan fountains, the palace of Satan (requiring three cut cloths and a backdrop), a medieval pavilion (also used for *Robert the Devil*); Durazzo (two cut cloths and a ground-row of town walls in front of the backdrop), a Turkish courtyard and a backcloth with a transparency showing Alcina's hell, depicted as a monster with a catlike mouth held open by two hands with long nails.

For *Pietro Micca* (1906), the Colla company commissioned scenery from Bosso of Vercelli and considerable research in art galleries and libraries went into the preparation of the show. They were moving towards the idea of a completely designed production and also towards a more modern type of staging which involved wing pieces angled forward from the background, creating a form of closed set.[92] A novelty for the marionette stage was the use of a dividing wall running from the front to the back of the set. This device allowing characters to pass from one room to another was popular on the French boulevard stage. Carlo Colla and the designer Lualdi spent time in Lecco, where the action is set, in order to re-create the authentic atmosphere for *I promessi sposi*.[93] The costumes and some of the sets were based on the illustrations by Francesco Gonin for Manzoni's novel.

A well-equipped permanent theater was an advantage for the staging of spectacular productions. However, the traveling marionette companies of Piedmont showed a remarkable ability to use their resources to the full. Franco Gambarutti mentions a *Flood* with a procession of 100 animals making their way into the ark. The rains were produced by countless silver threads hanging from a bar that was moved from side to side. This was supplemented by ground rows of waves that gradually covered the floor, while the ark sailed across the stage. A rainbow then appeared and the ark settled on Mt. Ararat.[94] Some glove-puppet showmen displayed considerable ingenuity in their staging. The glove-puppet performer Luigi Nespoli devised an effect which allowed for a large amount of real water on the stage for performances of the *Flood* or *Moses Crossing the Red Sea*.[95]

The collections of the Lupi and Colla families show that scenery in the great nineteenth-century tradition of scene painting continued to be used and even augmented right through the twentieth century. As scenery in the live theater became more solid and practicable, marionette scenery, like that for ballet, clung to its wings, backcloths and trompe l'oeil painting. During the nineteenth century the glove-puppet repertoires developed in parallel with the marionette ones and painted scenery acquired a similar importance. Desiderio Fontana of Bologna (1879–1924) was noted for his gifts as a theatrical scene painter and was as much in demand for the glove-puppet stage as the marionette one. When a puppeteer in Bologna obtained a Fontana backcloth, it was treated as something special and brought out only on great occasions. Many puppet families had one or more members who were very competent scene painters. The Salicis painted most of their own scenery and Peppino Sarina was specially noted for his skills. Giuseppe Burzio was also known as a painter of backcloths and Gualberto Niemen commissioned scenes of a palace and a town square from him.[96] The majority of puppeteers reinterpreted the techniques of the professional scene painters according to their own needs. The stock sets of the big theaters were an initial source of inspiration, but were rapidly translated into an idiom that was within the scope of the puppet theater.

Puppet scenery sometimes needed replacing or refurbishing, and when children or siblings formed separate companies they too needed scenery. In such cases the model was the company's existing scenery and this led to the perpetuation of a self-referential style that flowered as a form of folk art. Found with numerous glove-puppet companies, its most important development is in Sicily, where decorative motifs associated with the paladins exploded not only on the stage and all over the cloths or panels that formed the stage front and painted publicity, but also onto the painted carts that could be seen everywhere until a few years ago. Today Pina Patti Cuticchio is noted as a scene painter for the family companies. She stands in a class of her own as a folk artist with an exuberant love of color. She could be classified as a "primitive" and has developed a personal style that is distinct from other painters of scenery and cartelli.

At the end of the nineteenth century Nicolo Rinaldi, known as Faraone, was noted as a painter of backdrops and cartelloni and this work was continued by his sons Francesco (Ciccio) and Concettino. The latter decorated the Canino front curtain with the biblical episode of the angel leading the Maccabaeus brothers in battle. Most of the backcloths used in the Canino theater were by Giovanni Di Cristina, who painted a wood, a lake, the castle of Montalbano, a countryside, a piazza, a garden, a domestic interior, city walls, the court of Carlo Magno with a series of columns and a pagan camp with tents in oriental style.[97] Other gifted scene painters for the pupi were Rosario Napoli and Ernesto Puzzo.

Modern design reached the marionette stage in Italy with the opening of Podrecca's Piccoli Theater. The shows of the Piccoli were synonymous with modernity, color, synthesis and good taste and many members of the artistic avant-garde were involved. The attention given to mise en scène was new for the Italian theater. Podrecca brought to the marionette stage the notion of a single artistic vision as preached by Gordon Craig. In 1911 Diaghilev's Ballets Russes had visited Rome and the stunning painterly vision of a Bakst or a Benois heralded the replacement of the traditional stage painter with a creative artist as

The Barber of Seville as staged by the Teatro dei Piccoli, 1920s. (From *Paris et les Piccoli*, 1929. Author's collection.)

designer. The Ballets Russes suggested to Vittorio Podrecca the idea of the puppet stage as a picture made of forms and colors and images and resembling an illustrated children's book, opening its doors on a fantastic universe. He found an ideal designer for the puppet theater in the illustrator Bruno Angoletta (1889–1954).[98] In the early years Angoletta completely redesigned a number of existing productions, giving each its own specific design rather than using stock scenery.[99] To the costumes of *The Barber of Seville*, Angoletta added simple but pictorially exciting backgrounds that created a mood and were a complete departure from the realistic style of nineteenth-century scene painting. The simplified painting, usually with little detail on the lower part of the background, gave greater value to the figures, and the use of striped wallpaper proved a useful device to reduce the visibility of the marionette strings. For Mozart's *Don Giovanni* he emphasized non-realistic and fantastic skies and large areas of color. With *Guerin at the Trees of the Sun* (1919) and his subsequent striking designs for *The Tempest* (1921) he reached his full maturity as a designer, making brilliant use of chromatic effects and abandoning any idea of creating a realistic environment.[100] The Piccoli Theater led to a shift in emphasis towards the visual that would become the hallmark of modern puppet theater.

CHAPTER 8

The Twentieth Century

Awareness of Tradition

The social, political and technological changes of the twentieth century all had a profound impact on activities that dated from a pre-industrial era. The context of puppet performance was affected by changes which occurred more rapidly in the north than the south. These were not immediately obvious and many puppeteers continued until economic pressures forced them to abandon the profession. In 1970 Maria Signorelli was one of the organizers of a highly significant exhibition and festival in Bologna which brought together classic puppet theater and modern work. Signorelli found that according to figures produced by the Society of Authors in 1958 there were about 100 puppet companies still active in Italy, but that by 1970 only about 20 companies were in a position to give regular shows.

The reassessment of popular culture in the second half of the century led to a re-examination of the cultural values of the classic puppet show. Puppeteers were gradually acquiring a consciousness of the tradition of which they were a part. In 1936, with the collaboration of Francesca Castellino, Italo Ferrari published his memoirs, *Baracca e burattini*. In the same year he was one of the first puppeteers to appear on Italian television. His son Giordano hoped in the 1930s to make Parma the capital of the art of glove-puppet theater and set about learning as much as he could about its history. Realizing the ephemeral nature of the profession, he decided to record everything he could and also to collect puppets, posters, photographs and any other documentation. The result was the creation of an enormous collection that finally opened as the Castello dei Burattini in 2004.[1] In Palermo, Antonio Pasqualino and his wife Marianne Vibaek rescued material from the last practicing performers of the Sicilian pupi and created a museum where regular performances allowed activity to continue through the darkest days of the late 1960s and 1970s. It would be a mistake to think that today the classic tradition of Italian puppetry is dead. Audiences have changed and puppeteers have adapted to different circumstances.

Vittorio Podrecca and the Teatro dei Piccoli

A marked feature of the twentieth-century puppet theater is the growth of the idea of the puppeteer as a creative artist in his or her own right. For the classic puppeteer, the notion of métier remained uppermost, but puppetry was beginning to attract others who perceived it in a broader sense as a form of artistic expression. Vittorio Podrecca (1883–1959), the

Diaghilev of the Italian puppet theater, was a man of considerable artistic sensitivity. Coming from a professional family in Cividale and trained as a lawyer, Podrecca went to Rome and in 1911 started a children's magazine, *Primavera*. He moved in the circle of the artistic intelligentsia of the capital and planned to set up an art puppet theater for children. This is reflected in the name of his company, the Teatro dei Piccoli, which, together with Luigi Fornaciari, who provided some of the necessary capital, he opened in 1914 in the former stables of the Odescalchi palace. Podrecca was not a puppeteer, but he had seen the Neapolitan Giovanni Santoro with his "Fantocci Santoro," at the Teatro Umberto and he persuaded him to join the venture. The auditorium of the Teatro dei Piccoli was decorated by Bruno Angoletta (1889–1954), and the stage was specially designed to allow for either marionettes or glove-puppets. The initial idea was to present a spring and summer season of glove-puppets, while the marionettes went on tour.[2]

Performances involved a small group of singers and a live orchestra and from an early period Podrecca always introduced the show, appearing amongst marionettes performing a chamber music number. The opening program on February 22, 1914, consisted of Haydn's *Children's Symphony*, a prologue by Alfredo Testoni, recited by a marionette in tails with a top hat in his hand, and then *The Fairy Morgana*, a comic fable by Yorick, presented with glove-puppets by Ugo Campogalliani. After these came the Santoro company in Gounod's *March of the Marionette*, and Pergolesi's *La serva padrona*.

The reputation of Podrecca's company spread so quickly that on March 16 it was invited to perform at court at the Quirinale. The program included variety numbers by Santoro's marionettes and Ugo Campogalliani's *Fairy Morgana*. Podrecca could not attend because of his connection with his brother's socialist paper, *L'Asino*, but a presentation was made to him and the press made much of the occasion. Santoro was more or less ignored and decided to withdraw himself and his company from the association with Podrecca.[3] The latter now turned to another established marionette company, that of Ottorino Gorno Dall'Acqua, whose production of Valverde's *La Gran Via* was staged at the Odescalchi in April. Meanwhile Ugo Campogalliani was presenting Molière farces and pieces from the classic glove-puppet repertoire. Podrecca was called up between 1915 and 1919, but remained closely in touch with the theater which continued through the war; he also organized performances of puppets for soldiers in the trenches.

Fortunato Depero's *Balli plastici per marionette*, commissioned for the Teatro dei Piccoli in 1918, was the company's most notable contact with the experimental avant-garde.[4] The scenario was completely abstract and the simplified, stylized, and often flat marionettes were an integral part of their Futurist environment.[5] The *balli plastici* was accompanied by an exhibition of Depero's work organized by the Casa d'Arte Italiana. This association also used the Piccoli Theater to present Albert Birot's symbolic drama for marionettes, *Matoum e Temibar*, with sets and costumes by Enrico Prampolini, its director. In 1922, Prampolini directed a production of a versified *Little Red Riding Hood* for Podrecca. The marionettes were by Mario Pompei and the music by Cesare Cui. The well-known opera designer, Caramba (Luigi Sapelli, 1865–1936), was responsible for the costumes. The experiments of a Marinetti, a Depero or a Prampolini were of outstanding significance for the development of the art of puppetry, but their full impact would not be felt before the final decades of the century and the Teatro dei Piccoli did not continue in this vein.

For much of 1920, the Odescalchi Theater was left to the glove-puppets while the marionettes went on tour through the rest of Italy (Verona, Brescia, Bergamo, Milan, Turin).[6] Podrecca's proposal to open theaters in Turin and Milan so that shows could circulate had to be dropped in the face of furious reactions from the Lupi and Colla companies. The same year their *20,000 Leagues under the Sea* with a musical commentary by Giovanni Giannetti was precisely the sort of piece that the Lupi or Colla companies might have staged. The scenery, music and manipulation were highly praised and a special performance was given for the birthday of Queen Elena.[7] This was followed in January by Orio Vergani's adaptation of Shakespeare's *Tempest*. With voices provided by well-known actors and sets by Caramba, inspired by Arthur Rackham, this was regarded as a major event of the theater season.[8]

In 1922 the Piccoli embarked on its first foreign tour, visiting Argentina, Uruguay and Brazil. Back in Rome in January 1923 they presented a little-known Donizetti opera, *Betly; or The Swiss Cabin*, preceded by variety numbers, which were now becoming an important part of the repertoire and included the singer "Miss Legnetti" executing "O sole mio."[9] European renown came with a season in the New Scala Theater in London in 1923. After a triumphant first night on April 12, they were offered a contract for a further 45 days. All of fashionable London attended the shows, and after the Scala they were offered a contract at the 3,000-seat Coliseum Theater. The greatest accolade at this time came from Eleonora Duse in a congratulatory letter where she wrote: "The marionette too can be perfect when it is driven by a soul. His actors are silent and obey; mine speak and do not obey."[10] In London Podrecca employed Cissie Vaughan to replace his soprano. She was a pupil of Leoncavallo and Adelina Patti and currently working at Covent Garden. At first she was offended at the idea of singing for puppets and not appearing on the stage, but then she became interested, eventually married Podrecca, italianized her name to Lia Podrecca, and became one of the company's greatest assets. Carlo Farinelli, her son by a former marriage, went on to become company manager.

The English successes led to offers from America, and Podrecca sent part of the troupe there in September 1923. They appeared at the Frolic New Amsterdam Theatre, New York. Cesare Cui's *Puss in Boots* did not appeal, but the variety acts, Salome, a jazz-dancing "blackamoor" and a scene with the comic figure of Fortunello that involved a lot of little Fortunellos popping out of pumpkins was very successful.[11] Over this period touring continued to Spain, South America again and Mexico, Cuba, San Domingo and Puerto Rico. All the time the variety repertoire was growing in importance and some numbers were invented for the American audiences.

By the time of its tour of Switzerland, Berlin and Vienna in 1925–1926, the company had a huge repertoire, involved 24 people, including the 8 singers, a conductor and a pianist, and possessed some 800 puppets. It was now playing to larger audiences than any marionette theater had played to. In Magdeburg in June 1927 it filled the 4,500 seats of the Stadthalle for the German theater exhibition.

The company was in North America again between December 1932 and February 1934. Apart from the problem of having to have all the electrical equipment replaced and the scenery fire-proofed, its season at the 2,000-seat Lyric Theatre, Broadway, was a great success. The repertoire of lesser-known or specially composed operas seemed too elitist and was generally dropped in favor of better-known pieces and of entertaining and up-to-date comic numbers. Pressure to make the marionettes more realistic in their movements also led to some technical improvements. After Broadway, the company traveled across America presenting a ten-minute variety act in cinemas. This was far from what Podrecca had originally intended his company to do, but was economically necessary; puppetry as part of a ciné-variety show was popular in the 1920s, 1930s and 1940s. It was during this period that the company and the Yale Puppeteers became involved in making the musical film *I Am Suzanne* for Paramount Studios. In this, Lilian Harvey, the variety artiste Suzanne of the title, is doubled with a marionette. The idea behind the film is that the marionette can become more real than the human it represents. Two major sequences were performed by the Yale Puppeteers, but the Piccoli was central, and the film also allowed for a long nightmare sequence and short clips of the group's work such as the circus donkey, the quartet "Bella figlia dell'amore" from *Rigoletto* with the pianist, and four disjointing clowns.[12]

Over the next few years the Piccoli toured extensively in Europe and visited Egypt in March 1937. On June 20 that year they sailed for South America, starting what would become a 14-year exile. They were in Mexico in 1939 when war broke out, and the following year they found themselves in New York, and in danger of internment. The Italian ambassador advised them not to return to Italy. They had a contract in Brazil, but had run out of money. Arturo Toscanini provided a loan to help them leave and the American authorities turned a blind eye. Then Brazil too declared war on the Axis and also ceased to be a safe country. Moving to Argentina, the Piccoli played for three months at the Ateneo in Buenos Aires before visiting other towns and cities. The variety program focused more heavily on Italian dances and South American folklore.[13] In 1945 they were involved in Lucas Demare and Hugo Fregonese's film *Donde mueren las palabras*.

With the end of the war the Piccoli could not afford to return to Europe. Buenos Aires remained its base, but the group also toured Uruguay and Paraguay. When Eva Peron nationalized all businesses in 1950–1951 Podrecca was unable to pay the company and they had to cross the frontier hastily, making a short tour in Uruguay and Brazil. Finally they embarked for Italy on September 23, 1951. Podrecca was now a sick man. Back in Italy, he set up permanent home in Rome and handed over the management of the company to Carlo Farinelli. Desperate attempts were made to raise funds. In 1954 they visited Dublin, Oxford, Glasgow and Edinburgh with their variety show. Podrecca wished to return to the more artistic musical repertoire of the early years. He split the company and created a second group, Il Nucleo, which gave its first performance on March 12, 1956, at the Piccola Scala of Milan with singers from La Scala.[14] Setting up a second company accentuated the financial problems and led to a degree of bad feeling. Podrecca died in 1959, but the main company held together until 1964. Much material had been lost in a store bombed during the war, and more that had been left in Philadelphia was seized by a creditor there. Later this was bought back by a group of the artists who had collaborated with Podrecca for years. Finally Trieste provided money to set up the company again in 1979.

Like Enrico Salici, Podrecca discovered that what really appealed to foreign audiences were the variety acts. In addition to classic circus acts, he developed the "ethnic" dances beloved in the nineteenth century into complete scenes: ten minutes in Japan, the Neapolitan tarantella, and even the Charleston. A jazz orchestra became a very popular number, as did a Viennese one and a South American group of singers and musicians performing the rumba. Following the fashion for transforming music-hall stars into marionettes, Joséphine Baker and Maurice Chevalier graced the stage of the Piccoli. The Gorno company brought some of their own acts with them. In 1914 their concert singer, Miss Legnetti, was performing duets with Facanapa accompanied by a puppet pianist. By 1924 this pianist, now called Piccolowski, developed into one of the most popular acts of the company and was long remembered and much imitated for the care with which he arranged his stool, his piano and his tailcoat.[15] The comic singer developed into the absurd soprano Sinforoso Strangoloni, whose neck extended on a high note. A violinist, whose hair developed a life of its own, was a third musical solo performer.

Podrecca regularly employed puppeteers from existing marionette families — Santoro, Prandi, Corsi, Braga and Gorno dall'Acqua. Much of the early work of the Piccoli was the updating and re-staging of already existing productions. Podrecca's great skill was to group these talents together just as the family companies were failing to cope economically. His role was close to that of the director in the modern sense of the term. He was present at every performance and noted any mistakes, informing the performers and stage crew about them afterwards. In a sense the company was a summation of the classic marionette tradition, but the new emphasis on directing and production values, the idea that each show should have its own figures and scenery specially designed, and the overall artistic aims placed it in a new and resolutely modern context. Podrecca's aim was to create a national puppet theater, but sadly he was never able to cope even with the running costs of the Odescalchi, which was too small to be viable for an enterprise on this scale and which he ceased to use after 1923. Constant touring provided some income, but state subsidy never materialized and assistance sometimes had to be sought from wealthy patrons, such as Angelo Signorelli, a well-known radiologist and art collector.

The pianist Piccolowski, Sinforo Strangoloni and the violinist in performance with the revived Piccoli company. (Courtesy Teatro Stabile Friuli-Venezia Giulia.)

Maria Signorelli

Maria Signorelli (1908–1992) was the daughter of Angelo Signorelli and Dr. Olga Resnevic (originally from Riga), who wrote a biography of Eleonora Duse. Many of the great names in art, literature and theater visited Resnevic's salon. As a child Maria attended the Ballets Russes and Diaghilev presented her with her first box of paints. She studied art and came to know Nicola Benois, then in charge of the scenery at the Teatro Reale in Rome. Her special interest was in soft sculpture and the figures she produced in the 1920s had a strong expressionist quality. She exhibited successfully in Paris in 1929 and then went to study in Berlin, where she exhibited her work and also had contact with Rheinhardt, Brecht and Piscator. This was followed by a period designing sets and costumes for some of the main opera houses and theaters of Italy. Her first puppet shows were Debussy's *Toybox* and Mozart's *Bastien and Bastienne*, presented in Rome in 1937. Maria Signorelli would later devote the greater part of her activity to the glove-puppet and related techniques. Her soft-sculpture figures lent themselves to exaggeration of certain features that bordered on caricature. Her puppets likewise were physically represented by a single characteristic while other details faded into insignificance. Her stick-puppet ballerinas became celebrated. Many of the figures had a Cubist/Futurist quality that had clearly evolved out of her soft sculptures and she was already using unconventional materials long before this became general in Italy. Signorelli's first company was created in 1947 and acquired the title of L'Opera dei Burattini in 1949.[16]

Performances were often given for charities for causes such as Jewish orphans and some were presented in the garage of her home in the Via Corsini, Rome. She staged both classic fairy-tales and a broader repertoire of stories and legends. In 1947, her puppets appeared in Fernando Cerchi's film *Largo al factotum*, based on the *Barber of Seville*.[17] In 1949 her production of *Totonno the Giant* employed a human actor to play the role of the giant.[18] The Signorelli repertoire was close to that of the European avant-garde theater and included Shakespeare (*The Tempest*), Gozzi, Pushkin, Wilde, Dante's *Inferno* (with some 500 figures), a *Faust*, Brecht's *Antigone*, Guido Ceronetti's *La Rivoluzione Francese*, and a number of ballets danced by glove and rod puppets, including Prokofiev's *Cinderella* and De Falla's *Master Peter's Puppet Show*.

In 1957, after the hiatus of the war years, the international puppetry association UNIMA regrouped and Signorelli became heavily involved. Her awareness of what was happening on the artistic and puppet front in other countries, combined with her linguistic skills, made her an ideal person for this. More than anyone else she helped place the Italian puppet theater in the framework of world puppetry. In 1956 she produced an Italian translation of Sergei Obraztsov's *My Profession*.[19] In the 1960s she began to assemble a huge collection of puppet material (with a significant amount from the Podrecca company) and was involved in the creation of a number of exhibitions, including Burattini e Marionette Italiani at La Scala in 1961, and above all the magnificent Burattini e Marionette in Italia dal Cinquecento ai Giorni Nostri in 1980. In 1972, in an honorary capacity, she began to teach puppetry at the University of Bologna. Her work as a puppeteer has been continued by her daughters Giuseppina Volpicelli and Letizia Volpicelli with the Nuova Opera dei Burattini and is mostly geared for children.

Puppets as Children's Theater

As in most of Europe, puppet theater in Italy today operates primarily in the context of children's theater. Podrecca, Signorelli and others believed in the positive artistic value of puppets for children. Enrico Novelli (1876–1943), known as Yambo, had a similar aim. When he started his company in 1919 he invited Enrico Salici and his company to work with him. Talented as a journalist, writer, caricaturist and illustrator, he was fully capable of designing and making his own puppets and scenery and looking after the mise en scène. This limited Salici's input and the partnership lasted only a few years.[20] Yambo's second wife, Adelina Maud Pieri (1898–1980), also an excellent manipulator, later became the director of the company. The first performance of the "Burattini di Yambo" took place in the little auditorium of the Teatro della Pergola in Florence on December 19, 1919, with *The Adventures of Ciuffetino*.[21] Ciuffettino, the hero of a children's book written by Yambo, competed very successfully with Pinocchio in his appeal to young audiences.

Yambo staged operettas, operas and variety, but the main emphasis was on pieces specially written for children. He visited the main towns of Italy and also toured abroad.[22] The name of the company, which boasted 1,000 "wooden actors," was changed to the Fantocci Lirici. Carine Gallone's 1939 film *Marionette* involved Benjamino Gigli playing a famous singer incognito who sings in the wings of a traveling marionette show. Yambo's puppets were used and included a miniature Gigli and a group of tarantella dancers. In 1940 the wartime situation forced the Fantocci di Yambo to give up performing and the material was put into store in Florence, where much of it was destroyed by bombing.

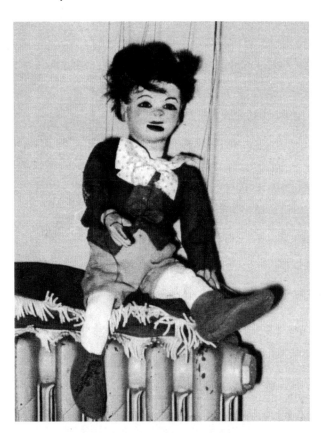

Ciuffettino, Yambo's original child puppet, the hero of children's books and puppet shows. A child puppet designed to appeal to juvenile audiences. (From Giancarlo Pretini, *Facanapa e gli altri* [Udine: Trapezio Libri, 1985]. Courtesy Giancarlo Pretini.)

In the 1930s in Communist Russia and Nazi Germany the ideological potential of puppetry as an educative tool sometimes took precedence over entertainment or notions of awakening artistic sensibilities. During the Fascist period in Italy there were strong parallels to the German Kraft durch Freude movement. In Italy the head of the Fascist youth group GIL turned to Giacomo Colla's company in 1940–1941 as flag-bearers of the Italian marionette tradition. They were seen as representing a renaissance of the art in Italy and even Mussolini was informed of this.

Giacomo Colla was both a Piedmontese patriot and an atheist, but, as his son pointed out, he was ready to "collaborate" on the cultural front to feed his family.[23] The company was based in Florence and new works were commissioned, with figures and costumes made by the Artigiani di Firenze. The Teatro Quattro Fontane in Rome was rented for a three-month season and the first performance was Antonio Petrucci's *There Is an Island at the Bottom of the Sea*. The aim was to create a specific theater for children with an avant-garde repertoire, to develop a new dramaturgy and to provide every production with its own director.[24] A tour of Sicily was planned, but events in the war prevented this. The company returned to Rome in 1942 and then set off on a tour of the north. The GIL proved to be completely incompetent and lost a large part of the material, and Colla broke off involvement with them. In 1945 the family came together to recreate a company and even considered abandoning marionettes to become live actors. Following the death of Giacomo, Gianni launched his children's theater, the Teatrino della Fiaba at the Palazzo Litta in Milan in 1949. Every show had puppets and scenery designed for that production alone.[25] In 1950 Gianni's daughter Cosetta joined the company and they began to use live actors alongside the puppets.[26]

For some performers television opened up a new way of communicating with audiences, especially young ones, but the change of medium had its effect on puppet performance. The notion of filmed puppet shows persisted for a time, but the real discovery was how to master the small screen and how to get the best possible value out of the close-up shot. Maria Perego became internationally famous with Topo Gigio, an entertaining mouse with a very strong character.[27] Created in 1958, Topo Gigio was a table-top figure operated with short rods by three people dressed in black against a black background. From the early 1960s he had a weekly television show. By 1963 he was on the Ed Sullivan Show in New York (92 episodes). Today he remains popular in Europe, the Americas and Japan. Tinin (Antonio) and Velia Mantegazza made their mark as television puppeteers. In 1985 they created a puppet figure, Dodo, who was the protagonist of *The Blue Tree*, a long-running children's series.[28]

Histories of puppetry often begin with a reference to small jointed dolls found in children's graves in Roman times. The great argument is whether these are dolls or puppets. In fact any doll played with by a child has life projected into it through the imagination. It is de facto a puppet and it does not really matter whether the context of use is entirely domestic and private or as

Dodo. Table-top puppet created by Velia and Tinin Mantegazza for the long-running RAI television program *L'Albero Azzurro*. (Courtesy Velia and Tinin Mantegazza.)

paid entertainment. A word associated with both acting and puppets is "play" (in Italian "gioco"). Today much puppet activity occurs in an educational context with groups of school children being brought to shows, or having shows brought to their schools. This is very valuable and is an extension of the paid engagements from which puppeteers have always derived a part of their income. In the latter part of the twentieth century another notion of the role of puppetry in education has developed. Here the emphasis is less on a notion of performance than on involvement of children in an activity that stimulates their own creativity and imagination. This activity is all the more important in a world where the young are exposed, sometimes for a number of hours daily, to forms of passive entertainment that make few demands on the imagination and in many cases fill up time that in the past might have been devoted to play. The focus of the present book has been on puppetry as a form of theater and entertainment, but another remains to be written on puppetry in the sphere of childhood activities.

Puppets and Politics

Beyond a generally populist ethos and the occasional joke at the expense of the authorities, nineteenth-century puppeteers could not be meaningfully described as politically involved. As socialist ideas spread, some began to pick them up. Antonio Sarzi (1863–1948), his son Francesco (1893–1984) and grandson Otello (1922–2001) all moved in a distinctly political direction. Francesco began his military service in 1913, in Messina, but ran into trouble because of involvement with anarchists distributing leaflets for the "settimana rossa." In 1921 he was involved in the foundation of the Italian Communist Party. During the Fascist period, membership of the Fascisti was extremely important for puppeteers to get permits to perform, and many puppeteers went along with this. Francesco Sarzi refused to join and on various occasions this created problems for him. Wherever possible he slipped Communist allusions into his shows and his audiences picked these up easily. There is an anecdote that after one performance the secretary of the local Fascist group came and shook Fagiolino's hand, saying "Bravo Fagiolino, we are colleagues with our sticks and we know how to strike." Sarzi instantly quipped back (as Fagiolino) "Oh no, we're not colleagues at all. First of all, I have the red beret, and you the black one, and I beat the baddies, robbers, bullies and the unjust, while you beat up poor working men."[29] During the Second World War, Sarzi and his family were all arrested a number of times, and narrowly escaped execution. At one point Otello was condemned to 25 years in prison, but escaped to Switzerland after two. On another occasion, Francesco left all his equipment with Communist friends in Caprara while he was on the run. The friends were executed, their house burned and Sarzi's own material, including a traveling booth, destroyed. He eventually escaped across the Linea Gotica of the Po and remained there for the remainder of the war. After the war Francesco Sarzi formed a Communist theater group presenting such works as Octave Mirbeau's *Les mauvais bergers*. He found he could express his political commitment better as an actor than a puppeteer. Otello was as committed as his father and after the war became involved with the Italian Pioneer Association for Communist Youth. In 1957 he moved to Rome. Together with a group of artists, intellectuals and journalists he set up an organization called T.S.B.M. (Teatro Sperimentale Burattini Marionette) whose aim was to renew and rediscover the specific language of puppet theater in harmony with the modern world.

Otello Sarzi became one of the strongest forces in twentieth-century Italian puppet theater, notably in the transformation of the glove-puppet repertoire from what had come to be regarded as a "traditional" form to a means of expression of contemporary relevance. He established puppet theater as a means through which serious issues could be examined and brought it into line with the experimental theater of the period, staging such pieces as Bertolt Brecht's *A Man's a Man* and *Round Heads and Pointed Heads*, Vladimir Maiakovski's *Radio October*, Federico Garcia Lorca's *The Little Theater of Don Cristobal*, Samuel Beckett's second *Act Without Words* and Fernando Arrabal's *Pique-nique en Campagne*. By aiming plays at specifically adult audiences Sarzi helped shift the generally held belief that glove-puppets were only for children. He took on board developments in the USSR and the work of Sergei Obraztsov and was one of the first in Italy to develop the idea of the operator performing in full view of the audience or stripping the glove-puppet right down to the human hand with a ball to represent a head. His career was marked by continuous experimentation, especially after 1969, when he established himself in Reggio Emilia, but he also remained one of the finest exponents of the classical glove-puppet theater of Emilia Romagna.

The association of puppets and politics became part of the raison d'être of a number of young companies that sprang up in the later 1960s. Two major influences were the theater of Bertolt Brecht and the Bread and Puppet Company, which visited Italy in 1970. The puppet lends itself to the Brechtian notion of alienation and its long tradition of parody and satire easily becomes a means of questioning the organization of society. The Compagnia dei Burattini di Torino, set up by Giovanni Moretti and others in 1968, initially wanted to return to a notion of popular puppet theater that was not reduced to innocuous entertainment for children. The aim was to mix traditional puppetry with work of contemporary artists, and to present classical and popular pieces using both actors and puppets. There was less emphasis on the traditional idea of animation and figures were often given life mainly by how they were positioned or moved on the stage and by the way in which attention was focused on them. In November 1968 the company presented *Sante Caserio*, the story of the anarchist who stabbed Sadi Carnot and was subsequently condemned to death.

Otello Sarzi with a rod puppet. (Archival photograph. Courtesy Castello dei Burattini/Museo Giordano Ferrari and of the Fondazione della Famiglia Sarzi.)

Caserio. Trial scene. I Burattini di Torino, 1970. (From catalogue of the "Primo Festival dei Burattini e delle Marionette — Bologna 1970." Courtesy Istituto per i Beni Marionettistici e il Teatro Popolare.)

This was adapted by Sandro Gindro from scripts of the Rame and Pallavicini companies.[30] In 1970 it featured at Maria Signorelli and Franco Cristofori's first puppet festival of Bologna, where the Compagnia dei Burattini di Torino was the only non-traditional puppet company to be invited.

In 1973 the *Martyrdom of Felicita and Perpetua*, based on letters written from prison in the third century A.D. and mixing large puppets and actors, received its first performances in a church and later transferred to the Teatro dell'Angolo. The Teatro dell'Angolo was founded and directed by Moretti with the aim of presenting serious material to children in a modern and non-patronizing way. It was not strictly a puppet theater, but until 1975 most of the productions involved puppets. Luisa Accati's *Massimone and the Gluttonous King* (1972), one of its greatest triumphs, was subsequently toured through Italy and abroad. The subject was the French Revolution. The revolutionary Massimone addressed the audience directly and tried to push them to revolution. On one side of him were the nobles and the court, represented by puppets made with hairdresser's equipment or, in the case of guards and soldiers, by pans and kitchen equipment; on the other side, puppets made of natural materials such as wood and bread stood for the peasantry and the poor.[31] *Massimone* was an example of serious political theater aimed at the juvenile audience.

Beyond Tradition

Just as the classical puppet theater reached its nadir in the 1960s a new generation of puppeteers began to emerge. Some came from puppet families, but many had no previous connection with puppet theater and a significant number had received third level education. They emerged at a historical moment when the value of popular culture was being reassessed and acquiring a new political dimension in the face of the rapid spread of mass culture and global consumerism. Activity in the field of popular culture was no longer merely a matter of earning a living, but a much broader assertion of humanist values under threat.

The Pasqualino brothers, Fortunato (1923–2008) and Giuseppe (1926–1999), came to Rome from Caltagirone in Sicily. They were familiar with the Catanian style of puppetry, but had no background in the activity. Fortunato was a writer and had a career in television. In 1969 they set up their Teatro Minimo and a little later opened a permanent puppet theater in Rome. Giuseppe (Pino) was responsible for the staging and the making of the puppets, while Fortunato created a repertoire with subjects ranging from Don Quixote to St. Francis of Assisi, Moses, Garibaldi, Amphytrion and even Pinocchio.[32] They always insisted they were using Sicilian pupi, not giving "traditional" pupi shows.[33] In *Pinocchio at the Court of Carlo Magno* (1972) Fortunato plays on the idea of Pinocchio's nose making the puppet sneeze whenever anyone, including the emperor, tells a lie. Nothing remains of Collodi's novel apart from the character who has taken on an independent existence. *The Triumph, Passion and Death of the Knight of La Mancha* is a meditation on violence with Don Quixote caught up in a cruel joke as members of the court dress up as the paladins that he still imagines to exist. *The Paladin of Assisi* opens with the battle of Roncisvalle and involves Orlando and Oliviero, but this is then conflated with the story of St. Francis trying to stop the crusades with his message of peace. Both plays explore the issue of the individual versus society in situations where St. Francis and Don Quixote are perceived as "mad." *The Temptation of Jesus* develops the role of Satan, who is dressed as a paladin, with a striking resemblance to Gano di Magonza.[34] In a curious ending, he appears in the desert with the dead Christ in his arms and prays to God that the innocent Christ should rise again. In *Garibaldi on the Waters*, the Pasqualinos intended to explore the conflict between idealism and reality, but this was banned because of the negative "antipatriotic" image it gave of King Vittorio Emanuele.

On the brink of extinction, the classic guarattella was revived in the 1980s by several individuals: Bruno Leone, Salvatore Gatto, Maria Imperatrice and Paolo Comentale. This coincided with a re-evaluation of popular entertainment and an ideology of the street as a performance space. The last exponent of the guarattella in Naples was Nunzio Zambello (1920–1984), but by 1978 he had virtually ceased to perform.[35] He was brought to Como for a festival and visited the university in Milan several times. Bruno Leone (b. 1950) came into contact with Zambello and asked to train with him. He refused but Leone attached himself to him, observed him and, according to age-old practice, "stole" his "tricks." For Zambello the voice was paramount. Leone gained valuable experience of the street by working for a short time with Zambello, alternating the roles of "guarattellaro" and "piattino" man.[36]

Leone mastered the swazzle, retained Pulcinella as his central character and evolved into an outstanding "guarattellaro," but differed from his predecessors by writing a number of new scripts with a pronounced political slant, such topics as the French Revolution, and characters such as George Bush and Osama Bin Laden. He also introduced a self-referential element by appearing in front of the booth dressed as Pulcinella, and holding a conversation with the puppet Pulcinella. After nearly 20 years of activity, Leone realized the need to pass on his accumulated knowledge of the art of the guarattella and ensure its continuance. He set up a school in the late 1990s and he has helped form a new generation of performers.[37]

Paolo Comentale (b. 1956) from Bari used the Ferraiolo family of Salerno as his model, and like them created his own original scripts. He began to work in 1983 and became an adept in the use of the swazzle. He created the Casa di Pulcinella in 1988 and aimed for a new Pulcinella that children might relate to in the later twentieth century. His Pulcinella was a positive figure, perhaps more similar to Gianduja or Gioppino than to the Pulcinella of Leone and certainly lacking the streetwise sharpness of the latter. The opera designer Lele Luzzati (1921–2007) had produced a series of brilliant animation films, including a *Pulcinella* with greatly simplified lines and shapes. Luzzati's Pulcinella transferred to Comentale's stage and Luzzati's wit enlivened many pieces, including a burlesque *Pulcinella Paladino* and even Niccolò Piccinni's opera buffa of 1776, *La Cecchina o la buona figliola*. Comentale lost his premises in the late 1990s, but then created an art center for the underprivileged children of Bari in the former football stadium, where the puppet theater is integrated with many activities, including a library and workshops. In this he has much in common with those puppeteers who since the 1970s have been concerned with both giving shows for children and exercising a form of cultural animation that develops the creativity of children through the use of puppets.

Sardinia had no obvious puppet tradition, but in 1980 Tonino Murru and Donatella Pau in Cagliari established Is Mascarredas, a traveling puppet group using a range of different types of puppet. In order to remain within a popular tradition they created their own local puppet figure, Areste Paganòs, for which they wrote a small repertoire.[38] Unlike the Sandrones and Gioppinos, Areste Paganòs was created as a cry for the maintenance of local and human values in the face of mass culture and globalization. The starting point of their 2007 production of *Giacomina e il popolo di legno* was the simple folk toys of Tosino Anfossi and Eugenio Tavolara that became almost symbols of Sardinia in the 1930s. These toys looked back to Sicilian folk tradition, but were interpreted in a resolutely modernist style and executed in wood. The central figure, Giacomina, is a little girl who goes through the village in a search for her donkey and encounters different characters and customs. For this production the wooden toys were blown up into table-top figures nearly one meter high with a minimum of articulation and the show itself successfully blended folk tradition, modernism and contemporary puppetry.

In recent years it has become very common for the puppeteer to appear onstage with the puppet and in some cases he or she has become an actor who performs directly for an audience and also uses puppets. A more presentational style and visible performers has resulted in the further distancing from any notion that the puppet, especially the marionette, exists only to present live theater on a reduced scale. In 1971, the Accettella marionette company of Rome encountered the sculptor Ferdinando Codognotto, who created figures carved in wood with minimal paint or costume.[39] The company wanted to emphasize and examine the theatricality of its performances. Its classic production was *Pinocchio in Pinocchio* (1979) and a part of the show's fascination was the possibility of seeing how it was done.[40] The company performed on an open stage, using a high bridge, but with the black-clad operators visible. They were separate from the puppets but incorporated in the same visual field as far as the audience was concerned.

Pinocchio. Teatro del Drago. A shadow sequence depicting the hanging of Pinocchio. (Courtesy Teatro del Drago, Ravenna.)

Mauro Monticelli was noted for his classic glove-puppet shows in the Emilian style.[41] In 1979, together with his brother Andrea, he set up the Teatro del Drago as a more experimental company exploring myth and legend and using a story-telling method of presentation.[42] Their *Pinocchio* (1990), a musical performance for actors, shadows, "pupazzi" and a wooden puppet, was treated as a visual collage evoking the main episodes of Collodi's story.[43] The performers were story-tellers, manipulators and actors.[44] There was no scenery as such, but on the bare stage a small number of significant elements from the story were introduced as required, including a door, a puppet stage, a tree, a circus or a piece of curtain against which shadows could be projected. This gave the production total flexibility in its use of stage space.

Nowhere is the blend of story-telling and puppet theater more clearly illustrated than in the work of Mimmo Cuticchio. Born in 1948 in a puppet theater (also the family's accommodation), he accompanied his father Giacomo to Paris to perform at the Italian embassy in 1967. The director of the Italian Cultural Institute persuaded Giacomo to sell his puppets and wanted Mimmo to remain in Paris. Mimmo decided to stay and a bookseller on the Boulevard Saint Michel made it possible for him to set up a teatrino for a season in the basement of his shop. Shows were reduced from two hours to one and a greater emphasis was placed on rhythms so that a foreign audience might understand more easily. The popular characters of Nofriu and Virticchiu spoke French.[45] After military service in 1968, Mimmo studied speech at the Pietro Sharoff school in Rome. Back in Palermo he found that his father was not interested in his "new" ideas. However, rather than break completely with tradition he saw his mission as being to react against it and to allow his own artistic vocation to emerge. Mimmo selected as his teacher the story-teller and puparo Giuseppe Celano. Celano restricted the use of dialect to terms that could be understood by a wider and not necessarily Sicilian audience. Celano's Orlando spoke correct Italian, while Rinaldo, perceived as a lovable rogue, used elements of dialect. Likewise Nofriu and Virticchiu, as squires to the heroes, also used Siciliano to amuse the audiences.[46]

As a puparo Cuticchio often exploits the contrast between Italian and Sicilian. As a contastorie, he dresses in ordinary street wear, but unlike the "cuntista," who simply gathered his audience round him in a semi-circle, often seated on chairs, he stands on a small platform when out of doors to help focus attention. He uses the classic wooden sword, the indispensable prop of the contastorie, and his movements are restrained and carefully chosen so as to maximize the effect of any action.[47] Where the older contastorie presented a different episode every day, Cuticchio, as a story-teller, has made the "cuntu" a one-off performance. He has remarkable vocal gifts and the rhythmic and musical aspects of his performance carry almost as much meaning as the words themselves.[48] In his combined role of puparo and story-teller he replaces straightforward linear narrative with flashbacks and other such devices.

Cuticchio established his teatrino in via Bara all'Olivella and here he, and now his son Giacomo, head a team that continues lively performances of the classic opera dei pupi. His more innovative work is usually presented in larger theaters, where he positions himself in front of a puppet stage and combines the roles of storyteller and puparo, plays a number of roles and engages in dialogue with the puppets. Cuticchio's work has a self-referential element and he delights in playing with the conventions of the genre. Many of the type scenes of the "op'ra" are retained, but the techniques used for the chivalric material have been extended to other subjects. The classic rod marionettes are carved by Mimmo's brother Nino and remain a basic element of the work but the emphasis has shifted away from the figures in armor. In his classical repertoire Cuttichio has tried to attenuate the bellicose aspect of the pupi and the presentation of Islam as the enemy. In *Francesco e il Sultano* (1997) he expressed a strongly pacifist message unusual for the opera dei pupi. In *L'urlo del mostro* (The Howl of the Monster, 1993), based on Homer, Cuticchio narrated and spoke for Polyphemos and Ulysses. The workings of the stage were exposed. Even the wind machine was visible and at one point a piece of cloth that had been used as part of the scenic structure became a sail.

The Brechtian notion of scenic writing, where every item on the stage was part of the language of the performance, lent itself to the new puppet theater. Audiences found themselves looking at a performance space in a way that focused their attention on what was happening in that space rather than on what it represented. Puppeteers began to use the much larger and more flexible space of the actor's theater, usually hung with black drapes so that the focal point now became the puppet, the properties and the puppeteer. In many cases techniques of black theater were also used. The conventional use of wings for entrances and exits was replaced by objects or figures coming into existence, apparently from nowhere, at any point of the performance area. A striking use of this was Claudio Cinelli's *Puccini en sortira* (1994), which depicts the last days of Puccini in a convent. Puccini himself is a life-size figure, operated by a group of large nuns (played by men), their faces concealed by black stocking beneath their huge starched coiffes. Music pervades the action and lets the audience into Puccini's mind as his delirious dreams conjure up images of scenes from his unfinished opera *Turandot*. These manifest themselves in mid-air out of the surrounding darkness.

Grimm's version of *Snow White* was the first production of the Teatro del Carretto of Lucca, established in 1983 by the stage-designer Graziano Gregori and the director Maria Grazia Cipriani.[49] The Carretto is not a puppet company, but an experimental theater company which, with its inventive ideas in design and lighting, is generally regarded as one of the most imaginative contemporary Italian groups. Like many companies both inside and outside Italy, its productions use live actors, puppets and masks and represent a significant trend in experimental theater, deliberately blurring the distinction between puppetry and other theater forms. As well as mixing puppets with actors, the group often aims to make actors behave in a puppetlike manner, while the puppets themselves seem if anything more real. This was particularly evident in its celebrated production of *Romeo and Juliet* (1986), a blend of Shakespeare's play and Bellini's *I Capuleti e i Montecchi*. The use of puppetry in experimental, alternative and sometimes mainstream theater by companies such as the Carretto has given the art a new status and the notion of reduced theater has receded into the background.

Towards a New Dramaturgy

Once the illusion of the marionette as a substitute actor was discarded, exciting new developments became possible. The glove-puppet stage already required a greater acceptance of non-realistic conventions, but realism no longer retained the significance it had had in the marionette theatre. Puppet companies began to create their own productions rather than interpret existing scripts. Some created new figures for every show. Proportions of figures changed and caricature was often pushed to the limit, while in children's shows figures representing animals were often the protagonists. Rod puppets of the East-European type, table-top puppets and more sophisticated use of shadow theater all extended the potential of puppet theater. They also meant that companies were less likely to remain tied to any one type of puppet, but rather would use whatever seemed most appropriate for a particular production. The materials used for puppet construction were also modified. Maria Signorelli had led the way, substituting soft sculpture for wood and papier-mâché. Otello Sarzi's group experimented with new synthetic materials such as foam, which, with polystyrene, became popular in the 1950s. Giovanni and Cosetta Colla used gauze, gesso and plastic for a production of *The Tempest* with students of the Scuola di Scenografia of the Academia di Brera (Milan) in 1960. Modern puppets could look like humans, but the human appearance was no longer necessarily the only point of reference. What did remain, if one leaves out abstract and object theater, were patterns of human behavior and reactions. The puppet was now a figure that existed for its own sake and was defined by its main characteristics and function. Metaphor and metonym took over from imitation or representation and this opened the door for a new dramaturgy of the puppet theater.

In the "classic" puppet theater language remains a vital component. One cannot imagine the opera dei pupi or Fagiolino deprived of the spoken word. Pulcinella has his swazzle and talks much of the time (even if the words themselves are often unintelligible). The same is true when plays are transposed or specially written for puppet performance. However, a full awareness that the dramaturgy of the puppet stage is not the same as that of the live theater is relatively recent.

In the late 1980s Mimmo Cuticchio began collaboration with the writer Salvo Licata. The challenge was to reconcile a tradition of improvisation with a fixed script, and this resulted in a series of pieces. The first, *Guided Visit to the Opera dei Pupi*, was less a piece for puppets than a piece with puppets. It was designed for performance in an empty space and was theater with all the elements exposed. Licata and Cuticchio used the bombing and destruction of large areas of Palermo, the end of the war and the arrival of the Allies to symbolize the departure of the old world and of the values of the pupi.[50] The puppets, with the visible operator, were handled in a way that made them a point of reference rather than actors. Cuticchio, playing an imaginary puparo, Paolo, picked up first one, then another. Scenes from the siege of Paris by Agramante and the madness of Orlando were inserted almost as quotations. These scenes were performed in Italian, but the atmosphere of a performance in the 1950s was evoked by the use of Siciliano in the verbal creation of a gallery of people discussing the mechanical piano, inserting their own comments on the action and hurling abuse at Gano, and even a local woman coming to the theater in search of her son, and having painted a picture of her own poverty wheedling her way into the show.

Gigio Brunello and Gyula Molnár's *Macbeth all'improvviso* (2001) is a piece that could only be written for the puppet stage. It plays in a Pirandellian manner with the whole notion of the reality of the performance.[51] On the stage stands a glove-puppet booth, denuded of scenery and over-painted with the well-known portrait of David Garrick as Richard III, through which the puppeteer emerges and tells the audience that the puppets for *Macbeth* are carved but not yet painted and that the scenery and costumes are not ready. The audience is informed that there will be no scenery, thus depriving the proscenium arch of the booth of its function as a picture frame. The puppeteer proposes to substitute a Goldoni play using the stock Commedia masks and embarks on this, but then the puppets decide to improvise their own version of *Macbeth*. Arlecchino takes control and plays Macbeth. Brighella wears a wig as Lady Macbeth. A running gag is the "generico" or utility actor, who plays a range of roles, generally with animal heads on his "human" body, except when he represents a soldier with Birnam wood, when the hand that forms the puppet's body becomes visible and the head is replaced by a sprig with a leaf. There is tension between puppets and puppeteer. When Duncan is murdered, a full-size sword appears on the stage. Arleccino thrusts downwards with it. A scream is heard and the audience understands that the puppeteer's arm has been cut off (for his final bow he appears in a shirt with a bloodied sleeve hanging free). After the murder Arlecchino becomes anxious at the direction in which things are moving and suggests a return to *L'emigrante geloso* (the imaginary Goldoni piece). When Macduff (Pantalone) reminds Macbeth that he was not born of woman, he says that the king (i.e., the puppeteer) was aware of this because he made him. Colombina appears at the end, announces the death of Arlecchino/Macbeth and, in a manner reminiscent of Mme Irma in Jean Genet's *The Balcony*, tells the audience to go home.

Visita guidata all'opera dei pupi. 1989. A performance with puppets rather than a puppet performance. Mimmo Cuticchio with the figures of Gano di Magonza and Rodomonte. (Archival photograph. Courtesy Associazione Figli d'Arte Cuticchio.)

Since the 1960s scenic language has developed to a point where there are many shows with no verbal element or only a much reduced one. Much derives from experiments in the visual arts in the early twentieth century. Oscar Schlemmer and the Bauhaus, Sophie Täuber-Arp, Alexandra Exter and a number of the Futurists, including Enrico Prampolini, Giacomo Balla and Filippo Tommaso Marinetti, all explored the possibilities of puppetry in their search for an abstract form of theater where a dynamic of forms, colors and sounds might replace the human element and the linear plot. In 1917 Balla and Igor Stravinsky created *Fireworks*, a five-minute abstract ballet. The "performers" were neither humans nor recognizable puppets, but abstract shapes of different colors sometimes lit from within, sometimes from outside, which moved around the stage according to a tightly controlled plot. Fortunato Depero (1892–1960) published *I colori* in the second collection of the *Teatro futuristica sintetico* in 1916. Instead of a setting he used a space defined by color (an empty blue cube). The actor was replaced by four abstract entities, moved by strings and emitting pure sounds that mirrored the chromatic and morphological qualities of each of these entities.[52] In 1917 Depero was commissioned by Diaghilev to design sets and costumes for Stravinsky's *Chant du rossignol*. He designed huge mechanical tropical flora and complex costumes that required animation by the dancer, who was enclosed in them. Such an experiment in pure form and color could have been exceptionally exciting as a puppet production, but went beyond what Diaghilev considered possible, and in the end the production was cancelled.

Depero's aim was a pure theater of puppets as distinct from theater interpreted by puppets. He required a technically far more advanced theater than could be found at the period to fulfill his vision of kinetic scenery, multiple levels and every imaginable trick effect, including what he called leaps in spatial and temporal dimensions using marionettes with "cadenzed angular movements." A major point of reference was the French cinema and the acting style of the silent movie. Like many artists of the period, he was looking for the ideal actor and was animated by a similar spirit to Foregger with his machine dances or Meyerhold and his idea of biomechanic acting.[53]

Many of the Futurist experiments would today come within the remit of puppetry. Marinetti's short pieces, *Le basi* and *Le mani* (1915), allow the audience to see only the feet in one case, and only the hands of the performers in the other. This idea of using hands as puppets has been taken up by a number of modern puppet companies across the world. In purely puppet terms what is happening is that the audience's attention is being drawn to extremities of the body, rather than the face. In *Le mani* a number of hands execute various recognizably human gestures.[54] Marinetti's *Vengono* (They Are Coming) was subtitled a "drama of objects." Under the direction of a butler, two servants arrange and rearrange the furniture of a very grand room. The piece ends as the terrified servants cower and the chairs march slowly out of the room.

Sergei Obraztsov in the USSR and Yves Joly in France led the way in using the performer's hands as puppets. This idea was especially developed by Claudio Cinelli in *One More Kiss*, a solo and highly amusing reduced version of *La traviata*. Helped out by little more than some balls for eyes and a few feathers, his hands became convincing if grotesque performers. Cinelli is a designer and opera director as well as a puppeteer. Whether focusing energy onto his hands or onto a piece of fabric, he can create the feeling that these are living entities and that a puppet does not have to be a carefully constructed and articulated figure. In the 1990s Hugo and Ines (from Peru and Croatia respectively) enjoyed great popularity in Italy. Hugo's own background as a street mime artist is fundamental to their work. They use different parts of their own bodies as puppets, projecting energy into arms, hands, legs, knees and feet and treating them as completely external to themselves.[55] These "puppets" then enact complete short scenarios.

Scatola Sonora. An abbreviated version of *La traviata* performed by the hands. (Courtesy Claudio Cinelli.)

Object Theater

In the 1970s the term "teatro di figura" came into general use because it was less limiting than burattino or marionette, but it soon proved inadequate as more and more performances were being given with non-anthropomorphic objects. The term "teatro di animazione" was coined because of the idea of giving life to inanimate objects.[56] After the 1960s an increasing number of performers began to use objects in a way that did not necessarily bring them to life or give them character and the label of "object theater" became widely popular. This was less a development of puppet theater than something that grew out of happenings, installations and kinetic elements in the visual arts. In the early 1980s the French performer Christian Carrignon, with his Théâtre de Cuisine, surrounded himself with a battery of kitchen utensils which were given added value as properties to accompany his performance, but emptied of any hint of human behavior or feeling. Carrignon always insisted that his performances had nothing to do with puppets.[57] The objects remain themselves, with their own characteristics, and never serve any existing text.[58] In this type of performance what matters is not the function of the object. It exists for its own sake, but once removed from its everyday function and placed on a stage where it becomes the focus of an audience's attention, it acquires a new energy and significance.

The Teatro delle Briciole (crumbs) of Parma was established in 1976 and is amongst the best-known practitioners of "object theater." The original members of the group had been with Otello Sarzi. At a period when virtually all puppet theater in Italy was designed for juvenile audiences they set out to appeal to all age groups and to place puppet theater firmly in the mainstream of contemporary experimental theater. The Briciole was fully aware of the importance of imaginative projection on the part of the audience and of the way in which metaphor and metonym constantly come into play on the puppet stage. From its first performances of *The Little Prince* and *The Wizard of Oz* the group set out to find a new language of theater using puppets and anything else it could. Members gave themselves freedom to work simultaneously at a number of levels and to develop a style that conjures up a poetic dream world.[59] Where puppets were used, the Briciole favored figures held directly by the performers, but they also used body-puppets and miniature figures. They employed black light to give a new value to objects in space that could appear and disappear at will and did not have any fixed setting to which they might be related. A Briciole production was notable for its almost cinematic fluidity as one image melted into another. With changes of scale they created the theatrical equivalent of a long shot and a close-up. The use of familiar things in an unfamiliar way was evident from their first productions. A known text, but seldom a dramatic one, was usually their starting point. In *The Wizard of Oz* the stage contained a number of shiny steel objects and the simple mechanical movements of pulleys, levers and so forth became integrated into the show. The company preferred to avoid the word puppet and to describe itself as a form of experimental theater using a theatrical language rooted in the experience of childhood.[60] Toys, dolls' houses and such things were often used to convey both a literal and a metaphorical meaning. In *The Call of the Wild*, based on the Jack London story, a square of cloth the size of a handkerchief came to read as a tent, while in *Genesi* (1981) the creation of the world was performed on a small table using cellophane bags of water, a small aquarium, some plastic figures and lumps of chalk. The Briciole integrated the actor and the object on an equal footing. In both *Topo and His Son* and *Ten Little Indians*, the human actor became a projection for the puppet and thus a curious distorting mirror of the puppet's reality.[61] Luigi Allegri described the Briciole as a theater of images sometimes manifesting itself as a theater of objects.[62] This is probably the best description of the work of a company which was one of the foremost exponents of object theater, but for which the sheer act of classification creates a straitjacket.

Minimal material means are the hallmark of the Hungarian Gyula Molnár, who performs a great deal in Italy. *Little Suicides* involves an actor sitting at a table telling stories and illustrating them with objects that retain their basic characteristics. *The Tragedy of the Aspirin* shows sweets playing on the table. An aspirin wishes to join in but is excluded, so it disguises itself as a sweet, but is discovered and in despair jumps into a glass of water, where it dissolves, releasing little bubbles. Molnár achieves a remarkable synthesis of the realities of children playing and the physical properties of the aspirin when dissolving in water.[63]

Luì Angelini and Paola Serafini of Bergamo began to work in the early 1980s with classic glove-puppets and called their company Assondelli e Stecchettoni (planks and nails). Their starting point was the contemporary avant-garde actors' theater transferred to the puppet stage, but they rapidly moved away from the classic idea of the puppet towards an examination of the underlying structures and this led to a form of object theater based on function and association. They began to look at the physical qualities of objects and to build a dramaturgy around these. Early experiments included five 15-minute versions of Shakespeare plays built around a cocktail bar. In *A Midsummer Night's Dream*, Demetrius and Lysander were

Odissea. Assondelli e Stecchettoni. Performers use objects, including rubber gloves and bicycle handlebars, to suggest rather than imitate. (Courtesy Luì Angelini and Paola Serafini. Courtesy Mauro Foli.)

represented by whiskey and gin and Hermia and Helena by red and white martinis. Othello became a Coca Cola and Desdemona a crème chantilly. During the early 1990s they embarked on the idea of apartment theater, where they presented a different piece in each room. The repertoire consisted of a restaging of three short programs they had earlier created: *Shaker-Speare, Dr. Jeykll and Mr. Hyde* and *Odissea.*[64] Later a fourth piece, *Snow White or The Misfortunes of Virtue,* was added. Angelini and Serafini have defined object theater as the story of heroes, but also of the things that represent those heroes.

Little Red Riding Hoods was a piece for puppets, objects and actors. The puppet stage became both a metaphor and an object to be explored. The story of *Red Riding Hood,* like a musical theme, was stated and then developed in a series of variations. First it was performed by stylized puppets with a mixture of narration and dialogue. The puppeteers intervened with comment to the audience. Suddenly the booth was split in half by an electric hedge-clipper and Luì and Paola emerged arguing. Luì retold the story, this time using bowls of different colors to represent the characters. In the next sequence the booth was turned around to become the grandmother's house. Paola was knitting and the needles were thrust into a ball of wool to create a "new" grandmother, while a radio message warned about wolves in the vicinity. Luì, wearing a pair of wolf's ears, arrived and devoured the grandmother by opening a little box and forcing the needles and wool ball into it. Red Riding Hood (a table-lamp with a shade) journeyed through a wood evoked by a strip of green fabric and rulers as trees. Her arrival at the grandmother's house was treated as a thriller with suitable lighting and sound effects. The grandmother's rocking chair swung forward onto the lamp, evoking the devouring of the child. The focus then shifted to the wolf's full stomach beneath a sheet. A film camera was placed in the wolf's "mouth" and the contents of his stomach were seen on video with an appropriate news commentary. Eventually the camera found Paola (now as Red Riding Hood) giving a television interview about being eaten by the wolf. Once the television had been turned off there was a discussion as to how to finish and the sheet covering the "stomach" of the wolf was popped back to reveal a porthole with Paola inside. The hunter pulled her out and they decided to get married. Finally the television came on again but the grandmother was found to have escaped and married the wolf. This company has always had a strong educational bias aiming to help develop creativity and imagination in children. Gradually performance became less significant for them than working directly with young people and in 2000 the name of the company was changed to La voce delle cose (the voice of things) to give a clearer definition of their aims.

The shift from giving shows to working with children and using puppetry techniques is particularly well represented by the Frenchman Albert Bagno (b. 1953), who has been an active figure in Italian puppetry since the mid–1970s. His formation is broader than that of many Italian puppeteers and he has been a central figure in Italian UNIMA. One of the earliest to use object theater, his work depends on the use of very simple materials such as paper and cardboard. He also employs a variety of puppet techniques, including very small rod marionettes. Rather than presenting a classic children's repertoire, he deals with social and political themes which he approaches with humor and poetry. Bagno makes himself a part of the performance both physically and verbally. He develops a special relationship with his audience and focuses on the individual child so that each can find its own place in relation to what is happening. Through play he tries to involve the child and help it realize its full potential. In 1978 he led the way in using puppets in the context of therapeutic work in hospitals and schools and in 1989 set up the first Puppets and Therapy association in Italy, and this, in conjunction with such organizations as UNICEF and the Red Cross, has also led him on a broader front to examine the whole question of puppets in a humanitarian context.

A Dramaturgy of Light

On the modern puppet stage, as in actors' theater, lighting has moved from a supporting role to being a central component. In the early 1940s the Costantini stage was still lit by four oil lamps with reflectors fixed to the sides of the proscenium, and this was considered to be adequate. By the 1950s they used two or three white electric lamps for daylight scenes and two or three others for night scenes, prisons and caverns.[65] The larger marionette companies were more ambitious and far closer to what was happening in the actors' theater. Mobile spotlights were being introduced and there was a greater possibility of more atmospheric lighting using dimmers and a range of colored gels. Depero and the Futurists anticipated developments in lighting that would not take serious effect for a long time. The points of reference for the scenic picture changed as space became defined by light rather than scenery.

A form of puppet theater that depends entirely on light for its existence is the shadow theater. It is the shadow of an object placed in a beam of light and not the object itself that is the main focus of attention. Ottonelli classified shadow theater performed by the "bianti ombranti" as a form of puppet theater. Shadow theater, often in conjunction with marionettes, continued through the eighteenth and nineteenth centuries. The Incisa diary entry for June 1786 mentions a "servo machinista" from Milan who brought his "visual optical theater in dark and light." Apart from showing views of scenery and architecture, like the many optical shows then popular, this showman also introduced moving speaking figures to these scenes in the form of "intangible shadows."[66] The following year Asti was visited by a Giulio Lombardi from Milan (possibly the same individual) calling himself the "inventor" and "director" of a "Chinese shadow machine."[67] This time the publicity also announced that the figures would perform farces, and that each scene would be accompanied by music by famous composers. Shadow puppetry had moved beyond scriptural scenes to a dramatic repertoire. For a long time it remained a minor (and seldom recorded) aspect of puppet theater. The cinema museum in Turin, for example, has some figures from an otherwise forgotten nineteenth-century shadow theater in that city.

It was only in the late 1970s that shadow theater in Italy blossomed. This happened thanks to the Gioco Vita company, whose contribution to puppet theater is arguably the most significant and influential Italian one of the last two decades of the twentieth century. Gioco Vita's name evokes both "play" and "life." It was set up in the early 1970s by Diego Mai as an experimental theater company aiming to use theater in non-theatrical spaces. In 1976 Mai encountered the inspirational shadow work of Jean-Pierre Lescot and decided to work in that medium. He acquired a valuable collaborator in Fabrizio Montecchi and a working relationship with Lele Luzzati helped them develop a new and exciting visual language from their first production, *Baron Munchausen* (1978). Just as other puppet forms broke out of the constrictions of the classical puppet stage, Gioco Vita has moved beyond a small and tightly framed white screen, stretched on all sides and illuminated by a single light source, and taken over the entire performance area.

The Chat Noir theater of late nineteenth-century Paris expanded the visual possibilities of shadow theater by creating a sense of perspective with scenic elements placed at varying distances from the screen to provide stronger and paler shadows. This was combined with a pair of projectors with a dissolve to project a scene or an image painted on a slide as was used in many optical shows. Montecchi embraced these techniques but increased the number and position of light sources, and above all developed a hand-held light that allowed the performer maximum mobility and a new control over the position of the light source and its relationship to the screen or the object placed in its beam.[68] This new flexibility permitted the shadow performers to use light expressively. The evolution of dimmers and the introduction of the halogen lamp also augmented the creative potential of light. Montecchi's work, however, has always depended on a sense of design and the technical aspect has remained surprisingly simple.

The traditional shadow figure is a flat shape (often in card, metal or leather) that is placed close to the screen. Following Jean-Pierre Lescot, Gioco Vita began to use a variety of different mediums placed between the light source and the screen. Semi-translucent materials, fabric and wire-mesh were all employed and the relationship with the screen became ever more flexible. Washes of colored light replaced the more traditional practice of inserting colored transparencies into a dark cutout silhouette. Articulation of the figures in a semi-realistic way with moving limbs or mouths made way for a new principle of creating a dynamic through the overall movement of the silhouette in space and in relation to the light source. Shadows were also thrown from the front of the screen as well as the back, and there was an increasing use of the shadow of a three-dimensional object, or even a human body. A major discovery was that the "screen" need not be a rigid divider between the audience and the show, and that it too can become a means of expression. With *The Toybox* (1986) Gioco Vita moved away from the idea of the two-dimensional screen in favor of a three-dimensional experience. The single screen was replaced by mobile screens and curtains, in various positions and often in different fabrics, which could catch beams of light and the shadows of interposed forms. Flexible screens or curtains were able to move with the needs of the production and the shadows now inhabited the full stage space and depended on the beams of light for their definition. Cracks were deliberately left in the curtains so that the audience could become aware of what was happening behind instead of merely looking at the projected shadow. Montecchi's approach had a conscious theatricality that was absent with the Chat Noir. Operators of the shadows were now turned into actors interposing objects or even their own bodies in the beam of light. *Il Corpo Sottile* (1989) explored the relationship of the human body to light and the shadow screen and marked a major change in the orientation of the work. Since then the human body has been as much a material for casting shadows as any of the objects which the performer might hold. In his reinvention of shadow theater Montecchi realized that it is not the cutout silhouette that is of primary importance, but way it is handled and its relationship to the light and the screen.[69] At one point he declared:

Gilgamesh. Gioco Vita, 1982. Designed by Lele Luzzati. Much of this shadow production depended on superimposition of images and multiplication of light sources. (Courtesy Teatro Gioco Vita. Photograph Stefano Rossi.)

The player has once again found his central point in scenic space. It is the player who creates the relationship between all the elements. He is the one who by moving screen, light and figure, gives this space its theatrical existence and so makes the whole thing possible.[70]

Gioco Vita has been a main force in bringing shadow theater into the mainstream and adding playing with light to the range of expressive skills of the performer. The company has also collaborated in co-productions with the Piccolo Theater of Milan, the Rome Opera, Venice's La Fenice and even Covent Garden, London. The organization itself has grown and now manages three theaters in Piacenza, including the magnificent 200-year-old Municipal Theatre.

Il Corpo Sottile. Gioco Vita, 1989. A shift from the cutout silhouette to shadows cast by the human body and flexible use of light sources and curtains as a medium to receive light and shadow. (Courtesy Teatro Gioco Vita. Photograph Stefano Rossi.)

The potential of shadow theater has been exploited by many groups; amongst the most important are Teatrómbria (Empoli) and Controluce (Turin). Grazia Bellucci created Teatrómbria in 1983 to explore the poetic potential of shadow theater and after 1998 the company began increasingly to combine shadow work with other puppet and theater forms. Claudio Cinelli collaborated with them on several productions, including *Macbeth* (1990), in which he combined a bunraku style of puppet with huge drapes that served as screens to take projections that made visible the subconscious thoughts and nightmares of the characters.[71]

Controluce (Alberto Jona, Jenaro Meléndrez Chas and Corallina de Maria), created in 1994, emphasizes the combination of music and the visual arts through the medium of shadow theater. *Naufragi* (Shipwrecks) juxtaposes Schumann's music and traditional shadow techniques. *Dido and Aeneas*, with an action spread over three screens, is a painterly reinterpretation of Purcell's work, blending cutout silhouettes with the shadow of a live dancer. The centrality of the live performer was more evident in their *Canto a Orfeo*, using music by Glück, which paralleled a production on the same subject by Gioco Vita. Where Controluce differs from Gioco Vita is in its attempt to create a dramaturgy whose starting point is not so much a text as an attempt to find structures in the relationship of music and visual images. Their work is also symbolic of one of the trends in twentieth-century puppet theater as a whole, which is a shift of emphasis from the textual to the visual.

Conclusion

Since the 1960s it has often become easier to speak of puppet theater in Italy than of Italian puppet theater. The puppet theater of the last half century has to be examined in the light of international puppetry without overlooking the significance of the regional element. The spread of UNIMA and the phenomenon of the puppet festival have led to a huge variety of exchanges and contacts. The establishment of festivals abroad and at home has exposed Italian puppeteers to all sorts of new possibilities. One of the oldest and most important festivals is that of Cervia, Arrivano dal mare, established by Stefano Giunchi in 1975. This festival brings a wide range of performance and companies to Italy and provides a showcase for home-grown ones. Cervia itself is a holiday resort on the Adriatic coast. The huge disused warehouses for the salt-works of the area provide a base for the festival and a number of performance spaces. In 1981 the Centro Teatro di Figura was established in Cervia. The center produced the valuable review *Burattini*, which allowed for the dissemination of information on Italian and foreign puppet theater, a study of the various puppet traditions and the development of a critical discourse on the art of puppetry. More recent developments of the center have included training in puppetry and the provision of resources, including a center of documentation and a small museum of puppets.

Festivals have provided a stimulus to many to explore the art of puppetry. In Sicily the Morgana festival of Palermo established by Antonio and Janne Pasqualino is based on the Museo Internazionale delle Marionette and combines local and international groups. Mimmo Cuticchio's Macchina dei Sogni, in various places in Sicily, is generally a grouping of exponents of the pupi, but also brings in other puppeteers working in the "traditional" field. In Turin Controluce, with Incanti, aims for very high artistic quality and this festival always includes an element of shadow theater and productions that extend the limits of what might be called puppetry. The Centro Teatro Animazione e Figure of Gorizia, on the borders of Slovenia, has used its geographical position to introduce a great deal of work from Central Europe, and encounters with these companies have given a new flavor to a number of Italian groups. There are now numerous other festivals, some devoted entirely to Italian companies, others to a mixture of the home-produced and shows from outside. Some take the form of several days of concentrated activity, while others are spread out over a number of weeks or weekends. Another important aspect of many festivals is the various outreach programs (workshops, schools performances, master classes) that accompany them.

The internationalization of puppetry has been increased by exchanges and the existence of puppet schools which often combine students from a variety of nationalities. The prestigious schools in Prague, Barcelona, Charleville-Mézières, Berlin and elsewhere have also led to the phenomenon of the puppet actor who is thought of more as a performer with puppets than a manipulator. Most of the younger generation of "puppet actors" carry no baggage of tradition and have been very open to new forms of artistic expression. Today many puppeteers are all-round theater people and the figures are merely one of the means used by them to direct their creative energy towards an audience. Terms such as "interference" have come into use in situations where the specificity of puppet theater is difficult to define. Puppets appear in festivals of alternative theater, mime and dance and many theater companies turn to the techniques of puppet theater for elements of their productions. The sixteenth-century commedianti and "teatranti" saw no real distinction between performing as a live actor and using puppets. After 200 years of being classified as a minor distraction, today puppets have re-emerged unashamedly as a significant element of theater and it has been realized that the puppet can sometimes make a stronger impact than the live actor on the imagination of the audience.

CHAPTER 9

Two Centuries of the Lupi Company of Turin (Alfonso Cipolla)

The Earlier Years

The Lupis are the oldest active marionette company in Italy. Today they are going through a critical and not very productive period, but their past history is a glorious one and is bound up with the history of Turin, the first capital if Italy. A look at their history opens the door on the complex theatrical system that characterized the Italian stage up to the first decades of the twentieth century. This was a system in which theatrical offerings existed in a continuous state of interchange of repertoire, performers, artists and métiers, laying the foundations for a close network of relationships, alliances, antagonisms, and rivalries that ran through the theater as a whole from opera to ballet, the dramatic theaters, equestrian shows, variety shows, and puppet shows.

Information on the origins of the Lupi family is fragmentary. Like many puppeteers, their history includes an element of myth-making. With the passage of time, their desire to predominate on a national scale led them to embellish their history and push their origins back as far as possible, blotting out the memory not only of rivals, but also of their various associates.

According to the romanced version of the story Luigi Lupi was born in 1786 or even earlier. An assistant in a chemist's shop in Ferrara, he is said to have followed a fellow citizen, the glove-puppet performer Francesco Jacoponi, whose daughter he married.

Documentary evidence from archives is much clearer. Luigi "Luppi" was born in Ferrara on April 30, 1794, and there, according to the Napoleonic census of 1812, he was employed as a miller's boy.[1] There is no sign of a Francesco Jacoponi in this census, and no Jacoponi was present in Ferrara at the time. It is possible that Jacoponi's company was a traveling marionette or glove-puppet one which has left no traces beyond this anecdote. It is unlikely that Luigi married Jacoponi's daughter, since there is a certificate of marriage between Luigi Lupi and Antonia Mirano that was celebrated in the cathedral of Turin on March 18, 1815, and this contains no indication of the fact that Luigi might be a widower. This document is significant since not only does it prove that Luigi Lupi was in Turin by 1815, but it also indicates indirectly that he had already taken up the profession. Antonio Mirano was in fact the sister of Vittorio Mirano, an actor and playwright (one of the very

215

few to be commissioned as a script writer by professional marionette companies). Other witnesses of the marriage were Carlo Cuniberto, a glove-puppet performer who used the character of Gerolamo and covered the circuit between Turin and Asti, and a certain Ignazio Jaccopone. We know nothing about the latter, but this might indicate a real connection with Francesco Jacoponi.

Between 1812 and 1815 Luigi Lupi left Ferrara and, probably by stages, reached Turin, where he began his professional career. Turin was not yet his permanent base. The following year we find the young couple in Mantua, where their son Enrico was born on January 30. The latter's birth certificate is the first official document that refers to Luigi and Antonia as "comici di marionette" (marionette performers).[2] They had therefore taken up that profession and their company was a traveling one.

In 1818 the company gave performances in Turin in a little theater in the palace of the Marquis of Paesana in via delle Scuole. It would be a matter of waiting a couple of years before they could take on a full winter season at the San Martiniano Theater, next to the church of the same name. In October 1820 they presented *La Gastalda veneziana*. The takings were good, amounting to 20 lire 15 soldi, if we are to go by the account of Caronte (Arturo Calleri) in *Le memorie di una marionetta* (Turin, 1902).[3]

The *Gazzetta piemontese* of 8 January 1822 contains a notice that reads:

> The associates Lupi and Franco who have been working with marionettes for the last two years in the theater next to the church of San Martiniano have the honor of announcing that they would be happy to give performances in convents or private houses, provided that they are informed in advance so that they can arranges things in such a way that their performances for the general public will not suffer any disruption.

Turin was a very lively city for puppet shows and at the period already had a tradition that went back at least half a century. The city that Luigi Lupi encountered was beginning to develop into the great capital it would become. Between 1815 and 1848 the population increased by 58 percent. The increase in population, industrial activity and circulation of money corresponded to urban growth not just in terms of the general population but above all in public works with ministries, offices, hospitals, schools, churches and theaters. With reference to the last it is important to note that in addition to the two main Savoy theaters (the Teatro Regio and the Teatro Carignano), a host of establishments from fixed theaters to temporary booths existed to entertain the audiences of Turin. Puppet shows enjoyed particular popularity at the time. In 1819 three theaters were devoted to this activity: the one in the courtyard of the Paesana Palace, the San Rocco and the San Martiniano.

The following advertisement appeared in the *Gazzetta piemontese* of August 8, 1818:

> Presently available for rent a new "teatrino" for marionettes and "Fantocci" with places for over 400 people: apply to Sgr. Pietro Mariano, agent for the former Garessio residence, at no. 19 "contrada" (quarter) of San Francesco of Turin, where the aforementioned theater is situated.

This refers to the San Martiniano, an attractive possibility for the young outsider, Luigi Lupi, to acquire a fixed base within the complex but dynamic theatrical system of Turin. Clearly Luigi Lupi was in a sound economic situation and had done well with marionettes if within the space of a few years he intended to abandon nomadic activity and settle for a fixed base, which also implies a more important professional set-up.

But from whom did Luigi Lupi learn his trade? Was it from Francesco Jacoponi, about whom we have no information, or from others? Within a very few years of his arrival in Turin he was able to offer complex and successful shows and was occupying a theater which could accommodate over 400 spectators. Shows of this type cannot be improvised and a marionette fit-up on this scale cannot be set up overnight. What puppets and equipment was he using? And above all, who were his associates? In the article from the *Gazzetta piemontese*, there appears the name of an associate, Franco, who would be Luigi Lupi's business partner until 1841, but of whom no trace remains. Lupi and Franco clearly had to fight every day to conquer their place in the complex system of the Torinese theater.

The undisputed rulers of the Savoy capital were the talented glove-puppeteers Giovan Battista Sales and Gioacchino Bellone, inventors of the character of Gianduja. Competition was acute. For example, in 1827–1829, two marionette performers, Boch and Carminati, opened a theater at the Piazza Vittoria, but failed to overcome the hegemony of the two glove-puppeteers and had to sell all their material at auction. Lupi and Franco managed to hold their own and gradually to become more firmly established. Given the shortage of surviving documents, the repertoire for this first period of their activity is difficult to establish. They appear to have passed from the shows common to the traditional marionette and glove-puppet repertoires, such as *Il Guerrino detto il Meschino*, to more spectacular productions based on the successful ones of the theater of the time, such as *L'idolo birmano* (The Burmese Idol). The heroic-comic ballet of this name was composed by Filippo Bertini for the Teatro alla Scala of Milan in 1820 and performed in Turin two years later. It was performed for the first time by the Lupi company in Novara on September 29, 1823, with the marionette title of *The Burmese Idol; or The Arrival of the English in the Kingdom of the Pegu, with Arlecchino as a Traveler in a Flying Balloon*.[4] This must have been an ambitious and highly successful production since not only was it chosen to be presented before Queen Maria Teresa at the Castle of Chatillon (July 11, 1830) but it remained in the repertoire for over half a century. In 1824 the death of King Vittorio Emanuele on the morning of January 16 forced all the theaters of Turin to close for a period of mourning. Luigi Lupi and his associate profited from this period of inactivity to renew and modernize their repertoire and make it more competitive, following the course on which they had embarked. They aimed at spectacular shows with major scenic effects so as to reproduce on the marionette stage those that were in fashion at the Teatro Regio, the Carignano or even La Scala of Milan. These included the ballets of *Pygmalion* and *The Triumph of Love*,[5] and emphasis on such productions would ensure the dominance of the Lupi company. The *Gazzetta piemontese* of November 6, 1828, carried the following announcement:

> The Lupi and Franco company who perform with marionettes in the newly renovated and painted theater near S. Martiniano announce that on the 7th of this month they will present the spectacular production based on the ballet recently given at the theater of HRH the prince of Savoy-Carignano entitled *Elizabeth; or The Exiles of Siberia*. Nothing will be left out in imitating the staging that can be seen in big theaters. The spectacle of Vesuvius will be displayed anew, not as was done last year, but using a new mechanism copied from that presented in Milan at the Royal Teatro alla Scala.

It can be gathered that the Lupi-Franco association was a solid one, going from strength to strength, since, in the space of a few years, it managed to establish firm roots in the region. In opposition to the character of Gianduja operated by Sales and Bellone they used Arlecchino. Gianduja as a glove-puppet who speaks the same language as his audience was ideal for satire, but the Lupis with marionettes set out to earn their spurs in the field of spectacular theater in Turin, a city in a continuous state of hegemonic expansion.

Articles in the press indicate that there was fierce competition not only between marionette and glove-puppet companies, but between all sections of theatrical entertainment. In 1831 the Lupis encountered competition from a new company boasting marionettes and figures much larger than usual, "richly dressed and brilliantly operated." This was the company of the Maggi brothers of Brescia and they ran a theater in Turin called the Monte di Pietà until at least 1836.[6] In 1832 the Teatro Regio of Turin staged the mythological ballet of *Castor and Pollux*, composed and directed by Salvatore Taglioni. A mere two days later Sales and Bellone announced performances of *Castor and Pollux* for the following week with "fantocci" and indicated that this would be "adapted from the spectacular ballet currently being performed at the Teatre Regio."[7] Some two months later it was the turn of Lupi and Franco to announce their own version of *Castor and Pollux*:

> Amongst the scenes that decorate it, particularly worthy of attention are the one of the Elysian Fields, where, to increase the pleasure of the illusion, can be heard the harmony produced by "nappi" or glasses, and the final scene of Olympus in which an ingenious and magnificent machine, the work of the always praiseworthy stage-manager of the Royal Theater, is specially notable.[8]

Continuous exchange is a feature of the theatrical system of the nineteenth century. Novelties and the general repertoire were shared between theaters, but so were skills, actors, scene-painters and a variety of other associated métiers. *Meleager* (1840), performed by Lupi and Franco as soon as performances at the Regio had finished, set out to offer a direct challenge to the Regio and not simply to imitate it:

> It may be asserted here that the scenery of this little theater reaches such a degree of perfection that, allowing for due proportions, they can put several theaters to shame, including La Scala of Milan, once the emporium of contemporary celebrity and the arbiters of the good and the beautiful.[9]

Luigi and his son Enrico, who now replaced the mysterious Franco in running the company, went from triumph to triumph, constantly on the lookout for novelty, not only as far as the repertoire was concerned, but also in terms of technological innovation. In 1845, for example, gas lighting appeared at the San Martiniano while the sumptuous Teatro Regio was still using candles and oil.[10] The great turning point came in 1849 with the staging of the Battle of Goito, with 160 marionettes in Sardinian and Austrian uniforms, which inaugurated a season of grandiose productions based on patriotic history. The theater was now firmly established and its dominant feature would become the presentation of contemporary events.[11]

At a period when visual illustration was not readily available, marionettes, fascinating in their very simplicity, managed to give a face to names and evoke events that could only be read about in newspapers or passed on by word of mouth. They managed to make audiences see history when it was still only news. The Lupis, who had now been more or less permanent in a fixed spot in Turin for some 40 years, were beginning to present themselves as the theater of the city. They were a theater that spoke to the city, told its history, and preserved its memory. It was one where the audience could recognize itself and recognize its own world. In other words this was a theater that had become the accepted expression of the society that had produced it. It is difficult to know whether the Lupis were aware of this, but certainly the daily struggle to attract large audiences and the solidity of the business required constant innovation.

The route they had embarked on with *The Battle of Goito* was a winner and riding on the wave of patriotism of the Risorgimento led to the staging of the numerous revues characteristic of the years to come. These were open shows stuffed with countless pieces of information, anecdotes, unusual events and odd items of local and international news, such as the almost journalistic re-enactment of *The Earthquake of Casamicciola.*[12]

During the politically turbulent 1840s Luigi, now in his fifties, was gradually replaced as director of the company by his son Enrico. During these years the business expanded and the Lupis went from being puppeteers to being theatrical impresarios. Around 1846 they opened a second theater, the Nuovo Teatro Lupi, in the suburb of Vanchiglia just on the edge of the "Moschino," one of the most ill-reputed parts of the city. Here they did not present marionettes but popular shows of various types. In this way the Lupis were following the example of their main rivals, Sales and Bellone, who 20 years earlier had profited from the growth of the city to open the Sales Circus in the Borgo Nuovo. This enormous arena had over 2,000 places and presented puppet shows, live theater and above all equestrian pieces that brought in generous profits.

The Nuovo Teatro Lupi, with its heterogeneous and extremely popular public, had the good fortune to host the company directed by Giovanni Toselli, later to become the greatest actor of the nascent Piedmontese dialect theater. Toselli performed as Gianduja, the mask created by Sales and Bellone, which now became the symbol of Turin and of the Piedmontese attached to the cause of Italian unification.[13] Toselli put Gianduja on the stage in the same way as the puppeteers did or else put him into existing plays, but reduced the element of the grotesque in favor of greater popular realism. The success was immediate and this first experiment laid the foundations for the theater in Piedmontese and for a highly profitable season of new plays, new actors and new companies. The initial Gianduja repertoire of Toselli was identical to that of the puppeteers precisely because it was made up of scripts allowing space for the insertion of this eccentric mask into the plot and into contemporary life. Additionally he could speak directly to the audience in their own dialect.

The death of Luigi Lupi on April 7, 1856, at the age of 62 was a shattering blow for the company, which ceased its activities for several months.[14] Thanks to the help of Giovanni Toselli the theater was able to remain open, and this was the first time that Gianduja appeared at the San Martiniano.[15] According to tradition, it was Toselli who persuaded the Lupis to give up Arlecchino in favor of the now very popular and modern Gianduja. Caronte (Arturo Calleri) wrote about this, referring to Enrico Lupi:

> Originating in Mantua he did not have the right accent for Piedmontese dialect, and his sons did not wish to hurt their father by encouraging him to change the traditional mask. Toselli persuaded the son to prove himself by writing little plays and inserting two characters, the Piedmontese and the Bergamask, and this continued for several years until about 1871, when the father retired from the exhausting work and Gianduja remained lord and master.[16]

The young Lupi referred to by Caronte is the eldest son of Enrico, who, following tradition, took on his grandfather's name and called himself Luigi I to distinguish himself from the second son, also called Luigi, who became Luigi II.[17] However, this is part of subsequent history when the Lupis, now uncontested masters of the stage in Turin, with a touch of coquetry put themselves forward as a sort of reigning dynasty.

From Arlecchino to Gianduja

The passing from one mask to another was certainly a psychologically significant moment not only in the history of the Lupi company, but also in that of the theatrical system of Turin. Toselli's advice is interesting, but it is also important to look at the situation of the Lupi's great rival, Giovan Battista Sales, the inventor and owner of Gianduja. Sales had for a long time concentrated on managing his circus and had gradually abandoned the puppets, possibly also for reasons of age. The Lupis were a family, but Sales apparently had no male heirs to continue the business. We do not know exactly when he died, but certainly during his lifetime no other glove-puppeteer or marionette performer could have put Gianduja on the stage.[18] A curious article appeared in the *Gazzetta piemontese* on October 1, 1868. This lets us know about the end of the puppets of the San Rocco Theater, where Gianduja had always lived. Now he was now almost an orphan:

Yesterday, Wednesday, a delighted audience witnessed a performance in the house of Gianduja performed by Signora S. and the bailiff and the auctioneer. It was a matter of no less importance than the passing of the theater and its actors under the auctioneer's hammer. In the middle of serious discussion about the best prices for Gianduja, the enchanter Sabino and the Queen of Spain, Signor L., the proprietor of the San Martiniano, arrived and with a noble gesture of disinterestedness paid off Signora S's creditors. Then he turned to the lady whom he had released from her debts and said "all these things, the stage, the scenery, and the puppets are still yours." An act of generosity always has its imitators. The bailiff and the auctioneer also renounced their fees. Everyone can imagine the delight of Signora S. Let the public find their own term to describe the action of Signor L.

We do not know exactly who the unidentified Signora S. (Sales?) might be, but the article lets us suppose that at this date the old puppeteer was retired or even dead, given his absence at such a crucial moment for his company. Certainly this is in contrast to the strong situation in which the Lupis now found themselves in relation to their former rival, and a loudly proclaimed act of generosity was the equivalent of a definitive victory. Performances had continued at the San Rocco on a more or less regular basis until this final closure.

With the disappearance of the theatrical empire of Sales the Lupis remained absolute masters of the theatrical scene and tended to forget, or encourage others to forget, their past history so as to emphasize this supremacy. This is probably why it is hard to reconstruct the history of the first 50 years of the company and why the names of the associates who helped make it a great company have disappeared from the memories that have been handed down. Not only is information on Sales and Bellone lost, but above all anything to do with Jacoponi and the mysterious Franco.

By the 1870s the Lupi had been permanently established at the San Martiniano for half a century, and apart from a few brief tours in the summer period had no need to take their show to any other venues in Turin. Permanency allowed them to enrich their repertoire. Having to rely always on the same audience, they had to continue to attract it by increasing their productive capacity and the number of "novelties." They also suffered more from economic pressures than the traveling companies, which, as they were continually changing audiences, could operate with a relatively restricted number of productions. The Lupi repertoire was therefore destined to increase all the time, as would the material for the show, the marionettes, costumes, scenery and properties, which piled up from production

TEATRINO DELLE MARIONETTE
vicino a S. MARTINIANO

Questa sera alle ore 7 precise si rappresenta
una PIACEVOLISSIMA COMMEDIA, intitolata:

LE DELIZIE
DELLA VILLEGGIATURA
ossia
I RIDICOLI EQUIVOCI DELL'ANELLO
CON ARLECCHINO Ladro per necessità.

Quindi avrà luogo

IL NUOVISSIMO GRANDIOSO BALLO
Mitologico in 5 Atti, intitolato:

LAOMEDONTE.

PERSONAGGI CHE AGISCONO NEL BALLO

LAOMEDONTE, Re di Frigia. - ESIONE, sua figlia amante di - TELAMONE, Principe di Tracia. - ERCOLE - NETTUNO - APOLLO - Gran Sacerdote, Sacerdoti, Sacerdotesse, Guerrieri di Laomedonte e di Telamone, Musicanti, Grandi, Popolo, Danzatori, Baccanti, Fauni, Eraclidi, Tritoni e Nereidi, le Ore.

BREVE DESCRIZIONE DELLE SCENE

ATTO 1.° Veduta di mare. — Da un lato sacro Delubro dedicato ad Apollo e Nettuno, con are accese ed offerte, dall'altro lato le Mura di Troia riedificate; segue una Cerimonia religiosa. Laomedonte è sul punto di unire le destre di Esione e Telamone, quando si presentano Nettuno ed Apollo sotto mentite spoglie di lavoratori, a chiedere la pattuita mercede per la riedificazione da essi compita delle Mura della Città, Laomedonte li disprezza, trattandoli da vagreggiatori. Ira dei Numi, i quali improvvisamente compariscono nella loro vera forma. Apollo sul suo carro vola all'Olimpo, Nettuno nella sua conchiglia s'inabissa nell'onde. Laomedonte furibondo rovescia gli arredi dei Numi; gran tempesta. Comparisce nel Mare un gran Mostro Marino; tutti fuggono. ATTO 2.° Altro che introduce al Tempio di Nettuno. — Vengono tutti a consultare l'Oracolo; comparisce la risposta, che condanna Esione ad esser preda del Mostro. ATTO 3.° Mare circondato da Scogli. — Un lugubre corteggio precede Esione che vien condotta allo Scoglio, ed ivi legata; sopraggiunge Ercole co' suoi seguaci, e si propone di liberarla a patto che gli sia la medesima concessa in isposa; il padre acconsente. Si presenta il tremendo Mostro Marino, e si slancia per divorare la Donzella; Ercole lo abbatte e lo uccide; giubilo comune; Esione viene sciolta, e tutti partono per la Città. ATTO 4.° Atrio nella Reggia. — Varii del Popolo, e Grandi incerti sulla sorte dell'infelice Esione, quando s'ode un lieto suono che annunzia il fausto evento.

— Gran Piazza di Troia. — Arrivo trionfale di Ercole sul suo carro tirato dai Leoni, e di Laomedonte con sua figlia sopra una biga. Succedono Feste e Danze di Baccanti e Fauni per festeggiare si lieto avvenimento. ATTO 5.° Galleria che introduce agli Appartamenti di Esione. — Ercole reclama al padre Esione per sua sposa, e questi gliela nega; alterco fra i medesimi. Accorrono Telamone ed Esione; Laomedonte snuda il ferro contro Ercole, ma questi, preso da furore, gli scaglia un colpo di clava e l'uccide. Terrore e confusione universale; intanto Telamone trasporta altrove Esione. — Intercolonnio magnifico della Reggia, dal quale si vede il Mare con Navi. — Telamone con i pochi suoi fidi fa trasportare alle Navi la desolata Esione, che subito partono. Giungono Ercole e gli Eraclidi, che vedono la partenza di Esione; Ercole ordina a suoi l'eccidio dei Troiani e l'atterramento delle Mura e della Reggia. Segue il conflitto. Alcide abbatte le principali colonne che crollano; in questo sorge Nettuno dalle acque sulla sua conchiglia circondata da Tritoni e da Nereidi; che gl'impone di desistere. Nel mentre si apre l'orizzonte, e si vede la Reggia di Apollo col Nume circondato dalle Ore; egli pure accenna essere compita bastantemente la loro vendetta. A tal vista Ercole abbassa la clava, e tutti i suoi seguaci in varie forme atteggiati di sorpresa e d'obbedienza fanno lo stesso; ed un QUADRO GENERALE chiude l'Azione.

PREZZI D'INGRESSO ALLA PLATEA cent. 25. — AL PALCHETTONE cent. 40.

TORINO, TIP. PSORATTI, via ....

Mid-19th-century bill for the San Martiniano Theater showing a typical program of light comedy followed by a spectacular "ballo." (Courtesy Istituto per i Beni Marionettistici e il Teatro Popolare.)

to production. To modify their offering each evening the Lupis were in the habit of dividing their shows into two parts. The first consisted of a farce or a light comedy with only a few characters and a limited amount of scenery, which therefore did not demand a complex set-up, and this was the element that changed frequently. This was followed, however, by the grand ballet, fairy piece or sumptuous pantomime with a huge number of marionettes, changes of scene, trick effects and displays of virtuosity designed to astonish audiences, with the emphasis on the greatest possible spectacle. This second part was complicated to prepare and remained on the program for several weeks.

A particularly interesting production for the understanding of the delicate moment of the passage from the mask of Arlecchino to that of Gianduja is *Aida*, based on Giuseppe Verdi's colossal "melodramma," the mirror of both a world and a period. Also interesting in this production was the attempt to fuse the initial farce and the spectacular ballet into a single performance. Both parts of the program are interdependent. The first part justifies the second and provides a plot that will lead to it. In presenting the theatrical event of the moment the Lupis' real hope was to fill the theater, and they knew their audiences. What interested the audiences was not so much the music and the singing as the possibility of being in the theater and gazing at places they would never see, such as the exotic world of the Pharaohs, the love story of Aida and Rhadames, and above all the triumphal march with its jubilant display and numerous extras. The Lupis created their own farcical comedy in three acts to justify the motley collection of music and the lack of singing. This is a comedy that opens with laughter and creates expectations from the preference for *Aida* turned into a ballet. A comic masked character was needed and this is where the problem started for the Lupis. Arlecchino, their main comic character, was not really suitable for situations relating to modern life. With his masked face and chequered costume he was too obviously a theatrical character to be involved directly with everyday events unmediated by conventions. The ideal would have been to turn to a character who was a contemporary, such as Gianduja, but Gianduja until a few years before had been associated exclusively with Sales and Bellone. Sales probably died in 1865, but seven years later the Lupis still did not feel ready to take on the inheritance of Gianduja. The comic possibilities of the dialect were being run in. Their native Ferrara was by now distant. Having reached the third generation, the Lupis were beginning to risk Piedmontese, but were doing so gradually, picking up Gerolamo, the forerunner of Gianduja, who had been made famous in Milan by Giuseppe Fiando. They therefore used Gerolamo in the comedy-pretext that served as a prologue to the ballet of *Aida*, but, additionally, as a foil to him introduced a second comic character who spoke Venetian. This allowed the Lupis to keep the language of Arlecchino in which they were confident but at the same time to introduce Gerolamo with his Piedmontese dialect.

The show pinpoints a liminal moment in the history of the company, placed between the final farewell of Arlecchino and the future taking on of Gianduja. In February of 1872 the Lupis were still using their traditional mask when they put on a classic of the marionette stage, *The 99 Misfortunes of Arlecchino*. In March 1873, exactly a year after the first performance of *Aida* with Gerolamo, they performed this again as *The 99 Misfortunes of Gianduja*. The character was now run in and Gianduja could appear at the San Martiniano without fear of comparisons. Eight months later, at Christmas, was the production of *The First Gianduieide* (Gianduja show).

The Lupi stage with a late 19th-century Gianduja. (Courtesy Teatro Gianduja — Museo della Marionetta di Torino. Photograph Roberto Parodi.)

The Great Years

With Enrico Lupi and his sons the reputation of the marionettes of Turin crossed national frontiers and extended as far as America, where they stayed for two years, starting with the Centennial International Exhibition in Philadelphia in 1876 and going on to Rio de Janeiro and São Paulo.[19] Amongst the shows on offer, apart from variety numbers and *Aida*, there were three sure-fire successes based on novels by Jules Verne, which allowed them to mix the fantastic and the exotic. These were *Around the World in 80 Days* (7 acts, 17 scenes and 200 marionettes), *From the Earth to the Moon*[20] and *Twenty Thousand Leagues under the Sea*, in which Arlecchino was used again since he was better known than Gianduja on the other side of the ocean. In Brazil the Lupis adapted their fantastic ballets to make them relevant to modern times. In their *Cinderella*, Pedro II (the emperor of Brazil), the king of Portugal, Napoleon, Victor Emmanuel II, Cavour and Garibaldi were all transformed into marionettes.

Meanwhile the San Martiniano was becoming less and less suitable for such a large company. An inspection in 1881 showed the lack of safety and the general state of deterioration. The gallery had only a single exit opening onto a spiral staircase, and the gas system, hailed 40 years earlier as a tremendous innovation, had now become a serious source of danger. The Lupis would have gone ahead with a summary reconstruction of the building, despite indications that it might be expropriated for urban development, which in fact happened a few years later when the San Francesco quarter was demolished with all its churches, theaters and palaces to make way for the brand new via Pietro Micca. However the historic Teatro D'Angennes became available and the Lupis seized the opportunity to buy it, which allowed them to move from a 300-seat theater to a 1,200-seat one. The Teatro D'Angennes had been the home of the first and only state company, the Royal Sardinian Company, in which all the major actors of the period had appeared. It was therefore a theater whose audiences were anything but popular, as is indicated to some extent by the elegant neo-classical façade and the four tiers of boxes. The Lupis, who had already worked in this theater in 1869 for a series of special performances, acquired it in the summer of 1884 and opened on October 4 with *The Great Ballet Excelsior*. The following day the *Gazzetta piemontese* described this memorable evening:

> In changing their residence, the Lupi marionettes have become more important and valuable. The Teatro d'Angennes was swarming yesterday evening and it was not only children who crowded the box-office. Two thirds of the stalls were occupied by serious people. The performance was a great success. People admired the little theater erected on the stage, the scenery and decoration and the company of comic dancing figures worked with strings by the clever director and his associates. Excelsior!

In 1891 the theater took on the name of Teatro Gianduja. Memory of Giovan Battista Sales had by now nearly disappeared and the name of Gianduja became associated with that of the Lupis. A few years later, on January 19, 1894, Enrico Lupi died,[21] but for a long time the company had been firmly in the hands of the two brothers Luigi I and Luigi II. Edmondo De Amicis described them in a long article[22]:

> The first, who is now over fifty, is the more original of the pair. One of the most notable aspects of his originality is that he has been employed for 34 years in the office of Turin's police department. He is a tall strongly built man with a large head who is not easily forgotten once he has been seen. He has an obstinate forehead, bold nose, and comic mouth, the lively resolute eyes of an imaginative and hard-working man, a neck and voice thickened by loud declamation and the behavior and habits of an artist. He speaks and writes correct Italian with the colored and sculpted language of an artist. And this is all the more attractive because of the passion that warms it when he speaks of his own affairs. These include the activities of his company which he has brought to Naples, Montevideo and Buenos Aires, performances which he has given with his father at the castle of Moncalieri for little prince Oddone and for princess Maria Pia, and journeys he has made to London, Paris, Chicago, Vienna, Berlin or Denmark to study the development of his art and to see the great exhibitions which he wished to reproduce in his theater. Above all, when we listen to him judge with a view to the possibility of adapting to his stage great dramatic and operatic works and political and martial events of every country, which he follows with the closest attention, looking to every corner of the horizon for potentially theatrical occurrences, people or material, we have the feeling that within him is a great impresario, the author, actor and director of a theater company, an opera company or a ballet company who thinks of working for the general public and seems astonished when he looks around him to see wooden actors hanging on the walls.

Their painstaking search for anything that might be theatrically exploitable found its fullest expression in the satirical revues. These end-of-year shows reproduced not only the most significant events taking place in Turin, in Italy and throughout the world, but also the tiniest details, unusual occurrences, and strange accounts, all capable of recreating the living image of a period and appealing to the tastes and the curiosity of an ever-increasing public. In short the Lupi theater had become to all intents and purposes the theater of the city where the stage and the audience each offered a mirror of the other. Leading up to the turn of the century titles included: *La rivista del'anno 1863, Il ficcanaso [the busybody] ossi i misteri di 1868, Il ficcanaso invisible, Gran rivista fantastica del'anno 1870, Rrrabagas* (the title jocosely evoking Victorien Sardou's popular play), *Rivista napoletana e pur cosmopolita del 1872–73, Vela! Rivista omnibus del 1874,* and eventually *Turin ch'a bougia* (Turin That Moves).

In 1885, after a triumphal tour in Europe, Thomas Holden reached Italy with his technically more complex marionettes entirely operated with strings, which allowed them lighter and more graceful movements. This was quite different from the type of marionette in general use, with an iron rod hooked onto the center of the head, and produced a very different type of movement. The older rod marionettes lent themselves to stylization, whereas those of Holden tended towards realism. As a result the whole nature of the show changed. Rather than emphasizing the scenic realization of a story and the shrewdness of the various regional masks, the emphasis shifted to the virtuosity of the manipulator endowing his "creatures" with an illusion of life so that the marionette passed from being a metaphorical reference to the human to being man in miniature. The shows became mainly a succession of brilliant numbers. In Italy the Holden phenomenon filled the theaters. In Milan, Bologna, Rome or wherever else he went reactions and reviews were enthusiastic:

> Holden's puppets overshadow everything: here we find ourselves faced with the creations of a man of genius and see perfected mechanisms combined with naturalness and even an enchanting degree of humour. Not only do these figures dance, walk, gesticulate, sit, play music or sing like live performers, they also have a sense of the comic in their behavior and all their movements. Just one more step and these marionettes won't be marionettes any more. It's terrifying. In Thomas Holden's autobiography can be read the following aphorism: "The decadence of dramatic art is demonstrated by the sheer fact that marionettes have reached a point where they can do virtually everything that the actor can." That is terrible.... And we don't have the strength to protest. Yesterday evening at the Brunetti theater there was a full house that would not be attracted to any other dramatic novelty.[23]

The reaction of Italian marionette showmen was immediate as they tried to pursue Holden's innovations. But the Lupis were ahead of the times and even before Holden presented his show at the Balbo Theater they were trying to forestall the competition by presenting the new type of puppet with the grandiloquent name of Ida Nugaj. The exotic name of this apparently foreign attraction was no more than an anagram for Gianduja. A stroke of genius as publicity, the identity of Ida Nugaj was revealed by the Lupis in the middle of Holden's performances in Turin. This can be read about in an article of February 21, 1885, glued onto the first page of the script used by the Lupis[24]:

> Now that the performances of the Ida Nugaj puppets are drawing to an end there are masses of stories from audiences who are more used to valuing foreign things than home productions.
> Ida Nugaj is no more than an anagram for the word Gianduja, and the show at the D'Angennes performed by phenomenal marionettes has been staged by Signor Lupi, who has shown that he can emulate the amazing Fantocci-Holden show even if till now the style of our marionettes has been rather different from that of the foreign ones.
> And Lupi without entering into impossible competition with doctor Holden, who has been perfecting his sort of puppet show for twenty years, has managed to convince everyone that he is still one of the greatest marionettists in the world and in no way second to any foreign

Gianduja Theater. "Comodino" or scene with figures used as a tableau depicting a military review in front of the Gran Madre Church, Turin. (Back scene 118. Courtesy Teatro Gianduja — Museo della Marionetta di Torino. Photograph Roberto Parodi.)

competition. And in fact parts of the show that is such a hit at the Balbo have been applauded for many evenings at the D'Angennes too.

As can be guessed, the Lupis were not afraid of any rivals. They showed that they had an extremely vital theatrical business and a solid basis in terms of resources and creativity, essential requirements to cope with a complex theatrical system and strong competition. The credit belongs to the untiring productive activity of Luigi I, who went on a number of trips in Europe and beyond, so as to enrich his theater with materials and ideas. A glance at some of the titles indicates their general character: *The Hero of the Two Worlds* (1887), *The Death of Duke Amedeo of Aosta* (1890), *Stanley across Darkest Africa* (1891), *From the Amba Alagi to Makallé* (1896), *Gianduja in Tripoli* (1912), *Gianduja in the Balkans* (1913), *Trieste, Turin, Trentin* (1916), *A Misfortune for the Kaiser* (1918). The list, which could continue for hundreds of titles, went from success to success. In 1917, in the middle of the Great War, *Turin Grey Green, a Dream Extravaganza in Three Parts with Gianduja as Aviator and Bomber in His Spare Time* ran to 172 performances with exceptional takings of 69,150 lire. This was the most popular show in Turin at the time, and no other was comparable. But every season was highly successful. The record was achieved in 1923–1924 with 97,421 spectators and stunning takings of 312,724 lire.[25]

Edmond De Amicis also wrote about the 800 or more scripts making up the extraordinary and in many ways unequalled repertoire of the Lupis:

> This is a repertoire which in addition to dramas, comedies, farces, revues, ballets and fairy plays embraces the universe in terms of space and time.... It contains the old Commedia dell'Arte

pieces, dramas drawn from the literature of every country, ballets by Pratesi and Manzotti, operas by Meyerbeer and Verdi, as well as every congress, earthquake, epidemic, flood, coronation, exhibition or great discovery that has happened on the face of the two continents in the last fifty years. Every ruler, every great statesman, general or hero, every famous Italian in whatever field, or for whatever reason, from 1821 to our own day has appeared on that stage, not just in name but in appearance, carved with amazing likeness, dressed as they dressed, and reproducing as far as possible their gestures and voices and presenting the most important activities of their public life and the best known details of their private one. The Lupi theater mirrors our new national life just as it is.

De Amicis also provided a vivid description of the work of the marionettists backstage, busy giving life to one of the battle scenes for which the family was famous:

> But to know the labors of the profession and the strengths of the Lupi family they need to be seen at work on a day when there are battles. The show on these occasions is more grandiose and terrible observed from the stage than from the auditorium. It is already magnificent to see the preparations for the battle: the crowds of armed figures gathered in the darkness, broken by the glint of the bayonets and lances; the cavalry in position behind the wings, as in a review; the mules loaded with munitions in long lines on either side of the stage; the commanders with their unsheathed swords waiting for the big moment on either side, their eyes wide open and staring as if watching out for the double mystery of the horizon and death. As the solemn moment approaches the directors offer the final advice and give the supreme orders.... The frontline troops exchange the first fusillade; the first cavalry skirmish; the first casualties bang the stage floor with their papier-mâché heads and lie stiffened; but some try to get up and these few are even more furious than before. Backstage someone bangs a big drum to imitate the sound of cannon, another blows the bugle, a third activates the machine that makes a regiment pass in the distance, a fourth rushes round the stage lighting rockets fixed to the wings that produce the crackling of shot. The horseshoes get warm: on the stage is a continuous succession of ferocious melees, a clashing of heads and chests, a hail of blows, a flailing of blades, a torrent of rushing horses, mules, cannons, and machine guns, falling from bridges and rocks with an infernal racket, while above, on the bridge, the Lupi brothers and their children wave their arms letting out furious yells, threats, groans, cries for help mixed up with orders and warnings to the helpers below.... The latter are the girls who move with the speed of light, every action being precise, every step measured, every second counted. They rush back and forth between the wings and the walls, taking down the marionettes, hanging them up, taking them again, hanging them up again, putting them back, catching in flight arms, helmets, cartridge pouches, flags, whirling round like ghosts in a dense haze of smoke and an acrid smell of sulphur.

Turin ch'a bougia

The greatest of all successes achieved by the Lupis came from an old script of Enrico Lupi written in 1886 on the occasion of the third Congress of Masks held in Turin during a historic Carnival on the Piazza Castello in the heart of the city. Gianduja's "ciabot" (his house in Callianetto) was erected and here he received in person masks coming from every corner of Italy. The manifest political intention was to state that all the inhabitants of Italy are brothers and that once the kingdom of Italy had been created it was necessary to make Italians. Lupi invented a scene in which Gianduja's house literally sets off to go to Turin. This was the origin of *Turin ch'a bougia* (Turin That Moves), staged for the first time in 1898 and running for nearly 1,000 performances.

The piece starts in the winter of 1848 in the midst of war and shortages. Gianduja and his wife Giacometta are in their house in Callianetto waiting for their daughter Marghitin and above all for the polenta flour she is to bring. Finally she arrives and the polenta can be cooked. This prologue allowed the Lupis to produce a scenic effect that would remain engraved on the minds of generations of spectators: Giacometta throws the flour into a pot and shortly after tips onto the table a fine lump of steaming polenta. The scene was immortalized on posters, publicity, programs and calendars and it became the company's visiting card for decades. Once the table has been set, Gianduja's youngest son, Pierino, arrives with two friars asking for hospitality. Gianduja shares his humble meal with them, talking of the war and of his third son, who is far away. One of the friars, who is more like a magician from a fairy story, or perhaps Jesus Christ come down to earth, offers to reward Gianduja by granting him three wishes. Gianduja has some strange and apparently incomprehensible requests (such as being able to stop a person coming down from a tree they have climbed), but in the course of the play these will prove to be providential. Left alone with his woes, Gianduja miserably calls on Death, who appears immediately with a crash of thunder. Gianduja pulls himself together and cunningly, thanks to the first of his strange requests, manages to trick Death and obtain an extension of 11 years so that he will not see him again until 1859. He does not waste time but summons his family and decides on the spot to quit Callianetto and leave no trace behind. This leads to the other big scene of the prologue. Everything comes to life for the move, not only people and animals, but the table, chairs, furniture, objects, walls and the house itself. This scene received great applause and the effect was accentuated by the use of a revolving panorama that gave the impression of movement.

In the second part of the show Gianduja and his family find themselves in the midst of the battle of Solferino amongst horses, fighting and shooting, which ends with nothing less than the appearance of the king. Gianduja looks for his eldest son, who finally arrives preceded by a fanfare from the bersaglieri. Their joy is brief because in the meantime a German soldier turns up. This is Death, who has come for Gianduja as the 11 years are up. But thanks to his second request Gianduja beats Death once more, obtaining a respite of another ten years, which takes us up to 1870.

The third part is set on the Piazza della Signoria in Florence, which in the meantime has become the temporary capital of Italy. Gianduja receives the news that Rome is about to be taken by the bersaglieri, but barely has a chance to rejoice about this before Death appears, this time as a policeman. He tries once more to defeat Death, this time playing mora, but the game is interrupted by the umpteenth coup de théâtre. Amidst detonations of cannons the curtain falls and the scene changes to the breach of the Porte Pia on September 20 and the flight of the pope's Swiss guard pursued by the bersaglieri under General Lamarmora. Rome is now the capital. After a musical interlude (the Lupis disposed of a real orchestra at the time), the action returns to Turin and to the modern period. Gianduja disconsolately wonders whether it is worthwhile to have to face so many hardships and mishaps, including battles, the African campaign, the economic crisis, etc. His soliloquy is interrupted by the arrival of an allegorical character, Fischietto (also the name of a celebrated satirical magazine at the Risorgimento), who consoles him by presenting him with a charming little girl who calls him "Daddy" and is an allegorical representation of the Universal Exhibition of Turin of 1898. Music, change of scene and we arrive at the Piazza San Carlo. The celebrations show a succession of cyclists, workers, trams and carriages whose purpose

Design for front curtain ("sipario") of Gianduja Theater, early 20th century. View of Turin and the Mole Antonelliana (today's cinema museum). (Courtesy Augusto Grilli.)

is to illustrate the Exhibition and the beauty to come for the Turin of the future. But Death does not forget Gianduja and now appears disguised as a coachman. A change of scene takes us to the cemetery. Gianduja sees the ghosts of all the great men who have contributed to the freedom of Italy, and this is the moment he should join them. However, he wants to see the inauguration of the Exhibition so badly that Death feels sorry for him. A change of scene leads to an apotheosis of the Exhibition, the arrival of the various Italian masks, and a grand finale in which all those who have caused Turin to "bougiè" (move) cross the stage. These range from Cavour to Mazzini and from Vittorio Emanuele to Brofferio, and the show ends with the music of Brofferio's song "Ij bogianen."[26]

As can be guessed *Turin ch'a bougia* is an open show that allows for the staging of salient events of history familiar to the audience. It also introduces the possibility of linking together in a single show the very best examples of marionette virtuosity from previous shows. This is why, enriched with new scenes to keep abreast of the times, it was revived in 1901, 1911, 1928 and even in 1948 and 1954. In this final version even the lawyer Agnelli, Fiat and the inauguration of the Motor Show were able to appear.

The Last Years

On October 4, 1934, there was a celebration of Gianduja's 50 years at the Teatro d'Angennes. A special publication was printed for the event and the program presented was divided into three parts. The evening opened with "Variety numbers that were performed in the San Martiniano Theater on 24 April, 1884, for the final closing down of the little theater."[27] These were followed by *Turin ch'a bougia*, and the show closed with *From the Earth to the Moon.*

This celebration of the Gianduja Theater was the last great manifestation of the Lupis.

The inexorable decline of the company resulted from a variety of different factors, some of which are a little obscure. Obviously the cinema was putting pressure on them (the first sound films date from 1932) and marionette shows were rapidly losing their social role, but there were other causes. For the 1934 celebration the Lupis spent an enormous amount of money to modernize their theater and to provide it with new boxes. This was certainly not an indication of crisis, and yet three years later in 1937 the Gianduja company presented its last show. What happened in this brief lapse of time? The Fascist regime, politically opposed to dialects, was probably a factor. About a year earlier, for example, they had forced the Familija Turineisa to wind up its activities. This was an organization which already in its title looked forward to a revival of the traditions of Turin, the most important of which were the glorious Giandujesque carnivals. Obviously the Lupis were in difficulties and these were made all the more acute by a decree of December 28, 1938, when the Service of the Monuments of Piedmont declared the Teatro Gianduja as being of "national importance," thus obliging it to embark on new activities.[28] Events were now moving rapidly and in addition a shadow of speculation now hung over the building. The coup de grace occurred on February 23, 1939, with the submission of an application to the magistrates of Turin by the architect Clemente Rocchetta on behalf of a developer who wanted to acquire the theater belonging to the Lupi brothers so as to turn it into a cinema-theater. The proposal would have guaranteed the historical façade of the building and its decoration, but would have gotten rid of the boxes and raised the stage. The following year the Angennes Cine-Theater Company was set up. Its official purpose was to keep the marionette tradition alive, but it was really a question of a radical transformation of the theater into a polyvalent auditorium mainly adapted for cinema, even if space was to be left for puppet entertainment between the films.[29] The Lupis had little choice. The sale or rather the selling-off of the theater was subsequently hastened following the bombing of Turin on the night of June 11, 1940. The theater was not directly involved, but neighboring buildings were destroyed or burnt. The Lupis received 400,000 lire but were faced with a project for reconstruction of more than 2.5 million lire. So, on June 24, 1940, the keys were handed over to the new owners. The same day Riccardo Lupi (1876–1940), son of Luigi I, shot himself in the head after an attempt to hang himself. The Lupis would never return to their theater. The extremely beautiful decoration of the ceiling of the D'Angennes was detached and probably lost during the war. The marionettes, equipment and scenery were divided up amongst members of the Lupi family and a large part of this immense treasure found its way to the Balon, Turin's flea market, where for some small change and without realizing it a part of the history of Italy could be carried home as a children's toy. Enrico Lupi (1871–1954), the artistic soul of the company at the time, so as to escape the overwhelming events and then the war, departed to a village near Asti, where he remained until his death. He lived in dignified retirement. Other more humble glove-puppet performers helped him eke out his subsistence with commissions for scripts or backcloths.

The company was de facto inherited by Luigi "Luisin" Lupi (1873–1964). Previously he had only a small part in the creation of shows, but was the voice of Gianduja, and now he tried to manage as best he could. Despite serious depletions the company still retained a significant amount of material, but the loss of a permanent theater was anything but painless. In 1941 the company gave a few performances for children at the *La stampa* show. The title of the piece was almost a challenge: *Gianduja l'è sempre viv* (Gianduja Is Still Alive).

Now began a long period during which, without a fixed base, the Lupis had to travel the province visiting tiny places or giving performances in the various theaters of Turin (the Carignano, the Alfieri, the Gobetti) but these were only occasional and generally, if not exclusively, for juvenile audiences. They also worked at the Romano on Piazza Castello before they found a home for 12 years in via Roma in an underground space made for a metropolitan railway that was never built. Then the marionettes acquired what has been their home up till now—a little theater under the church of San Teresa which naturally was renamed the Teatro Gianduja.[30] This marked the start of a new phase. In 1971 the Teatro Stabile billed the historic *Turin ch'a bougia* as homage to a glory of the city that should be saved. The theater and television director Massimo Scaglione created a production based on the various updatings of the script and the voices for the marionettes were provided by a number of well-known actors. Nine years later the Regio of Turin and La Fenice of Venice, still with Scaglione as the director, presented Marc'Antonio Ziani's musical drama *Damira placata*. Thanks to the intervention of Gian Mesturino this was followed by the magnificent productions of Luigi Manzotti's historical ballet, *Pietro Micca* (in the version by Mario Pasi) and Arrigo Boito's *Re Orso* (King Bear), both directed by Ugo Gregoretti, and by *Aida*, directed by Filippo Crivelli and based on the Cairo production. Meanwhile, in the spaces adjoining the theater in via San Teresa the Museo della Marionetta was set up. This was a permanent exhibition of the family treasures: backcloths, marionettes, furnishings, carriages, thrones, costumes, properties. But after the breaking up of the collections that followed the closing of the D'Angennes, this was a mere shadow of one of the richest marionette shows in the world.

At the San Teresa performances were generally restricted to Sundays apart from a few school performances in the mornings. The company had to take on young actors supplementing their income by moving some of the simpler marionettes and occasionally having their voices recorded for new tapes. The Lupi family now had other jobs. Gigi painted scenery for the big theaters and also posters, while his son Franco works as a lighting technician. Since the 1990s the there have been many difficulties and further losses of material. The company did manage to restage the historical production of *Aida* to celebrate the Verdi centenary, but it no longer contains a single member of the Lupi family, and is going through a period of uncertainty and artistic stasis. The purchase of the rich materials that still remain for a public collection was initiated a number of years ago, and this could finally give back to the city this unrepeatable theatrical experience indissolubly linked to two centuries of Italian history.

CHAPTER 10

The Fratelli Napoli
Puppet Company: The Catanian Opira
from 1921 Until Today
(Alessandro Napoli)

From the middle of the nineteenth century until 1973, when the Fratelli Napoli presented the story of *Erminio della Stella d'Oro* in daily episodes for the last time, the Catanian opera dei pupi offered serialized performances based on the literature of chivalry to a predominantly popular public (even if often composed of the middle classes and students). In Catania the chivalric repertoire was more extensive than in Palermo. Each episode was linked with the next and was divided into three acts or parts and between the second and third act came the "invito" (announcement) for the following day's performance.[1]

In eastern Sicily the show was referred to as the "opira" as opposed to the more western "opra."[2] For the traditional audience of the opira the numerous stories enacted were more real than any history documented by historians, since in popular culture truth and legend have equal historical value within the dimensions of myth. This audience was an initiated one and knew in advance the plot that might be performed on a particular evening and was familiar with the many different ways in which the stories were transmitted. They had been to previous seasons of puppets or had heard the stories told at home by their fathers and grandfathers, or by friends they met for a drink. The more literate had read the popular chivalric romances published in serial form by Giusto Lodico, Giuseppe Leggio, Costantino Catanzaro and others. Chivalric narrative was diffused in a variety of ways and even mothers would pull installments out of a chest and read them to children too young to go to the opira.

Audiences happily went to see the same things because the enjoyment and the function of the theatrical event was less to learn a story with anything new in it than to confirm already familiar stereotypes and allow them to relive the intellectual emotions and feelings where they had already experienced them. Lovers of the opira formed a culturally homogenous group united by attending it and by their consciousness of sharing the stories as an important form of collective knowledge and they went to the theater for the entirely social purpose of reconfirming their culture and consolidating every evening the identity and solidarity of the group in a ritual manner. People went to the opira to find on its stage a picture and an explanation of the world and a reflection on existence, with its irreconcilable contrasts, and on the ambiguities encountered in everyday life. An example of this is the much-loved hero Rinaldo, whose castle of Montalbano is razed to the ground by Carlomagno, who takes his family hostage after listening to the treacherous villain Gano di Magonza. At the theater audiences, as Buttitta has so aptly put it, were able to "redeem mythically their own subordinate situation" by projecting themselves and identifying with the social and reparative ascent of the vanquished hero. Rinaldo, banished by Carlo Magno, became emperor of Trebisond with 36 rulers under him who, after his supposed death, went so far as to threaten the stability of the Holy Roman Empire. Mythical redemption also occurred through Peppininu, the popular mask of the Catanian pupi, who punishes those guilty of treason by beating them, stoning them, whipping them and carrying out the death penalty. He thus becomes the symbolic expression of popular aspirations for natural justice. The opira provided a ritual catharsis through the true and appropriate rites for the exorcism of evil, as can be seen in the quartering of the Magonzan traitors, Galeone, Gano and Griffonello, always followed by the spectators falling on the dismembered body, whose limbs were eventually divided amongst the audience and burned in the street — which led to puppeteers preparing each time a straw doll that could be offered for public mockery.

The puparo's skills consisted in his capacity through the production to revive already familiar emotions and to involve and move the audience exactly where its expectations should be satisfied, thus confirming the spectator in the culture of his group. He offered all this and consequently enjoyed a special position in his own social context. He was the artist, the sage, the intellectual and the repository of knowledge of social relevance. He had the right to the honorary title of "Don."[3] If he was late he was anxiously awaited at the entrance to the theater. If disputes broke out amongst the spectators, he only had to appear on the front of the stage to calm them immediately. Giovanni Verga in his novel *Don Candeloro e C.i.* (1894) wrote: "If a dispute broke out in the theater and knives were produced, Don Candeloro had only to appear between the wings and say: 'Hey there, lads!' with his fine rich voice."

Like the Commedia dell'Arte the performances were improvised according to the division into acts, the succession of scenes and other summary indications in the hand-written scenario. The "upranti" or "upiranti" (showmen) were extremely jealous of these manuscripts and rarely allowed anyone to use or borrow them. Scenarios were obtained from a "parraturi" whose pupils they had been, or else acquired by luck or chance. Most often they were put together by the parraturi himself and based on a "book," that is to say a romance of chivalry published in installments and/or the memory of a staging of the story previously seen by him. Improvisation did not mean making the show up on the spot. Each upiranti had a very precise grammar for staging a story. This was learned orally and by following the practice of a performer he had chosen as his master. For the puparo this was picked up unconsciously in the same way that the speaker of a language knows how to use it but would not be capable of formulating the rules. The grammar of the performance of the opera dei pupi has been reconstructed in the same way as the grammar of a spoken language can be reconstructed.[4]

This analysis of the Catanian tradition of the opera dei pupi uses as its model the grammar of staging established by Pasqualino and Vibaek.[5] It is an indispensable tool for analysis and provides an effective comparative schema which is useful to bring out the similarities and differences between the Catanian and Palermitan styles as well as the similar-

Catanian cartellone showing Gano "quartered" by two Peppininus on horseback. (Courtesy Museo Internazionale delle Marionette Antonio Pasqualino. From Antonio Pasqualino, *L'opera dei pupi*. Courtesy and © of Sellerio, Palermo.)

ities and differences between the traditional opera dei pupi and the form that evolved between the 1970s and the present as a result of innovations introduced by the pupari. The work of Vibaek and Pasqualino is based mainly on the analysis of the Palermitan opra and the variants of the pupi theater found throughout western Sicily, and only occasionally on those of the Catanian opira widespread in eastern Sicily. The resemblances between the Palermitan style and the Catanian are numerous; for this reason, it isn't necessary to mention them individually. I shall, however, point out the most notable and significant differences and work on the assumption that whenever I do not indicate the contrary Catanian and Palermitan practices are fairly similar.

I shall expound a grammar of staging using micro and macro units. The micro units employed by the Catanian upiranti can be described as elements of codes and groups of codes. In both we find codes of characters and codes of places. The code is a system of signs made up by the relationship between two subsystems. Codes bring together two organized sets. One of these belongs to the expressive aspect and is made up of elements that can be perceived by the senses, which Umberto Eco calls the "syntactic system." The other relates to the content and is made up of signifieds that the sensory elements of the first system take on within a communicative praxis (in our case the conventional opera dei pupi, traditionally shared between audience and puparo), which Umberto Eco calls the "semantic system."

Pasqualino and Vibaek identified eight codes on which the opera dei pupi is based. These are the linguistic code, including a repertoire of stereotype phrases; codes of vocal quality; the code of noises and inarticulate vocal sounds; the code of music; the code of lighting; the kinetic code of movement and gesture; the figurative code of the characters; the figurative code of places. Some elements involving emotion employ several codes at the same time: vocal sounds show evidence of linguistic codes and codes of vocal quality; the visual images of the pupi contain both kinetic codes and ones relating to the figurative appearance of the characters.

Each of the codes of the *opira* corresponds to more general codes of life which are simplified or made more complex by a strategic choice of significant characteristics, or as it would be put in phonology, pertinent features.[6] The codes of the opera dei pupi have a degree of autonomy in the sense that some differ from the codes of everyday life only in the reduction of the number of pertinent features and others are different notably by the choice of pertinent features. In the second case the correspondence with the general codes of life is indirect in that the relationship is mediated by codes already constituted in theater practice of the nineteenth century, as for example is obvious in the kinetic codes. In any case, however, whether the system is simple or complicated, the pupi theater has produced a form of hypercodification.[7]

The codes also present differing degrees of complexity. The figurative code for the characters and that for places, together with elements from other codes, make up two more complex codes: the typology of the characters and the typology of places. These two typologies are a pair formed on the level of expression of several different materials, or from what De Marinis calls "*more elements of different significant material.*"[8] The typology of characters and the typology of places have two degrees of identification: generic and individual. The typologies of the opera dei pupi have been greatly crystallized in the sense that whatever the moment and whatever the theater a certain character and a certain place have been represented in the same way. Because of this the typologies transmit much information both in their individual aspect, linked to a single narrative cycle, and in their more general aspect, valid for any cycle.[9] The use of codes is determined partly by the rules for the formation of the type scene and partly by the narrative situation. Acts and scenes of a single "serata" (episode) are composed according to rules for the formation of scenes similar to the grammatical rules for a language with the micro units that constitute the vocabulary of that grammar. The rules for the formation of scenes are the expressive aspect of the system of signs, of which the content aspect is made up of the story and the world picture that is expressed in it.

The rules for the formation of scenes that pupari have only learned orally or by experience determine the macro unit: the type scene with a limited number of recurrent schemata. A type scene does not always coincide with the scenic unit taking place in front of a single backcloth, labeled from this and numbered sequentially in the scenarios of the parraturi who base their segmentation of the action on spatio-temporal criteria such as change of place and/or breaks in time. Such a scenic unit, which can include after the exit of characters the entrance of others, can correspond to more than one type scene, and sometimes a type scene can occupy the space of more than one scenic unit. The rules for the formation of the type scenes determine the music, the sounds, the entrance (to the left or right of the audience), the positions, the movements and a series of lines spoken by the characters according to their placing in the generic typology. Every scene is adapted to different narrative situations.

This can be resumed by saying that the narrative situations of the plot are divided up and set down in a sequence of type scenes selected from the limited number of models offered by tradition. The choice of the type scene is conditioned by the narrative situation only in the sense that it must be compatible with it. Thus the type scenes with the rules according to which they are formed predetermine the use of the greater part of the elements of the codes. The elements of the performance are determined not by rules for the formation of scenes but by the narrative situation and are a part of the discourse that makes up the individual typology of the characters and places.

In Catania at the end of the 1950s and then even more in the 1960s and 1970s the economic and consumerist boom and the mass media, notably television, upset the relationship between the puparo and his devoted traditional audience, which followed every evening's episode and loved the pupi as if they were real people. In the country towns this trend was not obvious until the 1970s, when the Napoli company made frequent tours to Misterbianco, Motta S. Anastasia, Aci Catena and Paternò. The new and relative affluence and its symbols — television, car, refrigerator, washing machine — had produced a dangerous cultural phenomenon. The popular classes now had free access to consumer goods, which they sought more as symbols of economic security than as things to be used. They identified the traditional elements of their culture as symbols of their earlier poverty and rejected them while following at the same time a leveling mass culture identified with wealth. Pupi and pupari bore the brunt of this cultural process. The former were no longer symbolic heroes in whom they could recognize themselves and with whom they could identify; the latter had to give up their status as "priests" of a rite of reconfirmation of a culture that was celebrated every evening.

The audiences of the pupari began to change. Gradually the subordinate classes were replaced by one-off audiences of the middle classes and of tourists. The former included enlightened people who came to the opera dei pupi out of honest and serious intellectual curiosity, partly aroused by Pitrè's studies and partly from an awareness that great literary works such as the *Chanson de Roland, Morgante, Orlando inamorato, Orlando furioso* and *Gerusalemme liberata* were the sources for the stories of the pupi. However there were also more prejudiced middle-class people who approached the opera dei pupi as a ridiculous show of little cultural value that could be comic because of the linguistic simplicity of the pupari and the machinelike movements of the figures. In the best of cases their attitude was one of condescending irony that masked a solidly negative assessment of popular culture in the wake of the misunderstandings provoked by the solemn mockery of the opira by literary celebrities of the island such as Nino Martoglio. The tourists in the audience were mostly those in search of local color.

The pupari were presented with a difficult alternative. They had to either sell the puppets and change their profession or invent shows that could break into a public that was middle class rather than popular, one of uninitiated people knowing little of the plots of the tales of chivalry and who would not be returning to the theater the next day. The pupi performance had to become a cycle of episodes that could be completed in a single evening. Not all the pupari took up the challenge and many sold their pupi and equipment. These were difficult years characterized by great hardship. In companies with a long tradition behind them this often caused bitter discussions and even quarreling between the exponents of the old and new generations. The work that the infinitesimally small number of companies still in existence did in those years and on into the 1980s and 1990s has been carefully documented and studied by Antonio Pasqualino.

Two avenues opened up for puppeteers. They could settle for artificial, insipid and meaningless shows, overdoing spectacular effects, filling them with battles and abbreviated dialogues in which they were prepared to exaggerate mistakes in grammar and syntax so as to delight a superficial bourgeois audience with solecisms. Otherwise they could take account of the full potential of the *opira* as a metaphor for the world and an instrument for reflection on contemporary reality and out of the consistent reality of its basic continuity find a theatrical formula that would overcome every social and cultural inequality so as to address every type of audience.[10]

There were two main types of problems in adapting the show for contemporary audiences. First and foremost shows had to be put together that would allow for the presentation of an action that was already complete. This meant giving up the presentation of a full traditional cycle, or reserving it for special occasions only. Then it was necessary to balance the traditional codes of performance with the tastes of an audience that was no longer a popular one and which, for the most part, as has already been indicated, very often had a patronizing attitude to the opera dei pupi, seeing it only as an amusing form of theater. To reshape the repertoire required a deep knowledge of the plots of the stories and a full command of the eight codes of staging identified by Pasqualino and Vibaek. These codes can be taken apart to adapt them to the new requirements of the audience without reneging on tradition, but only if they have been learned and handed down without a break over long years of patient apprenticeship with one of the renowned masters.

The studies of Pasqualino and Vibaek have encouraged the keenest of the traditional pupari, the Figli d'Arte Cuticchio in Palermo and the Fratelli Napoli in Catania, to reflect on their traditional way of staging, and this has led them to the acquisition of a real awareness of the codes and the rules of production of the show in performance. As a consequence the pupari of today not only know what to do but also how to formulate the underlying rules of their practice. This even applies to some pupari who remain unwilling to recognize any debt for their development to the world of scholars.

Between 1973 and 1978 the Fratelli Napoli experimented with several shows completed in a single evening.[11] With 60 years of theatrical activity behind them, they welcomed the proposals of Nino Amico, a descendant of the famous Catanian pupari Gaetano Crimi and Raffaele Trombetta.[12] He proposed that instead of the older technique of improvisation, the pupi should adopt a written text taking on the essence of the tradition and continuing to practice the rules of staging and that this should allow for a "theater of the word and of ideas performed by pupi" and for a dramaturgy that would use the content and theatrical means of tradition to express in contemporary language the underlying religious, social, existential and immediately human meanings of popular narrative and poems of chivalry. On this basis he established a distinction between "opera dei pupi performed according to a scenario on a subject relating to the paladins" and "theater with pupi performed with a text based on traditional content."[13]

The adoption of the extended script was justly associated by Nino Amico with the Catanian tradition as a natural development. The Catanian "parraturi" were already in the habit of writing out in full the texts of the more memorable set speeches ("parlate") of the opira. I can remember the speech where Namo di Baviera reproves Carlo Magno for persecuting Berta and Milone[14]; Angelica's set speech at her entry into the court in Paris[15]; Angelica's declaration of love to Medoro in the shepherd's hut[16]; the story of the accursed Lidia to Astolfo at the mouth of hell[17]; and the contrast between two different conceptions of knightly duties in the dialogue between Oronte of Morocco and general Sciantivaude from Berlin before their duel, the conversation between Soranzo of Russia and the "savage" Ideo in a cage, the monologue of Ideo, now Soranzo's general, after the passage of Evangelina's crusade in Metz and the account of the travels and deeds of Tigreleone upon his arrival in Berlin — all based on episodes from Salvatore Patanè's *Story of Erminio della Stella d'Oro*. The texts of significant speeches were appended to the scenario for the evening on separate sheets in the case of Raffaele Trombetta, or else written inside the script itself and noted as "corresponding scenes" as with Biagio Sgroi.

In the last decades of the twentieth century, the absence of a fixed theater where shows could be done added to the problem of adapting the opera dei pupi to a new audience. It became increasingly difficult to find spaces suitable for working puppets 1.3 meters high and it was not always possible to find halls where the stage and proscenium could be erected. To solve this problem and bring the pupi into smaller spaces such as gymnasia, school theaters, parish halls and lecture rooms for clubs and cultural associations, Natale Napoli, in 1973, had the idea of small pupi 80 centimeters high which together with a proportionately reduced stage made all these spaces suitable for pupi performances and allowed the Catanian tradition to perform to many more spectators than they could have done with the larger figures. This had been tried by Nino Amico in 1965 with puppets he had originally built for his drawing-room theater and subsequently used for public performances. The small pupi kept intact the codes, rules and techniques of the traditional performance and thus allowed a new audience of school children, university students, professional people and the educated middle classes to develop a love for the Catanian opira.

The new conception of theater with pupi, like the theater of words and ideas which clearly shows the influence of three or four centuries of European text-based theater, was substantially shared by the Fratelli Napoli (and myself) until 2000. But when what I like to define as an almost iconoclastic fury began to predominate in the texts of Nino Amico, Fiorenzo Napoli and I decided to develop scripts that would remain as faithful as possible to the scenarios and the traditional performance. Nino Amico's iconoclasm showed itself in three main areas: noticeable modification of traditional narrative material, radical changes of the figurative codes and of the individual generic typology of the characters, and above all an excessive weight given to reflection on philosophical and existential matters which, put in the mouths of the characters of the opera dei pupi, too often ran the risk of weighing down the dramatic dialogue and slowing the action, which resulted in a loss of the rhythm of the performance.

The regular adoption of a written script, which is a useful instrument to fix, wherever possible, the traditionally improvised dialogues of the parraturi, and the adoption of 80-centimeter figures have with time resulted in three types of change. Where the puppets are concerned there have been modifications of the internal and the mechanical structure. In the performance it is the codes selected and the type scenes, which it will be necessary to describe for the traditional Catanian opera dei pupi according to the model of Pasqualino and Vibaek, appropriately modified and/or integrated where it has seemed useful or suitable. At the level of form and content there has been a transformation of the dramatic structure and of the way of presenting the story.

A show written by this author and Fiorenzo Napoli will serve to describe the codes and changes, examining similarities and differences between old and new shows. Today's audiences, although they do not constitute a clearly defined social group as they did when the show was presented in daily episodes, have clearly recognizable preferences. They appreciate the dramaturgical style, the dialogue and the type of characterization exemplified in the texts created by Fiorenzo Napoli and myself. These resulted from a very careful combing through of the traditional sources, including the manuscripts of the "serate" (nightly installments) and the "parlate" (set speeches), and the eventual audio recordings of shows with dialogue improvised by the older parraturi. I am particularly proud of the research and selection which provided the raw materials on which Fiorenzo Napoli and I base our close examination of tradition. Usually once the necessary material in the scenarios and recordings has been selected I draft the first bits of dialogue, which Fiorenzo and I then hone, bearing in mind his speech rhythms as a parraturi and the amount of time needed for a show. There is often a degree of friendly debate between Fiorenzo and myself when we draw up the scripts. I prefer to keep much more of the formulaic expressions in the dialogues while he tends to limit them when they do not accord with his rhythm as a parraturi or, as he thinks, are too repetitive. Fortunately our collaboration and mutual esteem always lead us to find a suitable solution.

The characters are presented in such a way that the psychology is made obvious, the dialogue is explicit and carries an emotional charge and the contrasts are heavily underlined. By doing this we are following the path of a stylistic tendency of the Catanian opira. From the beginning of the twentieth century it borrowed from the naturalistic theater, to which its dramaturgy was linked in many ways. It is worth remembering that many great actors, such as Giovanni Grasso, began as parraturi.

To understand the process of transformation that the Catanian opera dei pupi has undergone in the shows currently being presented by the Napoli Marionette Company, we'll examine *Guerrino Meschino*, staged in 2007 and based on a script established by myself and Fiorenzo from the old scenarios of the Catanian opira. The story of Meschino, with literary origins in a romance by the fifteenth-century street singer Andrea da Barberino, was part of the general heritage of the Catanian repertoire, but the last performance known for certain in eastern Sicily was in 1949. In the Napoli family this story was, however, very familiar. Some of the last posters painted by Rosario Napoli, who died prematurely in 1934, depicted the exploits of Meschino, and Meschino's adventures were related every evening by the grandfather, Don Gaetano, to his grandson Fiorenzo when he cried because he was too young to be taken to the theater. Fiorenzo remembered this and wanted to stage it again. We were fascinated by a story that brings together all the typical elements of the romances of chivalry through the travels of Guerrino in search of his origins and his parents, which take him to the East, the West and the Otherworld and come over as a journey to find his own identity. This last aspect of the old popular romance seemed particularly suitable for a revival of Meschino in the twenty-first century. Just as it was in the old local theaters, this tale is still profoundly relevant and can provide keys for an understanding of reality and conceptual instruments suitable for finding one's way in the great labyrinth of the world.

Immediately we were faced with two problems. The first was to articulate in a single show the whole of the main narrative sequence of the novel running from the birth of Guerrino and the separation from his parents to finding them again 32 years later in the prisons of Durazzo. Condensing all these events into a single evening implied making significant cuts in the story and also introducing linking pieces to cover long intervals of time. Many of the events had to be narrated rather than acted out and the linking pieces had to be played at both the level of dramatic mimesis and also the narrative one. The second difficulty was that the Napoli company had not performed *Meschino* since 1933 and Gaetano, Pippo and Natale Napoli, who had staged this story, were no longer with us. The only sources for a new production were a very brief scenario and the visual material provided by the cartelli, which indicated how some scenes were developed (Meschino at the trees of the sun and the moon, or the recognition scene with his parents in the prison) and gave an idea of the physical appearance of the individual characters. To this could be added Andrea da Barberino's romance. More difficult for us was the reconstruction of all the scenes in which Peppininu with his quips lived the same adventures as Meschino according to the schemata of folkloric inversion, or took on the role of guardian and disenchanted counselor of the hero, embodying the audience's point of view of the events presented.

To resolve the first problem we decided to pick out the key moments of Guerrino's quest: the taking of Durazzo and the imprisonment of his parents Milone and Finisia; the jousts in Constantinople where Guerrino displays his valor for the first time; the farewell to princess Elisena, who had disdained him, calling him a re-sold slave and inciting him to go in search of his parents; the famous episode of the trees of the sun and the moon, when Guerrino learns his real name; the visit to the kingdom of Sibilla of Aspromonte; and finally the battle which allows for the re-conquest of Durazzo and the descent of Guerrino into the prisons, where he finds and recognizes his father and mother. Also to be linked were events of different periods, from Guerrino newborn, sold by pirates as a slave to Epidonio the merchant of Constantinople, to those of him as a young man in love with princess Elisena of Constantinople and going to fight in the jousts for which her hand is proclaimed as the reward. Further elements that had to be incorporated were the attack on Constantinople by the Turks following the outcome of the tournament (a war obviously won thanks to the strength of Guerrino's arm) and the innumerable wanderings of Guerrino. All these things had to be told, but we did not want to do this outside the action or outside the traditional rules of staging. The only person who could provide such an account was Peppininu as a metahistorical character with an independent existence outside specific limits of time or place and a long history as a "famiglio" (servant) to different knights. We therefore chose him to relate in his pleasant and witty dialect all the elements of the story that we could not for reasons of time. He did this in short interludes outside the main action or at the end of scenes in which he appeared following his lord Guerrino. So as to suggest to the audience that they had seen a whole cycle of the opira in a single evening, at the opening of the show we brought in front of the curtain a pupo with a visible manipulator for the "invito" as a way of linking the new audience with the ancient ritual of the traditional performance.

Once the framework of the show had been settled it was a matter of reconstructing the dialogue. The scenarios in the family's possession were of little help. I found some dialogue for the scene between Peppininu and the oracle at the trees of the sun and moon written by Giuseppe Crimi, but nothing more. Obviously Fiorenzo on the basis of his considerable experience as a parraturi was in a position to improvise Peppininu's lines, which established him as a comic counterpoint to the adventures of Guerrino. The servant had to show Meschino the same affectionate solicitude that is shown to the heroes of the other stories, such as Orlando. But it was still unclear how the key scene of the disdainful dismissal of Guerrino by Elisena would work, or how to handle the comic scene of the enchanted table laid out for Peppininu by the handmaid of the sorceress Sibilla, or to present the recognition scene between Guerrino and his parents.

A script of the *Guerin Meschino* of the Neapolitan pupante Luigi Luigini, held by the Museo delle Marionette Antonio Pasqualino in Palermo, was of great help. The scripts of the Neapolitan pupanti had dialogue written out in full, unlike those in the Catanian tradition, which usually present only the texts of significant speeches. The Neapolitan script presented substantially the same structure for staging the story as the Catanian scenario in our possession and, naturally, had Pulcinella instead of Peppininu in the role of the hero's servant. The fully written dialogue also allowed us to deal with some of the problem scenes. For example the dynamic of the notorious magic table scene was now clear to us. The remaining doubts were now cleared up and the difficult points of the Catanian scenario could be read and interpreted in the light of this extended Neapolitan script.

We now put our script together in the way I have already indicated. For some of the dialogue we decided to use the masterly prose of *Il Guerrino Meschino*, a romance by the Sicilian writer Gesualdo Bufalino. In so doing we were following an old custom of the Catanian opira, which liked to highlight the dramatic dialogue with pages from great literature (for certain episodes it was common to recite the verse of Boiardo, Ariosto and Tasso). Fiorenzo and his eldest son Davide made the puppets and armor for the production, Giuseppe Napoli painted the scenes and Agnese Torrisi Napoli, the wife of Fiorenzo, executed the costumes. Obviously all the characters reproduced the specific figurative codes as documented in the iconography of the cartelli.

Before proceeding, it will be necessary to describe the roles and duties which within a production fall to the individual members of the Fratelli Napoli company. Behind the stage right wings (that is to the spectator's left) are Fiorenzo Napoli, first parraturi and director of the show (his are the voices of Guerrino, Peppininu, Napar and Polinadoro), Italia Chiesa Napoli, parratrici, who despite her 85 years still gives her voice to the female characters, and Davide, the second parraturi (Madar, Prince Alessandro of Constantinople

The Napoli family rehearsing. Italia Chiesa Napoli on left. (Courtesy the Marionettistica dei Fratelli Napoli. Photograph Davide Napoli.)

and Milone of Taranto). Behind the backcloth on the bridge are the "manianti" (manipulators): Giuseppe Napoli, the chief manipulator, myself and Marco Napoli (the third son of Fiorenzo). Giuseppe taught us the codes for operating the Catanian pupi. Stage left, behind the speakers was Salvator Napoli, who looks after the lights and sound. His adoption of a complex switchboard with floods, spots, follow spots, gobos and black light vastly enriched the range of lighting codes of the opira, which before this was fairly basic and elementary. Agnese Torrisi Napoli looked after the stage-management, the entrances of the pupi and the positioning of the cutout pieces and props. She was helped by her son Dario, who, when required to manipulate, climbed onto the bridge. In addition to having collaborated on the drafting of the text and manipulating the pupi, I looked after the preparation of blood for death scenes where the armor fell away and blood issued from the main characters. I also prepared pyrotechnic effects.

As early as 1973, for reasons of time and having to face a very different audience from the usual one, the three acts of the traditional performance were reduced to two. But sometimes we observed that cutting the performance into two parts had a notable effect on the attention span of the audience, especially when the performance was not in a theater but in the open or in a school. Therefore we began to create some shows consisting of a single act in which any break in the narrative tension outside the conventions bound up with the theatrical rite of the interval would have seemed useless and inappropriate. *Guerrino Meschino* was a show of this type.

I shall now analyze the production following the succession of scenes and indicating the type scene or the combination of type scenes characterized according to the model of Pasqualino and Vibaek, and pointing out others encountered in the Catanian tradition, but not in the "op'ra" of Palermo. A scene-by-scene analysis will serve to describe the permanence of the codes and rules of traditional productions and the innovative solutions adopted from time to time to adapt the pupi performance to new contemporary audiences.

After the "invito," performed by Marco with a pupo in front of the closed curtain, the show proper began.

Scene 1: Rampart walk. On the glacis of the city of Durazzo a captain on sentry duty is speaking to the traitor Polinadoro. The latter approaches and stabs him. Polinadoro then has a speech, gives the pre-arranged signal to Madar and Napar by raising the lantern three times and runs to open the gates of the city to the Albanians. Polinadoro re-enters with the two Saracen brothers and they organize the taking of Durazzo.

Type scenes: dialogue, soliloquy, private council.

The linguistic codes of the characters are according to tradition. The register is heroic and the language is literary Italian without archaic features. A number of formulaic expressions can be found: Polinadoro turns to the sentry, calling him "bravo capitano," and when he has run him through apostrophizes him with the formula "e cadi!" (now fall), which, apart from expressing disdain for the victim, also serves as a spoken cue to the manipulators. The codes of vocal quality are also maintained: the dark and husky bass voice for the traitor and the clear and raucous baritone for the two "saraceni grossi."[18] The first innovation to be noted, and which is present in the rest of the show, can be found in the musical code. The traditional drum is supplemented by recorded classical or symphonic music, appropriately chosen to provide atmosphere at a particular moment of the drama or to accompany the exit of characters. The kinetic codes remain unchanged: the villain moves slowly and often bends over, arching his back so as to let the audience see his duplicity; the Saracens keep the movements and gestures that emphasize their pride and arrogance, raising the chin to address an interlocutor, wearing their scimitars on their left side and banging their swords on their shields. Obviously the villain keeps his individual figurative code unchanged. Polinadoro has the same head as Gano di Magonza. A more relevant innovation can be found in the figurative code of place in this scene. In the opera dei pupi there was no backcloth representing the walk behind the merlons of a castle. Giuseppe Napoli had to paint this new location because we wanted the signal scene to be more realistically located high up on the walls rather than in front of them or in a wood outside the city.

Scene II: The palace in Durazzo. To a thrilling roll of drums can be heard the voices of the Albanians forcing their way into the castle. Sefera, Guerrino's nurse, enters with the newborn child in her arms. In a short monologue she reveals her plan to lower herself from the walls to save the child from the fury of the Saracens and exits. Napar and Madar enter with Milone bound. Then Polinadoro enters, dragging the bound Finisia in front of the brothers. Napar bitterly reproves his sister and, on the advice of Madar, condemns the two prisoners to the rigors of prison until their death.

Type scenes: soliloquy, private council, sending of a character to perform a task.

This is the first scene in which the vocal and interpretative skills of the parratrici emerge. She has to express the anxiety and sorrow of an older woman worried about the baby entrusted to her. Milone, the father of Guerrino, has a tenor voice and the clear strong enunciation of positive heroic characters. The traditional lighting code, which for this scene would have required darkness, is balanced here with a suffused bluish light so as to suggest the atmosphere of rooms in a castle in nocturnal penumbra illuminated only by the torches. The most obvious innovation in the codes of production emerges in the music. On my suggestion, in addition to the drum, we used mainly music from Felix Mendelssohn's *Midsummer Night's Dream*, which seemed very much in keeping with the fairy-tale ingredients of the story of Guerrino. One detail of the figurative code for the characters was firmly maintained: Milone and Finisia caught unawares and arrested by night were dressed in full-length white night-shirts.

Interlude. At this point was introduced what was probably the most innovative element of the performance. As I have indicated, Fiorenzo and I had decided to use Peppininu to bridge the gaps between the events depicted on stage. Fiorenzo finally suggested a conversation between a puparo offstage and Peppininu operated by the visible Giuseppe. In addition to using Peppininu to tell how Guerrino got to the slave market in Salonika and became carver for the royal table in Constantinople, Fiorenzo improvised a few lines which allowed Peppininu to recall Gaetano, Pippo, Rosario and Natale Napoli, with whom he had performed since 1921, and also to mention the transmission of the métier of puparo to the fourth generation of the family represented by Davide, Dario and Marco. At first this idea did not appeal to me since it was too far from the traditional style of staging, but after I had seen the execution of what we had arranged in the script I had to agree that theatrically this interlude worked very well. In addition, thanks to Fiorenzo's skills as a performer and improviser it allowed the pupari to involve themselves again with their new audience. For this extraneous scene we thought of using the beautiful Peppininu of the large pupi, dating from the end of the 1800s. The choice of the antique puppet was all the more significant because of the reference to the continuity of the tradition.

Scene III: The lists. Third day of the jousting announced in Constantinople for the hand of princess Elisena. Prince Pinamonte of Turkey is the marshal of the tournament. Meschino enters the lists with his visor down to maintain his anonymity. One after another he defeats all his opponents. When asked to reveal his name he refuses. A constable and two soldiers come to arrest him but he knocks out one and puts the other to flight. Then he calls his horse Macchiabruna and leaves the stage. Peppininu comes in and tells the audience about the attack on Constantinople by Pinamonte and Torindo of Turkey and how Meschino defeats them.

Type scenes: tournament (a type not specified by Pasqualino), battle, soliloquy.

The tournament scene allows for recovering and restating many of the movements and gestures that belong to the kinetic code. Above all there is the entrance of Pinamonte, a haughty and arrogant Saracen who "trasi 'a malantrina" (enters like a bandit), that is striding out with his right leg and his scimitar sheathed on his left side. Then there are the so-called "corpu d'a giostra," a series of established movements divided into three phases: the two contenders take up positions on guard facing each other; they turn and rush apart towards the edges of the stage; they attack, clashing their swords and shields together, and one remains standing while the other, stretched on the ground, admits defeat and gets up again. In *Guerrino* the encounter concludes with a treacherous thrust from the defeated Saracen, who as soon as he has been beaten pretends to withdraw, then tries unexpectedly to smite the winner with his sword, but Meschino manages to avoid this and gives him a terrible beating. For the musical code, as well as drumming, the entry to the lists of each contender is reinforced by recorded trumpet blasts.

Peppininu. Catanian puppet dating from about 1880. (Courtesy the Marionettistica dei Fratelli Napoli. Photograph Davide Napoli.)

In this scene, for the first time the heroic protagonist of the story appears armed in the traditional manner. He is a handsome young man with black hair and wears over his armor a surcoat with a cross; the emblem on his helmet and shield is an eagle.[19]

Scene IV: The court in Constantinople. The emperor Raimondo with his son Alessandro and the faithful Costantino dell'Arciopelago express their delight at the victory of Meschino over king Astiladoro's Turks. Raimondo announces his intention to give him princess Elisena as his bride. Prince Alessandro asks his father to leave him alone with Meschino, as he sees he is troubled and wants to speak with him. Meschino reveals to his faithful friend Alessandro that he does not intend to marry Elisena because one day she scorned him and called him a bastard, and that his firm intention is to depart in search of his parents. After the conversation with Alessandro there is a desperate and ineffectual attempt by Elisena to persuade Meschino to love her and he departs having rejected her scornfully.

Type scenes : solemn council, dialogue, dialogue.

With respect to the linguistic code used by the characters in this scene, it may be said that the conversation between Meschino and prince Alessandro was the part of the text where Fiorenzo and I were most anxious to use the refined prose of Gesualdo Bufalino, and this seemed to correspond most fully to an expression of the sincere ties of friendship between the two young men. In the scene between Meschino and Elisena we made a particular effort to research and study the movements and gestures of the classic kinetic code. Meschino listening to Elisena with his shoulder turned towards her and the princess of Constantinople's vain blocking of his path in a final attempt to bind him to her are bits of play that characterize the best scenes of lovers' quarrels in the *opira*. This princess was as beautiful as she was proud and Italia Chiesa restored for her all the traditional modulations of tone that allowed the character to pass from the most open declaration of sincere love to bursts of temper at the sudden rejection, to extreme despair once aware that she was being definitively refused. I remember that the character of Elisena was the model used by Don Raffaele Trombetta for the character of the haughty princess Galatea in *Uzeta*.

Scene V: The trees of the sun and the moon. Meschino, accompanied by the faithful Peppininu, begs the oracle, already visited by Alexander the Great, to let him know the secret of his birth. The sun reveals that his real name is Guerrino. The moon says that his parents are still alive and that he must turn his steps back towards the West. Guerrino, furious at the incomplete reply of the oracle, smashes the sanctuary and kills the priest and the giant who are its custodians.

Type scenes: dialogue, receptions of news from a person encountered, fight, soliloquy, dialogue.

From the point of view of linguistic codes a noticeable feature is the particular way in which the priest expresses himself, using a rather archaic form of speech characterized by inversions and sentences constructed with the verb at the end. This traditional verbal play allowed for a comic dialogue with Peppininu which in his dialect and in his own register exaggerated and distorted the eloquence of the priest. This is also the scene which shows most clearly how Peppininu is not fixed to any period or place. There were numerous anachronistic references to problems and events in everyday life, often improvised by Fiorenzo, and an exchange of repartee with the audience, as happened traditionally with the *opira*. There were also interesting innovations in the lighting codes. Traditionally the sun and the moon which appear on the horizon in response to the voices of the oracle were two transparent discs, each with the face of the appropriate light and illuminated from within. We decided to keep the human faces of the sun and moon, but the light inside the shape was on a dimmer and increased or diminished according to the melodic curve of the voice of the *parraturi*. The representation of the sacred spot was close to the traditional staging as documented on the *cartelli* — two soaring cypresses at the sides of the stage and an altar with a burning brazier in the center.

Scene VI: The Mountain of Aspromonte. Peppininu, while Guerrino rests offstage, has a monologue made up of traditional commonplaces: he is tired and hungry, while his master thinks only of going on and on. They are now close to the abode of the sorceress Sibilla, who is to tell where the parents are imprisoned. Suddenly an enchantress appears, informs Peppininu that she is the handmaid of Sibilla and conjures up a richly laden table. Peppininu rushes at a huge plate of spaghetti, but every time he reaches it the plate escapes him, always leaving him without a bite. Defeated by the food, Peppininu seeks comfort with wine, but as soon as he approaches the jug placed on the magic table, snakes immediately come out of it. The beautiful maid is transformed into an ugly old woman and he is attacked by dragons, snakes, demons and animals. Guerrino enters and breaks the spell; both enter the kingdom of Sibilla, who shows Guerrino the faces of his parents in a magic mirror.

Type scenes: soliloquy, dialogue, breaking of a spell.

The scene reintroduces the comic lazzo of the enchanted table with the food that escapes and the dishes that hide diabolical apparitions. Two important traditional elements here are the generic codes of the characters and some of the old scenic tricks. The handmaid of the enchantress retained the traditional appearance of the "dangerous" sorceresses who turn the heroes aside from their duties and confine them in enchanting gardens of delights. They wear a diadem, and often the typical hennin, and their naked bodies are covered with a metallic bra with embossed nipples and a short skirt split up the side to reveal the thighs and ankle boots — in other words an outfit that tends to emphasize visually all their more erotic characteristics and fascination. A further scenic trick we retained was the fire spewed out by the dragon, produced by Bengal fire.

Scene VII: The papal court in Rome. Pope Benedict III sends Guerrino to Puglia to his unknown uncle King Guizzardo, who intends to attack Durazzo to avenge the supposed deaths of Milone and Fenisia.

This is a specifically Catanian type scene that is not recorded by Pasqualino. It brings together all the fixed elements of a council at the papal court in Rome. The pope is always followed by a cardinal who barely speaks and the almost obligatory close of the scene is the benediction with the sign of the cross given to the hero.

Figurative codes: The pope appears with the triple crown and a long white garment and the cardinal with a miter and a red robe. This scene also presents two interesting innovations firmly established in the shows of the Fratelli Napoli, especially since they began to use the "small" pupi. In their shows of the 1980s, with the aim of richer and more accurate scenery, Nino Amico and Natale Napoli began to use more furnishing. In Catania this was traditionally limited to those occasions where it was specifically required by the narrative situation. From the 1980s it became the norm to put on the stage thrones, chests, seats, candelabra, etc. In earlier productions the pontiff had received and blessed Guerrino standing up; now he listened to him seated on a throne in a court illuminated by a heavy baroque candelabrum. The introduction of thrones, seats and stools led to another interesting innovation. The Catanian pupi are known for their stiff legs without knee joints. However, all the characters who had to sit (and similarly those who had to kneel) were now constructed by Nino Amico and Fiorenzo with a knee joint to allow them to carry out the necessary movement less artificially.[20]

Scene VIII: Royal pavilion in the camp of King Guizzardo of Puglia. Guizzardo accepts Guerrino as the commander of his troops and the Christian army departs for Durazzo.

Type scene: solemn council.

Guerrino and Napar in the final battle. Fratelli Napoli production of *Guerrino detto il Meschino*. (Courtesy the Marionettistica dei Fratelli Napoli. Photograph Giancarlo Fundarò.

Here too the king has a jointed knee and is seated on a little camp throne. Traditionally this is the scene of reading the pope's letters in which he recommends Guerrino to Guizzardo and there is the classic theatrical action of two characters meeting each other, unaware of their relationship, but who feel the voice of blood speaking within them and reveal this to the audience in two brief monologues delivered by taking a step forward and speaking to the audience as an aside.

Scene IX: The walls of Durazzo. Battle: Guerrino leads the attack, slaughters the enemy and in single combat kills Arfineo, the son of Madar, by splitting his head in two. Then he faces Madar, kills him and "passa" (leaves the stage to go to another part of the battle). Prince Gerardo di Puglia comes onto the battlefield but after initial successes is knocked to the ground by the bestial Silonio, son of Napar. Guerrino comes back and kills Silonio, splitting him from stem to stern. There is a grand duel between Guerrino and Napar with the death of the latter and the entrance of the Christians into Durazzo.

Type scene: battle

In this show, as in many others written with Fiorenzo, we deliberately revived the transitional ritual of the "battaglie con i passagi" (battles with comings and going) of the old opera dei pupi that I remembered from my childhood. In the 1980s battles of this sort almost disappeared as they were felt to be too slow and repetitive for the new audiences of the pupi. To restage this today we had to count on the efficiency of the "pruituri" (stage hands) who pass the puppets and are thoroughly familiar with the rhythm of the performance. This allowed for much greater speed of execution than in the traditional opera and we realized that the contemporary audience still enjoys seeing the main heroes on the battlefield. Napar's death involves the hacking off of his armor and the grand preparation of blood to gush at the appropriate moment. The scene closes with the standard line that traditionally confirmed the victory in a battle: "the rest of the army is put to flight."

Scene X: Prison. Guerrino goes into the darkest dungeon in Durazzo. Seated on a rude pallet are two wretched, emaciated figures, a man and a woman. He approaches and recognizes in them the two figures seen in Sibilla's magic mirror. A few words are exchanged, followed by the recognition scene expected since the beginning of the show. The three embrace and this "bellissima rappresentazione" ends.

Type scenes: soliloquy, dialogue, recognition without outside intervention (a type scene not included as a model by Pasqualino).[21] Fixed elements of this type scene are the lines between the people who recognize each other and the final liberating embrace.

The tension that held the audience in suspense for the greater part of the evening was relaxed. Fiorenzo during the third performance inserted a short final piece for Peppininu that was not allowed for in the traditional production. Waving a handkerchief in his right hand, Peppininu bursts onto the stage to rejoice with his master and to connect again with the audience for a final speech. His lines point out the emotional participation of the audience during the show and emphasize that the atmosphere of involvement of the traditional show has been recreated. At this point Fiorenzo through Peppininu seized the opportunity to invite all the spectators to come to all the other fine stories that the pupari could perform. This final novel intervention by Peppininu, played entirely according to the tradition of the mask, seems to me to be one of the best possible theatrical solutions for attracting modern audiences to the cycles of the opera dei pupi and encouraging them to return for more.

Appendix. Diagrams

I. Rod Marionettes from the 18th Century to the Early 20th Century

These figures are drawn to scale to indicate the huge range of heights and sizes. Most bodies are unisex and may be shaped with additional padding. In some cases female breasts are carved in relief. The majority have one-piece bodies. Commedia dell'Arte masked characters and dancers often had bodies in two parts linked by a mortise joint, interlocking staples, leather strips or fabric. The commonest hip joints are mortise ones or ones where the legs are hung directly on a wire. Mortise joints are generally used for the knees, and a few companies also used ankle joints. The hand and forearm are mostly carved in one piece, with an upper arm in fabric, often lightly stuffed. Small eighteenth-century figures have cast lead hands and feet, whose weight helps the manipulability. The head rod is hooked onto a staple in the crown or sometimes implanted firmly in the head itself. For opening mouths a short wire attached to the back of the pivoted jaw emerges at the top of the head, where it is bent into an eyelet to which a string may be attached.

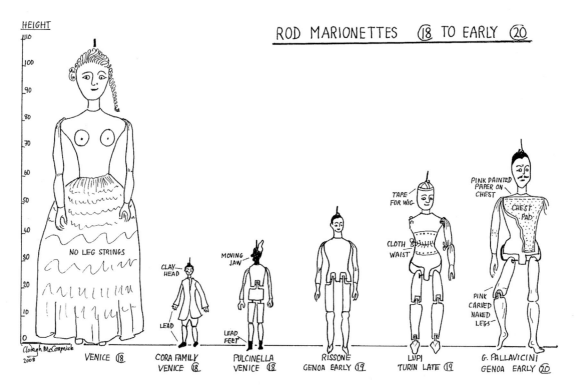

249

II. Pupi

These figures have been drawn to the same scale as those in diagram 1. There are variations in construction and control between regions and individual pupari. The Roman pupo is supported by a head rod attached to a staple in the crown of the head. In Sicily the head staple was reserved for female and unarmed figures (including angels, devils and animals). The control rod goes through the head of the armed figures of Naples and Sicily, hooks onto a staple in the neck opening and returns to lodge in a second hole in the neck. Sliding the head up the rod allows it to be unhooked and changed. Nineteenth-century Roman pupi often have the bodies covered by a layer of paper painted flesh color. Neapolitan pupi are the most heavily padded, but Catanian figures are often given shape, especially in the limbs, by padding over crudely cut wood. A pad or short skirt under the costume may be used to give more shape and to hold it out. The mortises for the hip joints in Palermo are sometimes set at an angle, splaying the legs. In Catania legs are generally unjointed, and some hang from two bolts set into a wooden piece beneath the pelvis. In Rome and Catania the upper arm was often a piece of wood linked to the forearm and shoulder with staples. Palermitan pupari tended to use a strip of fabric to link shoulder and forearm under the armor. In Sicily the sword arm is controlled by a rod rather than a string. In Catania the sword remains permanently fixed in the hand, but in Palermo (and sometimes Naples) a special string is used to draw it. Swords, guns and knives in Naples usually lodge in a hole running up the arm inside the wrist.

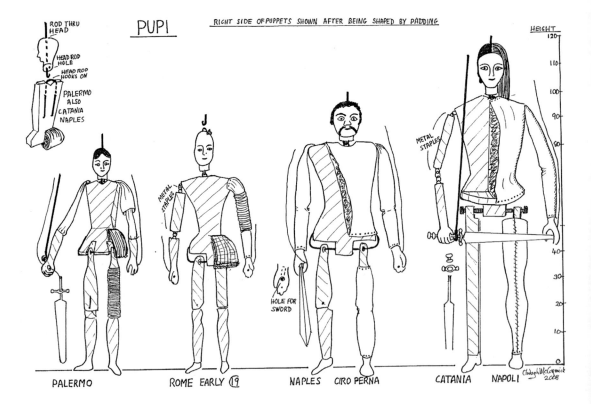

III. Classic Controls

The classic marionette (and pupo) control is an iron rod to the head, stout and short in Catania, lighter and considerably longer in Turin. Smaller figures have a relatively light wire,

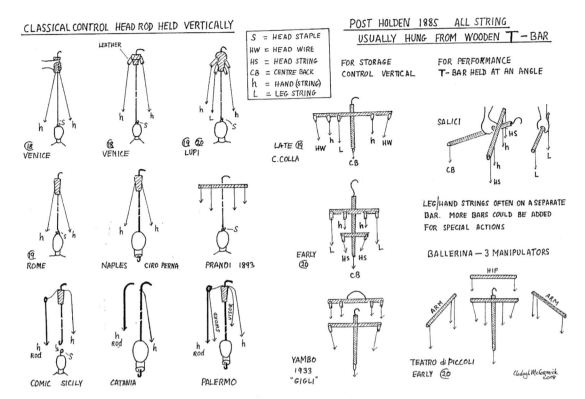

but this has the same function, which is to support the figure and propel it around the stage. Leg strings were seldom used for anything other than special movements (kneeling). Many figures have one leg slightly shorter than the other and a movement of the wrist of the manipulator causes the shorter leg to produce a swinging step. The top of the rod is bent over so that the puppet can be hung and there is usually a piece of wood, a wooden bulb or hand grip to which the strings are attached either directly or by means of leather tags. A separate hand rod may be attached to the top of the main rod by means of a piece of string (Palermo). A Prandi control of the 1890s shows a rod with a horizontal bar for hand and leg strings, but this appears to be a late development.

After the 1880s marionettes controlled entirely by strings and attached to horizontal bars became popular. Many used a T bar, sometimes with an additional bar (or bars) for leg strings, or other specialist ones. Head strings attached to the ears replaced the center head rod. When the marionette was hung backstage the tail of the T bar pointed downwards. In performance the control was held in an approximately horizontal position with the tail slightly lower.

IV. Classical Dancers

Many classical ballet positions are designed with the performer facing front. Many marionette dancers are constructed with legs that are splayed out and move laterally rather than from front to back. Additional help in the creation of balletic poses may be provided by a rod attached to the pelvis which supports the figure at this point and helps specially with leaps and fluid waist movement. Clock springs at the knees and sometimes in the arms allow limbs to spring back into position after a movement. Strings attached to the side of the calves with stops that allow them to be drawn up only a short distance allow for specific steps. An

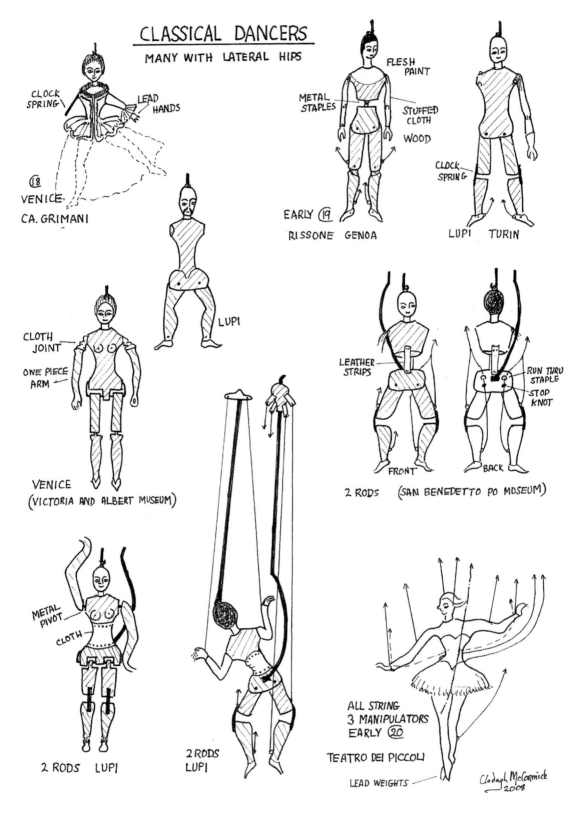

CLASSICAL DANCERS
MANY WITH LATERAL HIPS

CLOCK SPRING

LEAD HANDS

⑱ VENICE CA. GRIMANI

FLESH PAINT

METAL STAPLES

STUFFED CLOTH

WOOD

EARLY ⑲ RISSONE GENOA

CLOCK SPRING

LUPI TURIN

LUPI

CLOTH JOINT

ONE PIECE ARM

VENICE (VICTORIA AND ALBERT MUSEUM)

LEATHER STRIPS

RUN THRU STAPLE

STOP KNOT

FRONT

BACK

2 RODS (SAN BENEDETTO PO MUSEUM)

METAL PIVOT

CLOTH

2 RODS LUPI

2 RODS LUPI

ALL STRING
3 MANIPULATORS
EARLY ⑳

TEATRO DEI PICCOLI

LEAD WEIGHTS

Clodagh McCormick 2008

effect of arabesques can be produced by arms made in one piece and jointed only at the shoulder.

The Teatro dei Piccoli ballerina owes much to the Holden tradition. It requires three manipulators and the emphasis is on the arms (each equipped with three strings) and the hips, where strings create a quivering movement, particularly effective in the "Dying Swan."

Glossary

A puntate: presentation of a story in a series of episodes over a number of days, and sometimes weeks or months.

Appoggio: bar or shelf on which the marionettist leans when operating the puppets.

Bagateliere: street entertainer performing card tricks or juggling, and sometimes using puppets (see **Bagatelle**).

Bagatelle: common term for a street glove-puppet show in the seventeenth and eighteenth centuries, especially in the South of Italy. Probably of Spanish or Catalan origin (see **Bavastel**). Associated with the modern meaning of the term as something insignificant or a trifle.

Baiocco (plural: baiocchi): coin of slight value.

Ballare: to dance.

Bamboccio (plural: bambocci): young child ("bambino") or doll, but by extension used, especially in the eighteenth century, to refer to a marionette.

Bavastel: Provençal term used in the later middle ages to refer to a type of jigging puppet. Appears in various forms: "balastel," "babastel," "bagastel" and "magatellos," terms often used in a rather general way to refer to animated figures.

Bianti ombranti: seventeenth-century term for itinerant shadow performers.

Booth: see **Casotto**

Bunraku: a style of puppet that evolved in Japan in the eighteenth century, operated by short rods and generally requiring three manipulators.

Buratti: late medieval term for some itinerant entertainers.

Burattinaio: operator of "Burattini"; in modern Italian a "glove-puppeteer."

Burattino (plural: burattini): Second zanni of the Commedia dell'Arte. A general term for a puppet; in modern Italian usually a glove-puppet.

Canovaccio: scenario which outlines the plot and describes the action.

Carpenter's scene: scene set on the front part of the stage to allow the stage hands ("carpenters") to prepare a more elaborate scene behind it.

Cartello, cartellone: painted poster hung up outside a puppet theater to advertise the show.

Cartonaggio: flat cutout in pasteboard painted to represent either a scenic element or a figure.

Casotto: corresponds to the English "booth." Used to describe both a temporary theater complete with auditorium) and a small edifice, usually for glove-puppet shows, that contained the stage, scenery and equipment for the show.

Copione: the text for a puppet performance. It may refer either to a full playtext or to a scenario that simply describes what happens in each scene.

Crocera: a crutch or marionette control.

Fantoccio (diminutive: fantoccini): used from the later eighteenth century to the twentieth for a puppet viewed as a miniature human (cf. English "infant"). Fluctuating usage as to the type of puppet, but generally a complete figure (with legs).

Figure-worker: a marionette manipulator.

Forno: often noted in a register of a puppet company on an evening when there was not enough audience to make the show financially worthwhile.

Fraccurrado (plural: fraccurradi): similar to **bagatelle**, refers to glove puppets or stick puppets (**marottes**) in the sixteenth century. "Fraccurrado" had the general sense of a joke or **lazzo**. Origin of the name possibly Frate Corrado, an order of Franciscan friars (who may have used puppets).

Gel: a transparent medium used to add color to stage light. Originally made of gelatine.

Generico: a utility or small-part actor.

Glove puppet: puppet usually consisting of a head and trunk operated from below with the operator's fingers inserted into the head and arms.

Grembiule: literally "apron" — the cloth that covers the front of a glove-puppet stage and conceals the puppeteer.

Guarattella (plural: guarattelle): common term for a glove-puppet in Naples.

Guarattellaro: performer with **guarattelle**.

Guitto: strolling player.

Jigging puppet: jointed figure that moves when placed in contact with a vibrating board or is mounted on a string where changes of tension result in a similar effect. Found in many parts of the world.

Lazzo (plural: lazzi): a verbal or physical gag much employed by the masks of the Commedia dell'Arte.

Lycopodium: a powder made from dried lichen that produces a burst of flame when in contact with fire. Much used for theatrical effects, it could also be replaced by powdered resin.

Marionetta (marionette): word of French origin for a puppet. In modern Italian usage generally understood to be a figure operated entirely by strings.

Marotte: a medieval fool's bauble; a simple puppet mounted on a stick held from below, often without any other form of control.

Mestiere: generic term for a pupi stage and all its figures and equipment.

Motion: a common way of referring to a puppet show in Elizabethan England.

Muta: a set of puppets belonging to a company.

Ombres chinoises: popular term in the late eighteenth and first half of the nineteenth century for shadow puppets.

Oprante: the manipulator of a puppet, who does not usually or necessarily speak.

Paladin: one of the 12 peers or knights of the Emperor Carlo Magno, an equivalent of the Knights of the Round Table.

Piattino: dish used by street entertainers to collect contributions.

Piazza: implies the place where a puppeteer might set up in a town or village, often equivalent to the word "pitch" rather than the main square or open space.

Pivetta: see **Swazzle**

Planchette (literally a "small plank"): French term for a type of jigging puppet. The "planchette" supports a small upright to which is tied one end of a string on which the figures are mounted. The other end of the string is attached to the leg of the performer, who usually plays a bagpipe or hurdy-gurdy.

Playboard: shelf at the base of the opening of a glove-puppet stage. Often used for the placing of properties.

Popazzo/pupazzo (plural: popazzi/pupazzi): diminutive of "pupo" and in the non-modern period used in general way for an animated figure.

Producer puppet: a figure that separates into a number of smaller ones or "produces" them out of its clothing.

Pupante: the main puppeteer in the pupi theaters of Naples.

Puparo: the main puppeteer and speaker in the pupi theaters of western Sicily.

Pupo (plural: pupi): a doll or infant; by extension a puppet (especially in Southern Italy). Today implies a marionette controlled by metal rods as well as strings. In Naples and specially Sicily is associated with a heroic repertoire.

Risorgimento: literally "resurgence," the period of the nineteenth century leading up to and including the unification of the kingdom of Italy.

Soldo (plural: soldi): originally the same as the English shilling and made up of 12 denari. Twenty soldi amounted to 1 lira (pound).

Swazzle: a small instrument consisting of a membrane, sometimes of cloth, stretched between two metal plates. Placed against the palate this gives a high-pitched carrying sound to the voice.

Table-top puppet: simplified **bunraku** style figure operated on a "table" behind which the visible manipulator stands.

Tavoletta: see **Planchette**

Teatrino (plural: teatrini): diminutive of "teatro" (theater), used for a small puppet theater.

Vastasate: popular farce in Sicily.

Volatín: common term in seventeenth-century Spain for an acrobat or, more loosely, an itinerant entertainer. By extension "volatín" could refer to a puppet. Variants include: "volantín," "volatinero," bolantín" and " buratín."

Zanni: diminutive of the name "Giovanni" — used as a general term for the servant characters of the Commedia dell'Arte (cf. English "zany.")

Chapter Notes

Introduction

1. The collection was owned by the actor Checco Rissone, who gave it to the Civico Museo dell'Attore of Genoa in 1982. It includes over 100 marionettes and a large amount of scenery, properties, costumes and scripts.

2. "Marionette" is probably a diminutive of the name "Marie." For Magnin, the earliest use of it to denote a puppet is to be found in the *Sérées* of Guillaume Brochet, of which the first part was published in 1584 and the last two in 1608 (Magnin, *Histoire des marionnettes en Europe*, pp. 118–119). Campanini, *Marionette barocche*, p. 9, mentions a French song of 1536 which includes the lines:

Vous marchez du bout du pié, Marionette
Vous marchez du bout du pied, Marionet, Marion.

In this she sees a hint that the girl is being compared to a jigging doll. Magnin also states, without giving his sources, that between the 1590s and 1606 there were marionette theaters in Paris and that this word was used to designate them.

3. Cali, *Burattini e marionette tra cinque e sei cento in Italia*, p. 151.

4. Ibid., p. 150.

5. There is a theory that that the term originated in Venice and referred to the little statuettes sold during the ancient festival of the Marys (Giustina Renier Michiel, *Origine delle feste veneziane*, Milan, 1829, vol. 1, pp. 91–109). Few scholars take this idea very seriously today.

6. In recent years there has been a revival of the term "pupazzo" to cover figures that are neither glove-puppets nor marionettes. It is generally applied to table-top figures operated by a visible performer standing directly behind.

7. This can be observed with the rather lighter marionettes of eighteenth-century Venice, which do not always have leg strings either.

8. A similar mechanism can be observed with both the Antwerp Poesje and the St. Aleixo puppets of Portugal.

9. The Prandi company in the later nineteenth and early twentieth century retained a head rod five or six feet long, but used a separate rocking bar to which leg strings were attached.

Chapter 1

1. Michele Rak, "Il teatro meccanico" in *Quaderni di teatro*, 1981, p. 48.

2. Quoted by Cali, *Burattini e marionette*, p. 88.

3. Pietro della Valle, *Il pellegrino* (Bologna: Gioseffo Longhi, 1672), pp. 66–68.

4. *Burattini e marionette in Italia*, 1980, p. 29.

5. *Mondi celesti, terrestri, e infernale*, Vicenza, 1552. Quoted by Cali, 2002, p. 57.

6. *De rerum varietate*, book 12, "De artificiis humilioribus," ch. 63. Quoted in *Burattini e marionette in Italia*, 1980, p. 14.

7. Speaight, *History of the English Puppet Theatre*, 2nd ed., p. 55.

8. This dialogue exploits Florentine and Venetian dialects. It was published by Girolamo Righettini.

9. Cervellati, *Storia dei burattini e burattinai*, pp. 22–23.

10. Campanini, *Marionette barocche*, p. 154.

11. Ottonelli, *Della christiana moderazione del theatro* (Florence: Bonardi, 1652). The relevant sections are reproduced in Cipolla and Moretti, *Commedianti figurati*, pp. 23–38.

12. The use of a platform indicates a more prosperous ciarlatano.

13. Ottonelli, op. cit., p. 437. Reproduced by Cipolla and Moretti, op. cit., p. 31. Cali, op. cit., p. 69, sees this as the first time that "burattino" is clearly used in the sense of puppet.

14. Cali, op. cit., p. 70.

15. Ottonelli, op. cit., pp. 462 ff. (Cipolla and Moretti, op. cit., pp. 33–35). Ottonelli credits a Giuseppe Cavazza of Venice with the invention of these shadow shows. Cavazza is one of the earliest names that can be attached to this type of performance in Italy. There is a centuries-old tradition of shadow theater in Asia and this may be the origin of European shadow puppets. In late eighteenth-century France and England when "ombres chinoises" were at their height, they were sometimes called "Italian shadows."

16. Incisa's superbly indexed diary records every event in the town between 1776 and 1819 and is an important source of information about the activities of puppeteers in Piedmont. It is kept in the library of the Seminario Vescovile in Asti.

17. Ottonelli, op. cit., p. 462.

18. Request reproduced by Vezzani, "Il teatro dei burattini a Reggio," p. 226.

19. Ibid., p. 226.

20. Cali, 2002, p. 119. In England, Ben Jonson's *Bartholomew Fair* (1614) includes a puppet show in booth or tent with a specific admission charge: "What do we pay for coming in, fellows?" Twopence, sir." (Act 5, scene 3.)

21. Cali, op. cit., pp. 112–113. See O. Siliprandi, "Burattini e Burratinai a Reggio Emilia" in *Strenna degli Artigianelli, Reggio Emilia*, 1934.

22. Ademollo, *I teatri di Roma*, footnote to p. 127. He gives the date as 1671. M.G. Rak found an identical request, dated 1679 (the other was not dated), *Burattini e marionette in Italia*, 1980, p. 34. A female puppeteer, Camilla Biscona (1670–1738), made two unsuccessful attempts to obtain a

permit to perform in Bergamo in 1700 (Litta Modignani, *Dizionario biografico e bibliografia*, pp. 41–42).

23. Letter to Monsig. Spinola, governor of Rome, reproduced in *Burattini e marionette in Italia*, 1980, p. 42.

24. "Istanze di burattinai al Governatore di Roma" in Archivio di Stato di Roma, Camerale III, B.2140. D'Alibert came to Rome in 1656–1657 and became factotum to Queen Christina. He was much supported by the queen, who had obtained permission from Pope Clement IX to have this theater re-opened after a period of closure. D'Alibert was involved in the remodeling of this theater which reopened for the Carnival of 1671 with two new "melodrammi": *Scipione Africano* and *The New Jason*, probably both by Filippo Acciajoli. Acciajoli was the real artistic director of the theater, while D'Alibert was more an impresario. Acciajoli's own fortune helped subsidize D'Alibert's management (Ademollo, op. cit., p. 146).

25. The San Moïsè opened in 1620. Built as a theater for plays, it belonged first to Lorenzo and Alvise Giustinian, but was later inherited by their cousins, the Zane family, whose name was often attached to it (Mangini, *I teatri di Venezia*, p. 43). In 1623, in 1627 and again in 1633 the San Moïsè was occupied by the Commedia dell'Arte company of J.B. Andreini, I Fedeli. In 1637 it was the first public theater in Venice to present operas. In 1684 the San Moïsè was refurbished, with four tiers of boxes, and it reopened for Carnival 1685 and survived as a regular theater and later as a puppet theater before its demolition in the early twentieth century. It was situated in what is today the Via XX Settembre.

26. Mangini, op. cit., p. 43.

27. Ibid., p. 46, reproduces the description by Giovanno Carlo Bonlini in *Le glorie della poesia e della musica contenute nell'esatta notizia de teatri della città di Venezia*, Venice, 1730. The Tuscan resident minister, Matteo del Teglia, in a letter of October 14, 1679, mentioned that this show would happen with figures of a newly invented type (ibid., p. 47).

28. Cervellati, *Storia dei burattini e burattinai*, p. 39. Canon Antonio Francesco Ghiselli's *Memorie di Bologna* (ms) is in the University Library of Bologna. Ghiselli notes: "The burattini will start to perform on St. Stephen's night in the Galliera and at the Mercanzia. On the evening of Thursday, January 21, 1694 in the public theater, under the patronage of the Elders, performances of *Olympia avenged* will begin and then at San Paolo, then there will be a performance of the *Bernarda in musica*, a drama by Tommaso Stanzani."

29. *Burattini e marionette in Italia*, 1980, p. 38.

30. Leydi and Leydi, *Marionette e burattini*, p. 68.

31. Ibid., pp. 69–70.

32. Rak, op. cit., p. 53. One of these was Michele Luigi Mutio's *A Woman Always Holds onto the Worst*, with music by Tomasso di Mauro.

33. F. Valesio, *Diario di Roma* (Milan: Longanesi, 1977), pp. 264–268. Quoted by Cali, op. cit., pp. 170–171.

34. *Burattini e marionette in Italia*, 1980, p. 42.

35. Marzattinocci, *Cassandrino al Teatro Fiano*, p. 20, mentions various companies using this theater: Tommaso Carafa (1781), Nicola Bigacci (1785) and Filippo Filaja (1787).

36. Lanza, "Le leggende cavalleresche." The Capitoline Archives contain a number of documents on the Ornani Theater.

37. Maria Giovanna Rak, in *Burattini e marionette*, 1980, p. 35.

38. Malmani, 1897, p. 128.

39. In 2001, the Istituto per i Beni Marionettistici e il Teatro Popolare mounted a major exhibition at the Casa del Conte Verde in Rivoli, *I fili della memoria — percorsi per una storia delle marionette in Piedmont*. See, in particular, Cipolla, "Le marionette in Piemonte."

40. Cipolla, "Le marionette in Piemonte," p. 74.

41. A number of aristocratic families let out halls as commercial ventures. Such was probably the case here (Tamburini, "Fantocci, burattini, marionette a Torino," p. 22). By 1766 Martini and Mazzolino had left the company and been replaced by Giuseppe Trossarello, also a tailor. The company was also joined by a Stefano Poliano. After a couple of years Trossarello was replaced by Maria Radino, Ferdinando Pezza and Francesco Baima.

42. There was a director of a company of actors referred to as Signor Gandolfo. This may have been the husband of Felicita/Teresa. Cipolla, 2001, p.76, suggests that she may have taken on this identity to conceal the fact that she was a woman.

43. Cipolla, "Le marionette in Piemonte," p. 76.

44. Tamburini, "Fantocci, burattini, marionette a Torino," p. 23.

45. Bartoš, Jaroslav. *Loutkářská kronika*, p. 38, finds an "Antoni Rosi" from Savoy who performed in the Old Town in Prague in 1768. This could refer to the same company or family.

46. Incisa recorded 14 visits of puppet companies, 11 of which took place in the warmer months, between April and September (Bertonasso, "Burattini, marionette, ombre," p. 4). A company from Rome brought their marionettes to Asti in September 1792, and Incisa notes that their publicity was posted at the street corners and in the cafés.

47. Francesco Saverio Quadrio, *Della storie e della ragione d'ogni poesia* (Milan, 1744), vol. 3, part 7, pp. 245–249. Largely reproduced by Cipolla and Moretti, *Commedianti figurati*, pp. 38–44.

48. See Cipolla and Moretti, *Commedianti figurati*, p. 44.

49. Ibid., p. 41.

50. Leydi and Leydi, op. cit., p. 487.

51. *Burattini e marionette in Italia*, 1980, p. 48 (from a 1903 article by Corrado Ricci).

52. Giraldi diary entry for September, 9, 1729 — quoted by Cervellati, op. cit., p. 69.

53. This bill is in the library of Guastalla.

54. Parma, Archivio di Stato: Fondo: Rubriche, Registri e Copialettere — no. 257 — Register for 1789, 1790 and 1791.

55. Bertozzi, "Burattini e marionette a Parma," lists permits from the Archivio di Stato — Fondo Governatore di Parma, Busta 10.

56. Waxwork shows became fashionable in Europe in the later years of the eighteenth century, and many of these had an element of movement. In England of the 1860s a marionette show was sometimes referred to as "moving waxworks."

57. Probably what was known as the Malabaila theater. This was not in the main palace of the Malabaila family (Poggi, *All'Ombra dell'Alfieri*, pp. 32–33).

58. In June 1789 another marionette company occupied the Malabaila theater for three weeks (selling subscription tickets). The repertoire is sufficiently different to suggest that this was not the "Bolognese."

59. See Poggi, op. cit., pp. 33–35.

60. The stage was described as being sufficient for marionettes and their scene changes, but too low and narrow for live actors. Later it would be enlarged.

61. Alberti, *Il teatro dei pupi*, p. 13.

62. Archivio di Stato di Palermo, Real Segretaria, 5260, 1792. Quoted by Alberti, op. cit., p. 15.

63. Archivio di Stato di Palermo, Real Segretaria, 5260, p. 416. Quoted by Alberti, op. cit., p. 15.

64. Alberti, op. cit., p. 14.

65. Ibid., pp. 14–15.

66. Campanini, op. cit., p. 151, based on the findings of Margaret Murata, "Il carnevale a Roma sotto Clemente IX Rospigliosi," in *Rivista Italiana di Musicologia* 12, no. 1 (1977): 83–99.

67. Rospigliosi was an important figures in the development of opera and also helped promote the idea of Rome's first permanent theater, the Tor di Nona, in 1667 (*Burattini e marionette*, 1980, pp. 33–34.) The Palazzo Ludovisi, on the corner of the Corso, and the Piazza di San Lorenzo in Lucina would pass into the hands of the Ottoboni family, later dukes of Fiano, and this is where the Fiano theater of the nineteenth century was established. *La comica del cielo* was accompanied by a comedy with music by Filippo Acciajoli, probably *Il girello*. Acciajoli's comedy may well have taken the form of intermezzi between the acts of the more serious piece.

68. Ademollo, op. cit., p. 127.

69. After the Venetian experience, Acciajoli was back in Rome, where a production of his burlesque based on Ovid, *He Who Is the Cause of his Misfortune May Weep over It Himself*, for which he also wrote the music, was performed at the theater of the Colonna family. This does not seem to have been a piece for puppets.

70. As a painter, Neri executed frescoes for the Corsini Palace in Rome in the early 1650s. He also painted frescoes for the Palazzo di San Clemente in Florence in 1637 for Thomasso Guadagni, who had recently acquired it, and who was married to a relative of Filippo Acciajoli, Maria Acciajoli.

71. *Di Herone Alessandrino de gli automati, overo machine se moventi libri due* (Venice, 1589). Quoted by Cali, op. cit., p. 132. Baldi complains about the use of these "noble" things for commercial gain by vulgar mountebanks.

72. This type of theater is very similar to stages used for crib theaters in other parts of Europe. The figures of the Belem (Bethlehem) in Alcoy (Spain) also move in channels in the stage floor.

73. From Michele Giuseppe Morei, *Notizie degli arcadi morti* (Rome, 1730). This includes the biography of Acciajoli (quoted by Ademollo, op. cit., p. 124).

74. Letter in archives in Florence from P. Enrico di Noris, April 29 and May 16, 1684 (found in Ricciardi box in Biblioteca Nazionale Centrale, Florence).

75. Barocchi and Bertelà, *Arredi principeschi del Seicento fiorentino*, p. 80. The drawings are in the Biblioteca Nazionale Centrale, Florence, under the heading "Teatro dei burattini e teatro delle dame," Magl.III.380, c.89.

76. Ibid., p. 78.

77. Ademollo, op. cit., p. 179. This was performed in the casa Savelli.

78. Mentioned by Speaight, "Puppet Theatre of Cardinal Ottoboni," p. 9. The score of this work is in the British Library (Additional MSS.22.101.).

79. It has sometimes been wrongly assumed that the theater was in the Labia palace.

80. Allacci, *Dramaturgia*, p. 931. In 1780 an Italian company visited London, bringing with them a theater that was described as "in a small compass the exact model of the superb Teatro Nuovo at Bologna." Antonio Bibiena had completed the Teatro Nuovo of Bologna in 1756. The marionette theater was modeled on that and made for a young prince in Bologna as a house theater, but when he had lost interest in it, one of his servants had acquired it and brought it to London (Speaight, *History of the English Puppet Theatre*, p. 133. Information from the *Public Advertiser*, London, January 19 to May 20, 1780, and December 8, 1780, to May 2, 1781).

81. A. Groppo, *Cat. Dei drammi per mus. recit. nei teatri di Ven. Fino al 1746* (Venezia, 1746). Quoted by Mangini, op. cit., pp. 13–14.

82. There is ample evidence of marionette performers being engaged to entertain in private houses. One such figure in the Veneto was Girolamo Renzi.

83. According to Leydi and Leydi, op. cit., p. 73, performances of the theater of the counts of Ravegnani in Verona (also part of the territory of Venice at the time) were also celebrated.

84. Gorla, *Le marionette di casa Borromeo*, p. 27.

85. Ibid., p. 28.

86. Ed. J. Quincey Adams — Yale University Press, 1917.

87. Speaight, op. cit., pp. 55–56.

88. Purschke, *Die Puppenspieltraditionen Europas*, 1986, p. 69, from *Münchener codex Germanicus* 3587, sheet 200a.

89. Ibid., p. 66.

90. The last reference to him picked up by Purschke (op. cit., p. 118) was in 1698 in Basel, where he called himself Landolt from Malta.

91. Purschke, *Puppenspiel und verwandte Künste*, pp. 28–32. Also Purschke, *Die Puppenspieltraditionen Europas*, 1986, pp. 31–32, 70, 119.

92. Probably Pulcinella arrived as a puppet, but it is just possible that Brioché transformed the recently introduced popular stage character of Pulcinella (Polichinelle) into one. This could explain the multi-colored costume of French Polichinelle.

93. Anon. *Combat de Cyrano de Bergerac contre le singe de Brioché* (Paris, 1655).

94. Pierre Datelin's second son, Jean (b. 1632), was a musician but also worked with his brother François for the "menus plaisirs du roi."

95. Magnin, *Histoire des marionnettes en Europe*, p. 133. According to Magnin this document was to be found in the "cartons de Colbert."

96. Depping, *La correspondance administrative sous Louis XIV*, Paris, 1850–1855. Letter dated October 16, 1676.

97. Yorick confuses St. Germain and St. Germain en Laye.

98. Antoine Hamilton, *Œuvres* (Paris, 1825).

99. Fols. 44 and 47 of the royal registers. Quoted in Yorick 1902, p. 353.

100. Datelin sounds very French, but it may be worth noting that the name Datelino existed in Italy in the Jewish community of Correggio (Emilia).

101. *Dictionnaire critique de biographie et d'histoire* (Paris: Plon, 1872).

102. Document reproduced by Vezzani, "Il teatro dei burattini a Reggio," p. 224.

103. Purschke, *Die Puppenspieltraditionen Europas*, p. 31.

104. Ibid., p. 28.

105. Ibid., p. 30.

106. Elisabeth Mentzel, *Geschichte der Schauspielkunst in Frankfurt a.M.* (Frankfurt a. Main, 1882), p. 89.

107. Speaight, op. cit., p. 73.

108. Ibid.

109. The bill is reproduced in the *Revue d'histoire du théâtre*, vol. 4, 1950, p. 470.

110. Speaight, op. cit., p. 74.

111. Ibid., pp. 75–76.

112. Purschke, *Die Puppenspieltraditionen Europas*, p. 71.

113. Bartoš, op. cit., p. 15.

114. *Burattini Marionette, Pupi*, 1980, p. 293.

115. See Speaight, op. cit., pp. 129–131.

116. W.J. Lawrence, "Some Old Dublin Puppet Shows," *Dublin Evening Mail*, October 17, 1908. See also *Freeman's Journal*, Dublin, October 11, 1777. A major piece in the repertoire was *The Enchantments of Circe and Atlas* "with new decorations, wonderful metamorphoses, transformations and Grand Dancer" (*Saunders Dublin Newsletter*, October 6, 1777).

117. Speaight, op. cit., p. 133. The last puppet evolved into a very popular trick figure in England, the Grand Turk.

118. Goldowski, *Chronicles of the Puppet Theatre*, p. 192.

119. Ibid., p. 202.

120. Ibid., p. 203.

121. Ibid., p. 212.

Chapter 2

1. Pitrè, *Usi e costumi*, pp. 333–334.

2. An unusual case of glove-puppets with legs is the Pupi di Stac company of Florence, active since 1946. They use a two-level stage. The upper level works like a standard glove-puppet stage, but the lower level and main playing area is at chest height, with the performer standing behind the puppet which he/she can watch through a gauze. Glove-puppets with dangling legs are much commoner in Germany and Holland. English Punch is often provided with legs too.

3. Leone, *La guarattella*, pp. 41–42.

4. In such cases the Bergamask puppeteer used the thumb and middle finger for the arms. The standard Emilian practice involved placing the thumb in one arm, the index finger in the head and the remaining three fingers in the other arm.

5. Benedetto Ravasio of Bergamo devised a system of spring-loading, holding the arms in a position bent at the elbows and providing tension to these otherwise dead limbs.

6. When Sarina had crowd scenes with a dozen or more figures, he mounted glove-puppets on sticks jammed into a holder.

7. In the English Punch and Judy show, Polly (named after the character in the *Beggars' Opera*) was operated in this way — another reminder of the Italian origins of the show.

8. Crib theaters of Eastern Europe use simple rod puppets. Such theaters with their rod figures were almost certainly familiar to many in Italy.

9. Istituto per i Beni Marionettistici e il Teatro Popolare.

10. Niemen, *Autobiografia di un burattinaio*, p. 15.

11. Luigia also inherited a splendid set of puppets from her brother Attilio. In 1927 the recently widowed Luigia was joined by her nephew Renzo Salici (1904–1981), who continued the company until 1976. Their circuit was Friuli, the Veneto and Treviso. In 1943, touring had to stop. Much of their material, stored in a school gym that the Germans turned into a stable, was lost or destroyed. Between 1950 and 1974 the company worked on the Lido of Venice, doing shorter shows aimed at juvenile audiences.

12. This may be merely a portrait, where the artist has deliberately omitted the stage. However, there are many examples from India to Iberia of puppeteers performing without any sort of stage.

13. A nineteenth-century Portuguese engraving is reproduced in Passos, *Bonecos de Santo Aleixo*, p. 94.

14. *Ragionamenti sei giornate* (Rome: Newton and Compton, 1993), p. 44.

15. See Carlo Scotti, "Breve storia della famiglia Sarina," in *Trattenimento con burattini*, p. 4 (Porta, *Gente di Sarina*, p. 9). The son of a carpenter from Lodi, Sarina was caught up in the political movements of the time, including the five-day revolution in Milan. He was captured by the Austrians and pressed into military service in Styria. Liberated in 1857, he returned to his profession as a traveling peddler.

16. De Simone, *Le guarattelle fra Pulcinella*, pp. 13–14, describes such a routine. It is still performed by Salvatore Gatto.

17. Cremona in *Burattini e marionette in Italia*, 1980, p. 148. In the 1840s there is a mention of another Pulcinella performer who worked on the Molo (harbor), but the only detail that survives is that in 1847 his daughter replaced him, as he was sick. One of her performances, *Il cocchio scapalato*, described other street shows.

18. Ghetanaccio's Pulcinella puppet was given to Gaetano Moroni, chamberlain and confidant to Pope Gregory XVI (1831–1846), who appears to have helped obtain his release from prison on one occasion, and this puppet is now in the Signorelli collection.

19. Giovanni Giraud composed an invitation ticket in verse for a visit made by Ghetanaccio to Sig. Luigi Casciani, who indulged in amateur theatricals and had his own private theater at via Sebastaniello 11 (Cremona, op. cit., p. 97).

20. *Il volgo di Roma* (Rome: E. Loescher, 1890) (Cremona, op. cit., p. 98).

21. Engravings of the Piazza del Duomo of the period show a booth, which is probably his.

22. This refers to the five-day revolution of March 18–22, sometimes called the first war of independence.

23. In Verona two puppeteers, Giovanni Valetto, known for his use of the bagpipe to attract an audience, and Paolo Aldrighetti (1808–1875), are said to have ended in prison for similar gibes. The marionette showman Pietro Gualtieri was performing in Brescello on October 13, 1848. His performances were interrupted by a disturbance in which part of the audience shouted "Abbasso i burattini" (Down with the puppets!) and the other half "Avanti I burattini" (Up with the puppets!). Gualtieri was ordered by the "delegato politico" to leave the area within the day. Given the date and the Austrian domination of the area, the association between puppets and the local authorities may have been all too obvious.

24. Artists sometimes depict more than two characters on the stage in prints of "guarattella" shows. This is often done to portray several moments of the show simultaneously and is not necessarily an indication of more than one performer.

25. Dates established by Bertonasso, "Burattini, marionette, ombre," p. 23.

26. "Soldi" and "denari" correspond linguistically to the pre-decimal English shillings and pence, usually indicated by "s" and "d" in prices.

27. Tamburini, "Fantocci, burattini, marionette a Torino," p. 24. Another company to have a booth of the Piazza Castello was the Burzio company.

28. Louis Aubin Millin, the French archeologist (Cremona, op. cit., p. 131). Millin mentions the main figure as Girolamo, who in the Bellone and Sales shows had been replaced by Gianduja. It is not entirely clear whether this was the Bellone and Sales company, but the presence of Gianduja (together with a Venetian comic, Tartai, probably Tartaglia) makes it likely.

29. Viale Ferrero, in "Lo sfarzo di quelle microscopiche scene," p. 29.

30. Campogalliani was baptized as a Christian. His

godfather was the marquis Rango d'Aragona and Campogalliani was the name of a property he presented to the recently converted family (Jori, *Francesco Campogalliani*, p. 39).

31. Campogalliani's daughter Maddalena worked with her siblings up to her marriage in 1820.

32. Jori, op. cit., p. 44. Jori quotes a document dated Castell'Arquato, September 19, 1890, which seems to point to Francesco's first show on his own.

33. Ibid., p. 91.

34. Ibid., p. 56.

35. Ibid., p. 58. In 1973 the Santa Rosalia theater of Mimmo Cuticchio in Palermo carried over the door the words "arte — morale — diletto."

36. Bill of 1848 in the Communal Archives, Modena.

37. Costantini, *Vita*, p. 24, mentions this careful avoidance of politics.

38. Cervellati, *Storia dei burattini e burattinai*, p. 236.

39. Much of this information is from a manuscript of the Salici family communicated by Remo Melloni. Salici ms., pp. 48–49.

40. Ibid., p. 53.

41. Ibid., p. 175.

42. Niemen, op. cit., pp. 99–100.

43. Cervellati, op. cit., p. 220.

44. Ibid., p. 14.

45. Reproduced by Pandolfini Barberi, *Burattini e burattinai Bolognesi*, p. 44.

46. Ibid., p. 20.

47. During the First World War Galli returned to puppets to entertain the troops in the Casa del Soldato in Bologna. Another celebrated glove-puppet performer, Pirro Gozzi (1869–1940), who had started his career with Angelo Cuccoli (and later worked with Pietro Braga), also performed there. Gozzi was the son of Leopoldo Gozzi (1832–1908) and a grandson of Pietro Gualtieri, a traveling marionette showman, known only for some anecdotes and because his name appears on some of the scripts of the Rissone collection.

48. He wrote a satirical piece about this forced exile, but was advised not to present it as he might lose his license altogether. This text is reproduced in Pandolfini Barberi, op. cit., pp. 52–55.

49. *Gazetta dell'Emilia*, August 6, 1885. Pandolfini Barberi, op. cit., p. 62.

50. Sarzi, "I Sarzi, quattro generazioni di burattinai" (interview with Rosa Sarzi).

51. Ibid.

52. Ibid.

53. Bergonzini et al., *Burattini e burattinai*, pp. 150–151.

54. Ibid., pp. 153–154.

55. Another son, Erio, travelled up and down the Adriatic coast with his wife Ada and his Compagnia Italiana Burattinai, which became well known in the 1950s.

56. Capellini, *Baracca e burattini*, p. 48.

57. Valeria Cremona, op. cit., 1980, p. 141. The only document relating to this legendary figure is a poem by Pietro Ruggieri, "La Baracca del Bataja. Buratinada classega — romantega" in *Poesie in dialetto bergamasco* (Bergamo: E. Lorenzelli, 1831).

58. Strambelli was succeeded by his son Alfonso.

59. The Bergamask puppeteer, Cannella, gave shows in inns and church halls in the second half of the nineteenth century.

60. Capellini, op. cit., p. 75.

61. A small permanent glove-puppet theater was set up by Colombo at the Malpensata in the 1930s. Domenico Rinaldi (b. 1902), who worked with a number of the main

puppeteers, spent some time with Colombo and later opened his own teatrino. In the period between the wars he also performed frequently at the Mutuo Soccorso. Other well-known puppeteers in Bergamo included the Gotti brothers, well-known performers at the turn of the twentieth century, and their assistant, Carlo Sarzetti (1896–1970), who inherited his show. He continued as a solo performer, often performing in small halls.

62. The Cristini collection includes exceptionally fine scenery. The puppets, carved by Enrico Manzoni, are some of the best examples of the Bergamask tradition.

63. Liliana Ebalginelli and Paola Ghidoli, "Bigio, burattinaio bergamasco."

64. Ibid., p. 28. Using puppets to entertain armies was common in other European countries, especially in Germany. See Dorothea Kolland, *Front Puppen Theater — Puppenspieler im Kriegsgeschehen* (Berlin: Elefanten Press, 1998). In 1917, Attilio Salici performed for Italian and American soldiers at Pontelagoscuro. His first show was a classic piece of the repertoire, *The Exiles of Siberia*. Bigio Milesi was helped at the beginning by his older cousin Irmo Milesi, whose puppets he eventually acquired. Gualtiero Mandrioli of Bologna, in the midst of the devastation caused by bombing, set up his booth in the ruins of the Piazza di Marchi and almost as soon as the Allied troops entered the city, his Fagiolino was in full performance (Cervellati, op. cit., p. 268).

65. Capellini, op. cit., p. 56.

66. In the 1970s he had followed courses at the Teatro Verdi of Tinin and Velia Mantegazza and had also studied with Natale Panaro, one of the most important carvers of puppet heads of the later twentieth century.

67. Lucchesi's circuit was the area from Bergamo to Lake Como. A set of puppets in Bergamo consisted of anything between about 50 and 250.

68. Costantini, op. cit., p. 18. He liked to perform in a place where people were accustomed to seeing puppets, but sometimes found that a pitch that had been profitable one year did not necessarily produce audiences on a return visit.

69. A small number of glove-puppet showmen had their own portable theaters. Giacomo Onofrio (1904–1964), working near Lake Garda, acquired a 400-seat tent in 1937 and used it during the summer months. Giuseppe Foglieni (1918–1963), in the area of Brescia, had one that seated 1,400.

70. Costantini, op. cit., p. 33.

71. Museo Giordano Ferrari, *Il castello dei burattini*, p. 48. Their son Emilio became a violinist and sometimes provided music for his parents' performances, their daughter Ermelinda performed with the puppets until her marriage and their daughter Maura became a professional theater costumier (and dressed a huge number of the Ferrari puppets and many of the other figures in their collection).

72. Luciano's son Giordano and Gimmi's daughter Manuela now continue the company.

73. Porta, *Gente di Sarina*, p. 14. Antonio Sarina's extracurricular activities included embalming animals, manufacturing fireworks, and painting carriages and frescoes.

74. His second son, Andrea (1882–1915), a gifted violinist and puppeteer, died of meningitis during the First World War.

75. Porta, op. cit., p. 17.

76. Ibid., pp. 52–53, has useful maps. Prior to 1900 the company followed a wider circuit, including some towns north of the Po.

77. Niemen, op. cit., p. 27.

78. Niemen's autobiography gives an excellent idea of the route he followed and the places where he performed.

He went into brief associations with others, notably the Concordia and Garda marionette companies.

79. Ibid., p. 68.

80. Ibid., p. 88. He would write to the mayor of a town to request permission to erect this fit-up.

81. Through Monaldesca Gozzi, his wife, Attilio acquired an important set of glove-puppet heads which he used for extra marionettes.

82. They presented glove-puppet versions of operatic libretti: *The Force of Destiny*, *The Gioconda* and *L'Africaine*. Franco Gambarutti likewise converted the family marionettes into glove-puppets in the 1960s and travelled abroad, visiting Russia, Sweden, Germany, Israel and Formosa.

83. Some of the beautifully carved heads of the Monticelli marionettes were converted into glove-puppet ones and are recognizable from the fact that they are proportionately slightly smaller than the standard glove-puppet heads of the region.

84. In 1951 he bought the surviving Yambo material from Novelli's widow and today this can be seen in the Monticelli museum in Ravenna. It includes figures from the film *Le marionette*.

85. These converted figures have smaller heads than the glove-puppets of Emilia.

Chapter 3

1. Many are provided with cast lead hands and feet whose weight helps manipulation. Some eighteenth-century figures have terra-cotta heads. This may point to batch production or an overlap with crib figures.

2. Pictures of these figures are in *Gusto e passione*, p. 243. Two similar figures, originally from the same group, are reproduced in *Burattini, marionette, pupi*, p. 74.

3. Cervellati, *Storia dei burattini e burattinai*, p. 100.

4. Quoted by Marzattinocci, *Cassandrino al Teatro Fiano*, p. 155.

5. A document of 1829 indicates that the managers of the theater owed 183 scudi and 30 baiocchi to the duke of Fiano for the rent of the theater, the "botteghino" (probably the box office) and the marionettes.

6. MS 360 in the Vittorio Emanuele library. Quoted in Marzattinocci, op. cit., p. 84.

7. The marionettes used in the Borromeo private theaters in Milan and on the Isola Bella and the Isola Madre are of a similar size and were made by professionals who worked for the Fiando theater, from where some of the scripts also derived. The performers were servants and possibly some family members.

8. Emerson, *Things Seen in Sicily*, p. 68, credits Sebastiano Zappalà (1877–1953) with the increase in size of the Catanian pupi to a height of over 1 meter 30 centimeters.

9. These 60-centimeter. figures were probably part of a professional marionette company active in the first half of the nineteenth century. The finely carved heads and hair styles (including side whiskers) suggest the period between the 1790s and 1820s. The Musée Gadagne also has some very small figures in eighteenth-century costumes which are probably commercial ones from the 1820s and designed for domestic use.

10. The two Neapolitan figures in the Ferrari collection have the same system, which might suggest a Neapolitan origin for it. Some of the Casa Grimani figures have a head rod that passes through both head and body and emerges between the legs.

11. Cervellati, op. cit., p. 96. Gaetano Gioia (1764–1826) and Salvatore Viganò (1769–1821) were celebrated dancers and choreographers.

12. *Gazzetta di Bologna*, cited by Cervellati, op. cit., p. 98.

13. Samoggia used the comic character of Fighetto, who probably originated in Emilia Romagna and can also be found with the Monticelli company. The accompanying documentation shows that by the second half of the nineteenth century these puppets were used by a traveling company on the squares of Modena, Bologna and other towns. They were probably still in use in the early 1900s.

14. *Gazzetta di Bologna*, January 22, 1812 (Cervellati, op. cit., p. 100).

15. A bill for this is amongst the documents included with Incisa's diary. Reproduced in Bertonasso, "Burattini, marionette, ombre," p. 8.

16. Archivio di Stato Fondo Comune Serie Li-Polizia Busta 3551. Document found by Bertozzi, "Burattini e marionette a Parma" (cited p. 107).

17. Archivio di Stato Fondo Governatore di Parma Busta 532 (1800) — 22.11.1815 Sig.Nocchi domiciliato prov. On July 8, 1816, there is also mention of an "Avviso per le Marionette da affigersi al bisogno il cui autore è il Macchinista domiciliato provv. A Parma onde averne le rispettive Approvazioni" (cited by Bertozzi, op. cit., p. 117). This probably also refers to Nocchi.

18. The French marionette showman Comte described himself as a "physicist."

19. *Gazzetta di Milano* — July 4, 1824 (Litta Modignani, *Dizionario biografico e bibliografia*, p. 102).

20. Nocchi also retained the character of Arlecchino in pieces such as *Arlecchino Miller; or The Movement of the Red Cloak with Arlecchino in the Enchanted Castle and Barber of the Dead*.

21. Litta Modignani, *Dizionario biografico e bibliografia*, p. 102.

22. *La rivista teatrale — Giornale drammatico, musicale e coregrafico* 1, no. 9 (June 1833): pp. 8–9.

23. Pretini, *Facanapa e gli altri*, p. 71. The Calle Larga theater opened in 1834 in a former school for blacksmiths and was on the same street as the San Moïsè theater. The Gerolamo company of the Tuscan marionettist Antonio Macchi also used this theater.

24. See *Pictures from Italy*, pp. 605–607 (based on the 1867–1868 edition).

25. *La perseveranza*, October 23, 1882. Reproduced by Sanguinetti, *Teatro Gerolamo*, p. 53. Alfredo Edel of La Scala designed costumes for them.

26. Pretini, op. cit., p. 52.

27. Bill reproduced in Pretini, op. cit., p. 56. In Trieste the company also used the Teatrino delle Marionette al Acquedotto (later called the Teatro Apollo).

28. Pretini, op. cit., p. 90. There are the usual undocumented anecdotes about his making satirical comments about the Austrians in his shows and spending nights in prison or having the show suspended.

29. *Burattini, marionette, pupi*, p. 307.

30. They also had seasons at the Teatro Nazionale, in 1867 (the year it opened) and later in 1878.

31. Reproduced in Pretini, op. cit., p. 100.

32. Ibid., p. 75.

33. Pretini, op. cit., p. 116, established a list of some 400 plays performed by the Reccardini company. About 40 of these survive in typed copies from the 1920s. He lists the repertoire of October 1837–February 1838 in Venice and that for September–October 1900 in Udine (pp. 120–122).

34. Bertozzi, op. cit., p. 114. Document from Archivio di Stato Fondo: Comune di Parma Serie Spettacoli Busta 4109.

35. According to baptismal records, Giuseppe's father was Giovanbattista Colla. It is possible that Giovanbattista and Giovanni were one and the same person.

36. The Colla company's registers cover the periods 1835–1851, 1863–1879, 1883–1924 and 1924–1957.

37. A version of Shakespeare's *Tempest* was commissioned from Eduardo de Filippo and presented in 1985. De Filippo chose Neapolitan rather than standard Italian and cast Ariel as a Neapolitan street urchin. De Filippo's recorded voice was used for all the male voices (he died before the production took place).

Irma Pirr spoke for Miranda. The lengthy exposition was represented in visual form with a stage within the stage (inside Prospero's grotto) and included the marriage of Claribel in Tunis and the shipwreck. The masque became a marionette performance with Commedia characters organized by Prospero (photographs of the production in Young, *Shakespeare Manipulated*, ch. 5).

38. Formerly called the San Siro, this theater had housed marionette shows since 1805 (Bilello, "La primaria compagnia marionettistica," p. 15).

39. Gambarutti, *Una vita appesa ai fili*, p. 30.

40. The core of the company was Franco Gambarutti, his wife Fortunata, their son Massimo, born 1958, Franco's uncle Ugo Gambarutti and sometimes other family members or temporary assistants. Franco Gambarutti also worked for Carlo Colla e Figli and Gianni and Cosetta Colla (1972–1980), and was one of the earliest puppeteers to appear on Italian television.

41. He frequently modified the name of the company, which might range from "Fantocci Concordia" to "Primaria Compagnia Marionettistica e Varieta Giuseppe Concordia."

42. Publicity for 1920 mentions 500 scenes and 300 marionettes.

43. Tullio Lenotti, *I teatri di Verona* (1949), quoted by Pretini, op. cit., p. 106. Lenotti refers to them as Prando.

44. *Black and White*, p. 644.

45. The original company was directed by two brothers, Baldassare and Giovan Battista Dall'Acqua. Alessandro Gorno, probably their assistant, married Albina, daughter of Giovan Battista, and the names became linked for the new company. They appeared in Verona in 1869 and in Udine in 1876.

46. The Salici circuit was in Mantua, then in Emilia and finally the Marches, where the company remained until the 1880s.

47. It is said that he worked for Thomas Holden, but during most of this time Thomas Holden was traveling extensively abroad. He may have worked for John Holden, or simply used the name to impress.

48. Richard Bradshaw, "The Salici Marionettes" in *Journal of UNIMA Australia*, March 1997, p. 32.

49. Salici ms., communicated by Remo Melloni, p. 36.

50. Ibid., p. 65.

51. Ibid., p. 69.

52. Colla and Bonora, *Il popolo di Legno*, p. 17. Colla and Bonora also mention another much older practice that the Church may well have frowned on, which was to give performances at weddings and baptisms to ward off the evil eye.

53. Gambarutti, op. cit., p. 47.

54. Croce, *Pupari — storia di Girolamo Cuticchio*, p. 27.

55. Gambarutti, op. cit., p. 37.

56. In a letter of 1811, addressed to the viceroy, he mentions having been in Milan for 17 years (Sanguinetti, op. cit., pp. 28–29).

57. In 1841 it had a parterre furnished with benches with backs and three tiers of boxes (Magnin, *Histoire des marionnettes en Europe*, p. 84).

58. Sanguinetti, op. cit., p. 12.

59. Ibid., lists many of the shows presented at the Gerolamo theater over its 150-year existence.

60. Ibid., pp. 26–27. This strict control followed the rules laid down in France governing the opening of theaters and the repertoires they might present.

61. Ibid., p. 37. Their revised version of *The Last Days of Pompei* is today one of the most spectacular of the productions of the Compagnia Carlo Colla e Figli.

62. Ibid., p. 47.

63. *Corriere delle dame*, November 26, 1814, quoted by Sanguinetti, op. cit., p. 31.

64. Andrea Maggi (1810–1894), glove-puppet and later marionette showman. In October 1818 and in August the next year the Maggi company (possibly directed by Andrea's father Antonio) was in Bologna in the Teatro Marsigli-Rossi (strada Maggiore 229) and also appeared in the Civico theater and in the San Gregorio, where the program included Viganò's *Prometeo*. He also advertised for private performances.

65. Cremona in *Burattini e marionette in Italia*, p. 127.

66. Chesnais, *Histoire générale des marionnettes*, p. 146, quotes from Jal's *De Paris à Naples* (Paris: Allardin, 1836).

67. Cremona, op. cit., p. 129.

68. Cervellati, op. cit., p. 96.

69. The building was demolished in 1957.

70. Cervellati, op. cit., p. 102. Another little theater, the Teatro Privat, hosted marionette performances in 1824.

71. Vuoso, *Stella Cerere*.

72. Ibid.

73. Later, "pupante" could have the same sense, but it often applied to the operators as much as to the owner of the show.

74. Her cousin, Michaela Tomeo, was an actress and director of a puppet theater. Tomeo's father was involved in management of small theaters.

75. In the 1950s Jan Bussell saw the Di Giovanni company perform a number of marionette variety turns followed by a sketch with live actors (Bussell, *Through Wooden Eyes*, pp. 31–45). An *Orlando furioso*, with pupi, was still in their repertoire.

76. He also opened a theater for live actors, the Teatro Corelli (later to become the Politeama Cinema). Carmine Abbuonandi worked with Corelli in the early twentieth century, but then toured with his own company in Puglia and Calabria. His son Giovanni became a partner of Corelli's son Vincenzo between 1935 and 1937, when the company was mostly in Bari. Another son, Alberto, active in and around Naples, was also associated with the Corellis. He too alternated pupi and live actors. His son Mario set up his own portable theater in the 1950s, but had ceased to perform by the end of the decade.

77. Arturo Corelli opened a cine-theater at Boscotrecase, where Vincenzo sometimes performed. Amedeo Corelli became a well-known Pulcinella, but was also active as a pupante. In 1925 Vincenzo formed a company with Alberto Abbuonandi and toured in Puglia and Calabria, presenting a repertoire that combined puppets and live performances of farces and religious plays. In the 1930s he and his brother Amedeo had a little theater in Castellammare di Stabia. Vuoso (*Stella Cerere*) had access to family documents and a typescript by Nicola Furiati Corelli, whom he interviewed in 1993.

78. Vuoso, op. cit. In 1963 the theater officially had 120 folding seats, but could contain an audience of between 150 and 200.

79. Francesco Verbale (1870–1932) had a "teatrino" in Montesanto and his audience included the brother and daughter of the celebrated camorrist Salvatore De Crescenzo (Tore 'e Criscienzo). Ciro Verbale (1900–1982) had a grandson of De Crescenzo as his partner between 1944 and 1946 (Vuoso, op. cit.).

80. Izzo, *I pupanti e l'opera dei pupi*, p. 19. An element of xenophobia associated evil with the outsider or foreigner (the Saracen) or blamed "traitors" at home (Gano and the Magonzese) for problems.

81. In 1940 the Ministry for Popular Culture banned the sale in bookstalls of popular literature about brigands (Gambarutti, op. cit., p. 38).

82. Vuoso, op. cit.

83. Ibid.

84. E.g., Giulio Marchetti and his wife and Silvia Giulio in the 1930s (Vuoso, op. cit.). Local helpers were also recruited to handle figures in crowd scenes, and boys sometimes had the job of passing the figures to the puppeteers.

85. Vuoso, op. cit.

86. For a brief period the pupari (pupanti) were employed to read a script to accompany silent films, but this did not prove a great success (Izzo, op. cit., p. 19).

87. Giancane, *Angelica, Orlando*, p. 32. One of the first names recorded is Gennaro Balzano of Naples, who established himself in Foggia in 1864.

88. Giancane, op. cit., p. 34. The figures had papier-mâché armor, not metal, as the later ones.

89. *Il tesoro sepolto*, p. 10.

90. Giancane, op. cit., p. 37.

91. Ibid., pp. 45–49, lists the scripts owned by the company.

92. De Felice, *Storia del teatro Siciliano*, p. 45.

93. Croce, *Pupi, carretti, contastorie*, p. 22.

94. Sicily's long tradition of banditry and a terrain that was difficult to control meant that there were powerful secret societies. These are evoked in Luigi Natoli's popular novel, *I Beati Paoli* (1909–1910), and readers would have identified the Beati Paoli with the mafia, associated in the popular mind of the time with justice, not crime. *I Beati Paoli* joined the repertoire of various Sicilian puppet theaters.

95. The popularity of the chivalric material is indicated by a wide variety of names taken directly from the *Paladini di Francia* that have become regular family names and nicknames in Sicily (Luigi Natoli in "Le tradizione cavalleresche in Sicilia" in *Il folklore Italiano* 2, 1927, pp. 99–120).

96. A point made by Pitrè and others (Croce, op. cit., p. 14). See also Majorana, "Italia Napoli," p. 183.

97. The Calabrian puparo Giacomo Longo worked in Sicily and trained his stepson Don Michele Immesi (1864–1932), who traveled through Campania and Calabria, eventually opening a teatrino in Barletta (Puglia) in 1890. Immesi and his family worked with the Catanian type of puppet and repertoire. In 1909 he traveled to Paris for the first time and in 1926 constructed his first portable theater, "Il Barracone." The war interrupted activities of the company, but from 1945 to 1957 Immesi's sons Filippo and Giuseppe Carlo picked up the show again. When they stopped much of the material was sold off, but a year later, Filippo and his son Michele started up again and continued until 1964. Between 1987 and 1995 Michele, his sister Ada and her husband Giuseppe Chiumeo revived the company.

98. Agrippino Manteo began his career in Catania with Giuseppe Crimi, emigrated to Argentina at the beginning of the twentieth century, returned to Italy for the war and later settled in New York (1923–1936), performing mainly for Italian immigrants, first on Catherine Street and later on Mulberry Street. See Baird, *Art of the Puppet*, pp. 118–129.

99. In some cases admission was paid for in eggs, which the puparo would collect and sell. Emerson, op. cit., p. 63,

mentions the sale of water and dried melon seeds during the intervals.

100. One of the first names to emerge at the end of the eighteenth century is Domenico Scaduto, who possibly deserves some credit too.

101. Litta Modignani, *Dizionario biografico e bibliografia*, p. 80.

102. Adamo, *L'opra dei pupi*, p. 9; Emerson, op. cit., p. 66. One of Greco's assistants was Federico Lucchese, who later set up his own show in Trapani (Adamo, p. 49).

103. Pitrè, *Usi e costumi*, pp. 157–158.

104. Another son, Nino, set up in Termini Imerese. Other Palermitan showmen included Russo, Consiglio, Delisi, Giarratano, Pollicino and Pernice.

105. His skills included gilding and decorating carts (Litta Modignani, *Dizionario biografico e bibliografia*, p. 51).

106. This included a huge number of scenarios, scenery, puppets, a Fasoni organ, and the stage itself. There were about 100 figures — armed ones, giants, soldiers, "borghesi," a pope, a bishop, 2 or 4 monks, a lion, a horse, a mule, 3 snakes, 5 devils, a hippogriff, a vulture, a skeleton, a dog, a stag, and Pulicane + Christ and 12 apostles for the Passion (one of Canino's special pieces) and about 200 spare heads (some by Gaspare, some older ones by Bagnasaco, Mignosi and Alberto Canino). The armor was by Salvatore Delisi. Gaspare also painted carts with chivalric scenes and made armor and props for religious processions.

107. Emerson, op. cit., pp. 65–66, gives a detailed account of the Greco performance of the popular episode of the murder of Ruggiero. This ended spectacularly with the castle of Pinamonte (the murderer) in flames and large stones crashing down on the stage to the delight of the audience.

108. Litta Modignani, *Dizionario biografico e bibliografia*, p. 80.

109. Croce, *Pupari — storia di Girolamo Cuticchio*, p. 14.

110. The Argento and Mancuso and Sclafani families continued the opera dei pupi in the Palermo area. Vincenzo Argento (1873–1948) began his activity in the Borgo Vecchio of Palermo. His son Giuseppe (1922–1993) enjoyed considerable success in the years following the war. After occupying various teatrini he gave up performances in 1985. The family are skilled makers of armored puppets. This has become their main source of income and they have a small workshop and shop close to the cathedral. Since 1999 they have regrouped as the Associazione Culturale Agramante and have a little theater where performances are given on a more occasional basis, mainly for tourists. Their use of a recorded soundtrack has offended purists who see the live voice of the puparo as essential.

111. Achille Greco's two daughters, Nannina and Carmelina, are said to have provided female voices, but this was not usual (Majorana, "Italia Napoli," p. 187).

112. In Palermo the term "opranti" was preferred. At the Uzeta theater of Biagio Mirabella in 1948 the male speakers were paid 300 lire, the female speakers 250, and the 3 operators 150 lire each (Majorana, op. cit., p. 188).

113. Catanian speakers might also use a drum to cue the opening or closing of the curtain between the acts, to announce an entrance or to produce a rhythm appropriate to the character (Majorana, op. cit., p. 188). The bang of a clog might emphasize an important piece of speech or cue the musician(s) or pianino player. In Palermo the puparo uses this practice.

114. It is sometimes argued that there was a separate Siracusan "school" (Uccello, "L'opra dei pupi").

115. Between 1912 and 1936 Nini Calabrese had a little theater behind the Carmine church in Messina. Rosario Gargano (1863–1942) spent a few years with him, then ran his own theater from 1919 to 1935. Gargano enriched the repertoire with his own plays, including a *Belisario di Messina*. His son Venerando, daughter Tina and grandson Rosario restarted the company in 1938. They survived a disastrous fire in the late 1950s. Rosario died in 2000, but his family has maintained the company. Enrico Mezzasalma, originally an assistant of Calabrese, set up his Eden theater in a wooden booth in the late 1960s. Nini Cocivera and Michele Spadaro Cimarosa also continued the pupi in Messina (Mario Sarica). Between 1930 and 1960 Natale Meli, son of a Catanian puparo, Peppino Meli, was mainly active across the straits in Reggio Calabria, but also performed in Messina. He worked with both pupi and glove-puppets. Most of his material, including scripts, is in MIMAP in Palermo.

116. Crimi's son Giuseppe wrote memoirs around 1924. Part of these was included in Li Gotti, *Il teatro dei pupi*, pp. 158–164. Giuseppe gives Gaetano's date of birth as December 25, 1808 (1809 according to Majorana and 1807 according to Litta Modignani). The date of his death is generally thought to be 1874 (1877 in Litta Modignani).

117. Crimi had three wives and numerous children, most of whom died in the cholera epidemic of 1859.

118. Majorana, op. cit., p. 191. Giuseppe Crimi set up a theater in Siracusa and later moved to Franconforte. *The Flood* was one of his most spectacular productions.

119. Trombetta later worked with Angelo Grasso, but had his own Teatro Dante from 1899 to 1914. His assistant Sebastiano Zappalà ran the Dante very successfully from 1923 until the 1930s.

120. Another daughter, Nazarena, and her husband, Giovanni Cantone, had a teatrino at 55 via Celeste, Catania. Half the space was partitioned off as their home and the rest was the theater, with 13 fixed benches, seating about 80, and a raised area at the back for a further 16. Two windows let in daylight from the street. An oil lamp in the center of the ceiling, one on each side of the proscenium arch, and a further two on the stage provided the lighting. They emigrated to America in the 1890s.

121. De Felice, op. cit., p. 211, note 16.

122. According to Giuseppe Crimi, Grasso was a weaver taken on by his father as an assistant. His initial job was to pull the curtain and later he became a glove-puppet showman.

123. Via San Crispino, via della Lettera, via S. Maria del Rosario and via Cestai.

124. De Felice, op. cit., p. 211, note 22. A few years later Pitrè spoke of seats in Catania costing five cents, and the boxes ten.

125. Majorana, op. cit., p. 195. Angelo Grasso's elder brother, Giovanni, set up his Ariosto Theater in Messina, possibly with the help of Gaetano Crimi (Li Gotti, op. cit., p. 159). In 1877 he returned to Catania and opened the Teatro Popolare, but later abandoned the pupi to be an actor.

126. Majorana, op. cit., p. 194.

127. Nino Insanguine (1899–1980) went to Rome in 1927 to work as an actor with Giovanni Grasso, and also with puppets. He returned to Catania and performed with puppets at the Teatro Mazzini. After a period in Tripoli in the 1930s he returned to Sicily to work both as actor and puppeteer until 1957. An ebullient performer, he was noted for the theatricality of his puppet productions. His two sons continued the show for a time after his death.

128. Li Gotti, op. cit., p. 74. It then disappeared to make room for a Rinascente store.

129. The armor was made by Don Giuseppe Maglia (De Felice, op. cit., p. 60).

130. They then had a brief period in via Consolazione, but closed this in 1952.

131. Unlike most Catanian showmen, his puppets had jointed knees.

132. In 1929 he visited Tripoli.

133. Mauceri, *I fratelli Vaccaro*, p. 11. The influence of the Puzzos continued to be felt in Siracusa when the brothers Rosario (1911–1984) and Alfredo Vaccaro (1924–1995) had a pupi theater in a former convent on the via Nizza, from 1978 to 1995. They reduced the size of the puppets and made the heads out of papier-mâché. All performances were single-episode ones mainly for tourists. After 1995 the theater had to close as the building was unsafe. Shortly after this Alfredo's grandsons, Alfredo and Daniel Mauceri, opened their own tiny theater.

134. *Rome, Naples et Florence en 1817* (December 10, 1816), p. 18.

135. *Burattini e marionette in Italia*, 1980, p. 83, lists places where puppet shows occurred and marks them on the 1836 map.

136. Marzattinocci, op. cit., p. 29.

137. Toldo, "Nella baracca dei burattini," p. 93. One of the last marionette theaters in Rome that continued into the twentieth century was the Constanzi.

138. In 1835 the health inspectors required the Ornani to open the windows more often because of the bad smell occasioned by the "quality" of the audience (Marzattinocci, op. cit., p. 31).

139. Story, *Roba di Roma*, p. 272, mentions "live" performances at the Fico Theater, where admission to the first was five baiocchi, and to the second, two.

140. Marzattinocci, op. cit., ch. 4, provides a detailed study of the history and architecture of the Fiano Theater.

141. Legal documents concerning contracts and rent appear from 1812 onwards (Ottoboni collection, vol. 164, archive of the Vicariato of Rome).

142. List reproduced by Marzattinocci, op. cit., p. 176. The exact period to which it refers is not clear.

143. Marzattinocci, op. cit., p. 171.

144. Verdi wrote *Un ballo in maschera* for him.

145. It reopened as a variety theater in 1888 and continued into the twentieth century, when it became a store for official documents. In the late 1990s it reverted to entertainment as a cinema, the Nuova Olimpia.

146. Marzattinocci, op. cit., p. 157, quotes from a contract with the painter Vincenzo Pitorri, who freshened up the decoration and repainted the ceiling and the proscenium arch.

147. In 1822 Chinese shadow shows were being presented at the Ornani by a performer who was too poor to pay the rent (Marzattinocci, op. cit., p. 30).

148. *Briten in Rom* (Leipzig: Weller, 1940). Quoted by Cremona, op. cit., pp. 116–117.

149. Story, op. cit., p. 269. Story noted that the Emiliani was much cleaner than the Teatro delle Muse (the Fico), but had smaller audiences.

150. The premises later became a hardware shop.

151. The date of 1853 is based on a bill listing the repertoire mentioned by Gregorovius (Cremona, op. cit., 1980, p. 120).

152. Gregorovius, *Wanderjahre in Italien*, p. 87.

153. The files of the Deputazione dei Pubblici Spettacoli are in the Archivio Capitolino. Mazzoleni published a group of scripts of the Fiano theater for the years 1833–1834 together with the changes demanded by the censorship (*Cassandrino*).

154. *Registri della congregazione dei Pubblici Spettacoli,*

1823, section 6, Rubr. Spettacoli, note 38, cartella 6, pos. 38a. The Pace closed down altogether in 1844.

155. *Burattini, marionette, pupi*, pp. 286–287.

156. *Registri della congregazione dei Pubblici Spettacoli*, 1818, section 6, Rubr. Spettacoli, note 34, cartella 2, pos. 34a (Archivio Capitolino). (See Cremona, op. cit., p. 87.)

157. *Registri della deputazione dei pubblici Spettacoli*, 1825, Rubr. Spettacoli, note 7, cartella 7, pos. 7a (Archivio Capitolino, Rome). (See Cremona, op. cit., p. 87.) The Trastevere teatrini were probably not included because they were across the river and outside the city proper.

158. Lanza, "Le leggende cavalleresche."

159. Cremona, op. cit., 1980, p. 91.

160. This text is in vol. 11 of the *Opere* of Giraud, published in Rome in 1841.

161. Mazzoleni, op. cit., p. 60. The pedantic censor also corrected spelling mistakes.

162. *Il casotto dei burattini* appeared from September to December 1848 and was politically reactionary. At the top it carried an engraving of a puppeteer carrying his booth from one pitch to another and the motto "chi si sente scottar ritiri i piedi" (anyone who feels he is burning his fingers should pull back). In Bologna satirical papers with puppets' names were *Il sandrone* (1874) and *Fasulein* (1891).

163. The Gorno Dall'Acqua company inspired the Bolognese glove-puppeteers Chinelato and Cavadini to use marionettes at the Teatro Nosadella in 1910 (Cervellati, op. cit., p. 137).

164. The Lupis did this, but later reverted to the head rod, which they continued to use until the 1990s.

165. In 1925, when the film *Messalina* was popular, he wrote a short poem, "Caro — Pellicole" (Dear Film), where he played on the idea of the film costing 10 lire to see, while Messalina liked to exhibit herself for free.

166. Croce, *Pupi, carretti, contastorie*, reproduces one of Mancuso's leaflets (from the collection of MIMAP).

167. Colla and Bonora, *Il popolo di legno*, p. 15.

168. Gambarutti, op. cit., p. 47.

Chapter 4

1. Cervellati, *Storia dei burattini e burattinai*, p. 74.

2. Adriano Banchieri (1567–1634) in *La Catalina da Budri* (Budrio) and *Ursalina da Crevalcor* included characters speaking Bolognese. In another, untitled, piece three of the six characters respectively use Bolognese, Venetian and Bergamask.

3. Cervellati, op. cit., p. 221. This type of improvised performance disappeared towards 1914.

4. Beales, *Risorgimento*, p. 75.

5. Paolo Orano, "Il dialetto in Italia," *Corriere della sera*, Milan, March 30, 1930 (Jori, *Francesco Campogalliani*, p. 69).

6. Colla and Bonora, *Il popolo di legno*, p. 17.

7. Young, *Shakespeare Manipulated*, p. 17.

8. Cervellati, op. cit., p. 20.

9. This collection of scenarios, used by the Accesi company, was assembled under the title *Il teatro delle favole rappresentativo*.

10. Bragaglia, *Pulcinella*, p. 46. Bragaglia also found a woodcut from 1592 of a masked figure with a beaklike nose that bears a strong resemblance to Pulcinella, but could equally be Pascariello (p. 47).

11. Rak, "Il teatro meccanico," p. 50.

12. Bragaglia, op. cit., p. 89. According to Bragaglia, when Fiorillo played Pulcinella, the part of the captain, of which Scaramuzzia was a version, was taken by one of his sons, and finally by his son Tiberio Fiorilli, who became immensely popular in Paris and was said to have been imitated by Molière.

13. In the scenarios of the Casamarciano manuscript of Naples, which dates from 1700, Pulcinella is the main comic mask, often supported by Coviello (another descendant of the braggart Spanish captain), with Tartaglia, the Dottore and Pantalone as the older men.

14. Italian Commedia actors visited Russia in the 1730s with "at least four puppet companies" and performed plays about the adventures of Pulcinella (Goldowski, *Chronicles of the Puppet Theatre*, p. 115; Central State Archives of Old Documents, fund. 1239, inv. 3, f.51846, pp. 145, 160).

15. An engraving of the Fossard collection shows Arlecchino in a similar situation. Here the implication is that he is not the begetter of his own numerous family.

16. Cremona in *Burattini e marionette in Italia*, 1980, p. 95. Ferretti also mentions a scenario in which a servant has cheated his master and is dragged before the court.

17. One of the devils in the Borromeo collection has fowls' legs, and this representation is also found in a devil in the Scuola Civica Paolo Grassi. After the cloven hoof, this is quite a common attribute of the devil.

18. Sonnet of November 22, 1832 (Cremona, op. cit., p. 97).

19. Text published in De Simone, *Le guarattelle fra Pulcinella*.

20. Published in *I testi, il repertorio*, pp. 7–14. The Ferraiolo family of Salerno was active between 1900 and 1960.

21. These texts are in the Biblioteca Nazionale, Rome. Lanza, "Un rifacitore popolare," has established the authorship of Finardi.

22. Examples of figures with opening mouths are a devil and a Pulcinella in the Davia Bargellini collection, a Truffaldino, a Dottore and a Pantalone together with a Moor who is able to stick out his tongue in the Casa Grimani collection.

23. In 1815, Anna Maria Nardi, perhaps the widow of Nardi, was presenting marionette performances at the S. Romano Theater in Milan with Truffaldino (a mask popular in Venice and similar to Arlecchino).

24. Bartoš, *Loutkářská kronika*, pp. 43–47.

25. According to Cervellati (op. cit., p. 169), Balanzone, originally a victim of tricks, evolved into a more positive and responsible figure. Famous for his long tirades in Bolognese, his prolixity was considerably reduced during the nineteenth century.

26. He also used the mask of Brighella. His Lombard partner Andrea Ludergnani used Tartaglia and Gioppino. None of these found great success with Bolognese audiences.

27. The name appears in a list of characters for Giorgio Maria Rapparini's *Arlecchino*, published in 1718 by Muller in Heidelberg, but there is no obvious connection between this Fagiolino and the puppet (Cervellati, op. cit., p. 43).

28. According to Cervellati, op. cit., p. 203, the Bolognese Sandrone was closer to the Reggia Emilian type than to the Modenese one.

29. Gugliemo Preti's brothers Emilio and Enrico used Sgorghiguelo as their main character.

30. Cervellati, op. cit., p. 210. One short farce in which she appeared was *The Will of Old Pulidora Beccafichi*.

31. Galli also developed the Milanese mask of Meneghino with great success.

32. Sarzi, "I Sarzi, quattro generazioni di burattinai."

33. In the private marionette theater of the Borromeo family on the Isola Bella, Arlecchino remained the comic protagonist as a theatrical mask and was not replaced by the more popular and plebeian Gerolamo.

34. Included with the Incisa diary. When Cuniberto first appeared in Asti in 1811, he was performing out of doors. In 1816 he had moved indoors. The charge of 2.6 soldi for the pit and 4 soldi for the boxes at the Berruti indicates a more middle-class audience, which he flatters with references to the "generous and learned public of Asti" and "this respectable audience."

35. July 9, 1806, quoted by Sanguinetti, *Teatro Gerolamo*, p. 14.

36. Gambarutti, *Una vita appesa ai fili*, p. 35.

37. The season began on July 20, 1811, and ended abruptly on September 21. According to Incisa, audiences had been declining, but the performance of an anti-clerical piece of the Jacobin repertoire, *The Nuns of Cambrai*, was stopped by the mayor, who would not allow them to substitute a less offensive piece. The Asti performances were in the former convent of San Anastasio. Prices were three soldi for the pit and four for the balcony.

38. Monti, *Il Gerolamo*, p. 71.

39. Colla and Bonora, *Il popolo di legno*, p. 21.

40. Family tradition claimed that the character was created in 1828, but the first documented indication is on bills for 1837 (Pretini, *Facanapa e gli altri*, p. 73).

41. A good description was given by Edoardo Paoletti in *La scena illustrata*, Florence, December 15, 1888 (Pretini, op. cit., pp. 128–131).

42. The Donadino company used Arlecchino right up to the end of the nineteenth century. On its script for *Arlecchino Supposed Princess*, the name of Arlecchino is crossed out and replaced by Facanapa.

43. The Muchetti Cecchino had an opening mouth, mobile eyes and eyebrows and apparently the ability to smoke (photo in Poieri, *I Muchetti, marionettisti*, p. 75).

44. Melloni, "Burattini e burattinai nella tradizione bergamasca," p. 15, mentions a fresco of the crucifixion by Francesco Prata (1531) which depicts a Roman soldier with a triple goiter.

45. Capellini, *Baracca e burattini*, p. 44.

46. This scenario is very similar to the classic Guignol piece, *Les souterrains du château*. The Pupi di Stac in the last years of the twentieth century also used the subject for a piece using Stenterello, accompanied by Giovannin Senzapaura. A video was made in 1993 and distributed by Unicopli Giochi, Milan.

47. The name "Patacca" was taken from a small coin that represented a soldier's pay (Rossetti, *I bulli di Roma*, p. 56).

Berneri's Meo Patacca led a burlesque crusade against the Turks. He acquired a new popularity on the nineteenth-century Roman stage, and even on the pupi stages as a latter-day Orlando in episodic pieces set in a Rome besieged by the Turks (the Vienna of 1683 became the Rome of 1775).

48. Rossetti, op. cit., p. 72.

49. Ibid., p. 90. William Story mentions a bill for a puppet performance of *Belisario; or The Adventures of Orestes, Ersilia, Falsierone, Salinguerra and the Terrible Gobbo* (*Roba di Roma*, p. 271). The reference to the "terribile Meino," could of course be a passing one to the popular Piedmontese brigand hero of the puppet stage, Majno della Spinetta.

50. *Volgo di Roma*, 1820 (Rossetti, op. cit., p. 103).

51. Manuscript in the Vittorio Emanuele collections, National Library, Rome. The proprietor of the mausoleum at the time was Sgr. Settimo de Dominicis.

52. Another Rugantino play, Giovanni Giraud's *Malvinuccia; or The Little Girl of Four* (1832), was probably designed for performance in a noble house outside Rome during the "villegiatura."

53. Mentioned by Roger de Beauvoir in *Il Pulcinella* (Paris, 1834) (Marzattinocci, *Cassandrino al Teatro Fiano*, p. 116).

54. Cocchiara, *Le vastasate*, p. 32.

55. In Venice Arlecchino and Brighella fell into the same category. They were described as "facchini."

56. Cocchiara, op. cit., p. 11. He indicates that in more modern usage "vastaso" means an ill-educated boor.

57. Birlicchi and Birlacchi are devil's names used in much of Europe. In the puppet Faust plays in Germany they are called Perlico and Perlaco.

58. Jones, *Diversions in Sicily*, p. 188.

59. She is much used in the theaters of the Plaja quarter of Catania. A strange variant of Peppininu is Pippuzzu, who has a dark complexion and a page's costume and belongs almost exclusively to the theaters of the Picanello quarter (Alessandro Napoli).

60. Jones's reference suggests that Peppenino may still have been current in Palermo in the early 1900s. In Acireale Emanuele Macri had a variant of Peppenino which he called Famiglio, a name which simply means servant (cognate with English "familiar").

61. When the opera dei pupi was transplanted to Tunisia the main comic mask remained a Sicilian street boy, but his name changed to N'coula (Aziza, *Formes traditionnelles du spectacle*, p. 66).

62. Surviving comic elements in modern performances are a tendency for Saracen messengers to bump into the wings at their exit and the high-pitched voice given to the treacherous Gano to make him sound ridiculous.

63. Meli's figures are larger than the Neapolitan ones and also include an older man, Anselmo d'Artaglia (perhaps a deformation of Tartaglia).

64. He wears a red beret with a tassel which he can swing around in a similar way to Fagiolino. Sarina used a wide range of established masks and characters: Balanzone, Tartaglia, Pantalone, Brighella, Checco, Cavicchio, Ficcanaso, Arlecchino, Meneghino, Colombina, Rosaura, Sempronio, Battistino, Bortolino, Giovannino, Pasqualino, Bernadone and Gioppino and his family. Gianduja and Pulcinella are notable for their absence.

65. Porta, *Gente di Sarina*, p. 88. This is indicated in the scripts in the Fondo Sarina-Scotti.

66. Pampalughino has a brown costume with a rather military-looking beret, and his smile shows his teeth. Other folk types used by Peppino Sarina included La Vecchia Simona (the classic old woman), Il Nonno (the grandfather) and Mariollo, originally called Napoletano, who has a hooked nose and chin and may have been an attempt to create a Piedmontese equivalent to Pulcinella. Peppino's brother Andreino Sarina, who died during the First World War, invented a rather officious character, known as Barabba, and Rangognino, the long-nosed, bad-tempered, urbanized peasant, who was meant to incarnate the inhabitants of Broni.

67. Gambarutti, op. cit., pp. 55–56.

68. Palazzi, "La vocazione teatrale di Pinocchio," pp. 12–13.

69. Galleati, *Diario e memorie varie di Bologna* (Cervellati, op. cit., p. 312).

70. Cervellati, op. cit., p. 309.

71. Ebalginelli and Ghidoli, "Bigio, burattinaio bergamasco," p. 46.

72. Croce, *Pupi, carretti, contastorie*, p. 57.

73. Bergonzini et al., *Burattini e burattinai*, pp. 247–252.

74. National Museum, Prague. Reproduced in Patková, 1975, plate 2. The plays listed are: *Il gran basilisco*; *Pulcinella cuoco*; *Li quattro elementi*; *Pulcinella mago per fortuna*; *Pulcinella corrier straordinario*; *Comare Checa e la Co-*

mare Chaca; *Pulcinella Ladro in campagna e Galantuomo in città*; *I mondi novi ed i mondi vecchi*; *La nascita di Pulcinella*; *La gara de' Zanni: Il sicario innocente*; *Il cuccù immaginario*; *La confusione d' amore e gelosia*; *Le disgrazie di Pulcinella*; *I due simili*; *Il figliuol prodigo*; *Pulcinella assassino di strada*; *Pulcinella principio per magia*; *Pulcinella mercante di pignatte*; *Le astuzie di Pulcinella*; *Amore e gelosia*; *Pulcinella principessa*; *La casa con due porte*; *Pantalone schiavo in algeri*; *La testa incantata*; *Il servo sciocco*; *Pulcinella compagno del diavolo*; *Il gran convitato di pietra*.

75. *Le metamorfosi di Arlecchino*; *Arlecchino compagno del diavolo*; *La sfida di Arlecchino e Brighella pei loro padroni*; *Arlecchino bassa dei Turchi*; *Arlecchino finto prencipe*; *Le trentatre disgrazie di Arlecchino*; *Arlecchino servo sciocco flagello del suo padrone*; *La nascita di Arlecchino*. To these we can add *Il Demetrio*, with intermezzi by Arlecchino, and two classic Commedia pieces, *L'equivoco dei due annelli* and *Il convitato di pietra*. Apart from *Gli incanti di Circe* and *Nerone*, the remaining pieces were religious.

76. The pieces presented included: *La refugiata regina di Navarra e morte di D. Sancio ursurpatore* (June 15); *La morta di Davila gran tiranno d'America* (June 16); and *Il ratto d'Elena e l'incendio di Troia* (June 21).

77. These date from 1700 but may well have been around for a number of years.

78. Melloni and Bo, "Il repertorio del teatro," p. 7.

79. Speaight, *History of the English Puppet Theatre*, pp. 132–133.

80. Monti, *Il Gerolamo*, p. 24.

81. Bill for peformances in Asti (Bertonasso, "Burattini, marionette, ombre," p. 19). There is some confusion between the names of Renzi and Rizzi in 1777. The Rizzi family of 1810 may be the same family as Renzi (Rizzi) of 1777.

82. Cocchiara, op. cit., p. 43.

83. Jori, op. cit., p. 75. Jori, pp. 72–80, lists a number of pieces from Francesco Campogalliani's repertoire.

84. A video recording of a performance of the Ferrari production was made in 2000 (Officinema Produzioni Cinematografiche s.n.c. Parma).

85. A related piece in the puppet repertoire was *Leonzio il crudele*, in which a libertine visits the family tomb and insults the statue of his ancestor, after which he is dragged off to hell. Frequently staged in the eighteenth century, this may originate in a play performed at the Jesuit college in Ingoldstadt in 1615, but puppet showmen probably got the subject directly from cheap popular fiction (Cervellati, op. cit., pp. 275–278).

86. Leydi and Leydi, *Marionette e burattini*, p. 59. The chapter "Milano dai Romanitt a Gerolamo," especially pp. 256–274, has a valuable study of this piece, and is followed by the text of a version used by the Colla company, pp. 289–319.

87. The Mozart-Da Ponte *Don Giovanni* was only one of four new operas on the subject to be performed in 1787.

88. Remo Melloni in *Il tesoro sepolto*, p. 98.

89. Enzo Petraccone, ed., *La Commedia dell'Arte, storia — tecnica-scenari* (Naples: Ricciardi, 1927).

90. The Naples scenario included the Dottore and Tartaglia. Dell'Aquila omitted them and also compressed the two dinner scenes into one.

91. Toldo, "Nella baracca dei burattini," provides a valuable study of these sources for the puppet stage.

92. Sanguinetti, op. cit., p. 16.

93. Ibid., pp. 30–31.

94. According to Leydi and Leydi, op. cit., p. 140, parts of this adaptation also recall a musical version of *La castalda* performed at the Teatro Grimani di San Samuele in Venice during Carnival of 1755.

95. Jori, op. cit., p. 73.

96. A popular Commedia scenario that featured in Francesco Campogalliani's repertoire was *The Three Hunchbacks of Damascus*. This has nothing to do with Goldoni's *The Three Hunchbacks*.

97. Fiando's text belongs to the Colla company and is deposited at the Società Italiana di Autori e Editori (SIAE).

98. Stendhal, *Voyages en Italie*, p. 1200. Stendhal points out that in a city full of bachelors, many of them cardinals and monsignori, it did not take much for audiences to make this association.

99. Mercey mentions a couple of Cassandro farces in his long article, "Le théâtre en Italie" in *La revue des deux mondes* 22, Paris, April 15, 1840, pp. 185–213. In *Cassandrino dilettante* Cassandrino as a singer and impresario finds a rival in a youthful lady-killer, whom audiences could recognize as Rossini, while in *Cassandrino, Married Man* he is placed in a situation that contrasts his rather fastidious manners with those of the popular classes.

100. The Vittorio Emanuele collection of the National Library in Rome includes scripts belonging to the period 1833–1834.

101. Mazzoleni, *Cassandrino*, p. 66, suggests that this was written for performance by live actors. The dialogue is more realistic and fuller than in the other pieces and the censor does not indicate here that it is permitted "for performance by marionettes." This may be a case of the actors' theater cashing in on the success of the marionette one.

102. Marzattinocci, op. cit., p. 78.

Chapter 5

1. Gambarutti, *Una vita appesa ai fili*, p. 37.

2. In eighteenth-century Spain marionette shows were closely associated with cribs. In nineteenth-century Lyon the term "crèche" (crib) designated a marionette show.

3. Perucci's play's full title is *The True Light amongst the Shadows; or The Birth of the Word Made Man*. Palermitan-born Perucci was heavily involved in the late seventeenth-century Neapolitan theater and is especially known for his treatise on performance, *Dell'Arte rappresentativa, premeditata e all'improviso*.

4. Natale Meli and the Fratelli Napoli used very similar versions. The Meli script is in MIMAP (S.60).

5. Pepinninu upsets the shepherds by feeding the goats their entire supply of winter corn. In the Napoli version he brandishes a huge bunch of fennel, his offering to the holy child.

6. The script no longer survives (Leydi, *Gelindo ritorna*, p. 194).

7. Text in Leydi, *Gelindo ritorna*, pp. 341 ff.

8. Jones, *Castellinaria*, pp. 261–285.

9. Cipolla and Moretti, *I fili della memoria*, p. 94. This was performed at the Teatro San Simone in Tortona. Ringhieri wrote a number of religious dramas.

10. Jones, *Diversions in Sicily*, pp. 183–196.

11. Jones missed the final act that involved the cutting of Samson's hair.

12. Leydi and Leydi, *Marionette e burattini*, pp. 38–39, lists some of the more popular ones to survive: *Santa Margherita of Cortona*, *Santa Tecla*, *The Martyrdom of San Vittore*, *The Death of St. James the Apostle*, *Santa Filomena*, *The Journey of the Three Kings*, *Santa Rosa*.

13. As a Sicilian saint she also appeared regularly in Catania.

14. Sordi, "La materia cavalleresca," p. 218.

15. Both the Napolis and the Cuticchios have a Rosalia piece in their repertoire.

16. Salvatore Meli's scenario includes some dialogue passages written out in full (MIMAP, S62).

17. Script in MIMAP.

18. Niemen, *Autobiografia di un burattinaio*, p. 58.

19. The *Chanson de Roland* was composed after the destruction of a Christian army by the Saracens in Spain in 1086. The original defeat of Ronceveaux (Roncisvalle) in 778 had been of a French army by Basque fighters, and not Saracens. This reworking of events was to soothe French pride (Di Maria, "Risonanze storiche," p. 25).

20. The work of Ariosto and others became a regular point of reference for seventeenth- and eighteenth-century opera. Lully and Quinault used medieval romance for *Amadis de Gaulle* (1684), *Roland* (1685) and *Armide* (1686), derived from Tasso's *Gerusalemme liberata*. Händel had his *Rinaldo* (1711), *Orlando* (1733), *Ariodante* (1735) and *Alcina* (1735).

21. Clare Phillips in *The Illustrated History of Textiles*, ed. Madeleine Ginsburg (London: Studio Editions, 1991), p. 33.

22. Li Gotti, *Il teatro dei pupi*, p. 56, indicates that Pitrè mentions this.

23. The Locatelli collection was not assembled for a major known company. The material may have been put together for use by amateurs belonging to one of the many academies of the time (Pandolfi, *La Commedia dell'Arte*, vol. 5, pp. 207–208).

24. In another scenario, *La grande pazzia di Orlando*, Angelica, fleeing the amorous Ruggiero to seek Orlando, is captured by pirates but freed by Ruggiero. Orlando carries out glorious exploits and reunites the lovers Zerbino and Isabella. Angelica helps the wounded Medardo (Medoro) and Orlando, thinking they are lovers, goes mad with grief. Brandimarte is overcome by Rodomonte, and his lover Fiordalisi (Fiordiligi) is brought to an enchanted castle. Bradamante enters the castle and frees the prisoners, including Orlando, whose wits are brought back by Astolfo, who arrives from the moon on the hippogriff (Pandolfi, op. cit., vol. 5, pp. 252–253).

25. Rak, "Il teatro meccanico," p. 51. The first theater in Naples, it was replaced by a church in 1620. Silvio Fiorillo was the Matamoros of the company.

26. The Don Gaiferos and Melisandra episode used by Cervantes's showman was clearly familiar to many. A few years earlier, in 1609, on the day of the Holy Sacrament, a "danca de cascabel" on this subject was performed in Madrid. It involved four French dancers and four Moorish ones, the Infanta Melisandra, an enchanted castle and a painted paper horse for Don Gaiferos. The rich costumes included plumes, velvets, brocades, silks and gold trimmings and the castle had an opening door or drawbridge that could be set up wherever required. Document in Varey, *Historia de los titeres*, pp. 251–252.

27. Majorana, "Italia Napoli," p. 185. Generally performed exclusively by groups of men, this dance carries some of the signs of an initiation ritual. Similar elements can be found in the English Mummers plays with St. George and the "Turkey" (Turkish) champion. In the opera dei pupi, Agramante, the Saracen leader, is king of "Africa," today's Tunisia. The Aghlabid invasion of Sicily in 827 was launched from the Tunisian city of Sousse.

28. This document, reproduced by Bertozzi, "Burattini e marionette a Parma," probably refers to the company whose bill is discussed in chapter 1.

29. In a document of 1853 in the Archivio Capitolino, Finardi claims from the manageress of the theater, A. Maria Fabri, payment for himself and four more "opranti" (puppeteers) (Lanza, "Un rifacitore popolare," p. 138). Lanza established Finardi's authorship on the basis of internal linguistic and stylistic evidence and handwriting. Finardi, born around 1819, became a dragoon in 1837, was expelled from his regiment in 1841 and became a minor civil servant. Probably director of the popular Teatro delle Muse, he may have acted with Tacconi's company. His manuscripts are in the Vittorio Emanuele collection of the National Library, Rome.

30. This supreme moment moved audiences to such an extent that they left the theater in silence (Lanza, op. cit.," p. 144).

31. Ten parts covered the history of Fiovo and Rizieri, eight Fioravante, two Ottaviano and Gisberto, three Boveto, and the remaining ten Buovo d'Antona.

32. Durlindana is acquired by Orlando when he kills Almonte, a "good" Saracen, who is baptized as he dies. The sword itself was reputedly that of the Trojan hero, Hector.

33. The term "in paggio" (as a page) is employed for unarmed figures.

34. Li Gotti, op. cit., pp. 17–19.

35. The Rovenza episode is in many repertoires, notably those of Ciro Perna (Naples), the Fratelli Napoli (Catania) and the Teatro del Ippogrifo (Palermo). The Saracen princess, Rovenza, wields a mighty hammer. Protected by enchanted armor, her only weak point is the chink behind the knees. The Fratelli Napoli transformed this into her sex. She falls in love with Rinaldo and he kills her by feigning death and then thrusting his sword up into her as she comes to find his corpse.

36. Toldo, "Nella baracca dei burattini," p. 63.

37. Text in Giancane, *Angelica, Orlando*, pp. 125–152.

38. Sordi, op. cit., p. 217.

39. A collection of these scripts in the Civica Scuola, Milan, acquired via the Zaffardi family, includes *Carlo Magno*, *Bovo d'Antono*, and *Guerrino il Meschino*.

40. Cremona in *Burattini e marionette in Italia*, 1980, p. 89.

41. The original romance of Guerin continues with his marriage to Artemisia, princess of Persepolis, further military campaigns and the eventual death of himself and his wife.

42. Gambarutti, op. cit., p. 44.

43. Listed in Pandolfini Barberi, *Burattini e burattinai Bolognesi*, pp. 93–94. Cuccoli left three boxes of papers, including the scenarios of a large number of pieces also common in the marionette theaters. They are in the Biblioteca Communale of Bologna. Pieces relating to the heroic repertoire include: *Guerrino il Meschino, Ginevra di Scozia* and *The Exile of Rinaldo di Montalbano*.

44. Guerrino had no shield. Milesi saw the shield as belonging to the marionette theater (Ebalginelli and Ghidoli, "Bigio, burattinaio bergamasco," pp. 42–43).

45. According to the 1872 census about 90 percent of the population was illiterate. This was reduced to 80 percent in 1901 (Giancane, op. cit., p. 29). Children often did not go to school because their labor was too important for family survival. Giancane mentions schools that could not function for want of teachers, or for fear of brigands, and indicates that in Basilicata 122 out of 126 schools boasted only the most primitive conditions — often no drinking water or latrines.

46. "I 'Rinaldi' o i cantastorie di Napoli," *La Critica* 1, 1936, p. 771.

47. Li Gotti, op. cit., p. 56.

48. Croce, *Pupi, carretti, contastorie*, p. 31.

49. Li Gotti, op. cit., p. 51.

50. Croce, op. cit., p. 30.

51. Quoted by Li Gotti, op. cit., p. 53, from Federico de Maria, "L'epopea francese nella tradizione popolare siciliana," in *La Giara*, no. 2, 1954, pp. 39–44.

52. Gambarutti, op. cit., p. 45.

53. An example of this is a sixteenth-century engraving of the death of Saint Margherita, reproduced by Garbero Zorzi, *Teatro e spettacolo*, p. 132, together with a contemporary drawing of the mechanisms for such effects.

54. Orlando, Orlando
Morto tu sei per volere di Dio.
Faccio un sorriso
sul tuo pallido viso
e l'anima tua la porteremo lassù
nel celeste paradiso.
Interview with Mimmo Cuticchio, Palermo, November 2004.

55. Audiences often threw things at Gano di Magonza in the opera dei pupi, and even attempted to destroy the puppet. In Piedmont Franco Gambarutti relates how, at the end of a season, his grandfather was often approached by people wishing to buy the "villain" so that they could burn him publicly. Some companies discovered an extra source of income making duplicate figures in papier mâché, which were sold to be burnt. Peppino Sarina used a rod puppet of Gano di Magonza in the final episode of the Orlando cycle. Dressed in a paper costume, this marotte was burned at the stake (and rapidly dunked in a bucket of water backstage). A surviving figure was found in a rubbish heap (Pietro Porta interview, October 12, 2007).

56. Croce, op. cit., p. 60. Orlando's birth in a cave parallels Christ's in a stable.

57. In the Grasso *Passion*, Judas's soul was taken by the devil in the same way.

58. Recordings of interviews with pupari made by MIMAP in the 1960s and 1970s indicated that they knew this episode only through Lo Dico (Croce, op. cit., p. 61). Emanuele Macri of Acireale (1967) omitted the Rinaldo plot, since it was not in the *Chanson de Roland*.

59. Croce, op. cit., pp. 86–88.

60. Tradition attributes to Gaetano Crimi the invention of at least four cycles in the Catanian repertoire: *La storia greca*, *Farismane e Siface*, *Tramoro di Medina*, *Guelfo di Negroponte*. Less certain is whether he invented the story of *Guido Santo* and *Erminio della Stella d'Oro* (see Napoli, *Il racconto e i colori*, pp. 180, 217, 264, 280, 286).

61. The originator was either Gaetano Crimi, Ciccio Rasura (a speaker for the theater of Gregorio Grasso), or Angelo Grasso, who may have staged it for the first time at the Teatro Machiavelli. Salvatore Patanè published these stories as novels in serial form as *Erminio della Stella d'Oro e Gemma della Fiamma — Guerre ed avventure mediovali [sic]* in 1896, and also produced a sequel, *Azaleone* (1899). (Napoli, op. cit., pp. 217–228, discusses the attribution of the story and its narrative sources and plot.)

62. Napoli, op. cit., p. 223.

63. Published by Giuseppe Leggio in Palermo between 1904 and 1906. The subject became an important part of the Catanian repertoire.

64. Napoli, op. cit., pp. 228–229.

65. In Bologna between 1849 and 1855 191 bandits were condemned to death. Some were shot, others decapitated (Cervellati, *Storia dei burattini e burattinai*, p. 82).

66. Scarcella, *Il brigantaggio in Sicilia*, p. 90. Turriciano's arrest was thanks to a member of the Mafia, who felt he was intruding on their territory. Both Mafia and brigands depended on local support, including corrupt officials.

67. The association with crime and drug-trafficking came much later, when the Mafia had lost its original raison d'être.

68. Di Maria, op. cit., p. 21. He argues that the attitudes varied from religious and reactionary conservatism in Acireale, which retained Bourbon sympathies, to a more revolutionary spirit in Agrigento.

69. Uccello, "Copioni di briganti," p. 6.

70. Croce, op. cit., p. 13.

71. Uccello, op. cit., pp. 6–7. Canino's *Testalonga* appears to be based on V. Linares's *Il masnadiere siciliano*. Canino had a variety of brigand pieces, some probably used by his father Alberto. These included *Musolino*, *Testalonga*, *Marziale Brigand and Murderer*, *Giuseppina the Brigand* (one of the rare female figures) and *Varsalona*. Paolo Varsalona had a brief and violent career in the province of Palermo in the 1890s.

72. Uccello, op. cit., p. 8.

73. Both versions are published in Uccello, op. cit. Uccello dates the later one to the 1890s. This shorter version suggests a declining interest in brigand plays by this date. *Pasquale Bruno* was also in the repertoire of Giovanni Puglisi.

74. Capellini, *Paci Paciana*, pp. 3–8. Supposedly two acquaintances had stayed the night and stolen his watch and there had been a fight when he went to retrieve it. He was "unjustly" imprisoned for violence. According to legend he wore an iron bullet-proof vest that rendered him invulnerable.

75. Ebalginelli and Ghidoli, op. cit., p. 33 (interview with Bigio Milesi).

76. He also reached the live theater as a sort of folk hero in a play by Luigi Forti, published in 1843 and often reprinted, which became a frequent reference for puppet showmen.

77. Magnin, *Histoire des marionnettes en Europe*, p. 84.

78. His concern for exactness meant that he visited Spinetta Marengo so as to reproduce accurately the places where the action happened. Supposedly he went to Castellazzo Bormida (Alessandria), where there was a relative of Mayno della Spinetta, who forbade performances of plays on the subject. Andrea established a friendship with him and was told a great deal about Mayno (Porta, *Gente di Sarina*, p. 13).

79. Gambarutti, op. cit., p. 42.

80. The Civica Scuola of Milan has a copy of this script, dated November 27, 1939, made by Ettore Forni, to whom Salici had lent it. Forni also worked with Zaffardi. Characters include Fagiolino as a jailer, Sandrone as a brigadier (ultimately involved in Musolino's accidental arrest), and Facanapa as a carabiniere. After Musolino's escape from prison there is a long extempore comic scene between Fagiolino and Sandrone.

81. The organization was headed by a chief, or "capintesa," and 12 "capintrini" representing the 12 districts of Naples. The rank and file were known as "minore" and divided into "giovanotti" and "picciotti." The society had a common purse into which revenue was paid; they set up a school and also helped members in difficulty, especially those in prison (Franco Penza, "L'Onorata società," in *L'Infinito*, Naples, October 4, 1985).

82. A small cavity in the chest held a little bag of "blood" that could be released at the appropriate moment. This trick was also popular in Sicily. The Canino mad (and naked) Orlando had a similar arrangement to allow him to urinate.

83. Vuoso, *Stella Cerere*.

Chapter 6

1. Text published in *I generici di Arlecchino* 2. Some of the other texts in the Lupi and Colla collections may be early nineteenth-century copies of earlier ones.

2. The name of Arlecchino has been crossed out to be replaced by Gianduja, an indication that the piece was still in the Lupi repertoire after 1865. Giacometta has been added to the list of characters, but has no obvious role. This illustrates the way in which adapted texts often allowed for non-scripted interpolations.

3. The Rame family is a case in point.

4. Toldo experienced this problem in 1908. Many of the scripts studied by him were not particularly old themselves, but were copies or reworkings of much earlier texts.

5. Around 1800 paper was still very expensive and some scripts are written on the back or on the spare pages of other ones.

6. This usually appeared on the third or the final page.

7. There are two short examples of this in a version of *The Poor Baker of Venice* as performed by Angelo Cuccoli (Moretti, *Attori e barache*, pp. 67–68).

8. Cervellati, *Storia dei burattini e burattinai*, pp. 188 ff., publishes an immense list of titles performed on the glove-puppet stage in Bologna.

9. Cervellati, op. cit., p. 302. This applied to serious dramas. Popular farces were repeated more frequently.

10. Catalogues of these publishers are hard to find today. A valuable research tool is CLIO — *Catalogo dei libri italiani dell' ottocento (1801–1900)* (Milan: Editrice Bibliografica, 1991).

11. National Library, Rome, Fondo Vittorio Emanuele, ms. 68. There are indications of performances in 1827, 1834 and 1841, when it was stamped by the censor, who struck out a number of lines and wrote "no" against them.

12. Melloni and Bo, "Il repertorio del teatro," pp. 21–22.

13. Ibid., p. 20.

14. Remo Melloni in *Il tesoro sepolto*, 1997, p. 97. Other such printers were Ducci, Salani, La Biblioteca ebdomadaria teatrale, Barbini, Cesati and Ancora.

15. Moretti, *Attori e barache*, publishes the text of Ongaro's play.

16. Ibid., p. 35. For traveling acting companies this was also a very popular piece. By means of doubling it could be performed by 5 actors (2 men and 3 women).

17. The script was in existence until 1997, when much of the Lupi material was dispersed (Moretti, op. cit., p. 62).

18. A script that had belonged to the Pallavicini family is in the library of the Scuola Civica Paolo Grassi (Milan). There are indications that it was copied in 1922, and there is an authorization for performance in March 1930.

19. Moretti, op. cit., p. 55.

20. Ibid., p. 78.

21. This script has more stage directions than usual. In the prison scene, there are specific indications for the interpretation: "pause," "weeps," "sobs," "agony," "determined," and a couple of indications of a bell tolling.

22. Luigi Goro (Dall'Ongaro's Alvise) appears, saying he has had a good night; Loredano enters and stabs him, saying he is the seducer of his wife. All is observed by a masked figure who comments on it (Dall'Ongaro introduces a mysterious masked figure, but not until later in the action). Pietro then arrives, singing a song, picks up the sheath of the dagger (which will incriminate him) and goes off to sell it.

23. A second scenario includes both Gioppino and Tartaglia, and was probably used at the time when Angelo Cuccoli's partner was Andrea Ludergnani, who performed with these characters. A third version includes Meneghino and Sganapino (as bakers) and therefore dates from after 1876, when Augusto Galli was with the company. Brighella plays the jailer and Doctor Balanzone (or Tonino) appears

as a member of the Council of Ten. For the main characters this version reverts to the names in the original play, suggesting that Angelo Cuccoli possessed or had access to a printed text of the play. His father may have based his production on a live performance by another puppeteer (Moretti, op. cit., pp. 63–68). Antonio Sarina also had two versions of *The Poor Baker*, one apparently based on a performance by a semi-literate puppeteer and the other showing familiarity with the printed text (Moretti, op. cit., pp. 69–70).

24. The theme of class oppression in *The Poor Baker* had a special appeal in strongly Communist Bologna, where, during the Fascist period, pieces with a social or revolutionary message were banned. These included *Il passatore*, *No-one's Children* (which gave rise to the 1921 film dealing with illegitimacy), and the very popular *Nun of Krakow*, the horrifying story of a girl who was put into a convent to avoid an unsuitable marriage, imprisoned, and eventually died in a madhouse in Krakow in 1871 (Cervellati, op. cit., p. 148).

25. Dotti, "*I promessi sposi*," pp. 96–111, compares this libretto with the Manzoni novel.

26. A script in the Scuola Civica collection, Milan, bearing a stamp for Ugo Ponti and a written indication of belonging to Antonio Ajmino, uses Gianduja to play Abbondio. On the cover is noted that this "grandioso spettacolo" is based both on Manzoni's novel and Petrella's opera. The Ponchielli opera omits Don Abbondio. A version staged by the Fiando Theater in 1872 casts Gerolamo as a fisherman, which suggests that it was based on the recently staged Ponchielli opera. In the Colla revival of 1927 Don Abbondio was still played by Gerolamo, but his role was reduced and it was recognized that his dialect was no longer a great attraction.

27. Dotti, op. cit., pp. 10–12, includes a long list taken from the Tommasi catalogue of 1891 and published in *CLIO* 12, 1991, pp. 10034–10035.

28. Ibid., p. 21.

29. Text reproduced by Bergonzini et al., *Burattini e burattinai*, pp. 217–131.

30. *Aida* was published as a popular novel, which inspired Vittorio Busnelli's drama, *Aida or the Pharaohs*, 1887. This was the basis for the script of the Ajmino company's marionette drama of the same year, which also has a happy end.

31. Bill reproduced in Pretini, *Facanapa e gli altri*, p. 96.

32. *Robert the Devil* was staged by many companies. Ariodante Monticelli's script is in the family collection. The company also possesses a magnificent cut cloth of the auditorium of the Paris opera house used in this production. Meyerbeer's *L'Africaine* (1865) provided another popular plot for the marionette repertoire.

33. Text published in *Il tesoro sepolto*, pp. 19–37.

34. The first translation of *Hamlet* was the verse one of Alessandro Verri (1815). The tragedies published by Carlo Rusconi in prose (1819–1827) made the works more generally accessible. Rusconi's edition of the complete plays appeared in 1838.

35. Text reproduced in Young, *Shakespeare Manipulated*, pp. 160–186. It also includes later annotations, such as a list of the music for a revival in 1881 (and an indication of a ballo at the end, "L'Arbre de Noël"). In the early twentieth century the Gambarutti *Amleto* was also directly derived from Shakespeare, but used Gerolamo to play the role of Orazio (Horatio).

36. Young, op. cit., reproduces as an appendix a copy of this made by Alfredo Cagnoli (1906), now in the collection of the Carlo Colla e Figli company.

37. Ibid., p. 71. Her dating of c.1830 may be premature. Canino started his theater around that date. Uccello suggests that the puppet productions might have been inspired by such actors as Gustavo Modena or Tommaso Salvini. Modena started his Shakespearian performances in the 1840s. Salvini was born in 1829. This scenario is reproduced by Uccello, *Due tragedie di Shakespeare.*

38. One element that was abandoned was the customary stamping on the stage floor with a wooden clog to accompany the battles.

39. Cervellati, op. cit., p. 286.

40. Young, op. cit., p. 94.

41. Ibid., p. 31, mentions references to performances on March 21, 1821, March 4, 1822, and April 27 and 28, 1824. Macchi and his wife had a theater between 1819 and 1824 at Santa Catarinetta at the Ponte de' Fabbri near the Porta Ticinese.

42. Uccello, op. cit., reproduces this script but suggests that it cannot be dated much before the 1860s.

43. Young, op. cit., p. 75, mentions a 1912 version from the Palermitan puparo Giovanni Pernice which includes a scene derived from the Romani libretto of Bellini's opera where Romeo goes to see "Copelio" (Capulet) as an ambassador. As is common in the opera dei pupi, the love plot is subordinate to the conflict between the two families.

Natale Meli's *Giulietta and Romeo; or The Capulets and the Montecchi (Montagues)* (c. 1930) was based more directly on Shakespeare. The ball may have included a ballet interlude. In the final scene each of the lovers is provided with a soliloquy. Before killing herself Giulietta bursts into a song about how their spirits will be together again in heaven.

44. The first scene is not in the Bellini opera, but in one by Riccardo Zamboni with a libretto by Arturo Rossi. This cartellone is analyzed by Janne Vibaek in *Arte popolare in Sicilia*, pp. 346–347.

45. Gregorovius, *Wanderjahre in Italien*, p. 87.

46. When the Gambarutti company presented the brigand play *Mayno della Spinetta*, the guns of the soldiers were loaded with gunpowder stuffed into the barrel with a little wad of paper. A short fuse was lit moments before the entrance of the soldiers and when they pointed their guns there was a small explosion and a jet of flame came out of the barrel (Gambarutti, op. cit., p. 58). In Sicily, apart from its use in brigand plays, the gun was regarded as less noble than the sword.

47. Sanguinetti, *Teatro Gerolamo*, p. 39.

48. Cremona, *Burattini e marionette in Italia*, p. 141.

49. Antonio Colla had already performed this in Voghera and Meda (Sanguinetti, op. cit., p. 59).

50. Many of the middle class in Catania believed firmly in the new Italy and were especially fond of patriotic pieces with Garibaldi and Vittorio Emanuele. They especially enjoyed scenes in Garibaldi pieces when guns were pointed at the Borbone troops. Occasional disturbances at shows were usually sparked by the largely student element in the audience.

51. Sanguinetti, op. cit., p. 40.

52. A favorite piece with Gualberto Niemen, who successfully differentiated between the voices of the ten characters.

53. Gorla, *Le marionette di casa Borromeo*, pp. 73–74. This was also performed on the Isola Bella in 1831.

54. Script in the Biblioteca Nazionale, Rome. A note indicates it as the property of Filippo Tacconi.

55. An essential piece of equipment for the puppeteer is a flame-producer. This is like a rather long pipe for smoking. The bowl is covered with a perforated lid and inside there is a small candle. Around the candle is pow-dered lycopodium. By blowing down the pipe the puppeteer disturbs the lycopodium, which briefly ignites, throwing out a dramatic flame, temporarily dazzling the spectator and allowing a piece of magic to occur.

56. Collodi was the pseudonym of the Florentine Carlo Lorenzini (1826–1890), novelist, playwright, critic, author of a satirical journal and translator of Perrault's fairy stories.

Chapter 7

1. Vezzani, "Il teatro dei burattini a Reggio," p. 225.

2. La Gorce, "Un théâtre parisien," p. 224 (from Catherine Massip, *La vie des musiciens à Paris au temps de Mazarin* [Paris: Picard, 1976], pp. 80–81). The complete group would have included musicians, singers and stage-carpenters. By 1676 opera with its spectacular effects had reached the fairground puppet theaters in England:

While Author Punch does strange machines prepare
For their new Opera in Bartol'mew Fair
(Rosenfeld, *Theatre of the London Fairs*, p. 5. Epilogue to Duffet's *Armenian Queen*.)

3. *Les Pygmées* (Paris: Christophe Balard, 1676).

4. It is generally assumed that the reference is to Cardinal Ottoboni's theater, but Speaight ("Puppet Theatre of Cardinal Ottoboni," p. 9) quotes from Du Bos's *Réflexions critiques*, part 1, section 42, and suggests that the reference could be to Cardinal Cantelmo of Naples.

5. Mangini, *I teatri di Venezia*, p. 47.

6. This is a reworking of Aurelio Aureli's *The Fortunes of Rodope and Damira* (1657) (Campanini, *Marionette barocche*, p. 173).

7. *Burattini e marionette in Italia*, 1980, p. 38. The music was by Giuseppe Maria Righi.

8. Taddeo Wiel, *I teatri musicali veneziani del settecento* (Venice: Visentini, 1897), lists the operas performed at the San Gerolamo (see also Mangini, op. cit., p. 178).

9. For an adaptation of Pier Giacomo Martello's *Lo starnuto d'Ercole*, with music by Johann Adolf Hasse, the puppet actors were listed as Tuttolegno (all wood), Tacito, Silenzio, Senzalingua (without tongue), Muti (mute), Susta and Ordigni (contrivance). Hasse (1699–1783) was Kapellmeister to the Saxon court in Dresden and wrote music for a performance of *Didone abbandonata* there in 1742. He also provided music for the San Gerolamo's *Eurimedonte and Timocleone; or The Disappointed Rivals.*

10. The scenery was by Tomaso Cassoni and the costumes by Natale Canziani. They also worked on the *Didone abbandonata* of 1747. In 1748 Tomaso Cassoni is indicated as the "inventor and director of the scenery" and may have been a professional theater person engaged by Labia.

11. Magnin, *Histoire des marionnettes en Europe*, p. 90. Peisse's original article appeared in *Le temps*, September 2, 1835.

12. The text with indications of the changes required by the censorship is published in Mazzoleni, *Cassandrino*, pp. 71–79. Marzattinocci, *Cassandrino al Teatro Fiano*, pp. 84–85, prints a prologue spoken by Teoli dressed in a grey vicuna suit like that sported by Rossini.

13. Pappataci in Angelo Anelli's original libretto.

14. The robing of Cassandro as a "Kaimakan" or Moorish dignitary was dealt with in a way more manageable by marionettes — he leaves the stage and reappears dressed up (possibly a second puppet).

15. The final grand scene with its banquet for Mustafa takes place incongruously in the great mosque, an excuse for a large-scale oriental setting.

16. Translation from the French — Firenze, 1855.

17. Flaubert, "Voyage en Italie et en Suisse," in *Oeuvres complètes*, vol. 2 (Paris: Editions du Seuil, 1964), p. 467. *L'elisir d'amore* is probably the opera of which he was thinking.

18. For performances in 1898–1899 Gerolamo played Dulcamara (the quack seller of love potions).

19. Gambarutti, *Una vita appesa ai fili*, p. 48.

20. The singers were Marcella Luci (soprano), Nello Zacchia (tenor) and Egré (baritone).

21. Also from the Gorno repertoire were *La serva padrona* and Paisiello's *Barbiere di Siviglia*. The 1914–1915 season included *L'elisir d'amore* and *Don Giovanni*.

22. The conductor of the Piccoli orchestra, Giovanni Giannetti, made a reduced version of the score.

23. Libretto by Gian Biastolfi.

24. "I Piccoli di Podrecca e la musica," in *XXI Festival Internazionale di Musica Contemporanea della biennale di Venezia*, p. 10, September 1958, Teatro La Fenice, Venice.

25. The "melodramma" has been described as a "patriotic cement" that caught the mood of the Risorgimento (Dotti, "*I promessi sposi,*" p. 6).

26. A script for *Norma* in the Rissone collection refers to a religious march in the first act executed by the military band (Dotti, op. cit., p. 48).

27. Ibid., p. 138.

28. Ibid., p. 44.

29. Only with the Romantic ballet in France was the idea of a single composer for a whole work taken for granted.

30. The Carlo Colla e Figli company possesses music that was used for *I promessi sposi* from 1879 onwards. This is the only extensive music for the nineteenth-century marionette theater to survive and has been examined in depth by Dotti. She points out (p. 142) that Gounod's opera of 1862 was not widely popular in either France or Italy. The *Queen of Sheba* march (published separately in the Ricordi edition of 1900) was in the repertoires of the popular bands.

31. The omission of a composer's name may have been a way of avoiding paying royalties (Dotti, op. cit., p. 166). For the company's 1927 revival to celebrate the centenary of the novel it used the Ponchielli treatment of the story.

32. Dotti, op. cit., pp. 154–155.

33. Cervellati, *Storia dei burattini e burattinai*, p. 301, note 17.

34. Ibid., p. 301.

35. Vezzani, op. cit., p. 227.

36. *Prometeo* was performed at Turin's Teatro San Rocco in 1819. The presence of Gianduja as Prometheus's follower implies the Sales and Bellone company and presumably a glove- or perhaps rod-puppet version. The manuscript is in the Colla archive (program note for *Prometeo*, Carlo Colla e Figli, 1982).

37. *Giornale Italiano*, July 9, 1806, quoted by Sanguinetti, *Teatro Gerolamo*, p. 16.

38. This title does not appear in the register of performances published in Marzattinocci, *Cassandrino al Teatro Fiano*. The register seems to have been prepared after the event, so the piece may have been omitted, or have appeared under a different title.

39. When teaching at the Marinsky, Cecchetti and Lepri as dancing masters had a puppet theater set up where they worked out the choreography of many ballets most intricately, showing each movement of soloist and ensemble. One dancer observed: "I still recall with amazement the scores of pirouettes of 2 puppets in a pas de deux to music of Rubenstein's Valse Caprice, the male dancer lifting his partner in perfect timing and grace" (McPharlin, *Puppetry, a Yearbook*, p. 44).

40. A "ballo" with a classical theme as an afterpiece was common to many companies. Gautier saw the Zane company perform *Medea's Revenge*, in which Medea slaughtered her children, "two pupazzi with springs."

41. *Gazzetta teatrale* 7, 1829 (Marzattinocci, op. cit., p. 94). The Ottoboni documents in the archives of the Vicariato di Roma list the "balli" performed between 1813 and 1826.

42. Marzattinocci, op. cit., p. 89. In 1838 the censors banned the comic ballet *The Egyptian Magic Cabinet; or The Arrival in Rome of Cassandrino, Performer of Conjuring, Physical Experiments and Sleight of Hand*.

43. In 1873 they presented a comic ballet of *Lohengrin*, only a month after its unsuccessful premiere at La Scala.

44. Gerolamo, not Arlecchino, was chosen because he spoke Piedmontese.

45. *The Era*, June 2, 1888. Presented as the Royal Italian Opera and Grand Ballet Marionette Company, the Collas appeared at Hengler's Circus.

46. Most of the figures were closer to 60 centimeters than 80 centimeters. Briefly the Lupis abandoned the long head-rod for strings, but soon reverted to it except for trick figures.

47. Jones, *Castellinaria*, p. 77.

48. Chiumeo and Scommegna, *Don Michele Immesi*, p. 42.

49. Pitrè published three pieces, used respectively for a march, a call to battle and a battle (*Usi e costumi*).

50. The scissors movement is also used quite frequently as a way of lending emphasis and giving variety to a speech, such as a harangue by the emperor.

51. Salvatore Gatto, an expert user of the swazzle, builds his entire performance out of physical and verbal rhythms, and meaning is conveyed almost exclusively through these rather than speech as such.

52. In 2005 Cuticchio repeated this formula with Manuel de Falla's *Master Peter's Puppet Show*, this time using a visible singer and live music. A painted onstage audience evoked a circus and Cuticchio as puppeteer and presenter operated the large figure of Don Quixote. Behind him was a pupi stage where the story of Melisendra and Gaiferos was performed almost in quotation. Earlier in the twentieth century both Carlo Colla e Figli and Vittorio Podrecca gave relatively classical interpretations of this short opera.

53. Cipolla and Moretti, *Commedianti figurati*, p. 31.

54. Sarzi, "I Sarzi, quattro generazioni di burattinai." Usually the puppeteer plunges the hand down into the puppet. A few, such as the Ferraris, preferred to place the figures upright with the heads held between pegs and to push their hands up into them.

55. Cervellati, op. cit., p. 261. Rizzoli performed in the open air and his stage, together with some hundreds of seats, could be stored in a wooden kiosk. Many puppeteers achieved crowd scenes by combining rod puppets with glove-puppets and mounting the figures on stands.

56. Street fantoccini in England in the first half of the nineteenth century used a booth that resembled a glove-puppet stage.

57. Cipolla and Moretti, op. cit., p. 35. A similar screen of wires existed in eighteenth-century England and in nineteenth-century Belgium and survives today in Portugal with the Bonecos of Saint Aleixo.

58. Vuoso, *Stella Cerere*.

59. Gambarutti, op. cit., p. 45. The foot soldiers came in pairs, attached together by a rod concealed in their costumes. Referred to as a "doppietto," this was a pragmatic way for a small company to maximize the number of figures on the stage and was used in the pupi theaters in Rome in the nineteenth century.

60. This has been done by the Lupis in *Aida* and by Carlo Colla e Figli in *Il trovatore.*

61. This type of staging is also found in Antwerp, where theaters were usually in cellars with similar spatial limitations.

62. Adamo, *L'opra dei pupi*, p. 36.

63. *Architectura*, 1545, part 2, ch. 3 (Nagler, 1952, pp. 79–80).

64. Alberto Jona in Porta, *Famiglia Lupi, Aida*, p. 7.

65. Maffei, *Osservazioni litterarie del 1738*, p. 5. The stage, with an opening of about 30 palms or 6 meters, might have been used for chamber opera performance, but hardly for the grandiose spectacles that Juvarra conceived. However, the latter's designs for the public Capranica Theater indicate a proscenium opening of only 40 palms. Two sets of plans exist in the National Library, Turin (reproduced in Viale Ferrero, *Filippo Juvarra*, pp. 298–303).

66. Viale Ferrero, op. cit., p. 107, quotes Chappe's letter from A. De Montaiglon, *Correspondance des directeurs de l'Académie de France à Rome avec les surintendants des batiments*, vol. 3 (Paris, 1889), and uses this to argue that the "popazzi" were not puppets.

67. Ademollo, I *teatri di Roma*, pp. 127–128.

68. Cervellati, op. cit., p. 20.

69. An example is recorded at the Teatro Regio of Turin in 1689.

70. Viale Ferrero, *Scene per un teatrini*, pp. 21–23. Designs reproduced as plates 6 and 7. Viale Ferrero suggests that this might have been used for the "ballo" of *Fedra* (first staged at Teatro Regio in 1842), which included a scene of Neptune's grotto. The *Messagiere Torinese* in 1842 preferred the San Martiniano production to that of the Teatro Regio.

71. Jones, *Castellinaria*, p. 262.

72. Poieri, *I muchetti, marionettisti*, p. 102. Silhouettes reproduced on p. 103 and p. 105. This is the technique of the mechanical Teatrum Mundi, very popular in Germany.

73. In 1811 the Turin painter Luigi Vacca painted the death of Hippolytus for the sipario of the Fiando Theater in Milan (Sanguinetti, op. cit., p. 28).

74. With the disappearance of serial presentation, the perdomani scene has disappeared. Often there is a short comic prelude with Nofriu and Virticchiu, when the show is announced and the trick act of smoking a pipe or cigarette is executed.

75. A few separate items were used to satisfy particular requirements: fountains (whose waters cause forgetfulness or falling in love), tombs, thrones, beds or the mulberry tree under which Gano plans the betrayal at Roncisvalle and which rains blood on the plotters.

76. This was less common for the opera dei pupi. Ruggiero Dell'Aquila was unusual when he painted specific and recognizable scenes for the Teatro Aurora in the 1920s.

77. Filippo Filippi, *La perseveranza*, October 25, 1882 (reproduced by Sanguinetti, op. cit., pp. 56–57).

78. Speaight, *History of the English Puppet Theatre*, p. 133.

79. D.L. in *Museo civico d'arte industriale e galleria Davia Bargellini*, pp. 174–175. The proscenium arch has been made up of diverse elements, but D.L. points to the arms of the Albicini family, who had a villa in Forli where Antonio Bibiena designed a theater in 1763 (carried out after his death by Cosimo Morelli). The marionettes are probably Venetian, but appear to come from more than one collection.

80. In addition there are some wings without backcloths and a cut cloth of a gallery of mirrors and portraits with two pairs of wings. The Casa Grimani collection has a back scene of a bourgeois salon with a practicable door-

way in the center, flanked by two small portraits and suitable for almost any Goldoni comedy. According to old photographs, the theater in the Bethnal Green Museum had two backcloths (now lost) when acquired in 1923: an interior similar to that of the Casa Grimani, and a view of St. Mark's Piazza, Venice. It still has three sets of reversible wings, a rococo salon on one side and part of the view of Venice on the other. Another eighteenth-century domestic stage from the Carminati Palace, sold at the Hotel Druot in 1933, also boasted a view of St. Mark's Piazza. Amateur performances of comedies in many domestic theaters would have required little more than an indoor and an outdoor setting.

81. A set of designs in the Victoria and Albert Museum, London, has annotations in Juvarra's own hand, and often a sketch indicating the arrangement of the scenery.

82. The Biblioteca Marucelliana, Florence, has a copy of these. There are also some designs by Juvarra for a *Titus Manlius*, a *Heracles* and a *Royal Pastorale*. These include figures which, if drawn to scale, would be not much more than a meter high. There is a tendency to shrink figures in theatrical engravings, so as to make the scenery more imposing, but in this case, some of Juvarra's own original designs show equally diminutive figures, which are more likely to correspond to the scale envisaged by him.

83. Cecchini, "Provenienza," pp. 11–14.

84. Dario Cecchi, "Arte nobile e bella di una civiltà passata," in *Il teatrino Rissone*.

85. Alessandro Sanquirico (1777–1849), the official scene painter for La Scala, Milan, between 1827 and 1832, trained with Paolo Landriani at the beginning of the nineteenth century. He was also much influenced by Jacques de Loutherbourg in his use of local color and in the creation of an atmosphere by the careful use of lighting effects, both painted and real (Gorla, *Le marionette di casa Borromeo*, pp. 23–24).

86. When the Fiano was remodeled in 1813, the painter Vincenzo Pitorri provided a new front curtain, three cloths representing a wood, a room and a temple, a grid with nine "teli" (probably backdrops), 56 wings and various practicable pieces for the temple. The wings probably accompanied the "teli" to make up nine complete scenes. There is no clear indication whether this scenery was for live performances or marionette ones.

87. Viale Ferrero, *Scene per un teatrino*, pp. 24–25.

88. Gorla, op. cit., diagram, p. 98.

89. Listed by Gorla, op. cit., pp. 32–34. Fontana worked in conjunction with a Luigi Terzaghi, who made, dressed and maintained the marionettes.

90. I *teatri*, December 17, 1828, quoted by Sanguinetti, op. cit., p. 38.

91. Viale Ferrero, "Lo sfarzo," p. 29.

92. These scenes are still in the Colla collection. Lualdi may also have been one of the painters involved.

93. The Lombardy folk costumes were specially commissioned from Cantù.

94. Gambarutti, op. cit., p. 45.

95. Capellini, *Baracca e burattini*, pp. 66, 68. Nespoli also adapted a cartwheel to make a revolving stage to change scenery.

96. Niemen, *Autobiografia di un burattinaio*, p. 20.

97. Giovanni di Cristina began as a puppeteer but then dedicated himself to painting. The Caninos also painted much of their own scenery.

98. Ironically, Angoletta's few attempts as a designer for actors' theater were never very successful.

99. In the later years, for pragmatic reasons, Podrecca had to recycle material from previous productions. *Biancaneve* (Snow White, 1941) had scenery and costumes by Angoletta, Grassi and Caramba, and Satie's *Genoveffa di*

Brabante (1958) had designs and figures by Angoletta, Pompei and Saini.

100. Angoletta also designed several of the variety numbers, including "La piccola follia" (a super revue in three minutes), "The Jazz Orchestra," and "Mississippi."

Chapter 8

1. Cesare Maletti (1926–1992) was also anxious to preserve as much as possible of the tradition out of which he had emerged, and therefore collected old puppets and recorded as much as possible (Bergonzini et al., *Burattini e burattinai*).

2. Vergani and Signorelli, *Podrecca*, p. 62.

3. In 1923, when Podrecca had ceased to use it, the Fantocci Santoro took over the Odescalchi Theater. Santoro's daughter later worked for the Podrecca company. She married Pirro Braga, who was also with them, and their daughter Fausta continued the association with the revived Piccoli company of the Teatro Stabile Friuli-Venezia Giulia.

4. The *Balli plastici* received 11 successful performances by the Teatro dei Piccoli from April 14, 1918. Depero received financial help from his friend Clavel, with whom he was staying in Capri when he worked on this project. At the time, Picasso was also there and Depero had the opportunity to work with him on some of the costumes for *Parade* for the Ballets Russes.

5. This was divided into 5 "mimico musical" actions:

I pagliacci (the clowns) — in a luminous floral village a line of white "pinocchietti" marches rhythmically across, accompanied by a Russian folk tune on the piano. After they have gone a ballerina appears, and during her dance two marionettes in a red and yellow costume watch a chicken lay an egg.

The man with whiskers — a whiskered man walks down a golden street, then becomes a whole series of clones of different sizes. A blue ballerina appears while a black cat devours a white mouse. Finally a shower of cigarettes falls on a trio of dancing drunken whiskered men.

The savages — a row of red savages and a row of black ones, armed with shields, confront each other in a danced battle. Two savages in particular fight for possession of the heart of a giant female savage. The belly of the giantess opens suddenly to reveal a little theater inside in which a little silver savage is performing with the red heart in his hand. When he leaves his mother's belly the little savage is devoured by an enormous green serpent. (The brief theatrical actions are divided by moments of total darkness, during which disquieting green eyes glitter.)

The blue bear — a blue bear and a monkey dance, provoking hilarity with their awkward and grotesque movements.

Shadows, an abstract action based on lights, like Depero's *Colori*, with music by Bartók, was not used.

6. In 1915 Pirro Gozzi replaced Ugo Campogalliani, offering glove-puppet shows in the Odescalchi Theater. After 1922, when the Piccoli departed on tour, he remained in Rome.

7. Manipulation was by Gorno, Carlo and Anita Geirola, Morchio, Giovanni Pavero, Nicolò Corso and Ferrari (Vergani and Signorelli, op. cit., p. 72).

8. According to Leonardo Bragaglia, *Shakespeare in Italia* (Rome: Trevi, 1973), this was the first appearance of that play on the Italian stage (Young, *Shakespeare Manipulated*, p. 51).

9. Mussolini meant to come to the first performance, but could not. However a group of boys in black shirts arrived and climbed onto the stage, where they sang the popular Fascist song "Giovinezza" (Vergani and Signorelli, op. cit., p. 76).

10. Ibid., p. 79.

11. McPharlin, *The Puppet Theatre in America*, p. 282.

12. Further filmed records of the Piccoli are a series of four short films made in 1952 by Thetis films. Three are available from the Cineteca Nazionale in Rome. Both Sergei Obraztsov in his *Unusual Concert* and the Czech marionettist and creator of Spejbl and Hurvinek, Josef Skupa, as Edi Majaron has pointed out, found inspiration in the variety acts of the Teatro dei Piccoli.

13. The company also enriched its repertoire with De Falla's *Retablo di Maese Pedro* and *Fausto*, a new play by the Argentinian Estanislao del Campo.

14. Il Nucleo productions were *Master Peter's Puppet Show*, a double bill, *Visioni sinfoniche*, consisting of Debussy's *Toybox* and Ravel's *Mother Goose Suite*, and Prokofiev's *Peter and the Wolf*. The last production was Erik Satie's seven-minute piece, *Geneviève de Brabant*, presented at the Venice festival of 1958. More recently this has been staged both by Eugenio Monti-Colla and by Otello Sarzi.

15. In Poland in 1928 Paderewski, then president, came onstage and asked the puppet for his autograph.

16. For the Opera dei Burattini she also modeled heads in papier-mâché, but these had the same free contours as the earlier soft sculpture ones.

17. A number of the productions were also adapted successfully for television.

18. The voices for the shows were generally provided by actors concealed in a pit in front of the stage and supplied with mirrors to follow the action.

19. Obraztsov's visit to Bologna in 1961 was of seminal importance.

20. Pretini, *Facanapa e gli altri*, p. 341. Over time his collaborators included Edipo Cagnoli and Enzo Picchi and members of the Rame, Santoro, Burzio and Monticelli families. Sylvio Vanelli worked with him for a time, then joined Podrecca's Piccoli in 1930. Vanelli later became technical director of the Piccoli and when Podrecca died he set up his own company, I Piccoli di Vanelli, with 1,200 marionettes. When the Piccoli was revived he rejoined them.

21. Another Ciuffetino piece was called *Ciuffetino's Polenta*.

22. In 1930 he had a five-month tour of Hungary and Rumania and in 1932 visited Argentina, Brazil, Uruguay and Chile.

23. Colla and Bonora, *Il popolo di legno*, p. 30.

24. Ibid., p. 32.

25. A notable production was the 1981 staging of Stravinsky's *Soldier's Tale*, directed by Ugo Gregoretti, with marionettes, scenery and costumes by Luigi Veronesi, executed in a rather futurist style.

26. In *Pinocchio* actors were used for Gepetto, Ciliegia, Mangiafuoco and the fairy.

27. The recent discovery of foam for puppet construction made possible expressive flexible faces that particularly suited television.

28. Trained in the visual arts, the Mantegazzas created a cooperative in 1962 to explore different puppet techniques and forms. They worked in cabaret and fringe theater and also performed and gave workshops in schools. In 1975, under the name Teatro del Buratto, they established a small permanent base at the Teatro Verdi in Milan. Productions included Stravinsky's *Soldier's Tale*, which combined a human actor (the soldier) with puppets of similar size for all the other figures. Between 1991 and 1999 they were joined by Natale Panaro.

29. Sarzi, "I Sarzi, quattro generazioni di burattinai."

30. Gindro also composed the music. The puppets and scenery were by Francesca Moretti.

31. As an actor Moretti had been involved with the Teatro delle Dieci in the late 1960s. In 1983 he left the Teatro dell'Angolo to form a new theater company, the Teatro del Mediterraneo. With the Istituto dei Beni Marinonettistichi e il Teatro Popolare, Moretti, and later Alfonso Cipolla, built up a significant collection of puppets and established a major center of documentation on puppet theater. In 1999 Moretti introduced courses on the history of puppet theater at the University of Turin, and since 2003 these have been continued by Alfonso Cipolla.

32. Texts published in Fortunato Pasqualino, *Teatro con i pupi siciliani*, 1980.

33. Instead of live speech they had a prerecorded soundtrack. When they traveled to America, they used American actors for the voices, unlike the Manteo company, which addressed itself to the Italian immigrant population of New York but had less appeal for second-generation Italian Americans not so familiar with the language and culture of Sicily.

34. Photograph in Fortunato Pasqualino, op. cit., p. 172.

35. Amongst the last performers were also Renato Barbieri in the province of Naples, the Fratelli Ferraiolo of Salerno and Carlo Piantadosi in Rome.

36. Earlier Zampello had alternated with his partner Giuseppe Pino as the "guarattellaro" and the "artista di piattino" (Leone, *La guarattella*, p. 18).

37. "Schools" and courses have become an aspect of the work of many practitioners: Eugenio Monti-Colla, Stefano Giunchi, Mimmo Cuticchio, to name a few.

38. Is Mascareddas also does more experimental work. It runs an annual festival and extensive touring has given the company a more international profile. In 1999 it established the Yorick Library as an international center of documentation on puppet theater.

39. The company originated in 1945 when Ennio and Maria Accettella started their home theater to entertain their children and neighbors. Between 1948–1949 and 1962 they played regularly in a workman's club under the title of the Piccole Maschere. As they became more professional they moved into a church hall as the Marionette di Maria Accettella. In the 1980s the company found its own home, the small Mongiovino theater on the outskirts of Rome. This freed them to explore different techniques and in 1988 they received official recognition as a center for promotion, production and research.

40. The Accettella company presented three different versions of the story, in the 1940s, the 1950s and in 1979.

41. His basic figures are Fagiolino, Sandrone, Brighella and Dottore Balanzone. One of his notable productions was *The Abduction of Prince Carlo* based on an early nineteenth-century script.

42. Their sources have included the brothers Grimm and J.R. Tolkien

43. *Pinocchio* has remained a consistently popular theme for puppet shows. The Uovo (Egg) company turned Pinocchio into a glove-puppet in *Facciamo che Pinocchio era un burattino* (1979) and instead of becoming a child he rejoined the puppets of Mangiafuoco's theater. In 1981 Otello Sarzi's lively version transformed the story by removing its moralizing and edifying aspects. In the same year Gioco Vita presented a version using cardboard silhouettes. Emanuele Luzzati presented a large-scale and visually splendid open-air installation with the Teatro delle Tosse for the centenary celebration at Pescia, calling it *Pinocchio Bazaar in Heaven and on Earth*.

44. For *Cyrano* (2001), based on Edmond Rostand's *Cyrano de Bergerac*, they played on the idea of themselves as a strolling company of actors that included a singer and the story was presented with some of the very old marionettes of their collection.

45. Mimmo Cuticchio, "Lettere a voce, lettere scritte, racconti, viaggi," in Venturini, *Dal cunto all'opera dei pupi*, p. 42.

46. Croce, *Pupi, carretti, contastorie*, p. 38.

47. Ibid., p. 42. Croce also notes that Cuticchio often uses words with their least common meaning, as a way of heightening the speech and giving a slight sense of distance.

48. Ibid., p. 42.

49. Subsequent productions have included *The Lady of the Camelias* (1986), *The Iliad* (1988), *A Midsummer Night's Dream* (1991), Kafka's *Metamorphosis* (1992), and *The Odyssey* (2002).

50. In 1996 *Visita guidata* was performed in front of the old factories of the Zisa in Palermo. Sound, lighting, projections and commentary were used to evoke on a massive scale the hardship of the period and the background of homelessness, prostitution and black-market activity.

51. See Brunello and Molnár, *Macbeth all'improvviso*.

52. *I colori* can be compared with the moving colored forms in Giacomo Balla's designs for Stravinsky's *Fireworks*. *Fireworks* required some 49 different lighting cues — no problem with a modern computerized board, but an enormous challenge in 1917.

53. A reviewer commented on his entirely visual approach, uninterrupted by any narrative or logical development and depending on a rhythmic line established at the outset (*Il corriere d'Italia*, reproduced in *Fortunato Depero nelle opere e nella vita*, 1940, p. 217). Depero also explored new materials for puppet construction, such as rubber, fabric and sheet metal.

54. Kirby, *Futurist Performance*, pp. 58–59.

55. Like Cinelli with his extra eyes, Hugo and Ines often attach a small ball to a knee to turn it into a face or employ other minor modifications to turn the various body parts into recognizable human entities.

56. "Animazione" does not meet with general favor. Since the 1960s it has also been used in the context of groups or individuals using theater for social ends, generally in the context of schools, youth groups or among the socially disempowered.

57. Jurkowski, *Métamorphoses*, p. 188.

58. Ibid., p. 193.

59. Renato Palazzi in *Teatro delle Briciole*, p. 14.

60. *Teatro delle Briciole*, p. 89.

61. Allegri, "La materia e il suo doppio," in *Teatro delle Briciole*, p. 169.

62. Ibid., p. 166.

63. Jurkowski, op. cit., p. 191.

64. Where possible puppets and objects are made in a material appropriate to the show — wood for *Pinocchio*, metal for the *Iliad*.

65. Costantini, *Vita*, p. 56. In the 1950s Sandro Costantini (p. 26) mentions having his glove-puppet stage lit by four electric light bulbs, but no spotlights.

66. Incisa diary, June 18, 1786. This was presented in the private theater of the Casa Malabaila.

67. Incisa diary, August 25, 1787. Incisa included the bills for many of these performances, but virtually all have now been removed and probably stolen. In September 1796 a showman from Parma, Visioli, brought along his "teatrino di figure cinesi con ombre ed altre cose simile" and the program was padded out with tricks of balancing and skill.

68. Slides and cutouts also allowed for "negative" images that were light, not dark.

69. Montecchi, "Scenic Area," p. 98.

70. Ibid., p. 101.

71. A central element of *Macbeth* was Verdi's music, but the text was mainly Shakespeare's.

Chapter 9

1. City of Ferrara, Historical Archive, Napoleonic census 1812, vol. 3, f. 397.

2. Historical Archive of the Curia of the Diocese of Mantua, Registri Civili, vol. 1, from January 1816 to May 16, 1818.

3. The dating provided by Caronte is confirmed by various notices that appeared in the daily press of the period.

4. Script kept in the Museo della Marionetta, Turin.

5. Information from Caronte, but not found directly in the newspapers of the period.

6. *La gazzetta piemontese*, October 25, 1831.

7. Ibid., January 26, 1832.

8. Ibid., March 17, 1832. The sound referred to was produced by a finger rubbed around the moistened rim of a glass. Mozart wrote music for this "instrument."

9. *Il messaggiere torinese*, March 28, 1840.

10. Ibid., September 27, 1845.

11. A long series of shows inspired by the events of the Risorgimento would long remain in the repertoire of the company. *The Battle of San Martino, The Battle of Montebello, The Battle of Solferino, The Bombardment and Taking of Gaeta, The Piedmontese in the Crimea and the Taking of Malakoff* all appeared on their stage as mimed and danced performances. The exploits of Garibaldi were also reproduced in countless pieces such as *The Landing of the Garibaldians in Sicily and the Bombardment of Palermo*. The San Martiniano repertoire also included a large number of pieces relating to the Napoleonic epic: *The Memorable Days of Waterloo, The Disastrous Crossing of the Beresina* (which saw the extermination of an entire garrison, mostly made up of Piedmontese soldiers), *The Battle of Austerlitz, Napoleon on the Isle of Elba, The Death of Napoleon on St. Helena and the Arrival of His Ashes in Paris*. To these could be added *Caesar in Egypt*, based on Gaetano Gioja's ballet staged at La Scala and frequently performed because of the open references to Bonaparte.

12. Also known as *The Disaster of Casamicciola*, first staged in September 1883. Every disaster was potential material for a show: *The Breach of the Po, or The Flooding of Ferrara in 1872* (1873), *The Disaster of Nice* (1882), and *The Flooding of Verona* (1883) are just a few of the shows based on natural disasters — and to these could be added *The Wreck of the Medusa, Herculaneum Destroyed by Vesuvius* and *The Last Days of Pompei*.

13. Toselli anticipated the Albertine statute (law), which allowed some freedom to the press and led to the spread of satirical papers in which the major illustrators of the period came together to take Gianduja out of the puppet theater and turn him into one of the great icons of the Risorgimento.

14. Historical Archives of the city of Turin, deaths registered for 1856, death certificate no. 1794.

15. It is easy to suppose that the death of Luigi Lupi silenced Arlecchino, the central figure of the company, just as it is easy to suppose that the passing of the founder of the company, now firmly established, but still a family business, might have persuaded them to give up some of their activities. The San Martiniano got over the crisis by taking in Toselli's successes, but it detached itself from the

Nuovo Teatro Lupi, which remained open for the following season, presenting every type of show, including a variety of animals in combat with a Spanish bull (*La gazzetta piemontese*, April 11, 1857).

16. *Le memorie di una marionetta* (Turin: Lattes, 1902).

17. In 1842 Enrico married Eugenia Giacomelli. Their sons were Luigi Giovanni Antonio, known as Luigi I, born November 11, 1843, and Antonio Francesco Luigi, known as Luigi II, born January 29, 1846 (Historical Archives of the Curia Metropolitana, Turin).

18. Apparently Giovan Battista Sales was not born and did not die in Turin. Despite considerable research, he could not be found in any register or document kept in the archives of the city. The same is true of his associate Gioacchino Bellone, who according to tradition came from Racconigi, although no documents have been found as yet.

19. In 1887, Enrico's son Luigi II had another visit to South America, spending six months in Buenos Aires.

20. First performed at Kizalfys Theater. This was based on Jacques Offenbach's opera *Le voyage dans la lune*, staged with great success in Paris in 1875.

21. Registry office of the Comune of Turin, death certificate no. 198.

22. "Un piccolo teatro celebre," dated 1896 and published by De Amicis in *Ricordi di infanzia e di scuola* (Milan: Fratelli Treves, 1903).

23. *La patria*, Bologna, May 24, 1885.

24. This article unfortunately is not clearly identified. The script, now in a private collection and entitled "Fantocci," carries the date of February 14, 1885. On page 2 of the cover is glued a figure of a skeleton holding the words Holden and Ida Nugaj. This is a very mixed script, grouping together a heap of notes describing the various numbers prepared for the occasion, some of which use a modified version of scenes from the repertoire. Amongst the most significant numbers are the ballet of the clown, the "concerto dei mori" or minstrel show, described as a comic scene with singing and performed by black-faced puppets, and *Beauty and the Beast*.

25. This was not totally exceptional. There were other titles that were triumphantly received in the middle of the Great War. These included *Trieste, Turin, Trentin*, which remained on the bills for 182 performances in 1916–1917, and *A Misfortune for the Kaiser* (*N'assident al Kaiser*), which had 132 performances in 1918–1919. The information comes from the registers of the company that record all its activity between 1879 and 1935. This document of inestimable value for reconstructing the history of the company has inexplicably gone missing in the last few years. Fortunately some notes were copied in various theses for the Faculty of Letters and Philosophy of the University of Turin.

26. The song, which looks back to the period of the wars of the Risorgimento, describes the Piedmontese as "bogianen," or those who do not budge. This refers to their trustworthiness, which ensures that they will not budge when faced with danger.

27. It also included ballets and the fox-trot, with a Josephine Baker in ostrich plumes letting herself go in her "plantation dances," and then a Mickey Mouse jumping out of a grand piano on which a maestro with wild hair, after sitting down and pulling out the tails of his coat, accompanied two black singers.

28. Evidently to avoid the crisis they even staged some shows that showed obsequiousness towards the regime. In 1940 they produced *Balilla! A Comic Heroic Fantasy Action in a Prologue and Three Parts Dedicated to the Children of Italy Who "Are All Balilla,"* and then the ballet *A Shot at the Moon* in which the Lupis invited all the little Italian

girls and the Balillas of Turin to take part in a show in which all the little Italian heroes would parade, from the Balilla of Genoa to the Balilla of the Fascist era (*La stampa*, November 28, 1944). It is worth noting that as soon as the liberation came the Lupis rapidly adapted to the new political climate, staging a piece called *Gianduja Sergeant of the Partisans* (letter from Giorgio Agosti of Formation and Liberty, February 24, 1946). The booklet containing the official decree "for the reconstruction of the Gianduja Theater" was printed in Turin by V. Bona in 1941.

29. The 1941 booklet printed by Bona includes a piece signed by the head of the Monuments Service, Mesturino: "Continuing the noblest ancient traditions, a more thriving life will be renewed corresponding to modern social needs of an artistic nature following the directives of the Fascist regime and bringing decorum into a zone of the city in which some spaces currently used for shows are in premises that are too small, without respect or decorum and failing to correspond to the rules of hygiene and public safety."

30. The San Teresa theater and the Museo della Marionetta have always been run directly or indirectly by the Erba-Mesturino family, theatrical impresarios in Turin.

Chapter 10

1. The first part of a performance lasted between three-quarters of an hour and an hour, the second about half an hour and the third between ten minutes and a quarter of an hour. When the curtain opened for the third act one of the finest puppets announced the following day's show. He reached the center of the drop scene with a single stride, gave a ritual bow and greeted the audience with a fixed introductory formula such as "Esteemed and respectable audience, I have the honor to invite you to tomorrow's performance." Then followed a brief résumé of the following episode, finishing with a regular formula ("Do us the honor …"). Sometimes, on special occasions, the "invito" was given by three knights who all came onto the stage at the same time with a single stride, one in the center and one at each side, bowed and greeted the audience in perfect synchronization and gave the usual résumé, each one speaking immediately after the previous one.

2. In this essay after a re-reading of the work of the late Antonio Uccello, I use the word "opira" with reference to the Catanian tradition. Bernadette Majorana, *Pupi e attori*, notes "In my opinion, the historian's practice since Pitrè habitually, but incorrectly, extends the term 'opra' to Catania" (p. 2, note 3). Majorana's study with its wealth of documentary sources offers the most complete diachronic study of the Catanian opera dei pupi and can be placed alongside the work of Antonio Pasqualino.

3. Pitrè, *Usi e costumi*, p. 153.

4. The difficulty of analyzing a scenic text has sometimes been exaggerated on the grounds that a performance is both more ephemeral than a written text and more elusive. De Marinis, "Lo spettacolo come testo," p. 73, recognizes that the use of recording techniques and transcriptions can make the scenic text partially present. Vibaek, "Dal testo allo spettatore," p. 326, points out that the reading of a literary text by different individuals, or even by the same individual at different times, has different semiotic values.

5. See especially their writings of 1976, 1977 and 1984.

6. See Eco, *Trattato di semiotica generale*, pp. 188–190.

7. Pasqualino, "Codici gestuali nel teatro dei pupi," p. 84.

8. De Marinis, *Semiotica del teatro*, p. 117 — my italics.

9. Pasqualino, op. cit., p. 85.

10. A point strongly made in Pasqualino, "Tradizione e innovazione."

11. As far as the Napoli of Catania are concerned, a part of this journey towards self-awareness is due to my own studies of the opera dei pupi, which, up to my doctoral thesis in 1991, had followed unreservedly the methodological orientation of Antonio Pasqualino.

12. Nino (Antonino) Amico (born March 3, 1932) was a doctor. The son of Pasqualino Amico and Giuseppina Trombetta, he regularly attended the Fratelli Napoli theater where his parents worked as parraturi and learned from his father to work ("maniari") and speak ("parrari") for the pupi.

13. Amico, "Shakespeare coi pupi," p. 98. This aim was also indicated by Amico in the introduction to some of the scripts.

14. This episode from Lodico's *Storia dei paladini* derives from Ludovico Dolce's poem in ottava rima, *Le prime imprese di Orlando* (The First Deeds of Orlando). Namo di Baviera's speech, as set down by Raffaele Trombetta, is published in Amico, "*Teatrar narrando*" pp. 153–157.

15. Also from Lodico and based on chapter 1 of Mateo Maria Boiardo's *Orlando innamorato*. In this case the parratrici often quote the poem almost verbatim.

16. From the *Story of Orlando* developed by the Catanian pupari from episodes of Ludovico Ariosto's *Orlando furioso*.

17. Episode from the *Story of Orlando* from Lodico, based on canto 34 of Ariosto's *Orlando furioso*.

18. In the jargon of the Catanian opira, "saracinu rossu" ("saraceno grosso") is a strong, arrogant and proud Saracen warrior robustly built and usually having a bushy moustache and full armor. Saracini rossi include Mambrino, Gradasso and Agricane.

19. This was a matter of choice between the two emblems traditionally used for Guerrino, the eagle or the dragon.

20. They began to speak of the return to the jointed knee. In fact, according to the descendants of the Crimi it seems that originally all the Catanian pupi had jointed knees. Then, as they got bigger and heavier, the leg was made in one piece to allow it to set its full weight on the stage floor. The introduction of the unjointed leg most probably occurred in the last years of the nineteenth century. The hypothesis that the Catanian marionettes originally had jointed legs is supported by the fact that today we can still find pupi in the Catanian style with flexible knees in areas further from the center (for example the Siracusan pupi of the Puzzo brothers and those of Don Liscianniru Librizzi of Paternò, one of which is now in the Napoli material). As further confirmation of this hypothesis, the angels, devils and Peppininu, all smaller and lighter pupi, have retained the jointed leg.

21. There are two types of recognition scenes — those with an intermediary and those without. In the first and more general case a character stands between two others, perhaps separates a duel, and reveals that they are related, and they then embrace one another. The best example of this type of recognition scene is the revelation by the spirit of the magician Atlante to Ruggiero and Marfisa that they are brother and sister. In other cases it emerges from a dialogue between the protagonists and this too concludes with a final embrace.

Bibliography

Abbate, Vincenzo. *Quaderni dei pupi — Un patrimonio della cultura popolare siciliana.* Acireale: CSS Teatro Macri, 2007.

Accettella, Icaro, Bruno Accettella, and Anna Accettella. *Le marionette degli Accettella.* Rome: Accettella Teatro Mongiovino, 1997.

Adamo, Vito. "L'opra dei pupi ad Alcamo — la famiglia Canino." Thesis, Università degli studi di Palermo, facoltà di lettere, 1969–1970.

Ademollo, Alessandro. *I teatri di Roma nel secolo decimosettimo.* Rome: L. Pasqualucci, 1888.

Alberti, Carmelo. *Il teatro dei pupi e lo spettacolo popolare siciliano.* Milan: Mursia, 1977.

Allacci. *Dramaturgia.* Venice, 1755.

Allegri, Luigi. *Per una storia del teatro come spettacolo: il teatro di burattini e di marionette.* Universita di Parma, 1978.

Ambrosio, Franco, ed. *Il teatro ritrovato — l'edficio marionettistico di Cenderelli a Campomorone.* Catalogue, Palazzo Balbi, Campomorone. Milan: Skira, 1996.

Amico, Donata. "Una forma di spettacolo: l'opera dei pupi catanese (1882–1928)." Thesis, Universita degli studi di Catania, facolta di lettere e filosofia, 1992–1993.

_____. *"Teatrar narrando": l'opera dei pupi catanese le "serate" di Raffaele Trombetta (1882–1928).* Quaderni dell'Associazione Peppino Sarina. Azzano San Paolo (BG): Edizioni Junior, 2008.

Amico, Nino. "Shakespeare coi pupi." *Quaderni di teatro* 4, no. 13 (August 1981): pp. 96–105.

Angelini, D. *Maschere, marionette e burattini.* Milan: Ottaviano, 1981.

Anon. "I pupi di Giuseppe Cocchiara" in *Sicilia.* Palermo: S.F. Flaccovio, 1960.

Arte popolare in Sicilia, le techniche i temi i simboli. Catalogue. Siracusa: Italter, 1991.

Automi, marionette et ballerine nel teatro d'avanguardia. Catalogue. Ed. Elisa Vaccarino. Milan: Skira, 2000.

Aziza, Mohamed. *Formes traditionnelles du spectacle.* Tunis : Société Tunisienne de Diffusion, 1975.

Bagno, Albert. "Burattini e burattinai in valle San Martino." In *Il patrimonio culturale della valle San Martino,* edited by Fabio Bonaiti. Calolziocorte: Centro Studi, Ricerche e Documentazione, 2006.

Baird, Bil. *The Art of the Puppet.* New York: Macmillan, 1965.

Balzaretti, Erik, ed. *Dalla A. alla Ang. Bruno Angoletta, professione illustratore.* Turin: Little Nemo, 2001.

Barbagiovanni, Giusy. *Musica e marionette.* Turin: Ananke, 2003.

Barocchi, Paola, and Giovanna Gaeta Bertelà. *Arredi principeschi del Seicento fiorentino.* Turin: Utet, 1990.

Bartoš, Jaroslav. *Loutkářská kronika.* Prague: Orbis, 1963.

Beales, Derek. *The Risorgimento and the Unification of Italy.* London: Pearson Education, 2002. (Original edition George Allen and Unwin, 1971.)

Bergonzini, Renato, Cesare Maletti, and Beppe Zagaglia. *Burattini e burattinai.* Modena: Mundici e Zanetti, 1980.

Bertonasso, Giorgio. "Burattini, marionette, ombre — dal *Giornale d'Asti* (1776–1819)." *Linea Teatrale* 3, February 1982, Turin, Gruppo della Danza Contemporanea Bella Hutter e Teatro dell'Angolo.

Bertozzi, Cesare. "Burattini e marionette a Parma." Thesis, Universita degli studi di Bologna, 1996–1997.

Biggi, Maria Ida. "Scenari storici per un teatrini di marionette a Jesi." In *Il teatro delle meraviglie,* catalogue. Commune di Jesi, 2003.

Bilello, Ezio. "La primaria compagnia marionettistica Raffaele Pallavicini." In *Le marionette Pallavicini,* catalogue. Genoa: Sagep, 1995.

Black and White. May 27, 1893. London.

Boccascena. Quaderno semestrale. Milan: Associazione Grupporiani, 2000.

Bonlini, Gian Carlo. *Le glorie della poesia e della musica contenute nell'esatta notizia dei teatri della città di Venezia.* Venice, 1730.

Bouissac, Paul. *Circus and Culture, a Semiotic Approach.* Bloomington: Indiana University Press, 1976.

Bragaglia, Anton Giulio. *Pulcinella.* Florence: Sansoni, 1982. (Original edition 1953.)

280   Bibliography

Brenner, Anita. "A Corner of Sicily in New York" (photocopy of article in MIMAP, no source).

Brunello, Gigio, and Gyula Molnár. *Macbeth all'improvviso* (introductory essay by Pier Giorgio Nosari). Azzano San Paolo: Junior, 2003.

Bruschini, Nino. *Roberto di Roncaglia ovvero Pulcinella e il drago Fetonte*. Bologna, 1945.

Buonanno, Michael. "The Palermitan Epic: Dialogism and the Inscription of Social Relations." *Journal of American Folklore* 103, no. 409 (July–September 1990).

Burattini e marionette in Italia. Catalogue. Ed. Maria Signorelli. Milan: Museo della Scala, 1967.

Burattini e marionette in Italia dal cinquecento al giorni nostra: testimonianze storiche artistiche letterarie. Catalogue. Rome: Palombi, 1980.

Burattini, marionette, pupi. Catalogue. Milan: Silvana, 1980.

Burgaretta, S. "Intervista sul puparo Umberto Li Giol." *Il cantastorie* 51, 1980.

_____. "Intervista sul puparo Vincenzo Mangiagli." *Il cantastorie* 51, 1980.

_____. "Pupari ad Avola." *Il cantastorie* 51, 1980.

_____. "Il teatro dei pupi a Siracusa. I fratelli Vacaro," part 1. *Il cantastorie* 59, 1982.

_____. "Il teatro dei pupi a Siracusa. I fratelli Vaccaro," part 2. *Il cantastorie* 60, 1983.

_____. "Quale futuro per i pupi di Ignazio Puglisi." *Il cantastorie* 61–62, 1983.

_____. "Teatre dei pupi siciliani in lutto." *Il cantastorie* 72, 1986.

_____. "Cartelloni dell'opera dei pupi del Siracusano." *Il cantastorie* 80, 1988.

_____. "Cartelloni dell'opera dei pupi del Siracusano." In *Opra manifesta. Cartelloni dell'opra dei pupi*, by Anon. Taormina, 1991.

Bussell, Jan. *Through Wooden Eyes*. London: Faber and Faber, 1956.

Buttitta, Antonino. "L'opera dei pupi come rito." *Quaderni di Teatro* 4, no. 13 (August 1981).

Byrom, Michael. *The Puppet Theatre in Antiquity*. Oxford: DaSilva, 1996.

Cairo, Laura, and Piccarda Quilici. *Biblioteca teatrale dal '500 al '700, la raccolta della biblioteca casanatense*. Rome: Bulzoni, 1981.

Cali, Massimo. *Burattini e marionette tra Cinque e Seicento in Italia*. Azzano San Paolo (BG): Edizioni Junior, 2002.

Cammarata, Felice. *Pupi e Mafia—l'eroe carolingio nella demopsicologia siciliano*. Palermo: Renzo Mattone, 1969.

_____. *Pupi e Caretti—i mass media della Sicilia Liberty*. Palermo: Renzone Mazzone, 1976.

Campanini, Paola. *Marionette barocche—il mirabile artificio*. Azzano San Paolo: Junior, 2004.

Camporesi, Piero. *Il libro dei vagabondi*. Turin: Einaudi, 1973.

Capellini, Pino. *Un secolo di marionette—la famiglia Mazzatorta 1850–1950*. Bergamo: Quaderni del Vicolo, n.d.

_____. *Baracca e burattini—il teatro popolare dei burattini nei territori e nelle tradizioni lombarde*. Bergamo: Gutenberg, 1977.

Capellini, Pino. *Paci Paciana*. Bergamo: Fondazione Benedetto Ravasio, 1997.

Carozza, Maria, and Aldo Brigaglia. *Giacomina e il popolo di legno*. Cagliari: Tema, 2008.

Castellino, Francesca, and Italo Ferrari. *Baracca e burattini*. Turin: Società Editrice Internazionale, 1936.

Cecchi, Doretta. *Attori di legno*. Rome: Palomba, 1988.

Cecchini, Franco. "Provenienza e attribuzione degli scenari per marionette di Jesi. Ipotesi da una ricerca sul territorio." In *Il teatro delle meraviglie*. Commune di Jesi, 2003.

Cervellati, Alessandro. *Storia dei burattini e burattinai Bolognese (Fagiolino & C.)*. Bologna: Cappelli, 1974. (Original edition 1964.)

Chanson d'Aspremont, la chanson de geste du XIIe siècle. 2 vols. Ed. Louis Brandin. Paris: Honoré Champion, 1970.

Chesnais, Jacques. *Histoire générale des marionnettes*. Paris: Bordas, 1947.

Chiumeo, Filippo, and Francesca Scommegna. *Don Michele Immesi ovvero il teatro dei pupi a Barletta*. San Ferdinando di Puglia: Gianfranco Nezi, 1997.

Ciccarelli, Emmanuele. "Angelica nella tradizione cavallerescha popolare siciliana e nella tradizione letteraria." Thesis, Università degli studi di Palermo, facoltà di lettere e filosofia, 1973–1974.

Cipolla, Alfonso. "Dal segno al palcoscenico—l'avventura teatrale di Bruno Angoletta." In *Dalla A. alla Ang. Bruno Angoletta, professione illustratore*, edited by Erik Balzaretti. Turin: Little Nemo, 2001.

_____. "Dall'Alpi alle piramidi, da Callianetto al Nilo, ovvero L'Egitto in terra di Lupi, con Gerolamo redivivo, Gianduja alle porte e Aida che 'ai da.'" In *Famiglia Lupi—Aida*, edited by Pietro Porta. Azzano San Paolo: Junior, 2002.

_____. *Gianduja da Callianetto al gran teatro dei burattini dei fratelli Niemen*. Turin: SEB 27, 2003.

_____. "Le marionette in Piemonte—storie di famiglie e di compagnie." In *I fili della memoria—percorsi per una storia delle marionette in Piemonte*, edited by Alfonso Cipolla and Giovanni Moretti. Turin: SEB, 2001.

_____, and Giovanni Moretti, eds. *Commedianti figurati e attori pupazzani, testimonianze di moralisti e memorialisti, viaggiatori e cronisti per una storia del teatro con le marionette e con i burattini in Italia*. Turin: SEB 27, 2003.

_____, and _____. *I fili della memoria—percorsi per una storia delle marionette in Piemonte*. Turin: SEB, 2001.

_____, and _____. *Gianduja, una riscoperta in corso.* Turin: SEB 27, 2003.

Cocchiara, Giuseppe. "I cartelloni dell'opera dei pupi." *Sicilia* 5, 1954.

_____. *Le vastasate—contributo alla storia del teatro populare.* Palermo: Sandron, 1926.

Colla, Gianni, and Gustavo Bonora. *Il popolo di legno di Gianni e Cosetta Colla.* Milan: Imago s.r.l., 1982.

Colombo, Enrico. *Fiori e applausi per papà—20 anni di teatro con i burattini in provincia.* Cazzago Brabbia: Arti grafiche varesine, 2000.

Corrado Ricci, Corrado. *I teatri di Bologna nei secoli XVII e XVIII.* Bologna: Monti, 1888.

Costantini, Sandro. *Vita, spettacoli e incontri di un maestro burattinaio (1930–1997).* Memoirs presented by Remo Melloni. Brescia: Fondazione Civiltà Bresciana, 2004.

Cremona, Valeria. "'800" in *Burattini e marionette in Italia dal cinquecento al giorni nostra: testimonianze storiche artistiche letterarie.* Rome: Palombi, 1980.

Crimi, Melina. "Giuseppe Crimi e il teatro dei pupi in Sicilia." Thesis, Università degli studi di Catania, Facoltà di lettere e filosofia, 1970–1971.

Croce, Benedetto. *I teatri di Napoli dal Rinascimento alla fine del secolo decimottavo.* Bari: Laterza, 1966. (Original edition, Naples: Luigi Pierro, 1891.)

Croce, Marcella. "Aspetti della tradizione cavalleresca in Sicilia." Thesis, University of Wisconsin–Madison, 1988.

_____. *L'epica cavalleresca nelle tradizioni popolari siciliane.* Palermo: Distretto scolastico IV/42, 1997.

_____. *Pupari—storia di Girolamo Cuticchio dei pupi e di una tradizione.* Palermo: Flaccovio, 2003.

_____. *Pupi, carretti, contastorie—l'epica cavalleresca nelle tradizioni popolari siciliane.* Palermo: Dario Flaccovio, 1999.

Cuccoli, Angelo. *Burattini di Bologna—undici commedie dialettali.* Bologna: Insubria, 1921. (Reprint, Milan: Synthesis Press, 1981.)

Cuticchio, Mimmo, ed. *La macchina dei sogni.* 18th edition. Palermo: Associazione "Figli d'Arte Cuticchio," 2001.

_____, ed. *La macchina dei sogni.* 19th edition. Palermo: Associazione Figli d'Arte Cuticchio, 2002.

_____. *Storia e testimonianze di una famiglia di pupari.* Palermo: STASS, 1978.

_____, and Salvo Licata. *Visita guidata—Viaggio per parole e immagini nel teatro di Mimmo Cuticchio e Salvo Licata.* Edited by Roberto Giambrone. Palermo: Associazione Figli d'Arte Cuticchio, 2001.

Dalla caricatura al burattino—i grandi personaggi dalle teste di legno di Umberto Tirelli. Catalogue. Florence: Artifice, 1989. (Texts by Renato Barilli, Sandro Bellei, Giorio Celli, Luciano Guidobaldi, Remo Melloni, Emilio Vita.)

Dal Pos, Danila. *Burattinai et marionettisti a Castelfranco e nella Marca Trivigiana.* Venice: Corbo e Fiore, 1984.

De Felice, Francesco. *Storia del teatro Siciliano.* Catania: Giannotta, 1956.

Delle Muti, Mario, Angelo Capozzi, and Paolo De Angelis. *I pupari di Capitanata e l'esperienza di San Giovanni Rotondo.* San Giovanni Rotondo: Grafica Baal, 1998.

Delsante, Ubaldo. *Domenico Galaverna burattinaio e patriota.* Parma: Zara, 1988.

De Marinis, Marco. "Lo spettacolo come testo," part 1. *Versus* 21 ("Teatro e semiotica"), 1978.

_____. "Lo spettacolo come testo," part 2. *Versus* 22 ("Teatro e comunicazione gestuale"), 1979.

_____. *Segno.* Milan: Mondadori, 1980.

_____. *Semiotica del teatro. L'analisi testuale dello spettacolo.* Milan: Bompiani, 1982.

De Nigris, Fulvio. *Otello Sarzi.* Bologna: Patron, 1986. Reprinted in 1990.

Depero, Fortunato. *Teatro magico.* Catalogue. Milan: Electa, 1989.

De Simone, Roberto. *Le guarattelle fra Pulcinella, Teresina e la Morte.* Sorrento-Naples: Franco di Mauro, 2003.

Dickens, Charles. *Pictures from Italy.* Leipzig: Tauschnitz, 1846. (Reprint, London: Hazell, Watson and Viney, n.d.)

Di Maria, Vincenzo. "Risonanze storiche nel romanzo di gesta e il verismo epico del teatro dei pupi." *Quaderni di teatro,* 1981.

Dotti, Anna. "*I promessi sposi*" della compagnia Carlo Colla e Figli—il melodramma nella tradizione marionettistica.* Azzano San Paolo: Junior, 2004.

Ebalginelli, Liliana, and Paola Ghidoli. "Bigio, burattinaio bergamasco." In *Mondo popolare in Lombardia 1—Bergamo e il suo territorio,* edited by Roberto Leydi. Milan: Silvana, 1977.

Eco, Umberto. *Trattato di semiotica generale.* Milan: Bompiani, 1975.

Emerson, Isabel. *Things Seen in Sicily.* London: Seeley, Service, 1929.

Eusebietti, D. *Piccola storia dei burattini e delle maschere.* Turin: SEI, 1966.

Fagioli, Massimo. *La marionetta e il burattino.* Rome: A. Armando, 1974.

Ferrari, I., and F. Castellino. *Baracca e burattini.* Turin: SEI, 1946.

Fichera, Gaetano. *L'antico teatro delle marionette in Catania (opira dei pupi) anno 1920–1930.* Catania: Società Storica Catanese, 1968.

Freire, Susanita. *O fim de um símbolo—Theatro João Minhoca Compagnia Authomatica.* Rio de Janeiro: Achiamé, 2000.

Freri, Adriano. "Il bergamasco in commedia." *Quaderni dello spettacolo* 5, Bergamo, Ufficio Teatro-Scuola del Teatro "G. Donizetti," n.d.

Gambarutti, Franco. *Una vita appesa ai fili*. Azzano San Paolo (BG): Junior, 2005.

Garbero Zorzi, Elvira, and Mario Sperenzi. *Teatro e spettacolo nella Firenze dei Medici*. Florence: Leo S. Olschki, 2001.

Garzoni, Tomaso. *La piazza universale di tutte le professioni del mondo*. Venice, 1585.

I generici di Arlecchino, vols. 1 and 2. Bergamo: Fondazione Benedetto Ravasio, 2001 and 2003.

Giambrone, Roberto. *Visita guidata — viaggio per parole e immagini nel teatro di Mimmo Cuticchio e Salvo Licata*. Palermo: Associazione Figli d'Arte Cuticchio, 2001.

Giancane, Daniele. *Angelica, Orlando and Company — per una didattica della cultura popolare: le marionette di Canosa di Puglia*. Bari: Levante, 1989.

Gold, Donna Lauren. "Plucky Puppets Are the Stars in One Family's Saga." *Smithsonian*, August 1983.

Golding, Louis. *Sicilian Noon*. New York: Knopf, 1925.

Goldowski, Boris. *The Chronicles of the Puppet Theatre in Russia in the 15th–18th Centuries*. Moscow/Warsaw: Nina Gallery, 1994.

Gorla, Marina. *Le marionette di casa Borromeo*. Bologna: Cooperativa Libraria Universitaria, 1987.

Grano, Enzo. *Antonio Petito — autobiografia di Pulcinella*. Naples: Attivita Bibliografica Editoriale, 1978.

Greco, Franco Carmelo, ed. *Pulcinella, una maschera tra gli specchi*. Naples: Edizione Scientifiche Italiane, 1990.

Gregorovius, Ferdinand. *Wanderjahre in Italien*. Leipzig: F. A. Brockhaus, 1870–1877. (Reprint, Cologne: Agrippina, 1953.)

Gualdi, Germano. *Sagre fiere mercati d'Italia*. Carpi, 1980.

Guarraci, Giuseppe. *Pupi e pupari a Siracusa 1875–1975*. Rome: Meridional, 1975.

Guerci, Francis M. *Sicily, the Guardian of the Mediterranean*, 1938.

Gusto e passione teatrale fra otto e novecento — la raccolta Caccia di Romentino al Museo di Novara. Ed. Elena Cao, Emanuele Cigliola, Maria Laura Tomea Gavazzoli. Milan: Silvano, 2003.

Izzo, Michele. *I pupanti e l'opera dei pupi — racconti di un pupante*. Livorno: Quinci, 1992.

Jackson, Emily Nevill. *A Student in Sicily*. N.p.: Bodley Head, 1926.

Jal, Auguste. *Dictionnaire critique de biographie et d'histoire*. Paris: Plon, 1867.

Jansen, Steen. "Esquisse d'une théorie de la forme dramatique." *Langages* 12, 1968.

Jones, Henry Festing. *Castellinaria and Other Sicilian Diversions*. London: A.C. Fifield, 1920.

_____. *Diversions in Sicily*. "Travellers' Library" edition. London: Jonathan Cape, 1929.

Jori, Andrea. *Francesco Campogalliani burattinaio, poeta, commediografo*. Mantua: Banca Agricola, 1979.

_____. "Teoria e pratica del burattinaio Francesco Campogalliani." In *Mondo popolare in Lombardia*, 12, *Mantova e il suo territorio*, by Giancorrado Barozzi, Lidia Beduschi, and Maurizio Bertolotti. Milan: Silvana, 1982.

Jurkowski, Henryk. *Métamorphoses — la marionette au xxe siècle*. Charleville-Mézières: Institut International de la Marionnette, 2000.

Juvarra, Filippo. *Pensieri di scene e apparecchie fatte per servizio del Esmo Ottoboni in Roma per il suo Teatro nella Cancelleria da me suo Architetto l'anno 1708 sino al 1712*. Print room at Victoria and Albert Museum, London.

Kirby, Michael. Contribution to debate "La semiotica del teatro." *Versus* 21, 1978.

_____. *Futurist Performance*. New York: Dutton, 1971.

La Gorce, Jérôme de. "Un théâtre parisien en concurrence avec l'Académie royale de musique dirigée par Lully: l'Opéra des Bamboches." In *Jean Baptiste Lully — actes du colloque Saint-Germain-en-Laye — Heidelberg, 1987*, Heidelberg: Laaber, 1990.

Lanza, Maria. "Le leggende cavalleresche nei teatri popolari romani dell'ottocento." *Roma, rivista di studi di vita Romani* 9, no. 3 (March 1931).

_____. "Un rifacitore popolare di leggende cavalleresche: Adone Finardi." *Il folklore Italiano* 5, June–July 1930 — VIII, Catania, Libreria Tirelli di F. Guaitolini.

La Spisa, Elena, and Francesco Ballarini. "I 'Piccoli' di Vittorio Podrecca. Novità scenografiche e musica nel Teatro Stabile per Marionette (1914–1921)." In *Nuova Rivista Musicale Italiana* 27, no. 4. Turin: 1993.

Leggio, Antonio. *L'opera dei pupi*. Rome: Manzella, 1974.

Leone, Bruno. *La guarattella — burattini e burattinai a Napoli*. Bologna: Cooperativa Libraria Universitaria, 1986.

Leydi, Roberto, ed. "Che cosa sarebbe successo se il professore d'Ancona avese guardato I burattini." In *Arte della maschera nella commedia dell'arte*, Donato Sartori and Bruno Lanata. Florence: Casa Usher, 1983.

_____. *Gelindo ritorna — il natale in Piemonte*. N.p.: Omega, 2001.

_____. *Mondo popolare in Lombardia*, vol. 1. Milan: Sylvana, 1977.

_____. "Teatro da camera." *FMR*, March 1983.

_____, and Renata Mezzanotte Leydi. *Marionette e burattini*. Milan: Collano del 'Gallo Grande,' 1958.

Li Gotti, Ettore. *Il teatro dei pupi*. Palermo: Flaccovio, 1978. (First edition, Florence: G.C. Sansoni, 1957.)

Litta Modignani, Alessandra. *Dizionario biografico e bibliografia dei burattinai, marionettisti et pupari della tradizione italiana*. Bologna: Cooperativa Libreria Universitaria Editrice, 1986.

Lodico, Giusto. *Storia dei paladini di Francia cominciando da Milone conte d'Anglante sino alla morte di Rinaldo*. 4 vols. Palermo: Stamperia di Giov. Batt. Gaudiano, 1858–1860. (Reprint, La Punta: Brancato, 1993–2000.)

Longo, Mauro. *Pupi e pupari*. Catania: Greco, 1980.

Lo Presti, Salvatore. *I pupi*. Catania: Studio Editoriale Moderno, 1927.

Luzzati, Emanuele. *I paladini di Francia: ovvero il tradimento di Gano di Maganzo*. Milan: Ugo Mursia, 1962.

Maffei, Scipione. *Osservazioni litterarie del 1738*, vol. 3.

Magnin, Charles. *Histoire des marionnettes en Europe depuis l'antiquité à nos jours*. Paris : Michel Lévy, 1862. (Slatkine reprint, Geneva, 1981.)

Majorana, Bernadette. "Italia Napoli parlatrice dell'opera dei pupi catanese." In *Archivio per la storia delle donne II*. Naples: M. D'Auria, 2005.

_____. *Pupi e attori ovvero l'opera dei pupi a Catania storia e documenti*. Rome: Bulzoni, 2008.

Mancini, Franco. *Pulcinella nella vita napoletana dell'ottocento*. Naples: Società Editrice, 1982.

Mangini, Nicola. *I teatri di Venezia*. Milano: Mursia, 1974.

Marinetti, Filippo Tommaso. *Teatro*. Milan: Oscar Mondadori, 2004.

Marionette a Genova. Comune di Campomorone. Catalogue. Ente Decentramento Culturale, n.d.

Le Marionette degli Accettella. Rome: Accettella Teatro Mongiovino, 1997.

Marionette di Podrecca "Il Mondo della luna," *Quadern del teatro*, ns., no. 24. Trieste: Teatro Stabile Friuli-Venice, 1983.

Marzattinocci, Davide. *Cassandrino al teatro Fiano — il teatro delle marionette a Roma nella prima metà dell'ottocento*. Azzano San Paolo: Junior, 2006.

Mauceri, Alfredo. *I fratelli Vaccaro — un sogno chiamato "Opra dei Pupi."* Siracusa: Soc. Coop. Tipografica, 2000.

May, Esther. "Das sizilianische puppenspiel und seine literarischen Vorlagen, eine vergleichende Studie am Beispiel der Schlacht von Roncisvalle." Thesis, Bonn, Shaker, 2001.

Mazzola, Adriana. *Lo specchio dell'uomo — il teatro d'animazione in Trentino*. Trento: Curcu e Genovese, 1998.

Mazzoleni, Biancamaria. *Cassandrino, storia di una maschera romana del XIX secolo*. Rome: Arnica, 1977.

McPharlin, Paul. *The Puppet Theatre in America — A History, 1524–1948*. Boston: Plays, 1949, reprint 1969.

_____. *Puppetry, a Yearbook of Puppets and Marionettes*, Birmingham, MI: Puppetry Imprints, 1938.

Melloni, Remo. "Burattini e burattinai nella tradizione bergamasca." *Quaderni dello spettacolo 6*, Bergamo, Teatro Donizetti, n.d.

_____. "La collezione Signorelli." In *Il teatro delle meraviglie*. Commune di Jesi, 2003.

_____. "La crisi della commedia dell'arte e la sua continuità nel teatro dei burattini e delle marionette." *La rivista di Bergamo*, new series, nos. 22–23, July–September 2000.

_____. "Le marionette a Bologna nel XVIII secolo." In *Il teatrino Rissone*. Modena: Edizioni Panini, n.d.

_____. "Il teatro delle marionette." In *Le marionette Pallavicini*. Catalogue. Genoa: Sagep, 1995.

_____, and Maria Giuseppina Bo. "Il repertorio del teatro dei burattini e delle marionette della tradizione italiana." *Linea Teatrale 13*, Turin, 1990.

_____, Giuliana Manfredi, and Maria Giuseppina Bo. *Occhi di vetro occhi di legno — la tradizione burattinaia nella Bassa Regiana*. Reggio Emilia: Diabasis, 1989.

Montecchi, Fabrizio. "Oltre lo schermo." In *Schattentheater, Band I: Autoren + Akteure*, by Rainer Reusch. Schwäbisch Gmünd: Einhorn, 1997.

_____. "The Scenic Area." In *Schattentheater/Shadow Theatre, vol 2, art + technique*, by Rainer Reusch. Schwäbisch Gmünd: Einhorn, 2001.

Monti, Eugenio. *Il Gerolamo, c'era una volta un teatro di marionette....* Milan: Istituto Ortopedico Gaetano Pini, 1975.

Monti Colla, Eugenio. *Burattini & marionette — la storia del teatro di animazione e di figura*. N.p.: Prado, 2001.

_____. *Il melodramma e le marionette*. Milan: Associazione Grupporiani, 2000.

Moretti, Giovanni. "Ancora sul Caserio — note sulla Compagnia Pallavicini." *Linea Teatrale 7*, no. 14 (February 1991).

_____. *Attori e baracche — il Fornaretto nel sistema teatrale*. Turin: SEB 27, 2002.

_____. "Due copioni a confronto: il Caserio dei Rame ed dei Pallavicini." *Linea Teatrale 6*, no. 1 (1991).

_____, ed. *Mayno, il brigante della Spinetta — intorno a un soggetto cinematografico di Armando Mottura e Pinin Pacot*. Turin: SEB 27, 2008.

Mostra del burattino tradizionale. Raccolta Cesare Maletti. Catalogue. Modena, 1978.

Mostra-museo del burattino dell'Emilia-Romagna. Catalogue. Cervia, 1975.

Museo Giordano Ferrari. *Il castello dei burattini*. Edited by Remo Melloni. Milan: Mazzotta, 2004.

Museo-Laboratorio del Burattino e della Marionetta Tradizionali, *I burattini dei Maletti*. Modena: Industrie Grafiche Coptip, 1983.

Napoli, Alessandro. "'La Cantata dei Pastori' un percorso da Napoli a Catania." In *La Cantata dei Pastori*. Catania: Citta Teatro Libri, n.d.

_____. "Ettore, Achille e Alessandro Magno nell'opera dei pupi. La storia greca secondo i pupari catanesi." In *Epica e storia*, edited by Maria Gandolfo Giacomarra. Palermo: Associazione per la Conservazione delle Tradizioni Popolari, 2005.

_____. "La Marionettistica dei Fratelli Napoli: permanenze e mutamenti nell'opera dei pupi di tradizione catanese." Thesis, Universita' degli studi di Palermo, Facolta di lettere e Filosofia, 1990–1991.

_____. *Il racconto e i colori — storie e cartelli dell'opera dei pupi catanese.* Palermo: Sellerio, 2002.

Niemen, Gualberto. *Autobiografia di un burattinaio.* Tortona: Quaderni dell'Associazione Pepino Sarina, 2000.

_____. *La Iena di San Giorgio.* Porretta Terme: I Quaderni del Battello Ebbro, 1998.

Novelli, Sergio. *Materiali per una storia della compagnia marionnettistica Pallavicini.* Università di Bologna, 1983–1984.

Opera dei pupi. Teatro Angelo Musco di Catania, 1977. (Antonino Buttitta, "Il pubblico dell'opra"; Vincenzo di Maria, "L'ambiente popolare ed il carattere socio-politico dell'opera dei pupi"; Sebastiano Lo Nigro, "Il rapporto della tradizione popolare siciliana con l'epica cavalleresca poetico-romanzesca e relativi suoi innesti modificativi dei testi letterari"; Antonio Pasqualino, "Ideologia del teatro dei pupi"; Fortunato Pasqualino, "Il teatro dei pupi fra innovazione e tradizione").

L'Opra. Catalogue. Rodia, 1984.

Paërl, Hetty. *Pulcinella la misteriosa maschera della cultura europea.* Apeiron: Sant' Oreste, 2002.

Palazzi, Renata. "La vocazione teatrale di Pinocchio." In *Pinocchio, burattini e marionette.* Catalogue. Florence: La Casa Usher, 1982.

Palazzolo, Egle. "Aspetti socio culturali del teatro dei pupi (a proposito di due copioni di A. Musemeci)." Thesis, Universita degli studi di Palermo, Facoltà di Lettere, 1968–1969.

Pandolfi, Vito. *La Commedia dell'Arte. Storia e testo.* Florence: Sansoni, 1957–1961.

Pandolfini Barberi, Antonio. *Burattini e burattinai Bolognesi.* Bologna: Forni, 1923.

Paolucci, Daniela. *Pulcinella e Punch: due tradizione a confronto.* N.p.: Compagnia degli Sbuffi, 1997.

Parole consumate del teatro dei Piccoli di Vittorio Podrecca. Ed. Manuela Castagnara Codeluppi. Cividale del Friuli: Alea, 2003.

Pasqualino, Antonio. "Bibliografia delle edizioni cavalleresche popolari siciliane dell'ottocento e del novecento." *Uomo e cultura* 12, nos. 23–24(1979).

_____. "Codici gestuali nel teatro dei pupi." In *Intorno al 'codice.'* Florence: La Nuova Italia, 1976.

_____. *Dal testo alla representazione — le prime imprese di Carlo Magno.* Palermo: Laboratorio Antropologico Universitario, 1986.

_____. "Dama Rovenza dal Martello e la leggenda di Rinaldo da Montalbano." *I cantari — struttura e tradizione.* M. Picone e M. Bendinelli Predelli, eds. Florence: Leo S. Olschki, 1984.

_____. *L'opera dei pupi.* Palermo: Sellerio, 1977 (reprint 1989).

_____. *L'opera dei pupi a Roma a Napoli e in Puglia.* Palermo: Museo Internazionale delle Marionette Antonio Pasqualino, 1996.

_____. *I pupi siciliani.* Gibellina: Nando Russo, 1983.

_____. "Tradizione e innovazione nell'opera dei pupi contemporanea." *Quaderni di teatro* 4, no. 13 (August 1981).

_____. "Transformations of Chivalrous Literature in the Subject Matter of the Sicilian Marionette Theatre." In *Varia folklorica,* edited by Alan Dundes. The Hague: Mouton, 1978.

_____. *Le vie del cavaliere dall'epica medievale alla cultura popolare.* Milan: Bompiani, 1992.

_____, and Janne Vibaek. "Registri linguistici e linguaggi non verbali nell'opera dei pupi." *Semiotica della rappresentazione,* edited by Renato Tomasino. *Quaderni per l'immaginario.* Cattedra di Storia del Teatro e dello Spettacolo della Facoltà di Lettere e Filosofia, University of Palermo, n. 4. S. F. Flaccovio, 1984.

_____, and _____, eds. *Eroi, mostri et maschere — il repertorio tradizionale nel teatro di animazione italiano.* Catalogue. Florence: Artificio, 1990.

Pasqualino, Fortunato. *Teatro con i pupi siciliani.* Palermo: Vita Cavallotto, 1980.

Passamani, Bruno. *Depero e la scena.* Turin: Martano, 1970.

_____. *Fortunato Depero.* Rovereto: Comune-Musei civici-Galleria Museo Depero, 1981.

Passos, Alexandre. *Bonecos de Santo Aleixo — as marionetas em Portugal nos séculos XVI a XVIII e a sua influência nos Títeres Alentejanos.* Evora: Cendrev, 1999.

Patanè, Salvatore. *Erminio della Stella d'Oro e Gemma della Fiamma Guerre ed avventure mediovali.* Palermo: Giuseppe Leggio, 1896.

Patková, Jindriska. *Das Tschechische Puppentheater.* Prague: National Museum, 1975.

Perez, Massimo. *Scenari Casamarciano.* Rome: Teatro Laboratorio, 1987–1988.

Pitrè, Giuseppe. *Usi e costumi credenze e pregiudizi del popolo siciliano.* Palermo, 1889 (vol. 14 of his *Tradizioni popolari siciliane*). Reprinted, Palermo: Arnaldo Forni, 1979 (original edition, Palermo: Libreria L. Pedone Lauriel di Carlo Clausen, 1889).

Poggi, Fabio. *All'ombra dell'Alfieri, luoghi, spettacoli, personaggi della vita musicale astigiana dal Medioevo ai nostri giorni.* Asti: Provincia di Asti, 1998.

Poieri, Giacomo Bruno, ed. *I Muchetti, marionettisti in Adro dal 1750 al 1964 — una famiglia, una tradizione.* Adro: Commune di Adro, 2001.

_____. *Pinocchio, burattini, marionette e pupi.* Adro: Associazione del Teatro Minimo, 1994.

Porta, Pietro, ed. *Famiglia Lupi — Aida.* Azzano San Paolo: Junior, 2002.

_____. *Gente di Sarina — il burattinaio Peppino Sarina e le communità del Tortonese e dell'Oltrepo Pavese nella prima meta del novecento.* Vigevano: Diakronia, 1997.

_____, and Alfonso Cipolla, eds. *Famiglia Rame, la battaglia di Palestro — la battaglia di Solferino e San Martino.* Porretta Terme: Quaderni del Battelo Ebbro, 1999.

Pretini, Giancarlo. *Facanapa e gli altri — storia e storie di marionette, burattini e marionettisti.* Udine: Trapezio, 1987. (Original edition 1985.)

Purschke, Hans Richard. *Puppenspiel und verwandte Künste in der Freien Reichs-Stadt Frankfurt am Main.* Frankfurt: Puppenzentrum, 1980.

_____. *Die Puppenspieltraditionen Europas — Deutschsprachige Gebiete.* Bochum: Deutsches Institut für Puppenspiel, 1986.

Quaderni di teatro 4, no. 13 (August 1981). Special edition "I pupi e il teatro."

Racca, Carlo. *Burattini e marionette: il loro teatro ed i loro fantocci.* Trieste: G.B. Paravia & C., n.d.

Rak, Maria Giovanna "'500 e'600" in *Burattini e marionette in Italia dal cinquecento al giorni nostra: testimonianze storiche artistiche letterarie.* Catalogue. Rome: Palombi, 1980.

Rak, Michele. "Il teatro meccanico." *Quaderni di teatro.* Florence: Vallecchi, 1981.

Ricci, Corrado. "I burattini di Bologna." *La Lettura* 3, no. 12 (1903).

Rosenfeld, Sybil. *The Theatre of the London Fairs in the 18th Century.* Cambridge: Cambridge University Press, 1960.

Rossetti, Bartolomeo. *I bulli di Roma.* Rome: Newton Compton, 1979.

Sanga, Glauco. "La lingua di Gioppino e di Brighella." Note in "Bigio, burattinaio bergamasco," by Liliana Ebalginelli and Paola Ghidoli. In *Mondo Popolare in Lombardia, 1— Bergamo e il suo territorio,* edited by Robert Leydi. Milan: Silvana, 1977.

Sangrasso, Vito. *Il costume del pupo.* Catalogue. Palermo: Ispe Archimede, 1999.

Sanguinetti, Lamberto. *Teatro Gerolamo.* Milan: Uffizio Stampa della Commune di Milano, 1967.

Santino, Umberto. *I giorni della peste — il festino di Santa Rosalia tra mito e spettacolo.* Palermo: Grifo, 1999.

Sarina, Giuseppe. *Napoleone Bonaparte alla battaglia di Marengo.* Porretta Terme: Quaderni del Battello Ebbro, 2000.

Sarzi, Mauro. "I Sarzi, quattro generazioni di burattinai." Interview in *Biblioteca di Lavoro,* no. 79/80, February–March 1978.

Scafoglio, Domenico, and Luigi M. Lombardi Satriani. *Pulcinella il mito e la storia.* Milan: Leonardo, 1992.

Scarcella, Gaspare. *Il brigantaggio in Sicilia dagli antichi romani ai nostri giorni.* Palermo: Antares, 2001.

Scott, R.H.F. *Jean-Baptiste Lully.* London: Peter Owen, 1973.

Settecento anni di costume nel Veneto. Treviso, 1976.

Signorelli, Maria. *Ghetanaccio.* Padova: Amicucci, 1960.

_____. "Inizio dell'opera dei burattini." *Strenna dei Romanisti,* April 21, 1978.

_____. *Il teatro di burattini.* In L'Aquila, 1961.

_____, ed. *Il teatro di burattini e di marionette e l'educazione.* Rome: Istituto di Pedagogia dell'Università di Roma, 1962.

_____, and Guido Vergani. *Podrecca e il teatro dei Piccoli.* Pordenone, 1979.

Sordi, Italo. "La materia cavalleresca nel teatro di marionette e di burattini dell'Italia settentrionale." In *Burattini marionette pupi.* Milan: Sylvana, 1980.

Speaight, George. *The History of the English Puppet Theatre.* London: Harrap, 1955 (second edition 1990).

_____. "The Origin of Punch and Judy: A New Clue." *Theatre Research International* 20, no. 3 (1995).

_____. "The Puppet Theatre of Cardinal Ottoboni." *Theatre Research* 1, no. 2 (June 1958).

Stellefson, Sadie. "Sicilian Marionettes: A Didactic Form of Folk Art." Thesis, Columbia University, 1980.

Stendhal. *Voyages en Italie.* Paris: Gallimard, 1973.

Story, William Wetmore. *Roba di Roma.* London: Chapman, 1863.

Tamburini, Luciano. "Fantocci, burattini, marionette a Torino." In *I fili della memoria,* edited by Alfonso Cipolla and Giovanni Moretti. Turin: SEB 27, 2001.

_____. *I teatri di Torino.* Turin: Edizioni dell'Albero, 1966.

Il teatrino Rissone. Catalogue. Modena: Edizioni Panini, n.d.

Teatro dei Piccoli. *Spettacoli artistici di marionette. Opera giocose, fiabe, balli, varietà.* Rome: Tip. Armani e Stein, 1915.

Teatro delle Briciole — la materia e il suo doppia. Ed. Letizia Quintavalla. Parma: Edizioni Briciole, 1984.

Il teatro delle meraviglie. Catalogue. Commune di Jesi, 2003.

Teatro Gioco Vita. *C'era una volta un mare.* Bergamo: Juvenilia, 1983.

_____. *Odissea, spettacolo d'ombre.* Florence: S.E.S. s.r.l., 1984.

Il teatro ritrovato — l'edificio marionettistico di Cendrelli a Campomorone. Catalogue. Milan: Skira, 1996.

Il tesoro sepolto — le marionette di Canosa. Catalogue. Bari: Laterza, 1997.

I testi, il repertorio — quaderni sul teatro d'animazione in Campania — I Ferraiolo — Burattinai. No. 2, July 1993. Ed. Aldo Martino (note by Remo Melloni). Campania: Centro per la Ricerca e la Documentazione sul Teatro d'Animazione in Campania.

Toldo, Pietro. "Nella baracca dei burattini." *Gior-*

nale storico, vol. 51, fasc. 151. Turin: Vincenzo Bona, 1908.

Trattenimento con burattini — mostra di burattini, scenari, copioni, foto del maestro Peppino Sarina. Catalogue. Tortona, 1982.

Uccello, Antonino. "I cartelloni dei pupi nella Sicilia orientale." *Sicilia* 58, 1969.

_____. "Cartelloni publicitari del teatro dei pupi." In *Artigianato antiquario siciliano dalla collezione di Antonino Uccello.* Agrigento, 1970.

_____. "Copioni di briganti nel repertorio dell'opera." In *Bollettino del Centro di Studi Filologici e Linguistici Siciliani*, vol. 9. Palermo: Mori, 1965, pp. 5–21.

_____. "Due tragedie di Shakespeare nel repertorio dell'opra." *La galleria*, nos. 3–4, Palermo, 1965.

_____. "L'opra dei pupi nel Siracusano." *Archivio storico siracusano*, vol. 8, 1962 (later in *Siracusa.* Siracusa: La Società Siracusana di Storia Patria, 1965).

_____. "Pupi e cartelloni dell'opera." Siracusa, 1970.

Varé, Daniel. *Ghosts of the Spanish Steps.* London: Murray, 1955.

Varey, J.E. *Historia de los titeres en España.* Madrid: Revista de Occidente, 1957.

_____. "Titiriteros y volatines en Valencia: 1585–1785." *Revista valenciana de filología* 3, 1953.

Venturini, Valentina, ed. *Dal cunto all'opera dei pupi — il teatro Cuticchio.* Rome: Dino Audino, 2003.

Vergani, Guido, and Maria Signorelli. *Podrecca e il teatro dei Piccoli.* Udine: Casamassima, 1979.

Veroli, Patrizia. "Tra arte e teatro. Maria Signorelli scultrice e burattinaia." In *Il teatro delle meraviglie.* Commune di Jesi, 2003.

Vezzani, Giorgio. "Burattini, marionette, pupi." *Il cantastorie*, no. 47, 3rd series (January–June 1994).

_____. "Il teatro dei burattini a Reggio" (1). *Il cantastorie* 52, no. 1, 3rd series (April 1981).

_____. "Il teatro dei burattini a Reggio" (2). *Il cantastorie* 55, no. 4, 3rd series (December 1981).

Viale Ferrero, Mercedes. *Filippo Juvarra scenografo e architetto teatrale.* Turin: Fratelli Pozzo, 1970.

_____. *Scene per un teatrino di marionette nella vita di Torino ottocentesca.* Turin: Edizione, 1983. (Edition of fifteen copies — much of the text reprinted in *I fili della memoria*, edited by Alfonso Cipolla and Giovanni Moretti.)

_____. *La scenografia dalle origini al 1936* (*storia del teatro Reggio di Torino*, vol. 3). Turin: Casa di Risparmio, 1980.

_____. "Lo sfarzo di quelle microscopiche scene." In *I fili della memoria*, edited by Alfonso Cipolla and Giovanni Moretti. Turin: SEB 27, 2001.

Vibaek, Janne. "Dal testo allo spettatore." In *Per una storia della semiotica.* Quaderni del Circolo semiologico siciliano, 15–16. Palermo, 1981.

Volpicelli, Giuseppina, et al. *Piccoli personaggi grandi incanti — marionette triestine della Collezione Signorelli.* Treviso: Grafiche Antiga, 2002.

_____, and Patrizia Veroli. "La collezione Maria Signorelli" and "Regesto della mostra." In *Il teatro delle meraviglie.* Commune di Jesi, 2003.

Vuoso, Ugo. *Stella Cerere dizionario biografico dei pupari napoletani.* CEIC/Ed. Provv, 1997 (No page numbers).

Wolff, Lise-Lotte Neumann. "La Rotta di Roncisvalle" in "*Legends of Charlemagne or Romance of the Middle Ages* di Thomas Bulfinch e nella tradizione poplare siciliana." Thesis, Università degli Studi di Palermo, Facoltà di lettere e Filosofia, 1989–1890.

Yambo (Enrico Novelli). *La Bella e la Bestia ovvero le Astuzie di Lindoro.* Florence: Vallechi, 1927.

Yorick (Pietro Coccoluto Ferrigini). *La storia dei buratini.* Florence: Fieramosca, 1884. Also Florence: Bemporad & Figlio, 1902.

Young, Susan. *Shakespeare Manipulated — The Use of the Dramatic Works of Shakespeare in Teatro di Figura in Italy.* London: Associated University Presses, 1996.

Zanella, Vittorio. *Il museo dei burattini.* Commune di Budrio, 2000.

Zucchi, John E. *The Little Slaves of the Harp.* Montreal: McGill, 1992.

Index

Numbers in **_bold italics_** indicate pages with photographs.